PIRATES AND MUTINE
NINETEENTH CE

This book is for Felix Robinson, the littlest pirate, with all my love.

Pirates and Mutineers of the Nineteenth Century
Swashbucklers and Swindlers

Edited by

GRACE MOORE
The University of Melbourne, Australia

Routledge
Taylor & Francis Group

LONDON AND NEW YORK

First published 2011 by Ashgate Publishing

2 Park Square, Milton Park, Abingdon, Oxon OX14 4RN
711 Third Avenue, New York, NY 10017, USA

Routledge is an imprint of the Taylor & Francis Group, an informa business

First issued in paperback 2016

British Library Cataloguing in Publication Data
Pirates and mutineers of the nineteenth century :
   swashbucklers and swindlers.
   1. Pirates in literature. 2. English literature--19th
   century--History and criticism. 3. Piracy--History--19th
   century.
   I. Moore, Grace, 1974-
   820.9'355'09034-dc22

Library of Congress Cataloging-in-Publication Data
Moore, Grace, 1974–
   Pirates and mutineers of the nineteenth century : swashbucklers and swindlers / Grace
Moore.
      p. cm.
   Includes bibliographical references and index.
   ISBN 978-0-7546-6433-8 (hardback)
   1. English literature--19th century--
History and criticism. 2. Pirates in literature. 3. Pirates--History--19th century. 4.
Piracy--History--19th century. I. Title.
   PR468.P535M66 2011
   820.9'3556--dc22

                                                                        2010044374

ISBN 978-0-7546-6433-8 (hbk)
ISBN 978-1-138-25187-8 (pbk)

Contents

List of Figures   *vii*
Notes on Contributors   *ix*
Acknowledgements   *xiii*

Introduction   1
Grace Moore

1   Pirate Chic: Tracing the Aesthetics of Literary Piracy   11
Mel Campbell

2   The Pirate Poet in the Nineteenth Century: Trollope and Byron   23
Deborah Lutz

3   Playing Pirate: Real and Imaginary Angrias in Branwell Brontë's
Writing   41
Joetta Harty

4   Ho! For China: Piratical Incursions, Free Trade Imperialism and
Modern Chinese History, c. 1832–1834   59
Ting Man Tsao

5   The Wreck of the *Corsair*: Piracy, Political Economy and
American Publishing   79
Andrew Lyndon Knighton

6   Female Pirates and Nationalism in Nineteenth-Century American
Popular Fiction   95
Katherine Anderson

7   Mutiny on the *Orion*: The Legacy of the *Hermione* Mutiny and
the Politics of Nonviolent Protest in Elizabeth Gaskell's
North and South   117
Deborah Denenholz Morse

8   Acts of Piracy: *Black Ey'd Susan*, Theatrical Publishing and the
Victorian Stage   133
Kate Mattacks

9 The Perils of Empire: Dickens, Collins and the Indian Mutiny 149
Garrett Ziegler

10 Pirates for Boys: Masculinity and Degeneracy in R.M.
Ballantyne's Adventure Novels 165
Grace Moore

11 Piracy, Race and Domestic Peril in *Hard Cash* 181
Sean Grass

12 *The Pirates of Penzance*: The Slaves of Duty in an Age of Piracy 197
Abigail Burnham Bloom

13 'Dooty is Dooty': Pirates and Sea-Lawyers in *Treasure Island* 211
Alex Thomson

14 Staging the Pirate: The Ambiguities of Representation and the
Significance of Convention 223
Victor Emeljanow

15 Bram Stoker's *The Mystery of the Sea*: Law and Lawlessness,
Piracy and Protectionism 243
Carol A. Senf

16 Piracy and the Ends of Romantic Commercialism: Victorian
Businessmen Meet Malay Pirates 255
Tamara S. Wagner

Bibliography 273
Index 291

List of Figures

8.1	Frontispiece to Dicks' Acting Edition of *Black Ey'd Susan*	145
8.2	Frontispiece to Lacy's 1855 Edition of Black Ey'd Susan	146
12.1	Programme, *The Pirates of Penzance* by W.S. Gilbert, composed by Arthur Sullivan, D'Oyly Carte's London Opera Co., Fifth Avenue Theatre, New York City, 5 June 1880. Front cover	205
12.2	Programme, *The Pirates of Penzance* by W.S. Gilbert, composed by Arthur Sullivan, D'Oyly Carte's London Opera Co., Fifth Avenue Theatre, New York City, 5 June 1880. Back cover	206
14.1	Howard Pyle, 'Captain Keitt', *Harper's Monthly*, August 1907	224
14.2	J.K. Green, 'Characters and Scenes in *The Red Rover*' (1842)	227
14.3	Edward Fitzball, *The Red Rover*, frontispiece to Dicks' Standard Plays, No. 450 (undated, possibly 1843)	229
14.4	A.V. Campbell, 'Mr. Campbell as Blackbeard the Pirate'	232
14.5	'The Paradox Scene' from *The Illustrated Sporting and Dramatic News*, 10 April 1880	237
14.6	Gerald du Maurier as Captain Hook, *The Sketch*, 4 January 1905	240

Notes on Contributors

Katherine Anderson was raised on the pirate lore of 'the graveyard of the Atlantic', North Carolina's Outer Banks. She earned a PhD in English from the University of California, Berkeley, where she taught in the English and Comparative Literature departments. Anderson now works in Washington, DC, for an education policy non-profit organization.

Abigail Burnham Bloom teaches courses at Hunter College, CUNY and the New School and is managing editor of *Victorian Literature and Culture*. She is the author of numerous essays on the Victorians and her most recent book is *The Literary Monster on Film: Five Nineteenth Century British Novels and their Cinematic Adaptations* (2010).

Mel Campbell is a Melbourne-based journalist. She was one of the co-founders and editors of *Is Not Magazine* from 2004 to 2008, and is also editor of *The Enthusiast*, an Australian online cultural and entertainment magazine.

Victor Emeljanow is Emeritus Professor of Drama at the University of Newcastle, Australia and the General Editor of the e-journal *Popular Entertainment Studies*. He is the convenor of the International Federation for Theatre Research's Working Group, *Popular Entertainment: Circus, variety and the allied arts*. He is a professional theatre director as well as a theatre historian. He has published widely in the area of Victorian and Edwardian theatre: his most recent work, *Reflecting the Audience: London theatregoing 1840–1880* (co-authored with Jim Davis, 2001) was awarded the Society for Theatre Research's Annual Award in 2002. He is currently researching the career of the actor-manager Herbert Beerbohm Tree, for a book to be published by Pickering and Chatto in 2011.

Sean Grass is an Associate Professor of English at Texas Tech University, where he specializes in Victorian fiction and nineteenth-century British history and culture. He has published essays in *Nineteenth-Century Literature*, *JEGP* and *Dickens Studies Annual*, and won the *South Atlantic Review* Essay Prize in 2001. His first book, *The Self in the Cell: Narrating the Victorian Prisoner*, appeared from Routledge in April 2003, and he is now at work on another book manuscript called *'Portable Property': Theft and Identity in Victorian Narrative*, which addresses the commodification of identity in mid-Victorian autobiography and sensation fiction.

Joetta Harty recently received her PhD from the George Washington University in Washington, DC. Her dissertation, entitled *The Islanders: Mapping Paracosms in the Early Writing of Hartley Coleridge, Thomas Malkin, Thomas De Quincey, and the Brontës*, explores the charting of imaginary kingdoms in the era of geography militant. She has published articles on the image of the child in children's writing, and imagining Africa in the Brontë juvenilia. Currently she teaches literature courses at the University of Maryland University College, and is working on projects on Hartley Coleridge and Thomas Malkin, as well as a monograph about Romantic motherhood and the production of the child.

Andrew Lyndon Knighton is Associate Professor of English at California State University, Los Angeles. He holds research interests in the intersections between philosophy, political economy and literary and visual discourses, and is currently completing a book about the concept of unproductivity in nineteenth-century American literature and culture.

Deborah Lutz is an Associate Professor at Long Island University, C. W. Post. Her first book – *The Dangerous Lover: Gothic Villains, Byronism, and the Nineteenth-Century Seduction Narrative* (Ohio State UP, 2006) – traces a literary history of the erotic outcast. Her second book – *Pleasure Bound: Victorian Sex Rebels and the New Eroticism* (Norton, 2011) – explores the lives and collaborations of mid-nineteenth-century pornographers. She is currently working on a third book, supported by an ACLS Fellowship, about the materialism of Victorian death culture and 'secular relics': little things treasured because they belonged to the dead.

Kate Mattacks is a Senior Lecturer in Drama at the University of the West of England, Bristol. After completing a PhD on M.E. Braddon at Keele, she has worked on two Arts and Humanities Research Council (AHRC) projects within the field of Victorian drama: the Victorian Plays Project, a web-based resource of over 350 Victorian plays and the 'Buried Treasures' Project based at Royal Holloway/ the British Library, extending the catalogue for the Lord Chamberlain's Collection of licensing manuscripts. She has written articles on subjects including Braddon, the theatrical publisher T.H. Lacy, Victorian anti-feminism, spiritualism, staging speech disability and dramatic piracy. She is currently working on a monograph entitled *After Lady Audley: M.E. Braddon, Sensation Fiction and the Stage* and a project on perceptions of disability on the Victorian stage.

Grace Moore teaches and researches at the University of Melbourne, Australia. She is the author of *Dickens and Empire* (2004), which was shortlisted for the New South Wales Premier's Biennial Award for Literary Scholarship (2006), and co-editor of *Victorian Crime, Madness and Sensation* (2004). She is also author of a number of essays on Victorianism and neo-Victorianism and is at present working on a guide to the Victorian novel and a project on representations of Australian bushfires in the nineteenth century.

Deborah Denenholz Morse is Professor of English at The College of William and Mary. She is one of the Inaugural University Professors for Teaching Excellence at the College, and a recipient of the Phi Beta Kappa Award for Excellence in Teaching and the Thomas Graves Award for Sustained Excellence in Teaching. Professor Morse is the author of the first feminist study of Anthony Trollope, *Women in Trollope's Palliser Novels*, and the co-edited anthologies *The Erotics of Instruction* (with Regina Barreca [UPNE 1997]), *Victorian Animal Dreams: Representations of Animals in Victorian Literature and Culture* (with Martin Danahay [Ashgate 2007]), and *The Politics of Gender: Anthony Trollope in the Twenty-First Century* (with Regenia Gagnier and Margaret Markwick [Ashgate 2008]). Professor Morse is currently writing a book on Englishness and history in Anthony Trollope's novels that is under contract at Ohio State University Press. She has published articles on Anne Brontë, Maxine Hong Kingston, Mona Simpson, Elizabeth Gaskell, Anthony Trollope, Hesba Stretton, Elizabeth Coles Taylor, A.S. Byatt, and Kay Boyle.

Carol A. Senf is Professor of English at Georgia Institute of Technology, where she teaches courses in Victorian studies and the Gothic. She is the author of *Science and Social Science in Bram Stoker's Fiction* (2002), and her 'Dracula: Between Tradition and Modernism' won the Lord Ruthven Society prize in 1995. She has edited editions of *Lady Athlyne* (Desert Islands Dracula Library, 2007) and *The Mystery of the Sea*, both by Bram Stoker (Valancourt Books, 2007). Her most recent work is *Bram Stoker* published by the University of Wales Press in 2010 as part of its series Gothic Writers: Critical Revisions.

Alex Thomson is Senior Lecturer in Scottish Literature at the University of Edinburgh. He is the author of two monographs, *Deconstruction and Democracy* (2005) and *Adorno: A Guide for the Perplexed* (2006) and the projects on which he is currently working include an edition of *Memories and Portraits* for the New Edinburgh Edition of the Collected Works of Robert Louis Stevenson.

Ting Man Tsao is a Professor of English and teaches composition and literature at LaGuardia Community College of The City University of New York. With native fluency in Chinese, he majored in English at Hong Kong Shue Yan College, and holds a PhD in English from The State University of New York at Stony Brook. The title of his dissertation is 'Representing China to the British Public in the Age of Free Trade, c. 1833–1844.' His research interest is colonial discourse studies with a focus on late eighteenth- and nineteenth-century British imperialism in China.

Tamara S. Wagner obtained her PhD from Cambridge University in 2002 and is currently Associate Professor at Nanyang Technological University in Singapore. Her books include *Financial Speculation in Victorian Fiction: Plotting Money and the Novel Genre, 1815-1901* (2010), *Longing: Narratives of Nostalgia in the*

British Novel, 1740-1890 (2004), and *Occidentalism in Novels of Malaysia and Singapore, 1819-2004* (2005), as well as edited collections on *Consuming Culture in the Long Nineteenth-Century* (2007; paperback edition 2010), and *Antifeminism and the Victorian Novel: Rereading Nineteenth-Century Women Writers* (2009). Wagner has also guest edited special issues on silver-fork fiction (2009) and on the religious writer Charlotte Yonge (2010) for the journal *Women's Writing* and co-edited a guest issue on the Victorian Orient for *Critical Survey* (2009). Her current projects include a special issue on Frances Trollope and a study of Victorian narratives of failed emigration.

Garrett Ziegler received his PhD in English and Comparative Literature from Columbia University in 2010. His articles and reviews have appeared in *Victorian Studies*, *Race/Ethnicity, Space and Culture*, and the *Journal of British Studies*.

Acknowledgements

This book has suffered a number of delays and I thank its contributors for continuing to believe in it when emigration, childbirth, illness and a whole host of other difficulties stood in its way. I am enormously grateful to Ann Donahue of Ashgate, who has patiently supported this project and who has, as always, been a wonderful editor. I am also very grateful to the manuscript's anonymous reader, who made a number of important and helpful suggestions.

Kristine Moruzi (now of the University of Alberta) worked as my research assistant when a broken hand threatened to delay progress still further, and I thank her for her meticulous attention to detail and careful assistance with the final typescript. Mike Rickard at the Bill Douglas Centre for the History of Cinema and Popular Culture at the University of Exeter provided valuable help with the cover image and I am grateful to him and the trustees of the collection for permission to reproduce the beautiful magic lantern slide from *Peter Pan*.

At the University of Melbourne Ken Gelder, Peter Otto and Stephanie Trigg have each provided support at different times and in varying ways as heads of programme. I am especially thankful to Peter for his regular help and advice during a professionally challenging time. Thanks are also due to the university for a Career Enhancement Fellowship and an Early Career Researcher Grant, both of which enabled me to offload some of my teaching responsibilities.

I would also like to thank Andrew Robinson, Sharyl Kammerzell, Claire Knowles, Cathy Scott, Charlotte Smith, Owen and Indigo Jones and Clara Tuite for differing forms of support and distraction. This project would not have been possible without the expertise of the members of the superb VICTORIA-L listserver, moderated by the indefatigable Patrick Leary.

This book is for my son, Felix Robinson, with all my love.

Introduction

Grace Moore

> Public curiosity in the subject of piracy is no new thing. It has always existed, though at the present time there is probably a greater interest in the history and the activities of the pirates since the last were hanged at Execution dock than there ever was before.
>
> Philip Gosse, *My Pirate Library*, 14–15

I

The nineteenth century heralded the great age of the literary pirate, even as piracy in the real world was on the wane. While piracy has been identified as the 'third oldest profession' (Stanley 22) and pirates continue to plague sea traders to this day, the 1800s saw a lull in pirate activity, particularly in the Atlantic Ocean. Perhaps as a direct consequence of the decline in pirate attacks close to home, the pirate underwent a metamorphosis in the nineteenth-century literary imagination in both British and American literature. Representations of the pirate shifted from the dangerous, uncouth cutthroats like the notorious Blackbeard, to the brooding Romanticism of Byron's corsair and the swashbuckling charisma of figures such as Captain Hook and Long John Silver.

As the popularity of recent movies like *Pirates of the Caribbean* demonstrates, our appetite for pirate tales remains as hearty as ever. The historian Linda Grant de Pauw has attempted to account for the pirate's curious mystique, noting that:

> pirates have fascinated writers for centuries in a way that shore-based cutthroats have not. Pirates are often heroes and heroines in novels and plays in which they would more rightly be cast as villains. It is easy for writers of fiction to romanticize pirates, partly because hard, factual knowledge about them is scarce. (19–20)

A number of the chapters in this collection examine the voracious public appetite for pirate tales, and our ongoing attraction to the myth of the pirate. The contributors chart the change in representations of pirates in the nineteenth century, focusing particularly, but not exclusively, on piracy in the waters of the Atlantic and the Caribbean. The chapters explore how and why literary pirates developed from the sensational, ruthless and demonic figures of texts like Charles Johnson's *A General History of the Robberies and Murders of the Most Notorious Pyrates* (1724) to the more benign and even humorous pirates who appear by the middle of the nineteenth century in works by the likes of Charles Dickens and Wilkie Collins.[1]

The so-called 'golden age of piracy' had lasted from 1694 until 1724 or thereabouts – a period when mythical figures like Captain Avery and Captain Kidd ruled the waves, plundering ships and terrorizing sailors. Piracy is likely to have appealed to the nineteenth-century imagination because of its brief resurgence in the early 1800s. The end of the Napoleonic Wars and the Wars of Liberation in South America left a large body of privateers without any source of revenue, and these desperate men turned to piracy in their droves. The fight against piracy in Caribbean waters involved both the US and the British navies in a sustained campaign to eradicate this threat against their trade interests. By the late 1820s incidents of piracy in the Caribbean had dwindled and, with this diminished threat, the pirate was gradually reinvented. The pirate expert David Cordingly has remarked of this reinterpretation, 'pirates have acquired a romantic aura which they never had in the seventeenth century and which they certainly never deserved' (xiv). Cordingly continues to suggest that the nineteenth century was the great age of pirate narratives, an idea that is compellingly supported by Hans Turley's provocative conjecture in *Rum, Sodomy, and the Lash* that the pirate came to replace the libertine as the embodiment of sexual and cultural anarchy (39). For Turley, the eighteenth century marked the beginning of the pirate's transition from villain to hero, and he cites Johnson's *General History* as a pivotal text in this redefinition. Indeed, while there are a number of studies of literary pirates in the eighteenth century, this collection offers the first detailed, chronological examination of the nineteenth-century pirate.

As Jo Stanley notes in her important collection on female pirates, *Bold in Her Breeches*, there is a wide gap between the pirate of fantasy and the reality of the pirate's fugitive existence. Stanley comments:

> The preoccupation in these fantasies is with bloodthirsty pirate leaders' deeds accomplished with ease rather than with the daily life of the mass of workers on pirate ships. This legendary sort of piracy has a similar eroticised thrill about conquering as that of westerns, but to find it exciting we have to make ourselves blind to the brutality and sexist and racist attitudes that have accompanied it. We have to ignore the viciousness the pirates showed towards captives from other ships, to people ashore whose services they needed and to each other. (5–6)

Following Stanley's lead, this collection is concerned primarily with the imaginary pirate. When contributors like Ting Man Tsao venture into the domain of the real, it is always to examine the ways in which pirate mythology permeates reality, whether through the exoticism of the foreign pirate as a stateless 'other' or through the wish fulfilment associated with creating and reading about piracy.

---

[1]   For a thorough account of the representation of the evils of piracy in eighteenth-century literature, see Hans Turley's *Rum, Sodomy, and the Lash: Piracy, Sexuality, and Masculine Identity*. New York: New York UP, 1999.

The pirate aficionado Philip Gosse captures the allure of the pirate when recounting his childhood fascination with tales of the sea and his encounter with an influential teller of pirate tales:

> It happened years ago when I was a child, that there used to call upon us a certain, romantic-looking gentleman, an old friend of my parents. I remember now little about him except that he came to see us on warm summer evenings, and that he used to wear over his shoulders a red silk shawl borrowed from my Mother, as he sat on our balcony, and that we children eagerly leant up against him while he told us wonderful stories.

> Such stories: All of the sea, wrecks, mutinies and pirates. Tales of blood-curdling adventures and disaster. After the nice gentleman had gone, we children went to bed, but not to sleep, our little minds being all too excited by the stories we had just been listening to.

> It was on these occasions that our nurse would say, with a vexatious sigh, 'Whenever that there Mr. Stevenson comes here I never can get you children to sleep.' (Gosse, *My Pirate Library*, 9)

Gosse was, of course, fortunate in that his father's circle included Robert Louis Stevenson, the creator of one of the world's best-known pirates. However, his comments neatly demonstrate the transformation of the pirate from the dangerous ruffian of the eighteenth-century novel, to an essential figure in children's bed-time stories by the close of the Victorian era.

As the historian C.R. Pennell has noted, our modern-day perception of the pirate owes a great deal to Stevenson's *Treasure Island* (1883) and the fearsome pirate who so excited Gosse, Long John Silver. The story first appeared in serial form in the periodical *Young Folks* between October 1881 and January 1882. However, it was only when the work became available in its entirety that it captured the public imagination. The story of Gladstone reading into the small hours of the morning in order to finish the tale is well known and, as David Cordingly has contended, 'Stevenson linked pirates forever with maps, black schooners, tropical islands, and one-legged seamen with parrots on their shoulders' (7). Certainly, there are many connections between the pirates of today's movies and television shows and the villains depicted by the likes of Dickens and Stevenson and the chapters to follow map out the shift in pirate-lore that is such a striking nineteenth-century phenomenon.

II

The pirate was radically reconfigured during the nineteenth century, his reputation undergoing a significant process of rehabilitation as his role shifted from the terror of the high seas to a much more mainstream figure. One of the key texts behind this refashioning of the pirate was Byron's *The Corsair* (1814), which swiftly became an early nineteenth-century publishing sensation. It sold over 10,000 copies on the day it was published and, as both Mel Campbell and Deborah Lutz discuss in Chapters 1 and 2, this influential poem reshaped perceptions of the pirate forever. Indeed, Joetta Harty's chapter 'Playing Pirate' charts just one instance of the pervasive influence of Lord Byron by drawing parallels between Branwell Brontë's childhood creation, Percy 'Rogue' Northangerland, and the brooding Byronic outlaw. Examining the Brontë children's famous Angrian saga (begun in 1826), Harty draws on Branwell's 1,000-page long narrative of an imaginary kingdom in West Africa, reading Angria as a transgressive site and reading the kingdom as a 'parodic, carnivalesque space'. Harty importantly resists the urge to equate Rogue with his creator's subsequent hell-raising ways, arguing instead for connections between pirates and insurgent nations at a time when Britain had tried and failed to build a colony in West Africa.

Mel Campbell distinguishes between fictitious pirates and their real-life counterparts, examining the shift in the pirate's reputation from feared villain to Romantic hero. Through an analysis of Sir Walter Scott's *The Pirate* (1821) and Byron's *The Corsair*, Campbell helpfully examines the origins of the nineteenth-century fascination with piracy, focusing particularly on what she terms the 'hybridity' of the Romantic pirate. For Campbell, the pirate is a hypermasculine figure who deploys a feminized aesthetic vocabulary, exploiting a position of freeplay in between two 'contradictory aesthetic properties'. Deborah Lutz develops some of these ideas in Chapter 2 where she considers the romanticization of the gentleman pirate, a phenomenon at odds with the working-class origins of most real-life pirates. By comparing Byron's Medora with Anthony Trollope's Lizzie Eustace, Lutz examines the erotics of piracy, concentrating particularly on the pirate as lover. Through juxtaposing Byron's Romantic idealism with Trollope's Victorian realism, Lutz asks why Lizzie Eustace is attracted to Byron's corsair and traces the conflation of Lord Byron with his pirate.

One of the major attractions of the pirate life was its democracy when contrasted with the existence of a sailor in either the Royal Navy or the merchant navy. Many pirates were former sailors and David Cordingly has attributed their extraordinary organization to this fact. They had often been lured to piracy by the fairer and more relaxed working conditions aboard ship. Angus Konstam has pointed to the level of wish fulfilment invested in the popular image of the pirate, observing, 'Pirates may be portrayed as violent, but they are also free-living, lying in a hammock in the sun, and kicking over the traces in a port; things that many people would like to do, but feel that they cannot because of the society in which they live' (8). Conditions for pirates were often extremely unpleasant; food could be scarce in between raids and, as with all sailing ships, the work required to keep the ship afloat was onerous. Pirate communities were notable, however, not only for sharing plunder equally between men, but also for the fact that their leaders were elected.[2] Pirates lived by an agreed code of conduct which regulated their interactions with one another, from their sexual behaviour down to their gambling habits.

The pirate code offers an important backdrop to Alex Thomson's analysis of pirate democracies in *Treasure Island*, 'Dooty is Dooty'. Thomson scrutinizes pirate democracies, looking closely at the pirate's outsider status and drawing upon the work of Peter Linebaugh and Marcus Rediker to re-evaluate the pirate ship's hierarchy. For Thomson, the pirates are a 'headless community' and, he argues, Stevenson offers us a vision of the 'making and remaking of the law' through which the pirates legislate for their own downfall. With the exception of Long John Silver, the novel's pirates are inordinately committed to following rules and regulations and, as Thomson puts it, 'Part and parcel of the degeneracy of *Treasure Island*'s pirates is their quaint and irresponsible addiction to a heavily legalistic but formally democratic mode of decision-making'. Asking what it means to do one's 'dooty' in *Treasure Island*, Thomson offers a reading of the novel that draws on both Derrida and Hannah Arendt, examining Long John Silver as a substitute father for young Jim Hawkins. Contrasting Silver's prudence (he has a bank account) with the fecklessness of his crew, Thomson considers him as a role model, before going on to examine how Jim learns to manipulate the 'improvisational violence' underpinning the law.

Thomson's chapter draws upon late Victorian attempts to challenge the idea and meaning of duty, and this climate is of key importance to Abigail Burnham Bloom's reading of Gilbert and Sullivan's operetta, *The Pirates of Penzance*. Examining the pirates as 'noblemen who have gone wrong', Bloom considers the conflicts that arise between different forms of responsibility, paying attention to the tensions between duty to the nation and duty to the self and focusing especially on the marriage market. Duty is also a key concern in Deborah Denenholz Morse's chapter on Elizabeth Gaskell's *North and South*, in which she explores the fine line between acts of heroism and acts of mutiny. Looking at the parallels between Gaskell's novel and a real-life mutiny that took place aboard *The Hermione* in 1797, Morse argues that Gaskell uses the shipboard uprising as a trope to examine broader problems aboard the British ship of state. She examines how Frederick Hale is exiled from Britain for an act of rebellion against a cruel captain and highlights the parallels between Fred's position and that of the industrial workforce in mid-Victorian Manchester. Finally, Morse argues that Frederick's story forms part of an attempt by Gaskell to construct an 'alternative politics of tolerance' that rejects violence in favour of mediation and understanding.

Gaskell is never explicit about the degree to which Frederick Hale is guilty of mutiny and rebellion, although several characters in the novel allude to

---

[2]   As David Cordingly notes, both the captain and the ship's carpenter (a crucial figure who kept the ship in a seaworthy state) received a larger share, as did the ship's surgeon. For an excellent, detailed discussion of the pirate code, see Cordingly, *Under the Black Flag*, 96–103.

Fred's hot temper and childhood misdemeanours to suggest that he has always displayed transgressive tendencies. Frederick might therefore be considered an 'accidental pirate', a figure Grace Moore examines in her chapter on pirates in R.M. Ballantyne's stories for boys. Analysing Bloody Bill from *The Coral Island* (1857) and Richard Rosco in *The Madman and the Pirate* (1883), Moore argues that Ballantyne used his pirates to examine European degeneracy and to warn his young readers of the dangers of being seduced into a life of crime. Resisting the impulse to glamorize the pirate that characterized so many nineteenth-century nautical dramas, Ballantyne's accidental pirates are, according to Moore, psychologically complex figures who enact the perils that result from impulsive behaviour and a lack of discipline. As one of the nineteenth century's best-selling authors of stories for boys, Ballantyne was ideally situated to re-cast the pirate and to put him to work to promote rigidly moral conduct within his boy readers. As such, Ballantyne's novels are an important source for understanding how representations of piracy shifted and conflicted, making the pirate an enthrallingly ambiguous figure.

The impressionable juvenile is an important figure for Victor Emeljanow, who charts the history of the stage pirate in the nineteenth century. Arguing for the development of a tradition of the spectacular pirate that was connected to a need to showcase an actor's skills as a stage villain, Emeljanow shows how melodrama gave way to a more refined type of play in the middle of the century – before the emergence of great stage pirates, including Long John Silver and J.M. Barrie's terrifying Captain Hook, as the century drew to a close. Conscious of the dialogue between page and stage, Emeljanow delineates the links between juvenile theatres and juvenile fiction and draws attention to the many ambiguities within the anti-authoritarian stage pirate. Like Moore, he looks at the role of the adventure story in shaping the iconography of the corsair, not to mention his popularity. He also considers the connections between today's screen pirates and their Victorian predecessors, arguing for a continuity of representation.

Both Katherine Anderson and Andrew Lyndon Knighton consider the pirate in the literary marketplace, where, as *Treasure Island* exemplifies, the public lapped up tales of his exploits. Knighton considers the weekly gazette *The Corsair*, founded by T.O. Porter and Nathaniel Parker Willis in 1839. The publication covered literature and the arts and ran for just 52 issues. Knighton asserts, 'Drifting upon the unregulated seas of transatlantic literary exchange, *The Corsair* mobilized and modified the conventions of pirate mythology to intervene into debates surrounding the relationship of intellectual property to the market and meaning of antebellum authorship.' Knighton examines the interplay between literary piracy and the nautical pirate, drawing attention to the gazette's deliberate use of piratical tropes to draw attention to its editors' flagrant disregard for intellectual property rights. Plundering works by overseas authors to fill their pages, the editors of *The Corsair* sent out a series of decidedly mixed signals on the copyright question. On the one hand they joined with prominent members of the literary establishment, like Charles Dickens, to demand an international copyright treaty to protect authors, while at the same time they wilfully abused the absence of such an agreement to reprint works without any regard for the rights of the author.

In her analysis of mid-nineteenth-century American pirate fiction, Katherine Anderson considers the female pirate as an incarnation of American expansionism and independence. Focusing her discussion on Fanny Campbell, a cross-dressing female pirate captain who accidentally founds the American navy, Anderson considers the politics involved in impersonating a male pirate, whilst aligning Fanny's vulnerable, disguised body with the fragile, new American nation. Jo Stanley has discussed what she calls the 'empowering pleasure of the woman pirate', arguing that for women 'piracy symbolises the freedom from having to graft obediently for the means to survive' (10). By examining the paradox of the 'vulnerable yet victorious soft conqueror', Anderson takes issue with this idea, arguing that the woman pirate is both a 'colonized victim and an (absent) imperial perpetrator'. She then continues to examine what Janet Myers has labelled the 'portable domesticity' of the female pirate's ship, drawing compelling parallels between the dislocatedness of the vagabond ship and the rootlessness of the newly emancipated United States. For Anderson's pirates, the ocean becomes not a means of leaving home, but rather an extension of American domestic space, signalling the mobility of American identity at this time.

In many ways the nautical dramas of this period were highly subversive, discussing contentious issues that included free trade and Abolitionism and often drawing attention to the pirate's liberating statelessness. With the expansion of the British Royal Navy, the genre became increasingly popular, as did the figure of the sailor-hero. While Victor Emeljanow argues for the influence of the stage play *The Red Rover* (an 1829 adaptation of Fenimore Cooper's novel) in Chapter 14, Kate Mattacks examines Douglas Jerrold's hugely popular play, *Black-Ey'd Susan*, in Chapter 8, 'Acts of Piracy', to consider T.H. Lacy's 'illicit trade' in Victorian plays. Mattacks probes the connections between the stage pirate and the dramatic piracy that were rife in the Victorian theatre and considers how nautical drama allowed playwrights to address the regulation of dramatic piracy on stage. For Mattacks, Jerrold uses the male lead character, William, to articulate his position as a writer beset by piracy. Arguing that the hapless William's defence of the eponymous Susan represents the awkward position of the playwright in the face of pirate publishers and 'adaptors', Mattacks draws attention to analogies between dramatists and pirate crews, while also focusing on the unstable definitions of piracy and mutiny both on stage and in the wider world.

Garrett Ziegler picks up on the importance of the pirate drama to broader political concerns in his chapter, 'The Perils of Empire'. Beginning with an analysis of the *Household Words* article 'Blown Away' by George Craig, Ziegler looks at public reactions to the so-called Indian 'Mutiny' of 1857. Charles Dickens, the editor of *Household Words*, was notoriously vehement in his initial responses to the uprising. Ziegler skilfully explores the story he penned with his friend Wilkie Collins to commemorate events for the journal's Christmas edition in 1857. While Dickens wrote chapters one and three, Collins was responsible for the middle chapter, and Ziegler probes the curious differences between Dickens's vitriolic chapters and Collins's much gentler, almost comedic, contribution. Collins's contribution to the story is frequently ignored by critics who are eager to seize upon Dickens's more incendiary offering. However, it was Collins who chose to relocate the events of the narrative from India to South America, and to transform the Sepoy rebels into a band of nationless pirates. Following Lillian Nayder, Ziegler addresses the tensions between Dickens and Collins's styles and emphases in this story and offers a compelling analysis of Collins's attempts to undermine his mentor's demoniacal characters.[3] One of the story's most memorable figures is the absurdly foppish, guitar-strumming Pirate Captain, whom Collins deploys to downplay Dickens's almost obsessive focus on the alleged violation of British women at Cawnpore. Collins displaces concerns about the vulnerability of the female body on to the effeminate Pirate Captain, creating a counter-threat to British masculinity.[4] By comically depicting the Pirate Captain as flamboyant and camp, Collins, argues Ziegler, successfully sabotages Dickens's furious attack on the sepoy rebels and offers a critique on the builders of empire and their lack of tolerance for racial others.

Race is also a concern for Sean Grass, who examines Charles Reade's sensation novel *Hard Cash* to explore how Reade adapts the pirate genre to examine domestic concerns. Focusing on the otherness of the pirate, Grass argues that for the Victorian reader piracy was 'an explicitly racial peril, an outrage committed against "white Britons" by dusky savages at the limits of culture'. Taking the eponymous 'hard cash' as the novel's central protagonist, Grass demonstrates a much less exotic form of piracy in the wheelings and dealings of British venture capitalists, 'a domestic peril rooted in the financial and textual practices of mid-Victorian England'. Grass suggests that the pirates' role in the plot is to force the reader to form a sequence of connections between domestic fraud and terror on the high seas. As he observes, 'The racially 'other' pirates who attack [the ship] are … just the first and most transparent iteration of what the novel suggests is the more civilized rapacity of financial life in mid-Victorian England.' Anticipating late nineteenth-century debates surrounding atavism, Reade shows that beneath the British veneer of cultivation, there lurks the potential for piracy within all citizens, as is evidenced by Reade's battle scenes, in which a number of Englishmen seem to metamorphose into pirates. Reade's pirates are, then, not the increasingly conventional swashbucklers of adventure stories, but the more mundane, yet equally dangerous embezzlers and speculators who posed an ongoing threat to the financial equilibrium of individual Britons and of the nation as a whole.

Looking back to Daniel Defoe's parallel between the 'pyrates' of the London Exchange and their nautical counterparts, Grass traces the historical parallels between sea-farers, speculators, financial sharks and literary pirates. He then makes a compelling case to regard Charles Reade himself as a pirate, noting that

---

[3]   See Lillian Nayder, *Unequal Partners*. Ithaca and London: Cornell UP, 2002.

[4]   For discussions of pirate sexuality, see Turley, *Rum, Sodomy and the Lash*.

'Reade's authorial practice seems often to have been at odds with his vigorous attacks on those who pirated his work', since he frequently lifted plots from other authors without their permission. Notwithstanding the fact that he attempted to reimburse those whose works he adapted, Reade stands out as an author who both agitated against and participated in artistic piracy. As Grass registers, this was piracy reconfigured for the industrial age and in a form which could not be banished to distant, exotic shores.

Throughout the nineteenth century, piracy was an important trope for depictions of capitalist robber barons, highlighting the lawlessness of the stock market gambler and the currency speculator. Writing of Daniel Defoe's *Captain Singleton* (1720), John Peck has asked the important question, 'what is it … that distinguishes the trader from the pirate, for the mercantile trader is equally an opportunist and equally likely to break the law?' (20). Peck's research demonstrates that parallels between the businessman and the pirate coincided with Britain's shift to a capitalist economy and, according to this logic, it makes perfect sense for Defoe to explore the morality of money-making through the character of a reformed pirate. Indeed, as Kristie Allen has commented, the 'melodramatic figure of the pirate is a fascinating early nineteenth-century receptacle for tensions surrounding national authority in the commercial arena'.[5]

Tamara Wagner demonstrates a similar conflation of piracy and commerce in her chapter, 'Piracy and the Ends of Romantic Commercialism'. Looking at writers as diverse as Catherine Gore, G.M. Henty, John Conroy Hutcheson and James Greenwood, Wagner argues that pirate narratives chart changes in the literary representation of colonial South East Asia and the growing attraction of Borneo in pirate novels. Wagner reads piracy as a metaphor for threats of native resistance and points to the dangers of succumbing to piracy as akin to 'going native'. The novels examined in this chapter respond to a growing public demand for exotic colonial narratives at the end of the nineteenth century. By examining the work of the colonial administrator Hugh Clifford, Wagner reappraises late nineteenth-century representations of British Malaya and re-evaluates racial hierarchies aboard pirate ships. Wagner also pays attention to the process of revising and questioning stories of piracy in South East Asia and how this 'embodies the death of a Romantic commercialism that has run aground in an imperialist commercialism that is exposed as an outgrowth of, rather than a benign counterpoise to, piracy'.

Wagner's chapter forms a useful companion piece to Ting Man Tsao's contribution, 'Ho! For China: Piratical Incursions, Free Trade Imperialism and Modern Chinese History', which examines the considerable tensions in the run-up to the Opium War of 1840. The question that perplexes Tsao is the absence of

---

[5] Arguing that the highly popular *Black Ey'd Susan* blended nautical concerns with domestic melodrama, Allen reads the play as a seditious text, exposing the dangers of failing to do one's duty. Drawing comparisons between the 'slavery' of the press-ganged sailor and the slave, Allen offers a series of parallels between the sailor, the slave and the pirate as free-trader. Page numbers not available at the time of going to press.

the pirate hero from imperial discourses surrounding China. While pirates feature prominently in narratives of the Caribbean, South Pacific and the Americas, they appear for only a brief period in British stories about China – probably, as Tsao notes, because piracy was not deployed as part of Britain's expansionist policy in the Far East. Tsao examines the accounts of how H.H. Lindsay, working for the East India Company, and Charles Gutzlaff, a German missionary, entered the forbidden ports of China in disguise in 1832 and transformed themselves, through narrative, into piratical heroes. By examining how Lindsay and Gutzlaff broke with narrative traditions and offered a new perspective on connections between piracy and empire, Tsao shows how they 'opened' China to the British middle-class male reader and legitimized commercial and religious intervention in the region.

Like Thomson and Wagner, Carol A. Senf concerns herself with fin-de-siècle piracy in her chapter on Bram Stoker's curious novel *The Mystery of the Sea* (1902). The novel's central protagonist, Marjory, is an American descendant of Sir Francis Drake, who comes to be represented as a pirate. Akin to Elizabeth Gaskell, Bram Stoker uses piracy as a trope to examine broader contemporary abuses of power that affected maritime communities. Senf argues that in addition to pursuing treasure, Marjory is also working to cleanse herself of her ancestor's 'taint of piracy', reminding us of the shifts that take place between the 'hero' and the 'pirate'. She also examines Bram Stoker as a coastal dweller, and looks at his representation of the plight of impoverished fishing communities as well as the legal forms of theft that can occur at sea.

This collection as a whole considers the dramatic appeal of the pirate, a figure who should really occupy the status of villain, rather than hero. Hans Turley has remarked, 'pirate fiction is not a reputable genre. Witness the huge number of "penny dreadful" novels and romances in the 1830s, 1840s, and 1850s, and the notable dearth of critical studies about this genre' (74). Furthermore, David Cordingly has commented, 'Romance tells us that pirates were no more than common criminals, but we still see them as figures of romance' (xiii). Many of the contributors ponder the paradox of the pirate and the way in which he has been re-evaluated by nineteenth-century poets, dramatists and novelists. The chapters probe the charisma and flamboyance of these bold forebears of Captain Jack Sparrow and their, at times, awkward relationship to the literary canon. They also chart the ambiguity of these attractive, but dangerous, villains who seek shortcuts to economic dominance and who continue to enthral readers with their cunning, bravery and sheer ruthlessness.

Chapter 1

Pirate Chic: Tracing the Aesthetics of Literary Piracy

Mel Campbell

When we imagine pirates, more often than not we conjure up fashion plates: dashing rogues waving Jolly Rogers and sporting puffy shirts, parrots, rakish bandannas, gold earrings, wooden legs, eye-patches and velvet coats. This image would seem at odds with the economic, political and legal realities of piracy in eighteenth-century Europe (Turley 37–42), and the unsentimental brutality that has been documented among real-life pirates. It also ignores privateering, the state-sanctioned looting of enemy ships in wartime, and elides the breadth of historical piracy, which ranged from China to Yugoslavia and from the Caribbean to the Mediterranean. From an historical perspective, C.R. Pennell points out that 'the behaviour of pirates is so dramatic in its context, apparently romantic in its action, and so photogenic in its possibilities that the temptation to ignore the one-two-three for the yo-ho-ho is very attractive' (3). In popular culture – and, Pennell contends, sometimes in scholarly endeavour as well – piracy is apparently 1 per cent crime and 99 per cent swashbuckling.

The origins of what I shall term 'pirate chic' are both intriguing and subject to debate. Hans Turley argues that it is 'impossible to separate the "real" pirate who preyed on legitimate traders from the romanticized version accepted as the "reality" in the twentieth century' (36), but that 'the *way* this fabric is woven can be examined' (7, original emphasis). Turley describes how historical and fictional representations of the pirate merged the legally defined 'pirate as criminal' with the popular 'pirate as hypermasculine transgressor', creating what Turley calls the 'piratical subject' (41). He goes on to describe the production of this subject in the early eighteenth-century fiction of Daniel Defoe, including *Robinson Crusoe* and its sequels (1719–20) and *Captain Singleton* (1720). However, I shall argue that what twenty-first-century audiences understand as 'pirate chic' was more decisively shaped by a Romantic literary tradition in the early nineteenth century. Importantly, I want to depart from Turley's thesis that the key marker of the piratical subject is a transgressive sexuality. Instead, I will consider the *aestheticization* of the piratical subject in Captain Charles Johnson's hugely influential *General History of the Robberies and Murders of the Most Notorious Pyrates* (1724) and the impact that this text had on two of the most significant Romantic works on piracy to follow it, Lord Byron's *The Corsair* (1814) and Sir Walter Scott's *The Pirate* (1821).

The Romantic piratical subject is particularly interesting because it is a hybrid: it represents a hypermasculine figure using an aesthetic vocabulary that at the time was decidedly feminized. A detached and intellectual mode of aesthetic appreciation, known as 'disinterested', was defined as 'good taste' (R. Jarvis 174), and it was seen as the prerogative of gentlemen, who were not distracted from their appreciation by having to work for a living. Byron dismissed his cycle of Oriental tales, including *The Corsair*, as worthless, citing their popularity among women (Watkins 15); while the tendency of Scott's reviewers to focus on his novels' historical context rather than their plots 'reflects the general lack of esteem in which contemporaries held the loosely structured romance form' in which Scott worked, which was often dismissed as a 'women's genre' (Robertson 35). Specifically, I want to argue here that the nineteenth-century piratical subject operates in the hybrid aesthetic mode of the picturesque, which has its origins in an Italian word 'denoting a bold and vigorous technique drawing attention to the medium of representation' (R. Jarvis 181). In Romantic aesthetics, the picturesque was situated somewhere between the feminized mode of ideal beauty and the masculinized mode of the sublime. Further, I contend that the nineteenth-century piratical subject was shaped by two discourses of Romantic aesthetic hybridity: heroism and historicism. *The Corsair* epitomizes the trope of the pirate as anti-hero that is first evident in Johnson. Neither hero nor villain, he is a morally ambiguous personality to be admired but never understood. Scott depicts this anti-hero somewhat more ironically; but in manufacturing an historical background for its fictional protagonist, *The Pirate* combines fact with fiction, in a sense taking up where Johnson left off.

The Pirate as Anti-Hero

The piratical subject has its origins in two bestselling 'true-crime' novels. In 1678, Alexander Exquemelin (called John Esquemeling in early English editions) wrote *The Bucaniers of America, a True Account*, which told of seventeenth-century European pirates of the Caribbean.[1] First published in Dutch, it was translated into German, Spanish, English, French, Russian and Italian. It remains a curiously partisan text, because each translation played up the pirates of its respective country and criticized the others. Then, in 1724, Captain Charles Johnson published *A General History of the Robberies and Murders of the Most Notorious Pyrates*. This was a bloodthirsty, lavishly illustrated account of the British pirates whose

---

[1]   When seventeenth-century European traders discovered the rich resources of the Americas, they became sitting ducks for rogue ships to plunder their cargo. The Caribbean Sea became the centre of a so-called Golden Age of piracy that lasted until around 1725. The pirates hid out among the area's many islands, living on the local smoked beef known as 'boucan'. Hence, they came to be called 'buccaneers'.

exploits had recently made news headlines on both sides of the Atlantic. It was so popular that it ran to four editions and two volumes within two years.

The *General History* deliberately pandered to the British public's taste for the exotic, revelling in graphic stories of murder, rape, pillage and torture on the high seas. One of its most powerful accounts is that of Edward Teach, the notorious Blackbeard. Johnson reports that Blackbeard shot his first mate through the knee, laming him for life, to ensure his crew would not 'forget who he was' (84). He also forced his wife 'to prostitute herself' to his crew members, 'one after another, before his face' (76). Blackbeard is one of Johnson's more unambiguous sadists, along with Captain England, whose crew tortured a man by lashing him to a mast and throwing glass bottles at him (115), and Captain Low, who cut off a sailor's ears and forced him to eat them, seasoned with salt and pepper (334). Yet in recounting Blackbeard's death, Johnson writes: 'Here was an end of that courageous brute, who might have passed in the world for a hero had he been employed in a good cause' (82). Blackbeard is granted an anti-heroic status as a piratical subject *despite* and even *because of* his brutality.

Johnson is able to produce Blackbeard – and other pirates – as piratical subjects through a process of aesthetic fetishization. This process is best introduced in the case of the pirate flag, the Jolly Roger. Today, the skull and crossbones on a black background is seen as the 'quintessential' pirate motif; it would be easy to suppose it was flown by every historical pirate ship. Certainly, 'Old Roger' was an eighteenth-century name for the Devil, and seventeenth-century French buccaneers flew a red flag known as 'Jolie Rougere', which showed they took no prisoners. But the Jolly Roger we know today is an amalgam of various black pirate flags. Captain Spriggs's flag in Johnson's *History* had 'a white skeleton in the middle of it, with a dart in one hand striking a bleeding heart, and in the other, an hour-glass' (352). 'Calico Jack' Rackam, whose nickname came from his striped pantaloons, had two crossed cutlasses below the skull on his flag. The notorious Bartholomew 'Black Bart' Roberts ordered a new flag made after being insulted by the governors of Barbados and Martinique. It portrayed Roberts, a flaming sword in hand, standing on two skulls labelled 'A Barbadian's Head' and 'A Martinican's Head'. It was so terrifying, says Johnson, that other ships 'immediately struck their colours and surrendered to his mercy' (234).

Why does Johnson describe these flags in such detail? First, they provide a mode of representing pirates that refers to their actual atrocities in an indirect, aesthetically pleasurable way. Second, and more importantly, Johnson wants the reader to realize that these flags are not arbitrarily terrifying: there is a *logic* to their manufacture and display. Likewise, Johnson builds a detailed picture of how pirates look and act that initially suggests an unnerving but alluring spectacle:

> This beard was black, which he suffered to grow of an extravagant length; as to breadth it came up to his eyes. He was accustomed to twist it with ribbons, in small tails, after the manner of our ramilies wigs, and turn them about his ears. In time of action, he wore a sling over his shoulders with three brace of pistols

hanging in holsters like bandaliers, and stuck lighted matches under his hat, which, appearing on each side of his face, his eyes naturally looking fierce and wild, made him altogether such a figure, that imagination cannot form an idea of a fury, from hell, to look more frightful. (84–5)

While Blackbeard is described as ready for 'action', Johnson implies that it is the way he *looks* that enables him to perform his criminal acts (carrying pistols, cowing onlookers). And this appearance, rather than any crimes as such, marks Blackbeard as 'piratical'. In the *General History*, these 'pirate aesthetics' form a universal visual code for piracy that is instantly identifiable by readers – and by the textual pirates themselves. In one tale, two pirate ships try to rob each other and hoist their respective flags, but when they realize their 'happy mistake', 'the satisfaction was great on all sides, at this junction of confederates and brethren in iniquity' (Johnson 174).

This idea of a visually signified pirate brotherhood is elaborated in Johnson's discussion of pirate clothing. The real-life pirate was likely to go without washing for months, his skin turning so black with grime that he occasionally needed to be dunked into the sea to recover its colour (Turley 18). Pirates wore whatever they could: 'Put together from the clothes of dead or captured sailors, booty, and what they can scrounge up, their clothing was patched and falling apart' (Turley 90). Yet in Johnson's account, pirates are connoisseurs of menacing display, combining signifiers of danger with their sartorial choices: 'they were extravagantly nice, endeavouring to outdo one another, in the beauty and richness of their arms … These were slung in time of service, with different coloured ribbands, over their shoulders, in a way peculiar to these fellows, in which they took great delight' (180). According to Johnson, Roberts' crew 'appeared gay and brisk, most of them with white shirts, watches, and a deal of silk vests' (241). Roberts himself is 'a gallant figure' in:

a rich crimson damask waistcoat and breeches, a red feather in his hat, a gold chain around his neck, with a diamond cross hanging to it, a sword in his hand, and two pairs of pistols hanging at the end of a silk sling slung over his shoulders (according to the fashion of the pirates). (Johnson 243)

As Turley notes, the word 'fashion' in the early eighteenth century bore all sorts of contemptible, emasculating connotations (90–91), but the idea of a 'pirate fashion' 'suggests that their world was in fact a society, with its own standards of fashion' (91). In this way, aesthetic markers move beyond mere exotic spectacle, instead becoming signifiers of this alternative society. Just as the black flag acted as a universal sign of 'brethren in iniquity', a particular semiotic repertoire rhetorically 'flags' for the reader that pirates are not inexplicably evil villains: they are anti-heroes who operate under a different moral code.

Conrad, the protagonist of Byron's poem *The Corsair* (1814) is just this sort of anti-hero and in many respects Byron owes a considerable debt to Johnson. He is a corsair, a pirate who raids ships and cities on the Mediterranean Sea. Bidding farewell to his beloved Medora, Conrad and his crew raid the palace of the Muslim Pacha, Seyd, but Conrad is captured. He is freed by Seyd's queen and concubine Gulnare, whom Conrad had chivalrously saved from the burning palace; but when Conrad arrives home, he discovers that Medora, thinking him killed, is herself dead (whether of a broken heart or by suicide, Byron leaves to the reader). Devastated, Conrad disappears, never to be seen alive again. Thanks to Johnson and the writers who followed him, the anti-heroic piratical subject had become a truism; and for Byron, pirates were attractive figures because they operated outside the legal and moral constraints of mercantile bourgeois society.[2]

The opening pirates' song in Johnson establishes piracy as an alternative society that is appealing because of its 'freedom' from conventional hypocrisies. The trade-off of a short criminal life for 'freedom' is widespread in the *General History*, which presents it as a positive and noble personal choice. 'Black Bart' Roberts' motto is given as 'A merry life and a short one', and his favourite toast as 'Damn to him who ever lived to wear a halter' (Johnson 244).[3] Before his execution, Calico Jack Rackam is allowed to see his lover, fellow pirate Anne Bonny; but instead of comforting him, she tersely informs him that, 'if he had fought like a man, he need not have been hanged like a dog' (Johnson 165). However, Byron presents the pirates' freedom in purely aesthetic terms by likening it to the sea: 'Our thoughts as boundless, and our souls as free' (1.2). The pirates are kings, their domain the Mediterranean: 'Our flag the sceptre all who meet obey' (1.2). Byron dramatizes Conrad as 'Man as himself – the secret spirit free' (1.248), and Conrad shares the tendency of Johnson's pirates to find shame in capture. At first, he rejects Gulnare's offer to help him escape: 'Unfit to vanquish – shall I meanly fly/ The one of all my band that would not die?' (2.472–3).

In the character of Conrad, Johnson's piratical subject becomes a classic Byronic hero: defiant, alienated and misanthropic (and misogynist), yet also sensitive, honourable and faithful. For Byron, Conrad is heroic because he realizes and accepts his own worst nature:

> He knew himself a villain – but he deemed
> The rest no better than the thing he seemed;
> And scorn'd the best as hypocrites who hid
> Those deeds the bolder spirit plainly did. (1.265–8)

Importantly, Conrad's anti-heroic qualifications also manifest in aesthetic terms, and Byron spends considerable time detailing Conrad's appearance. 'Unlike

---

[2]   *The Corsair* was written when Byron's disillusionment with Regency society and politics had reached a point where he was considering leaving England forever (Watkins 69), which, two years later, he did.

[3]   This is a pun: pirates referred to the hangman's noose as the 'halter'. Roberts means that the finest pirates never allow themselves to be captured alive.

the heroes of each ancient race' (1.194), Conrad is not particularly tall or good-looking, but 'his dark eyebrow shades a glance of fire' (1.196) and he has 'sable curls in wild profusion' (1.204). When he reveals himself to Seyd, he makes a Blackbeard-style apparition:

> His close but glittering casque, and sable plume,
> More glittering eye, and black brow's sabler gloom,
> Glared on the Moslems' eyes some Afrit sprite,
> Whose demon death-blow left no hope for fight. (2.148–51)

Byron's description of Conrad is strangely hybrid. The poem's perspective shifts between modes of representation that, at the time, were gendered 'male' and 'female': 'disinterested' observation of Conrad's appearance and empathetic description of his emotions and values. Byron describes Conrad as a 'closed book', difficult for the 'disinterested' observer to understand; yet he evokes Conrad's temperament and emotions by presenting Conrad as mysterious:

> Love shows all changes – Hate, Ambition, Guile,
> Betray no further than the bitter smile;
> The lip's least curl, the lightest paleness thrown
> Along the govern'd aspect, speak alone
> Of deeper passions (1.229–33)

Curiosity, R. Jarvis notes, 'is the chief mental effect of the picturesque' (183). Perversely, Conrad's ability to repel observation – 'He had the skill ... At once the observer's purpose to espy/ And on himself roll back his scrutiny' (1.219–20) – simply stimulates the reader's curiosity. So, Byron presents Conrad as an aesthetically constructed anti-hero, but also gives him a complex and compelling interior world of the sort that fascinated Romantic readers.

In several memorable moments, Byron highlights the tension of the piratical subject between violent acts and gallant appearances. As Conrad commands his ship, he leans 'o'er the fretting flood,/ And calmly talked – and yet he talked of blood!' (1.605–6) As he rescues Gulnare from her burning harem, she wonders: 'T'was strange – that robber thus with gore bedew'd,/ Seem'd gentler then than Seyd in fondest mood' (2. 263–4). These are distinctly picturesque images, by which the early nineteenth-century reader would understand that they have a striking balance which is neither soothing nor terrifying, but vigorous and intriguing (R. Jarvis 182–3). The poem's other Romantic conceits further transfigure the piratical subject. Conrad's voyage to Seyd's palace is set up as a fateful trip before it even happens: he tells his men that 'many a peril have I past,/ Nor know I why this next appears the last' (1.311–12). The voyage is fateful, of course, because it will have grave repercussions for the one exception to Conrad's general villainy: his love for Medora. Like Johnson's sexually voracious and perverse Blackbeard, Conrad's depredations continually supply him with attractive, desirable women ('fairest captives'), but he is unable to betray his beloved: 'None ever sooth'd his most unguarded hour' (1.292).

Ultimately, it is Conrad's ability to love that produces him as a Romantic piratical subject. In Johnson's epitaph, Blackbeard's qualities could have made him heroic if he had not turned them to evil; likewise, for Byron, Conrad's 'heart was form'd for softness – warp'd to wrong' (3.662). In a way, he is redeemed through his love for Medora and his grief over her death. As Byron concludes, 'He left a Corsair's name to other times,/ Link'd with one virtue, and a thousand crimes' (3.695–6).

The Pirate as Historical Fiction

As a qualifier to his description of female pirates Mary Read and Anne Bonny, Johnson remarks that the 'odd incidents of their rambling lives are such, that some might be tempted to think the whole story no better than a novel or romance' if it were not 'supported by many thousand witnesses' (153). Turley argues that Johnson does this to 'explain' the sheer oddness of women intruding into a male homosocial world (97–8), but this is not the only point at which Johnson intervenes in his own narrative to attest to its veracity. He quotes the trial transcripts of various pirates, government proclamations and large slabs of reportage about places including Brazil and Madagascar. Of Captain Avery, who notoriously robbed the Great Mogul's ship and established a pirate community in Madagascar, he writes: 'I have given all that could be collected of any certainty concerning this man; rejecting the idle stories which were made of his fantastic greatness' (57).[4]

As Turley points out, any beliefs in the 'truth' of the *General History* 'have to be based on the same assumptions about "history" that one makes about the authenticity of … *any* eighteenth-century fiction and histories based on the

---

[4] In the preface to the 1925 edition, Philip Gosse writes that 'it was the custom to smile indulgently at Johnson's *History* as being a mixture of fact and fancy', but that archival evidence has largely proven Johnson accurate 'in date and circumstance' (qtd. in Cordingly ix). But as Turley points out, Johnson's real genre 'is difficult to pin down because he makes up pirates within the metanarrative of a wholly factual 'history' (3). The aristocratic and idealistic Captain Misson, whose utopic 'pirate kingdom' of Libertalia is described in the two-volume 1726 edition, did not exist outside Johnson's imagination; and it is also probable that when Johnson 'introduces conversation into his biographies he uses considerable license' (Cordingly ix).

The same ambiguity present in Johnson's text is also present intertextually in the matter of his identity. Although a hack playwright named Charles Johnson was active in London at the time and had even written a play based on Captain Avery's life called *The Successful Pirate*, for many years Johnson was thought to be a pseudonym of Defoe himself. This idea has largely been debunked (Cordingly xii–xiii; Turley 7–8; Pennell 4–5), but we are still no closer to discovering if Johnson really could back up his protestations of eyewitness and objectivity.

narrator's protestations of "truth"' (101, original emphasis). Alexander Welsh argues that the prevailing Enlightenment values meant that eighteenth-century literature 'pretended to a knowledge of things and a loyalty to facts' (92). Defoe's *Robinson Crusoe* and *Captain Singleton* were written in the first person, purportedly as 'true histories', and it is highly likely that Johnson's insistence on his own reliability as a narrator was a canny tactic to situate his book in the same bestselling genre. First-person travel narratives, especially to exotic locales, remained hugely popular well into the nineteenth century (R. Jarvis 27).

Ann Rigney writes that history's claim to objectively represent social realities has always been dubious because of its entanglement with 'the novelistic genre, whose role has traditionally involved the portrayal of manners and daily experience in such a way as to engage the sympathies of readers' (2). For Rigney, 'history' and 'fiction' are such slippery categories because of the nuances contained within the very idea of fiction. It can be something that is constructed rather than discovered ('fictive'); invented rather than real ('fictitious' and 'imaginary'); legitimate in its make-believe nature ('fictional'); or literary in genre ('novelistic') (5–6). As Rigney argues, we take aesthetic pleasure in 'historical' writing because 'real events may not only be much stranger, but also more exciting, than stories that have been merely imagined' (7). Johnson's prose heightens this excitement because, despite its protestations of objectivity, it is often self-consciously literary. For example, Blackbeard fights Lt Edward Maynard ''till the sea was tinctured with blood round the vessel' (Johnson 82). His description of Blackbeard's brief reign of terror in Charleston, South Carolina, reads like some kind of maritime Western. The townsfolk are 'fired with the utmost indignation' as the pirates swagger through the streets, but 'durst not so much as think of executing their revenge, for fear of bringing more calamities upon themselves, and so they were forced to let the villains pass with impunity' (74–5).[5]

The Corsair operates entirely at the level of fiction, within a hazy time and place that is evoked mainly by references to 'old-fashioned' clothing ('casque' and 'corselet'), names like Juan, Pedro and Gonsalvo, and Medora's offer to serve Conrad 'sherbet' (1.427) and serenade him with her guitar (1.437–8). Byron

---

[5]   There is even a dry wit to Johnson's description of the (probably fictitious) early life of Anne Bonny. A bourgeois wife enjoys a night of passion with her husband, with only one thing to spoil her pleasure: she was in her serving-girl's bed at the time, and her husband thought she was the maid. She resolves to punish the girl, without considering that 'to her, she owed the diversion of the night before, and that one good turn should deserve another' (Johnson 163). And when it comes to Mary Read's affair with a fellow pirate, Johnson's language is decidedly flowery. Read had revealed that she was actually a woman by showing 'her breasts, which were very white', to 'the young fellow, who was made of flesh and blood'. His liking for her ''twas now turned into fondness and desire; her passion was no less violent than his, and perhaps she expressed it, by one of the most generous actions that ever love inspired' (Johnson 157). According to Johnson, Read discovered that her lover was to fight a duel with a fellow pirate. She challenged the other sailor to a second duel one hour earlier than the first, and shot him dead.

makes no attempt to create an internal temporal or cultural logic. He probably named Conrad after a German prince in a book he was reading at the time he wrote *The Corsair* (Watkins 70); it certainly does not 'fit' with the names of his crew. However, Byron does take pains to be 'true' in the sense of being authoritative, adding footnotes, often with their own references, that aim to lend the events of the poem an air of plausibility. Importantly, these invoke the author's first-hand experience of European and North African geography and culture. For example, 'The time in this poem may seem too short for the occurrences, but the whole of the Aegean isles are within a few hours' sail of the continent, and the reader must be kind enough to take the *wind* as I have often found it' (446). Rather than being excited because of the knowledge that its events *did* happen, the reader can appreciate totally fictional events knowing that they *could* have happened.

Scott's *The Pirate* (1821) offers a more complex and ambivalent melding of history and fiction. One of Scott's more obscure Waverley Novels (the better-known include *Ivanhoe* and *Rob Roy*), it was first attributed only to 'The Author of *Waverley*', lending Scott the same kind of pseudonymous authority as Johnson. The novel draws on Johnson's account of a particular 'real' pirate, Captain Gow, who was born at Cariston in the Orkney Islands off the coast of Scotland. According to Johnson, in his youth he had courted a local gentlewoman 'and was not ill received', but 'as Gow's circumstances in the world were not in any extraordinary condition', his prospective father-in-law told him, in effect, to come back when he was rich (363).

After launching his piratical career, Gow's thoughts turned to home, and he told his crew there are riches for the plundering at Cariston if they could only go 'undercover' for a time as merchantmen. Johnson is unclear as to whether love or avarice was foremost in Gow's mind; but his father-in-law was certainly impressed by his changed fortunes. However, only the day before Gow was to marry his beloved, a young boy 'discovered the whole scene of roguery to the magistrates' (365), and Gow was captured and executed. Johnson is unable to resist a delicious pun: 'Here ended the short reign of this piratical crew, who might have done considerable more mischief, had they not been so infatuated, as to court, as it were, their own ruin' (368).

In *The Pirate*, Scott does not re-imagine Gow himself, as he does with other historical figures like Richard the Lionheart and Mary, Queen of Scots. Instead, as Rigney suggests, Scott 'uses his freedom as a novelist to invent tailor-made exempla for mixing, matching, and supplementing the properties of actual individuals' (25). In Scott's hands, Gow's story of love thwarted by piracy becomes a convoluted Gothic maze of secrets, grudges and taboo affairs. Moreover, Scott proposes that *The Pirate* is 'true' where the *General History* is not. Introducing the novel, he writes that the 'particulars of the commonly received story' are 'inaccurate, since they will be found totally irreconcilable with the following veracious narrative, compiled from materials to which he himself alone has had access, by THE AUTHOR OF WAVERLEY' (8).

For Rigney, Scott 'mixed up two genres: historiography, traditionally seen as one of the most elevated, serious and instructive of genres, and the upstart romance, a more recent genre with a much lower literary status (typically a female genre) and a reputation for sensational entertainment' (34). The genre of historical romance encapsulates a tension between these two genres: 'it provides a conscious critique of society through the presentation of a past world ... [and] strings together a number of romantic incidents whose popularity arises more from their mythic quality than any pretensions they may have to realism' (Hughes 11). *The Pirate* is set in Zetland at the end of the seventeenth century. Misogynistic Basil Mertoun and his son Mordaunt move to the area, where Mordaunt befriends the two Troil sisters, serious Minna and fun-loving Brenda. When Mordaunt rescues the pirate Clement Cleveland from his wrecked ship, he finds himself being left out as Minna and Cleveland fall in love. Cleveland decides to give up the pirate life to be with Minna, but his pirate friends ruin everything by showing up and exposing him. Worse, Norna of Fitful-Head, a tormented local witch woman, comes out in support of Mordaunt, believing him to be the illegitimate child she bore years earlier to Mertoun. But after Cleveland is arrested, Mertoun tells Norna that Cleveland, the pirate she schemed against, is actually her son. Luckily, Cleveland is reprieved from the scaffold for having spared a Caribbean governor's life years earlier, and he leaves Zetland, while Mordaunt marries Minna's sister, Brenda. Later, Minna hears that Cleveland was killed on one of his depradations.

As I have argued in regard to *The Corsair*, the piratical subject is produced in the tension between contradictory aesthetic properties. In *The Pirate*, however, the tension between romance and 'real history' produces an ironic, self-reflexive piratical subject. The aesthetic contradictions of piracy are actually dramatized in the plot. One telling scene lampoons the poetics of piracy: buffoonish bard Claud Halcro rhapsodizes about ships, 'once the water-dragons of the world, swimming with the black-raven standard waving at the topmast, and their desks glimmering with arms' (138). It is an image that could have come straight from Byron.[6] But Magnus Troil, father of Minna and Brenda, abruptly shatters this romance with the cold hard 'fact' that 'your voyage may bring up at Execution-Dock' (138). Later in the same scene, an old man relates how he was press-ganged into maritime service years earlier, and fled when his ship was attacked. The romantic Minna and the poetic Claud are shocked:

> 'You might have died with him,' said Minna.
> 'And lived with him in all eternity, in immortal verse,' added Claud Halcro.
> (139)

The old man replies that he actually prefers having stayed alive in the intervening years. Cleveland, showing an alternative kind of realism (the reaction

---

[6]   The epigraph to Chapter 9 is a description of Conrad from *The Corsair* (Scott 199).

of a ship's captain), disgustedly opines that the deserter should have been lashed and pickled (139).[7]

Cleveland certainly fits the aesthetic mould of a piratical anti-hero: Norna tells him he is 'bold, haughty, and undaunted, unrestrained by principle, and having only ... a wild sense of indomitable pride, which such men call honour' (343). But for Fiona Robertson, Scott's depiction of Cleveland is ironic, 'firmly rejecting the charismatic misanthropy' that Byron's Conrad 'had substituted for heroism' (169). Moreover, Cleveland is not mysterious, as Conrad is. Mordaunt notes that he has 'the frank and open manners of a sailor' (80). Later, Cleveland tells Minna: 'I have not disguised from you that I have reason to fear the English laws' (204). Indeed, Scott presents Cleveland as almost a *deus ex machina* to dispel the mysteries that enshroud Zetland and that torment its inhabitants (Robertson 172).

In passing, Scott alludes wryly to a feminine tendency that could just as well characterize his readership as his characters: 'Women are always particularly desirous of investigating mystery ... especially when these circumstances are united in a handsome man about the prime of life' (12). The wilful Minna loves Cleveland as a romantic fantasy – a mysterious sea-king plucked from the waves (188) – but the novel sets up an inevitable clash with the realities of his life. 'What say you to shooting the man at the wheel, just as we run aboard of a Spaniard?' Cleveland asks Mordaunt (82). By the novel's conclusion, the scales have fallen from Minna's eyes. She tells Cleveland: 'I have seen your associates – need I tell you more – need I say that I know now what a pirate is?' (336). As Scott puts it, 'equally romantic and ignorant, she had built the fabric of her happiness on a quicksand instead of on a rock' (376).

We can see, therefore, that Scott's piratical subject is considerably more ambivalent than Johnson's or Byron's. Importantly, this ambivalence is produced through the same aesthetics Johnson and Byron use to create the piratical anti-hero, but by distancing them from the reader through the device of 'history'. When Cleveland leaves Zetland to rendezvous with his fellow pirates, Scott tells us his dress was 'considerably altered' (238). Scott's description is pilfered largely from Johnson's description of Black Bart:

> Cleveland himself was gallantly attired in a blue coat, lined with crimson silk, and laced with gold very richly, crimson damask waistcoat and breeches ... He had a gold chain several times folded round his neck ... Above all, he wore a decoration peculiar to those daring depredators, who, besides one, or perhaps two brace of pistols at their belt, had usually two additional brace, of the finest mounting and workmanship, suspended over their shoulders in a sort of sling or scarf of crimson ribband. (307)

---

[7]   This punishment involved whipping the sailor with the cat o' nine-tails and then immersing him in salt water or rubbing salt into his wounds. The pain was part of the punishment but the salt also served to help the wounds heal.

Moreover, where Johnson makes repeated use of phrases such as 'the fashion of the pirates' to suggest an alternative pirate society, Scott repeatedly mentions that these clothes are *historical* dress. Cleveland is also wearing 'white silk stockings, and red-heeled shoes, which were the extremity of finery among the gallants of the day' (307). Earlier in the book, Scott twice uses the phrase 'according to the fashion of the times' to describe clothing (112, 126). He also portrays Cleveland's pirate friend, Jack Bunce (who, in another jibe at the romance of piracy, thinks the name Frederick Altamont far more suitable for his profession), as having a manner of 'the free and easy rake of the period' (277).

Scott wants his narrative to be regarded as 'true', but at the same time he cannot immerse his reader completely in the historical setting. By emphasizing the temporal distance between the reader and the characters, Scott's simultaneous claims to history and romance allow him to present the piratical subject as anti-hero, while questioning the legitimacy of such a subject position. For example, the pirate Goffe is far less anti-heroic a spectacle than Cleveland, despite wearing very similar clothing. He 'looked like a boorish clown in the dress of a courtier, or rather like a vulgar-faced footpad decked in the spoils of some one who he had murdered' (307). Indeed, what he looked like was exactly what he was. So, Scott introduces an interesting qualification to the aesthetic piratical subject. Yes, the piratical subject can be visually signified; but it is the pirate's youth, good looks and ability to wear clothes well that really paper over his crimes.

Just as Johnson facilitated Byron and Scott's complex portraits of the pirate at the beginning of the nineteenth century, so *The Corsair* and *The Pirate* paved the way for both further consolidation and further parody of the aestheticized piratical subject. Gilbert and Sullivan's comic operetta *The Pirates of Penzance* was written in 1879; and J.M. Barrie's play *Peter Pan*, with its stage-ish villain Captain Hook, in 1904. But the text that most wholeheartedly takes on the Romantic project of aestheticizing piracy is Robert Louis Stevenson's 1883 novel, *Treasure Island*. For C.R. Pennell, *Treasure Island* is 'remarkably well told ... It rings true, even if it is not' (4). One-legged pirates like Long John Silver certainly existed, and *Treasure Island*'s language demonstrates a familiarity with ships and sailors. But some pirate practices, like the map with an X 'marking the spot' of buried treasure, are entirely inventions in the tradition of Johnson. Meanwhile, the genre of historical romance continued Scott's triumph of style over historical substance. Rafael Sabatini's early twentieth-century piratical adventure novels became the basis for canonical pirate movies like *Captain Blood* and *The Black Swan*. By interweaving fact and fiction, and transforming villain into anti-hero, a common maritime criminal has become a figure of enduring popular fascination. So, the spectacle of pirate chic in contemporary popular culture may irritate the historian with its 'inaccuracy', but its aesthetic appeal does not diminish its importance.

Chapter 2

The Pirate Poet in the Nineteenth Century: Trollope and Byron

Deborah Lutz

As a schoolboy at Harrow, Anthony Trollope, like his self-identified character from *The Small House at Allington* (1864), Johnny Eames, 'knew much, – by far too much, – of Byron's poetry by heart' (148). To know *too much* of Byron's writing portends a character's susceptibility to Romanticism's grand gestures, its deep pathos, its running after sublimity.[1] Yet Trollope's famous admirer of Byron, the delightful Lizzie Eustace of *The Eustace Diamonds* (1872), wants her corsair not only to 'be rough with her' but also to have 'an island of his own in the Aegean Sea' (405). Lizzie, in fact, has very little romantic sincerity and earnestness about her; she is not only an ambitious social climber and a genius at attracting and holding on to her capital, but she loves nothing more than to cleverly cheat and lie her way through whatever social difficulty confronts her. Another 'shallow' lady out for her own gain, Blanche Ingram of *Jane Eyre* (1847), informs Rochester that a 'man is nothing without a spice of the devil in him' and that a husband to her taste would be something of a 'wild, fierce, bandit-hero' (202): 'Know that I doat on Corsairs' (203), she pronounces, and goes on to remark, 'An English hero of the road would be the next best thing to an Italian bandit; and that could only be surpassed by a Levantine pirate' (209). Brontë means for the reader to see Blanche as 'showy' and 'not genuine'; 'she was not original: she used to repeat sounding phrases from books' (210). Like Lizzie, Blanche develops a repertoire of fashionable ideas to be expressed at parties, and a series of performances to attract men. Thus to be sophisticated, with a dash of daring, is to express desire for a pirate lover.

To set Byron's lover of the corsair, Medora, side by side with Trollope's Lizzie is to see a starkly rendered picture of the differences between Byron's Romantic idealism and Trollope's Victorian realism that colours erotic attraction in light of social and financial gain. She wants poetry in her lover, but also those other accompaniments of love: 'poetry was what her soul craved; – poetry, together with houses, champagne, jewels, and admiration' (654). While Lizzie's desire for

---

[1]   Trollope teased his mother, the writer Frances Trollope, for her Byron worship. She wrote a satirical poem in the style and verse of *Don Juan* about the refusal of the vicar of Harrow, John William Cunningham, to put a marker on the grave of Byron's daughter, Allegra, when she was buried at Harrow at Byron's request.

a corsair is presented as full of levity and even irony, an anatomy of this desire describes a particular articulation of the literary pirate-as-lover figure in the nineteenth century, strongly influenced by Byron.

Today, the pirate lover in historical romance erotically attracts largely because of his tinge of sadism – born of his own disappointments and of his tormented, oppressed past – tempered generally with a passionate tenderness.[2] The magnetism of the rough lover-bandit was already in place by the nineteenth century; Lady Eustace desires her corsair to be a sexual sadist, yet – and this also holds true for twentieth-century romantic pirates – she does not want him to be a financial one:

> he had fine Corsair's eyes, full of expression and determination, eyes that could look love and bloodshed almost at the same time; and then he had those manly properties – power, bigness, and apparent boldness – which belonged to a Corsair. To be hurried about the world by such a man, treated sometimes with crushing severity, and at others with the tenderest love, not to be spoken to for one fortnight, and then to be embraced perpetually for another, to be cast now and then into some abyss of despair by his rashness, and then raised to a pinnacle of human joy by his courage – that, thought Lizzie, would be the kind of life which would suit her poetical temperament. But then, how would it be with her, if her Corsair were to take to hurrying about the world without carrying her with him; – and were to do so always at her expense! Perhaps he might hurry about the world and take somebody else with him. Medora, if Lizzie remembered rightly, had had no jointure or private fortune. But yet a woman must risk something if the spirit of poetry is to be allowed any play at all! (437–8)

It is easy to recognize that Lizzie desires the moody, misanthropic, indeterminately tortured Byronic hero, whose sublime interiority presents the impression, as viewed from the exterior by the lover, of an inexplicable variety of fevered emotions and actions. Like many of his Victorian contemporaries, Trollope was himself drawn to dashing, bold outsiders – to Byronism – but also felt distaste for what he saw as the impropriety of such behaviour, even its immorality.[3] He seems to revel in the creation of such characters as George Vavasor in *Can You Forgive Her?* (1865), the rake with a Cain-like scar across his face, who simmers with barely suppressed violence. Trollope allows his romantic brutes a good deal of play before they are ultimately banished from the narrative realm, often in a punishing manner.

---

[2]   There are hundreds of twentieth-century pirate historical romances; in fact, they could be defined as their own subgenre; a few are Connie Mason's *Pirate* (New York: Leisure, 1998), Sabrina Jeffries' *The Pirate Lord* (New York: Avon, 1998) and Jayne Ann Krentz's *The Pirate* (New York: Harlequin, 1990).

[3]   Other Victorians who had similarly complicated love/hate relationships with Byronism were Carlyle, Ruskin and Bulwer Lytton.

In *The Last Chronicle of Barset* (1867), Lucy Toogood remarks jocularly that a certain type of nostalgic, Gothic love and the corsair have come to be folded together. Lucy, who 'knew Byron by heart', hopes that John Eames will continue to be in love, 'because it is such fun':

> I don't mean to be caught till some great swell comes this way. And as great swells never do come into Tavistock Square, I shan't have a chance. I'll tell you what I would like; I'd like to have a Corsair, – or else a Giaour; – I think a Giaour would be nicest. Only a Giaour wouldn't be a Giaour here, you know. Fancy a lover 'Who thundering comes on blackest steed, With slacked bit and hoof of speed.' Were not those the days to live in! But all that is over now, you know, and young people take houses in Woburn Place, instead of being locked up, or drowned, or married to a hideous monster behind a veil. … I know I'd go back and be Medora, if I could. Mamma is always telling Polly that she must be careful about William's dinner. But Conrad didn't care for his dinner. (396)

No Byronic lover will whisk her off into a violent adventure, but rather love has come to represent dull domesticity – dinners and setting up house in mundane Woburn Place. Trollope would say this was a good thing, as Lucy would probably admit too, if pressed.

Byronic characters were, well before the 1860s and 1870s when Trollope published *The Eustace Diamonds* and *The Last Chronicle of Barset*, already well-recognized stereotypes, satirized as early as 1818 in Thomas Love Peacock's *Nightmare Abbey* – particularly the 'gloomy brow' and 'tragical voice' – and used often by Silver-Fork novelists such as Edward Bulwer Lytton and Catherine Gore in the 1820s and 1830s, as dramatic elements easily identified by readers, or as a means of parodying romantic melancholy, titanic character or poetic dandyism.[4] Byron anticipated his critics, with alacrity, by commenting upon his own literary creations soon after their appearance in print, in his letters and more completely and carefully in *Don Juan* (1819–24). Byron wrote with amusement of his 'Harry and Larrys, Pilgrims, and Pirates' (*Ravenna* 3.169). He wanted to write of deep passions and abyssal subjectivity yet, knowing what an easy target such drama was, he also felt the need to circumvent cynical ridicule by a sometimes debilitating self-deprecation. Trollope continues this tradition of poking fun at grandiose desires by immediately following Lizzie's erotic thoughts of being mastered by the corsair with worries about the expenses of keeping her own pirate and the possibility of his villainy affecting her property. The quandary that comes from questioning the value of love for an inaccessible and potentially destructive other continues to be a problem for Lizzie and those faced with similar desires:

---

[4]   A number of scholars have studied the use of Byronic characters in nineteenth-century literature. Of particular value are Andrew Elfenbein's *Byron and the Victorians*, Frances Wilson's *Byromania: Portraits of the Artist in Nineteenth- and Twentieth-Century Culture*, and Samuel Chew's *Byron in England: His Fame and After Fame*.

how much is she willing to risk for a dangerous lover? This question could be asked of Byron or Trollope as well – how much are they willing to risk for their attraction to such a perilously dramatic and dangerously camp figure? The answer would be: Byron, much; Trollope, very little. Or more pointedly, how can one be both mastered (by unmitigated passion in the case of Trollope and Byron, and by a pirate in the case of Lizzie) and maintain mastery whenever one might want it? Because Lizzie herself is a master and something of a sadist ('she liked the power of being arrogant to those around her' [51]) who proves to be the most domineering and cleverest character in the narrative, one wonders what she wants with a pirate at all. This brings us to a central question of this chapter: what does Lizzie Eustace find erotic about Byron's corsair or, more generally, what were some of the ways in which the literary depiction of the pirate in the nineteenth century became linked with erotic visions of the perfect lover?

In the quotation above, Lizzie feels the need to feed the fire of her 'poetical temperament', and she realizes the outlaying of some risk is required 'if the spirit of poetry is to be allowed any play at all' (438). Lizzie describes her interest in Byron and Shelley as proof of her deep-rooted feeling, her sublime emotions and her propensity to love hugely, to pine eternally. Perhaps Lizzie even believes (or at least would certainly like to have us believe) that the perfect life for her is living in seclusion at her castle in Scotland, reading poetry and thinking. She tries to work up the proper feeling when reading Shelley's *Queen Mab: A Philosophical Poem* (1813) – 'Ah, how true it is; how one feels it; how it comes home to one!' (232). Yet she reads merely the first stanza, and with no real comprehension and certainly no understanding of the radical politics of the poem. Lizzie reads poetry in order to memorize it, so that she can later quote it to others:

> And so the piece was learned, and Lizzie felt that she had devoted her hour to poetry in a quite rapturous manner. At any rate she had a bit to quote; and though in truth she did not understand the exact bearing of the image, she had so studied her gestures, and so modulated her voice, that she knew that she could be effective. (233)

Romantic poetry works as Lizzie's proof of her 'cultivated tastes'; she reads poetry only to turn it into cultural capital. Lizzie wants to appear to be refined, with the least amount of work possible; she wants to garner admiration, particularly from men, for having a poetic temperament or being the type of person who loves the solitary life, who lives inwardly, who spends most of her time reading and brooding with pathetic melancholy and emotion – characteristics of the 'man of genius' popularized by Byron.[5] Lizzie works to cultivate the demeanour of the deep thinker and intellectual because she knows the power of poetry and its related

---

[5]   Dino Franco Felluga discusses the way brooding melancholy became linked with the poet, and Byron in particular, in *The Perversity of Poetry: Romantic Ideology and the Popular Male Poet of Genius*.

emotionality in the art of seduction. She uses poetry to win Sir Florian Eustace – 'Lizzie read poetry well, and she read verses to him – sitting very near to him, almost in the dark … . He was astonished to find how sweet a thing was poetry' (44) – a masterful move which brings her a fortune, a title, and a husband who dies before the year is out.

Lady Eustace has no real passionate desire for knowledge or love, yet she knows the value of appearing, at least occasionally, to have them. Poetry, in fact, comes to *represent* 'love' in *The Eustace Diamonds*; it represents the means to fire up desire in the heart of another; the path to upper-class sophistication which leads to proper marriages, settlements and jointures; the quick path to feeling profound, pathos-producing emotion. In Lizzie's mind, to be in love is to be in love with a corsair:

> Now she desired to be so in love that she could surrender everything to her love. … [S]he was alive to the romance of the thing, and was in love with the idea of being in love. 'Ah,' she would say to herself in her moments of solitude, 'if I had a Corsair of my own, how I would sit on watch for my lover's boat by the sea-shore!' (81)

The pirate becomes linked – in Trollope and, I will argue below, in Byron, Scott and later pirate narratives – with social refinement, with intellectual achievements and with a cultivated melancholy, represented in Lizzie's mind by Romantic poetry and the Byronic lover. The pirate then comes to encompass these seemingly paradoxical elements: he embodies the height of discrimination, he is linked to the most seductive poetry, yet he is also the dark and dangerous lover, an outcast and villain with a masterful power to seduce, to rape, to pillage.[6]

The cultivated pirate who reads and who has a history of learning was, for the most part, a product of nineteenth-century nostalgia. By 1814, when Byron wrote *The Corsair*, the days when gentleman buccaneers roamed the open seas were long gone.[7] The legendary British pirates whose names and stories would be familiar to the reading public in the nineteenth century were Elizabethan or seventeenth century, such as Sir Francis Drake (ca. 1540–1596), Sir Henry Morgan (ca. 1635–1688) and William Kidd (ca. 1645–1701). Western pirates of Byron's time were generally land-based marauders or small-scale privateers, part of the French Revolutionary and Napoleonic Wars of 1793–1815 or the War of 1812, such as Jean Lafitte, one of the historical sources for Byron's corsair, a

---

[6] Another literary-historical trajectory of the erotic pirate that should be mentioned here is the gay-coded pirate; see for instance B.R. Burg's *Sodomy and the Pirate Tradition* (New York: New York UP, 1995) and Hans Turley's *Rum, Sodomy, and the Lash: Piracy, Sexuality, and Masculine Identity* (New York: New York UP, 1999).

[7] Byron's lasting interest in pirates can be seen in his regular use of them in his poetry. Not only did he write *Lara*, a sequel to *The Corsair*, but 'Prisoner of Chillon', *Manfred* and *Don Juan* all mention pirates.

Franco-American privateer who marauded ships off the Gulf of Mexico.[8] Byron's appropriation of the pirate narrative emerges from a particular kind of nostalgia – a longing for the past that we also see, as Mel Campbell demonstrates, in the central tone of Scott's *The Pirate* (1821) – that desires lost myths and long-gone grandeur. Nostalgic longing appears as a central motif of Romantic era poetry: the focus on time passing, an interest in the ruin, the cemetery, the dead, the attempt at revivification of what has gone before.[9] With Scott especially, this nostalgia points to the desire for a connection to a great time, full of ancient magic and folklore, now lost in the mysterious past.[10] Both Scott and Byron – not to mention many other Gothic and Romantic writers in love with medievalism or other reconstructed historical periods (Coleridge, Keats, Radcliffe, Lewis, Beckford, Walpole, just to name a few) – wished to revivify archaic narrative forms such as the epic, the romance and the tale of chivalry. The pirate narrative belongs to this historiographical project whose central work is redemption – here the work becomes the literary revisioning of the historical pirate into a glamorous figure representing love, refinement and rebellion.

Given the Romantic and Gothic interest in the noble, self-willed outlaw, who, in his superior passions, sees through society's petty interests and has the courage to defy them with a misanthropic villainy, it is easy to see how the pirate would naturally be appropriated as a ruling figure. Such a character is almost entirely a literary construct. For the most part, pirates were obscure men – mostly drawn from the working class or lower middle class – who wanted to make money, even if it meant breaking the law, stealing and murdering; in effect, they were violent criminals. The historian Marcus Rediker points out that in the early eighteenth century pirates were almost always merchant seaman or Royal Navy sailors who defected from their oppressive and hard-working occupations to enter the comparative egalitarianism of the pirate ship, where authority was placed in the collective hands of the crew. However, both Byron and Scott's pirates come from the upper classes or the aristocracy; they are gentleman in bearing, speech and dress.[11] It is quite difficult to find a historical pirate who fits the Romantic

---

8   Alexander Cowie points out that Byron made Lafitte famous when he described his exploits in a footnote to *The Corsair*. A flurry of historical novels were written in America on the Lafitte legend, from 1826 to 1836, such as the bestseller *Lafitte, The Pirate of the Gulf* (1835) by Joseph Holt Ingraham.

9   As in Wordsworth's 'Tintern Abbey' or *The Prelude*, which call up past joys and experiences and refashion them with thought; or Byron's *Manfred* or *The Giaour*, haunted by the dead lover and a sense of the irrevocable; or the beauty and pain of mortality, in Keats's 'Ode to a Nightingale' or 'When I have fears that I may cease to be'.

10   Scott's historical fiction and poetry call up this desire for a more magical past, especially in such works as *The Bride of Lammermore* with its ancient curse and *Ivanhoe* with its grandiose medievalism.

11   Scott's Captain Cleveland in *The Pirate* is based on John Gow, a buccaneer of the Orkney Islands in the early eighteenth century.

construct; most of the 'pirates' educated as gentlemen were privateers working for the most part within the law, or at least were not 'noble' misanthropic exiles, such as Morgan, John Oxenham (ca. 1550–1580)[12] and Prince Rupert of the Rhine (1619–1682). And then there were the unredeemable pirates, who seem, given the little true information we have on them, to be cruel and savage men who had nothing noble or gentleman-like about them, such as Edward 'Blackbeard' Teach (ca. 1680–1718) and John 'Calico Jack' Rackham (1868–1720). However, such a discussion misses the point of the pirate figure altogether. The pirate attracts because he is a character of legend or myth; truth and historical accuracy fall away almost immediately as soon as the pirate story is recounted.[13]

Much of the movement and resonance of Byron and Scott's narratives comes from the pathos-producing difference between the position the pirate chief was meant to hold in society and the one he has now chosen to pursue. The very gestures of Scott's pirate illustrate this: 'He spoke in a tone at once impassioned and insinuating, and his whole language and manner seemed to express a grace and elegance which formed the most striking contrast with the speech and gesture of the unpolished seaman which he usually affected or exhibited' (203). Marked by tragedy, the pirate lives a cursed life, often glorying in his cursedness.

The pirate chief in Byron's *The Corsair*, 'that man of loneliness and mystery' (1.173), inspires fear and awe in his band by his scorn for human emotion and needs, in his bold crimes, which demonstrate an utter disregard for his own life as well as those of others. An *avant la lettre* Nietzschean Übermensch,[14] 'Lone, wild and strange, he stood alike exempt / From all affection and from all contempt' (1.271–2), the corsair is pained by a vague interior blightedness attributed indefinitely to being 'warped by the world in Disappointment's school' (1.253). Part of the sexual attraction of the utterly blackened and unredeemable criminal is a fantasy of bold sadism, as we have seen with Lizzie Eustace, yet the pirate must have one or two added elements in order to embody enough complexity to fascinate, as Lizzie puts it after she finally sees through her 'corsair': 'Lord George

---

¹²   In Charles Kingsley's historical novel *Westward Ho!* (1855), Oxenham appears as a character.

¹³   Byron and Scott were not the first to glamorize pirates; they themselves were surely familiar with extremely popular books written in the seventeenth and eighteenth centuries about pirates, such as Alexander Esquemelin's *History of the Buccaneers of America* (1678); *General History of the Robberies and Murders of the Most Notorious Pyrates* (1724), thought by many to be written by Defoe but published under the name Captain Charles Johnson; Defoe's novels *The King of Pirates* (1719), *Captain Singleton* (1720) and others. The tales in these first two books spawned many pirate novels and stories, including Scott's *The Pirate*, parts of R.L. Stevenson's *Treasure Island* (1883) and J.M. Barrie's *Peter Pan* (1904).

¹⁴   In fact, the influence goes the other way. Nietzsche was a great admirer of Byronism. He wrote in *Ecce Homo*, 'I have no word, only a glance, for those who dare to pronounce the word 'Faust' in the presence of Manfred' (254).

was no longer a Corsair but a brute' (621). The most obvious added element in
Byron's poem as well as Scott's novel is, in the depths of his hellish interiority, the
capability of loving passionately. His misanthropy and expressions of inhumanity,
paradoxically, lead to his seeing all that is good, beautiful and true in the other,
who embodies everything that the rest of the world and humanity lack. Byron's
corsair, Lord Conrad, says to his beloved after she asks him to quit his violent and
roaming life,

> Yea, strange indeed – that heart hath long been changed;
> Worm-like 'twas trampled – adder-like avenged –
> Without one hope on earth beyond thy love,
> And scarce a glimpse of mercy from above.
> Yet the same feeling which thou dost condemn,
> My very love to thee is hate to them,
> So closely mingling here, that disentwined,
> I cease to love thee when I love Mankind. (1.398–405)

The pirate's love depends on a process of expulsion from divine and human
forces, which causes the full intensity of his desire to fall on one woman, who
becomes his only possibility for salvation. This could be called 'outcast love'; a
love that depends upon near wholesale rejection – of a god and a societal bond.
Byron defines the pirate as the ruined man whose only redemption could come
through romantic love. *This* is the kind of love that would suit Lizzie's 'poetical
temperament' – in other words, one that constructs her as full possessor. Lizzie's
subjectivity revolves around possession and display, and the corsair's love, as
she imagines it, would be fully legible to others as *her own*. Other than this one
obsessive love, the pirate's subjectivity is filled with an emptiness resulting from
dispossession.

The corsair also has the finely wrought melancholy which, to the minds of
Victorians like Lizzie Eustace, marks a Romantic sensibility in tune with reasons
to mourn the past and feelings of loss because modernity has brought a break
with the natural world. Caught often in 'pensive posture' (131), Conrad has a
'murkiness of mind' (211) within which 'worked feelings fearful' (212). Although
Lizzie does not fully understand the melancholy stance, she does see it as genteel,
even aristocratic. If Lord Byron and Shelley, in line for a baronetcy, were doing
it, shouldn't she? Lizzie gets caught up in the cult of Byronism, described by
Andrew Elfenbein, Frances Wilson and other Byron scholars, that led to a slavish
imitation of qualities associated first with Byron's imaginary characters and then,
through a subtle confusion, with Byron himself.[15] Young men in the 1820s and
1830s imitated 'Byronism' in order to express a sophisticated eroticism. Elfenbein

---

[15]   See Andrew Elfenbein, *Byron and the Victorians*. Cambridge and New York:
Cambridge U Press, 1995 and Frances Wilson (ed.), *Byromania: Portraits of the Artist in
Nineteenth and Twentieth-Century Culture*. New York: St Martin's Press, 1999.

quotes John Edmund Reade from 1829, who comments that 'open shirt-collars, and melancholy features; and a certain dash of remorse, were ... indispensable to young men' (67). At least one friend appropriated the corsair attitude. The swashbuckling Edward John Trelawny, who joined Byron and the Shelleys in Pisa in 1822, seemed to Byron to be 'the personification of my corsair. He sleeps with the poem under his pillow, and all his past adventures and present manner aim at this personification' (qtd. in Marchand 3: 963).[16]

As with *Childe Harold's Pilgrimage, The Corsair* was thought by readers to be about Byron's own experience. Byron was never averse to milking such simplistic thinking in his admirers, which made him seem more interestingly dark and dangerous and made his characters more vivid, since they seemed to be partially taken from life. In fact, in his journal of 18 February 1814, Byron mysteriously alludes to the possibility of his tale of the corsair being a representation of his own adventures in Greece: '"The Corsair" has been conceived, written, published, &c., since I last took up this Journal. They tell me it has great success; – it was written *con amore*, and much from existence' (qtd. in Marchand 3: 243). His friend Hobhouse told Byron of the rumours on 10 March: 'He told me an odd report, – that I am the actual Conrad, the veritable corsair, and that part of my travels are supposed to have passed in privacy [piracy?]. Um! – people sometimes hit near the truth; but never the whole truth' (qtd. in Marchand 3: 250). Whether or not Byron practised piracy is irrelevant; what is important is that in the popular imagination Byron may have done so, and thus the pirate figure became conflated with Byron, the famous artist and fashionable dandy. Hence, although his corsair is not a poet or an artist, the common identification of Byron with his pirate paints the pirate as a gifted, dashing young writer, for a time a member of the most exclusive circles of Regency London. It is thus that the pirate becomes the gorgeous, melancholy poet and even comes, for Lizzie Eustace, to gesture toward representing the state of being in love itself.[17] In Byron, melancholy usually develops out of insatiable desire, thus sadness takes on an eroticism, with characters such as Manfred, Childe Harold and the corsair. Erotic melancholy, according to the rulebook of Byronism, most aptly expresses itself in poetry, which is certainly a belief Lizzie holds.

While the pirate must be dispossessed, he must also be very much in possession. Often he embodies his capital to the farthest extent by displaying his wealth in his

---

[16]   Trelawny went on to write an almost entirely fictional autobiography, *Adventures of a Younger Son* (1831), in which he becomes a pirate.

[17]   William St Clair points out that the majority of commonplace books of the period have copied-out excerpts of Byron's poems and that these fragments show that he was treasured, by women especially, as the poet of 'long-suffering constant tragic love' (10). Elfenbein feels that the commonly noted propensity for women to fall for Byron and Byronic heroes was something of a stereotype got up by literary critics. A number of Victorian novels depict women comically falling all over Byron, such as Arthur Clough's *Amours de Voyage* (1858), George Eliot's *Felix Holt* (1866) and Samuel Butler's *Way of All Flesh* (1903).

clothing.[18] Captain Cleveland, the pirate of Scott's novel, sallies forth in just such a fully signifying outfit: 'Cleveland himself was gallantly attired in a blue coat, lined with crimson silk, and laced with gold very richly, crimson damask waistcoat and breeches, a velvet cap, richly embroidered, with a white feather, white silk stockings, and red-heeled shoes, which were the extremity of finery among the gallants of the day' (307). Scott links the pirate with another popular hero of the Regency and post-Regency period, the dandy. While the Silver-Fork novel – the most popular chronicle of the dandy's exploits among the rich and fashionable – did not appear until the late 1820s, the dandy's appearance in both society and literature can be traced back to at least the late eighteenth century, and particularly to Fanny Burney's satirizing of the dandy pose and costume in *Camilla* (1796). The dandy, obsessively attentive to appearances, creates an inimitable style that becomes the benchmark for fashion. His work entails dropping in his cunning wit in apt situations – having a 'devil of a tongue' (17), as does Vivian in Benjamin Disraeli's Silver-Fork, *Vivian Grey* (1826–1827) – and manipulating and leading an exclusive circle that must be both secret and known by everyone as the most fashionable and desirable place to be. That Scott presents his pirate as a dandy expresses the importance of the pirate's place as not only fully outside, but, paradoxically, at the very centre or pinnacle of society. The play between inside and outside brings us back to Lizzie Eustace and her corsair who, representing poetic love and refined intellectuality even though he is also an outcast and outlaw, might mask her ambitious vulgarity by giving her the intellectual sheen of the cultured classes. The dandy attracted using a similar dual sleight of hand. He had to be well-read in order to develop his cutting wit – constantly referencing a large range of contemporary and classical culture. In Bulwer Lytton's Silver-Fork novel, *Pelham* (1828), the eponymous hero admits that 'there has not been a day in which I have spent less than six hours reading and writing' (201). Yet everything needed to appear effortless for the jaded, cynical dilettante who spun his web by not caring, yet being always perfect in those aspects where he seemed most careless. Trebeck, in Thomas Henry Lister's Silver-Fork *Granby* (1826), is 'gracefully indolent', with a 'reputation of being able to do a great deal if he would but condescend to set about it' (52). Lizzie, without being a scholar or an intellectual, wants to *appear* to know and feel poetry. The pirate also exemplifies this hinged interior/exterior, which I shall discuss more fully below, which manifests itself in an oft-changing array of rough villainy and refinement moving from hidden to manifest and back again.

Many dandies, including the most famous real-life Regency dandy and friend of Byron (another famous dandy), Beau Brummel, so carefully and fully master the paring away of all that would seem to express a running after position, a desire to be admired, that they dressed in the simplest manner, usually all black, with a plain but perfectly cut coat. The façade of *not* dressing to impress masks the strongest desire to represent and create exclusivity and the most sophisticated

---

[18]   The pirate as dandy dates back at least to the Elizabethan period, however. The flashily dressed pirate remains today a popular way of representing and satirizing the figure.

fashion. Unusual in later literary depictions of pirates (such as Long John Silver in *Treasure Island* or Captain Hook in *Peter Pan*), Byron's poem presents the corsair as an ascetic man, who despises luxurious clothing, food and drink.

> Ne'er for his lip the purpling cup they fill.
> That goblet passes him untasted still –
> And for his fare – the rudest of his crew
> Would that, in turn, have passed untasted too;
> Earth's coarsest bread, the garden's homeliest roots,
> And scarce the summer luxury of fruits,
> His short repast in humbleness supply
> With all a hermit's board would scarce deny.
> But while he shuns the grosser joys of sense,
> His mind seems nourished by that abstinence. (1.67–76)

Conrad shuns the sensual world for an interior life full of extravagant emotion, excessive passion and transcendent meaningfulness. The inward life is hidden behind an opposite exterior. In his ability to both veil and reveal, the pirate's impenetrable wholeness is both unreadable and signifying endlessly, it both presents and then represents, in a kind of seductive striptease of subjectivity.[19]

The pirate-lover's possession of a good deal of cultural capital as well as literal capital – he must have both his island in the Aegean sea, or at least some pirate treasure somewhere, like Captain Cleveland in Scott's *The Pirate*, and a refined and

---

[19]   This complicated duality of the pirate as one of his attractions also appears in Shelley's unfinished poem *Drama*, where two women are in love with the same pirate. An Indian 'Enchantress' falls for the pirate, 'a man of savage but noble nature', as Mary Shelley describes him in her introduction to the poem, when she saves his life. But he already has a lover, and in the fragment the two women meet and describe their pained love. 'He was as is the sun in his fierce youth, / As terrible and lovely as a tempest' (58–9) …

> He was so awful, yet
> So beautiful in mystery and terror,
> Calming me as the loveliness of heaven
> Soothes the unquiet sea: – and yet not so,
> For he seemed stormy, and would often seem
> A quenchless sun masked in portentous clouds;
> For such his thought, and even his actions were;
> But he was not of them, nor they of him,
> But as they hid his splendour from the earth.
> Some said he was a man of blood and peril,
> And steeped in bitter infamy to the lips. (103–13)

These women cherish the pirate's secret interior, the mystery of his self that can be 'so beautiful' yet 'so awful', 'terrible' yet 'lovely', 'calming' yet 'stormy'.

cultured sensibility – is usually deeply hidden and follows the classic pirate trope of buried treasure. Many nineteenth-century pirate narratives centre on hidden treasure of some sort, the most famous being *Treasure Island* (1883). Even pirates who do not ostensibly possess treasure depend on unknown or barely glimpsed stores. As mentioned above, the act of hiding, of keeping secret something of surprisingly large value, is a key element of the pirate figure. Byron's corsair has a mask-like exterior – 'Though smooth his voice, and calm his general mien, / Still seems there something he would not have seen' (207–8) – which serves to cover, often with only minor success, a roiling interiority, 'as if within that murkiness of mind / Worked feelings fearful, and yet undefined' (211–12). And Captain Cleveland of Scott's *The Pirate* also has an 'iron mask':

> for on that spot of barren sand I found, or rather forged, the iron mask which has since been my chief security against treason or mutiny of my followers ... I bargained with myself then, that, since I could not lay aside my superiority of intellect and education, I would do my best to disguise, to sink in the rude seaman, all appearance of better feeling and better accomplishments. (210)

Cain, the pirate chief in Frederick Marryat's *The Pirate* (1836), has a secret past trauma – that the woman he loved died from a blow from his own hand – that curses him and drives him to violent despair. With the pirate all lies within and this 'all' represents 'deeper passions', vastness, an abyssal infinity. To expose 'the naked heart' of the corsair is to see a sublime depth of pain, a 'secret spirit' that cannot be represented: 'No words suffice the secret soul to show, / For Truth denies all eloquence to Woe' (*The Corsair*, 3.1812–13). The secret interior or buried treasure of the corsair, whether this treasure holds pain or a huge capacity for desire, becomes erotically attractive because of its inaccessible quality; the lover is drawn toward the untouchability and the unknowability of the pirate soul, to a longing for that which withdraws, just out of reach. Elfenbein, through a reading of *The Corsair*, argues that Byron created a figure whose profound subjectivity, linked with unfulfillable desire, made subjectivity itself erotic. 'The key to the naked heart in Byron', he writes, 'is the eroticization of all inner emotions in terms of desire so profound that they can never be fulfilled' (18). Thus, the structure behind the pirate's compelling magnetism involves the one outside looking into the obscured interior, eternally secluded; yet, paradoxically, she will be invited to step in and be herself the erotic centre. To be the one who looks in and witnesses the buried treasure – the beloved such as Medora or Scott's Minna Troil – is to be in the position of becoming the redeemer, the only chance of grace in the world. This position is a powerful one, one which Lizzie, herself masterful, covets.

Similarly, in Scott's story, Minna Troils's attraction for the pirate-as-lover evolves out of his ability to narrativize his experience, to make of it a vast store of adventure and knowledge that Minna wants to possess. He 'tells Minna romantic stories of foreign people, and distant wars, in wild and unknown regions' (149) and she imagines she has found in him a kindred spirit, another who is a 'lover of solitude, and of those paths of knowledge in which men walk best without company' (122). Minna pictures him stepping out of the past; she believes she sees in him one of her great and noble ancestors, a sea-king or a Norse champion, heroes because of their daring deeds and courage. She wants to love the mythical wronged man with a great well of passions; she wishes him to embody all her fantasies of greatness. Like Lizzie, she wants her lover's hidden treasure to become as legible as her own, possessed because only she recognizes it, only she witnessed it and can heal his soul with her intimate understanding.[20] Once he loses his connection to the storied past, she refuses to entertain the idea of him as her lover.

The pirate as thinker and scholar – his enigmatic brooding – adds further erotic depth to what is already a vast interior, increasing an already manifold subjectivity. The sudden uncovering of his surprising capacity for thought awes, fascinates and finally seduces. Following the famous lines in Byron's *The Corsair*, 'That man of loneliness and mystery', the corsair's mindscape, and thus the reason behind this mystery, is described:

> That man of loneliness and mystery,
> Scarce seen to smile, and seldom heard to sigh;
> Whose name appals the fiercest of his crew,
> And tints each swarthy cheek with sallower hue;
> Still sways their souls with that commanding art
> That dazzles, leads, yet chills the vulgar heart.
> What is that spell, that thus his lawless train
> Confess and envy – yet oppose in vain?
> What should it be, that thus their faith can bind?
> The power of Thought – the magic of the Mind! (1.173–82)

One of the clearest pictures of the erotic reaction the corsair elicits, the swarthy cheeks of his men are painted with the desire to rebel, to be fascinated and to love their magical chief and his enigmatic actions. The sensual mixture of being both chilled and dazzled casts the spell of the pirate, and a prime ingredient of this heady concoction has to do with 'the power of Thought'. The thinker is one who sways souls by appearing to close off from others a world whose power comes

---

[20]   The woman who wants to plumb the depths of the immense soul of her mysterious lover is common in stories with Byronic characters. *Jane Eyre* and *Wuthering Heights* are prime examples. Jane looks into Rochester's face and eyes:

> and as for the vague something ... that opened on a careful observer, now and then, in his eye, and closed again before one could fathom the strange depth partially disclosed; that something which used to make me fear and shrink, as if I had been wandering amongst volcanic-looking hills, and had suddenly felt the ground quiver, and seen it gape ... Instead of wishing to shun, I longed only to dare – to divine ... the abyss. (213)

from its mystery. One who broods holds himself aloof from the everyday bustle, and draws the interest of others through his self-containment and self-reliance; he can entertain himself with his mind, always finding fresh scenes and activities within. His power comes from the attraction of his disconsolate independence.[21]

Thus, in addition to a limitless secret interior that might be possessed by a lover, the pirate must also have buried in his subjectivity a learned mind, a dark reflectiveness that comes from the solid education of a gentleman. Interior stores of knowledge and education must be hidden like treasure, as we see from the Scott quotation above; it became a matter of survival for Captain Cleveland to hide his gentlemanly and humane temper – which includes Latin and Greek: 'I have travelled books as well as seas in my day' (165) – from the rest of his pirate crew. Cultivation makes the pirate poetic, as Lizzie knows; otherwise he is just a brute. This further romanticization of the pirate as sensitive intellectual becomes common in the pirate narrative after Byron and Scott.[22] In fact, Byron's *The Corsair* refitted the pirate figure as a scholar, gentleman and sometimes even an artist, and many later pirate narratives reflect this influence.[23] While it may be difficult to believe that a poem by Byron could have such a heavy and lasting influence, it is hard to overstate the popularity of Byron's writing throughout the nineteenth century and into the twentieth. William St. Clair estimates *The Corsair* sold to 36 per cent of the readership and was the most popular of Byron's poems in terms of sales until *Don Juan* was published (216). *The Corsair* sold 10,000 copies in a single day in 1814. Sales of Byron's poems consistently broke records, even topping those of the immensely popular Walter Scott, and *The Corsair* was almost immediately carried into other media. David Blayney Brown, in his description of paintings and illustrations of Byron's poems, points out that *The Corsair* appealed to readers visually, and was 'the most painted and illustrated of Byron's poems' (28). Brown

---

[21]   The pirate is more of a brooder than a thinker, as Walter Benjamin would define it: a brooder being a kind of thinker who never solves the puzzles he sets his mind to, but rather finds endless food for more brooding. Benjamin describes the sadness of the brooder, as opposed to the simple thinker:

What fundamentally distinguishes the brooder from the thinker is that the former not only meditates a thing but also meditates his meditation of the thing. The case of the brooder is that of the man who has arrived at the solution of a great problem but then has forgotten it. And now he broods – not so much over the matter itself as over his past reflections on it. The brooder's thinking, therefore, bears the imprint of memory. (367)

[22]   Wim Tigges's 'A Glorious Thing: The Byronic Hero as Pirate Chief', traces the romanticization of the pirate in nineteenth- and early twentieth-century children's fiction, and also discusses Byron's impact on boys' adventure stories.

[23]   One historical pirate who has some affinity to the Romantic pirate was William Dampier (1651–1715). While not exactly a gentleman, Dampier was highly literate and eager for knowledge about the world. He kept careful journals on his travels, and they were published in four volumes between 1697 and 1709 under the title *A New Voyage Around the World*. Becoming a bestseller, the book was used by a number of writers for research, such as Defoe and Jonathan Swift, for *Gulliver's Travels*.

relates that in 1814 paintings of scenes from *The Corsair* by Henry Singleton and Richard Corbould appeared at the Royal Academy. During the same year, the Princess of Wales requested that Johann Heinrich Fuseli paint her a subject from Byron, and he chose one from *The Corsair*: 'Conrad Liberates Gulnare'.[24]

Byron felt that the pirate-scholar was such an important element of his corsair character that he included a lengthy endnote with an account of a buccaneer-scholar.[25] Though apocryphal, the story of Archbishop Blackbourne is presented by Byron as possibly having some basis in fact. Byron does not give his reasons for including the endnote, but he does write: '... there is a singular passage in [Mark Noble's] account of Archbishop Blackbourne; and as in some measure connected with the profession of the hero of the foregoing poem, I cannot resist the temptation of extracting it' (298). It seems that Byron included such an involved and tangential story as a kind of proof that pirate-scholars did possibly exist, and thus his Conrad, he tries to convince us, is not such a fanciful construction of his mind, but indeed had some basis in historical fact.[26] He quotes from the 'singular passage' in Mark Noble's *Biographical History of England*:

> There is something mysterious in the history and character of Dr. Blackbourne. The former is but imperfectly known; and report has even asserted he was a buccaneer ... How is it possible a buccaneer should have been so good a scholar as Blackbourne certainly was? He who had so perfect a knowledge of the classics (particularly of the Greek tragedians), as to be able to read them with the same ease as he could Shakespeare, must have taken great pains to acquire the learned languages; and have had both leisure and good masters. (298–9)

As Byron (and Lizzie) knew, the pairing of the buccaneer and the scholar, whether possible or not, created the kind of complexity, the kind of paradox, that led to erotic attraction.

Practically every literary pirate of the nineteenth and early twentieth centuries was influenced by Byronism and the re-imagining of the pirate as a gentleman with interior, hidden treasure. As Alex Thomson notes in his chapter in this collection, Long John Silver of *Treasure Island* 'was that genteel' (98), had 'good schooling'

---

[24]   Eugene Delacroix painted a watercolour, around 1831, of Gulnare saving Conrad. Also, books of illustrations of Byron's poems proliferated, such as William Finden's *Byron Gallery* and *Byron's Beauties* (1830s). The Italian composer Giuseppe Verdi created an opera of *The Corsair* in 1848 – *Il corsaro*.

[25]   Other historical sources of Byron's corsair, in addition to the already mentioned Lafitte, are discussed in Harold Wiener's 'Byron and the East: Literary Sources of the "Turkish Tales"'. *Nineteenth-Century Studies*. Davis, William DeVane and Bald (eds). New York: Greenwood, 1968, 89–129.

[26]   In the sequel to *The Corsair*, *Lara*, Conrad becomes Lara – a landed gentleman who is a reader: 'Books ... / With eye more curious he appear'd to scan, / And oft, in sudden mood, for many a day, / From all communion he would start away' (1.130–34).

(54) and was an exceedingly quick thinker. Captain Hook in *Peter Pan* manages to be a dirty, vulgar, evil figure, but also a sympathetic, sophisticated, dandified gentleman. The children are afraid of Hook, with his 'cadaverous and blackavised' (63) countenance, who 'was Blackbeard's bo'sun ... the worst of them all. He is the only man of whom Barbecue was afraid' (54). Yet his ugliness falls away with his Byronic melancholy: 'His eyes were of the blue of forget-me-not, and of a profound melancholy' (63). No matter how vicious he becomes, still 'in manner, something of the grand seigneur still clung to him ... The elegance of his diction, even when he was swearing, no less than the distinction of his demeanour, showed him one of a different caste from his crew' (63). Some of the observations about Hook clearly mimic lines from *The Corsair*, such as 'Ever a dark and solitary enigma, he stood aloof from his followers in spirit as in substance' (147) and 'This inscrutable man never felt more alone that when surrounded by his dogs [his men]. They were socially so inferior to him. Hook was not his true name. To reveal who he really was would even at this date set the country in a blaze ... he had been at a famous public school ...' (164–5). Like the corsair's crew in Byron, the children admire Hook, in the midst of their fear. After Peter Pan kills him, he wears 'Hook's wickedest garments', and 'sat long in the cabin with Hook's cigar holder in his mouth and one hand clenched, all but the forefinger, which he bent and held threateningly aloft like a hook' (190).

Who doesn't want to be a Byronic pirate? Certainly a huge raft of pirate stories for children in the nineteenth and twentieth centuries were influenced by *The Corsair*, such as many of those serialized in boys' 'penny dreadfuls' – cheap and sensational magazines – like *Boys of England*, *Sons of Britannia* and *The Boys Standard*.[27] W.H.G. Kingston's children's adventure stories often included pirates with Byronic qualities, such as Zappa in *Pirate of the Mediterranean* (1851), who is a 'man of mystery', decorates his island hideout with 'silk cushions', 'valuable oil paintings' and 'priceless musical instruments' and has a beautiful captive wife (qtd. in Carpenter 72).[28] A number of influential pirate novels for adults appropriated the Byronic ideal, probably the most famous being the numerous stories by the American James Fenimore Cooper (1789–1851) such as *The Pilot* (1823), *Red Rover* (1828), *The Wing-Wing* (1842) and *The Sea Lions* (1849). Cain of Marryat's *The Pirate* 'had received an excellent education, and it was said that he was of an ancient border family' (73). Moreover, W.S. Gilbert and Arthur Sullivan's *The Pirates of Penzance* (1879) works as a send-up of the Byronic pirate. Not only are all the pirates 'noblemen, who have gone wrong' (II.584), but they are too tender-

---

[27]   Kevin Carpenter discusses nineteenth-century boys' pirate narratives in these magazines and others, as well as in novels. Interestingly, he argues that the glamorized pirate was more readily available to working-class boys than middle-class ones, as it came to be thought immoral to present the criminal as romantic by mid-century.

[28]   Other children's novels that have Byronic pirates include R.M. Ballantyne's *Gascoyne, the Sandal-Wood Trader* (1865), *Rob the Rover* (1871) and *The Madman and the Pirate* (1883).

hearted to be pirates, are thought at first to all be orphans, and finally just want to fall in love, get married and be domesticated:

> Here's a first-rate opportunity
> To get married with impunity,
> And indulge in the felicity
> Of unbounded domesticity. (I.426–9)

In the final analysis, it is because of the influence of Byron's *The Corsair* that the pirate took on qualities of the 'perfect' lover: high passion and drama, dashingly self-exiled, sadistic, rich, cultured, gentlemanly. A certain type of Gothic desire came to be characterized as love for a corsair, exemplified by Trollope's character Lizzie. Lizzie wants the odd mix that the corsair seemed to contain, post-Byron – a man who will pull her into a higher class but who somehow carries qualities stereotypically associated with the underclass: criminality, the propensity for violence, exile from society. This pirate-brooder carries his treasure within, and the lover must penetrate his interiority in order to have access to it. Such penetration is an act of possession, one marked by 'gaining' the pirate's knowledge, his social position and, paradoxically, his complete lack of social position, all at the same time. Lizzie, if she ever gets her corsair, imagines she will then become poetic, aristocratic, perhaps even pirate-like herself, with the privilege of being so entrenched in society that she can choose to be on the outside. Unlike Lizzie, caught in her feminized world of petty interests, the pirate can be as large as the world, can scorn the world, yet still possess as much power in it as he pleases. This figuration of the corsair shaped by Byron keeps the pirate alive today as an erotic mainstay.

Chapter 3

Playing Pirate: Real and Imaginary Angrias in Branwell Brontë's Writing

Joetta Harty

Well Friend I have taken you to see the navy since you last saw me why man I've been on my voyages ha! Ive turned Merchant you see no not so I am an Admiral. But Ive not hit it yet Im more I'm Rougue I Im all three Im Three in one you know ha. dont you? … Yes I tell you Im not one of your pitiful land. Louping Merchants who when they send out there vessels can never make sure of being able to send them back again no no Bankruptcies and tempests and losses can never hurt Rougue ha! nor *piracys* neither ha! (here he drank again and turning suddenly round he fixed his eyes upon me I feared he would fall into some fit but he continued) Sir Sir I say did you ever know of a man whose wealth was in danger of being lessened by the very means he used to get wealth you dont understand me how should you (he paused) its all long of this (laying his hand on his forehead) I say sir Im as near foundering as Life can be I say Im a Perfect wreck why (drinking again largely) why I could'nt keep body and soul together if it wasnt for this Body and soul did I say. Fool who in the name of nonsense ever heard of two things separating that were never together? ha.

Branwell Brontë, 'The Pirate' (1833)[1]

As his disregard for the rules of grammar and punctuation in the excerpt above indicates, the character Percy 'Rougue' Northangerland, the pirate hero of Branwell Brontë's Angrian narratives, exists at odds with himself and the world that he both mocks and rails against. Typical of Branwell Brontë's writing about the imaginary kingdoms of Glass Town and Angria, this lack of regard for syntax, punctuation and capitalization, and the irregular spelling and grammar in the pirate's speech emphasize the absolute roguery of the Angrian antihero. The writings about the imaginary kingdom of Angria are part of a game, referred to by Charlotte Brontë as a 'play' (Alexander *Early Writings* 25), begun by the four Brontë siblings, Patrick Branwell and his sisters Charlotte, Emily and Anne

---

[1] Patrick Branwell Brontë, 'The Pirate' in *The Works of Patrick Branwell Brontë: an edition*. 4 vols. Ed. Victor A. Neufeldt (New York: Garland Publishing, 1997–99). Vol. I (1997), p. 241.

in 1826.[2] Charlotte, the eldest, was 10, Branwell nine, Emily eight and Anne Brontë two years younger than Emily when they began the first games of imaginary kingdoms.

Over the more than 20-year period that Branwell Brontë's Angrian writing spans, Rougue figures prominently in the manuscripts (Alexander *Early Writings* 199).[3] A child of the Glass Town Federation, Rougue plays an important role in the formation of the Glass Town Empire and is one of the two key figures behind the creation of Angria, where he heads the government as the first prime minister.[4] His fate is intrinsically linked to that of the imaginary kingdom, and his biography charts the rise of new kingdoms in a new world. It is therefore all the more interesting that Percy/Rougue, the antihero of Branwell's paracosm, is a pirate.

Born in Percy Hall on the Gambia River in Wellington's Land, one of the four kingdoms that made up the original Glass Town Confederacy, Alexander Percy is a first-generation Anglo-African or Angrian, as the inhabitants of the imaginary world proudly refer to themselves. Rougue's former tutor-turned-fictional biographer, Captain Bud, one of Branwell Brontë's pseudonyms, describes Percy's birth as an adverse event for the nation: 'all I have yet spoken of (and I fear, Africa) must mark with a black cross the year 1793. Then, on the first of December, on a bleak, stormy morning was born at Percy Hall his country's pride and scourge – Alexander Percy' (R. Collins 11). Visually, the allusion to a 'black cross' marking Rougue's birth date on the calendar suggests the inverse image of the Jolly Roger or King Death, the black flag with white representational images including skeletons, skulls and weapons, flown by pirates.[5] This inverse pirate flag

---

[2]   Charlotte Brontë began 'The Play of the Islanders' in December, 1826; Branwell's earliest extant work is *Branwell's Battel Book*, 1827. For the history of the plays see Branwell Brontë, *The Hand of the Arch-Sinner: Two Angrian Chronicles of Branwell Brontë*, ed. and reconstructed by Robert G. Collins (Oxford: Clarendon, 1993), p. liv.

[3]   One of Charlotte's first attempts at novel writing was a failed attempt to recast Alexander Percy as the main character in a novel set in England.

[4]   Percy/Rougue's development as a character occupied Branwell even after he was no longer concerned with Angria. Branwell published all save one of the 19 total poems that appeared in various Yorkshire newspapers before his death in 1848 under the pseudonym 'Northangerland', the name of the earldom of Alexander Percy/Rougue; and the incomplete manuscript of Branwell's novel, *And the Weary Are at Rest*, features a protagonist based on Percy.

[5]   Against the black background, pirates placed white representational figures, including a weapon, often a sword, cutlass or dart, an hourglass and a skeleton or skull. The most common of these symbols, according to Marcus Rediker, was the human skull, or 'death's head', sometimes isolated but more frequently the most prominent feature of an entire skeleton which held the weapon or hourglass in its bony hand (Rediker, *Between the Devil* 279). The symbols themselves were pirated from graveyard art and ships' logs, in which captains traditionally drew a skull in the margin to note the death of a sailor. Rediker argues that these symbols were given new meanings in the context of piracy, when '[p]irates seized the symbols of mortality from ship captains who used the skull "as a marginal sign

on the Angrian calendar marks Percy's birth date as the antithesis of a national holiday and alludes to Rougue's treacherous career and his deleterious impact on the imaginary kingdom.

Rougue's biography, 'The Life of Feild [sic] Marshall The Right Honourable Alexander Percy, Earl of Northangerland', was written in 1834. At the same time, Branwell Brontë was writing a separate narrative entitled 'Angria and the Angrians', chronicling the history of the Glass Town Confederacy, its civil wars and the Angrians' struggle for independence. The simultaneous production of the two texts – one charting the ascent of the new nation, Angria, the other the man who makes her, 'Angria's Prime Minister, Verdopolis's arch agitator' (Collins 5) – links the character of the rogue and the new nation together in the manuscripts. Both 'his country's pride and scourge', Rougue's nature is intrinsically tied to that of the imaginary Africa. Indeed, his dichotomous character is created in conjunction with the landscape of the imaginary world into which he is born, which is at once Africa and England.

Initially the Glass Town Saga was based on the adventures of Branwell's toy soldiers, 'The Twelves,' as the children narrated the wooden soldiers' adventures in founding a new country, an 'African Babylon' called Glass Town or the Verdopolitan Confederacy (Alexander *Early Writings* 18). Six years after they began, Emily and Anne Brontë started a separate, independent saga about imaginary kingdoms of their own. Around the same time Charlotte and Branwell expanded the Glass Town Confederacy, creating a new nation called Angria. Charlotte abandoned the Angrian Saga in 1839, but Branwell continued to write stories and poems about the imaginary kingdom for many more years.

A number of nineteenth-century authors are known to have played at the game of imaginary kingdoms: Thomas de Quincey could be found ruling over one such land at the end of the eighteenth century, as could Hartley Coleridge, the eldest son of Samuel Taylor Coleridge, a few years later. Later in the century, C.S. Lewis and Robert Louis Stevenson invented the kingdoms of Boxen and Encyclopedia respectively. All of these games consist of elaborate, carefully constructed worlds that restage contemporary cultural and historical events of interest in Britain, such as newly discovered islands, battles, and political debates, against imaginary landscapes and geographies. Branwell and Charlotte Brontë's Angrian Saga is a particularly well-developed example, with Charlotte contributing several hundred pages and Branwell almost a thousand pages of writing about a kingdom established in Western Africa at a time when the British had just attempted, and failed, to introduce a colony there. Robert Collins, a transcriber of some of Branwell Brontë's manuscripts, observes that:

---

in their logs to indicate the record of a death"' (279). These piratical associations were infused with another meaning, though still associated with death, when officials raised the Jolly Roger on the gallows during pirate hangings, reappropriating the flag for the public spectacle (279).

> In fact, the associated kingdoms of the Verdopolitan Confederacy are an empire;
> to spend much time in the great mass of surviving manuscript, particularly that
> of Branwell, is to realize quickly that it represents a fictional reproduction of the
> imagined political life of the United Kingdom itself, fraught with the scheming
> and intrigue of Shakespeare's history plays, with an added heavy emphasis on
> the more modern contest between republican and conservative views, as well as
> the logic behind the extension of empire. (Collins xx)

Featuring historical personalities including Napoleon Bonaparte and the Duke
of Wellington, as Collins suggests, the imaginary kingdom mirrors political events
in contemporary Europe to the extent that an attempted French invasion culminates
in an African Waterloo, while parliamentary debates between the various republican
and aristocratic factions lead to threats of civil war. Furthermore, Branwell uses
the pirate figure not only to restage imperialist endeavours or domestic political
differences, but also to interrogate the overlap between disparate modes of
existence.

Angria is more than a mirror image of history, however. Like the novel, it
provides a space where historical and political elements – historical personalities
and conflicts – are replicated alongside the literary with all 'the scheming and
intrigue of Shakespeare's history plays' (Collins xx). Through the deliberate 'mis-
reproduction' that results from appropriating historical facts and literary details
in the creation of a new world, the imaginary kingdom becomes a place where
historical and literary texts are perverted and, in the process, parodied. Furthermore,
the use of an inherently ambiguous figure like the pirate as the protagonist asserts
a challenge to 'the logic behind the extension of empire' (Collins xx). The pirate
figure is thus crucial to gaining an understanding of the complex Angrian text.
Branwell's Angrian pirate draws on the historic and mythical significance of the
pirate in British culture. As a mythologized rule-breaker or outlaw, the role of the
pirate protagonist of the Angrian 'play' forms a critique of the inherent flaws in
colonial, capitalist culture.

As it was not transcribed in full until the 1990s, Branwell Brontë's writing has
not received as much critical attention as it deserves. Many biographers of Branwell
and his sisters, including Winifred Gérin (1961) and Daphne du Maurier (1960),
have read the antihero of the Angrian tales psycho-biographically, as the author's
alter-ego (Miller 135).[6] Some literary critics do the same: in his introduction to
The Hand of the Arch-Sinner (1993), a transcription of two of Branwell's tales,
Collins suggests that Branwell 'created an Antichrist in his own image' which
he then 'becomes locked inside' (xvi). This type of analysis, with its slippage
between Branwell and Rougue, does a disservice to the text's literary qualities, for
Rougue is only of interest '[a]s a projection of Branwell' (Collins xvi). Reading

---

[6]   See Daphne du Maurier, *The Infernal World of Branwell Brontë* (London: Gollancz,
1960); Winifred Gérin, *Branwell Brontë* (London and New York: T. Nelson, 1961); Lucasta
Miller, *The Brontë Myth* (London: Anchor, 2005).

Rougue as the 'involuted ego' of Branwell Brontë reduces an otherwise complex character to a mere manifestation of his author's repressed psyche. The purely psycho-biographical reading denies the value of the text as a cultural commentary on mid-nineteenth-century imperialist activities.

While not applicable to the author, Collins's synopsis of the rogue character, Alexander – a truly desire-driven egotist and master rebel – occupies a place in the imaginary world that parallels the historical positioning of the pirate witnessed in eighteenth- and early nineteenth-century literature. This 'man who stands as the Lucifer figure in the chronicles' and 'rages against the limitations of this world and finally stands, like all creatures of ruin, as a metaphor for the limitations of the stalwart individual confronted by indifference, hostility, or persecution … is an exemplar of the destructive impulse, the defiance, even hatred, of the involuted ego towards anything that would restrain it in any way' (Collins xvi). He embodies, as Hans Turley suggests of the eighteenth-century pirate, 'all kinds of economic criminal desires … and deviance' (3). Considering how the pirate figure came to be portrayed by eighteenth-century writers as 'both the criminal and the romanticized antihero *par excellence* in the following centuries' (2), Turley describes the cultural positioning of the pirate:

> [He] lived outside the boundaries of conventional European society … [and] threatened society because he embodied all kinds of economic criminal desires *and* cultural transgressions and deviance. Paradoxically, despite his very real criminality, during these same years [the eighteenth century] the pirate came to be seen as the romantic antihero still popular to this day. (2)

Through his positioning as an independent agent and voluntary outlaw in historical and literary accounts, the pirate exposes the flaws in the political, economic and social systems (Rediker 255). Branwell's Glass Town/Angria Saga consists of an elaborate, carefully constructed world that restages cultural and historical events occupying contemporary British interest. Through the transplanting or pirating of facts, figures and events, the imaginary kingdom can be read as a parody of Georgian English values, including military prowess, politics and honest trade. 'Parasitic on the very merchant navy that they refused,' writes Erin Mackie, 'pirates expose, even as they mimic, the aggressive self-assertion and ruthless greed of early modern global capitalism' (54).

Branwell Brontë's Angrian world caricatures or rectifies unsuccessful British attempts to establish a colony in the Niger River delta in western Africa in the 1820s. At the same time, and as seen in the Angrian Saga, the pirate functions as a symbol not only of the individual, but of the very nation he rebels against. The principles of defiance and self-destruction that govern the Byronic hero are also the guiding principles embraced by the new republican Americanesque nations of the Glass Town and, to an even greater extent, Angria when Rougue is elected as the first prime minister. A 'romantic antihero', Rougue forces the reader to admire his transgressions even while he acknowledges his criminality. With his cursing and love of drink, the pirate figure in Branwell Brontë's imaginary world shares in the stereotype of the pirate portrayed in eighteenth-century literary portraits, including Johnson's *A General History of the Robberies and Murders of the Most Notorious Pyrates* (1724) and *The King of Pirates* (1718), a pseudo-autobiographical account of Captain John (also known as 'Henry') Avery, who founded the pirate kingdom on Madagascar.[7] Interestingly, and as Grace Moore discusses in the introduction, this image of the pirate as 'action hero' was formed even as the threat of piracy was being dispelled by the increased enforcement of British authority over the seas.

Historically, the pirate is a deviant figure *par excellence*. The presence of the pirate in Angria underscores how the imaginary kingdom functions as a transgressive site. By placing the antihero outside mainstream culture in this way, Angria engages in a Bakhtinian 'dialogism' (Bakhtin 9) representing an alternative way of viewing the real world. Not only do outcasts marginalized by the dominant cultural ideology gain a voice or presence in the paracosm, but their voices speak volumes about the ideologies seeking to outlaw or silence them. The island paracosm becomes an unofficial, 'second world and a second life outside officialdom' (Bakhtin 6), and the appropriation of the pirate as the antihero lends itself to reading the kingdom as a parodic, carnivalesque space. Beyond this use of the pirate character, Branwell's evocation of the pirate within Angria exposes a discomfort with the economic and political systems that made up the culture of British imperialism. The drive to colonize and perpetuate trade around the globe, and in particular in Africa, is threatened by the character and exploits of the pirate. With his 'swashbuckling' ways, Rougue satirizes the image of the comfortable, clean-handed merchant, thus mocking the businessmen of the Glass Town capital whose greed he exploits by soliciting investments in his shipping company, which doubles as a pirate operation, taking the ships of its own investors as prizes.

Through the transplanting or pirating of facts, figures and events, the imaginary kingdom can be read as a parody: Branwell Brontë's Angrian world presents not only a portrait, but also a caricature of Britain's activities in the Niger delta. These political developments were discussed in *Blackwood's Edinburgh Magazine*, which the Brontës were reading during this time.[8] Thus, the imaginary world does the same cultural work as Bakhtin's Renaissance 'carnival'; it provides a site of deviance within the community. Contrary to the 'official feasts of the Middle Ages,

---

[7]   'Swashbuckling' pirates also figured in several of Daniel Defoe's novels, among them *The Life, Adventures, and Pyracies of the Famous Captain Singleton* (1720) and *The Farther Adventures of Robinson Crusoe* (1719). Pirates were also featured in Walter Scott's novel *The Pirate* (1821), and were serialized in *Blackwood's Edinburgh Magazine's* 'Tom Cringle's Log' (appearing sporadically from 1831 to 1832). The Brontës were known to have been enthusiastic readers of *Blackwood's* and admirers of Walter Scott.

[8]   Christine Alexander, who has transcribed all of Charlotte Brontë's early writing, discusses the extent of the influence of *Blackwood's* on the Brontës in 'Readers and Writers: *Blackwood's* and the Brontës', *The Gaskell Society Journal* 8 (1994): 54–69.

whether ecclesiastic, feudal, or sponsored by the state, [which] did not lead the people out of the existing world order and created no second life', the unofficial feast, or carnival, overthrew existing hierarchies and added to an individual's identity (Bakhtin 9). An unofficial feast of literary activity, an imaginary world based on geographic sites of historical British colonialist activity like India and Africa, a fantastic, alternative space within that space, the paracosm shapes a commentary on the culture within which it is based and which it parallels.[9] It reflects, in the sense of Lewis Carroll's Looking-Glass world, a new, unique place, and is simultaneously useful as a place of '"modelling" at once utopian and counter-hegemonic' (Stallybrass and White 18). As a literary endeavour, the imaginary kingdom is not envisioned as a utopia; on the contrary, it is often, as in Angria, conceived as a place of war and strife. A collection of the historical and the fantastic, the narration of an imaginary world models the way real events become interwoven in the fabric of fiction so that, like the carnival, the imaginary world acts 'as a *catalyst* and *site of actual and symbolic struggle*' (Stallybrass and White 14).

As the hero of the Angrian narrative, the piratical rogue reinforces a reading of the kingdom as a carnivalesque place, a site of cultural, social and economic transgressions. Historically, the pirate's social transgression and refusal to participate in the legitimate forms of marine trade and defiance of maritime law earned him the name 'Hostis humanis generis, a common Enemy with whom neither faith nor oath is kept' (Johnson 377). The pirate was the proclaimed enemy of all humanity, but he was a *voluntary* outlaw. In addition to the great economic peril that it represented, the piratical community posed a threat to the nation and a sense of nationality, of affiliation with and loyalty to one's country.[10] Voluntary exiles who established an alternative society complete with its own rules and regulations (Rediker 264–5), in their agreement to attack all non-piratical ships regardless of nationality, pirates renounced their citizenship and refused to recognize any loyalties outside the pirate community.

Reading the Angrian pirate as a Byronic hero points to the complicated nature of cultural transgression. As a romantic antihero, the pirate functions as a privileged transgressor, one whose infractions against the social and cultural 'norms' are glorified even as they parody Georgian culture. Rougue's socio-economic status is ambiguous, as he himself proclaims he is simultaneously admiral/merchant/pirate. In his tri-part identity he embodies contradictory roles within the economic

---

[9]   'Carnival is presented by Bakhtin,' write Stallybrass and White, 'as a world of topsy-turvy, of heteroglot exuberance, of ceaseless overrunning and excess where all is mixed, hybrid, ritually degraded and defiled' (8).

[10]   Marcus Rediker has a chart of the connections among Anglo-American pirate crews from 1713 to 1726, showing how they were all 'related'. *Between the Devil and the Deep Blue Sea: Merchant Seamen, Pirates, and the Anglo-American Maritime World, 1700–1750* (New York and Cambridge: Cambridge UP, 1987), p. 268.

system, highlighting the difficulty of distinguishing between legitimate and criminal systems of trade. As Robert Collins observes,

> 'The Pirate' ... was an integral part of the Percy saga ... For Branwell, as for Byron before him, the Pirate figure is very important. It becomes an avatar of the Luciferian figure in the actual world of physical strife and contest, a world where men are not saved by sentiment. While much has been said concerning the influence of the Byronic hero on the Brontës generally, it is probably equally true to say that the Pirate figure was a parallel influence on first Byron and then Branwell, for the Pirate was a real identity in the eighteenth and early nineteenth century. He was not simply lawless but a law unto himself. (xxx–xxxi)

Throughout the seventeenth century, and during the early eighteenth century, piracy was a real threat to maritime trade, with more than 5,000 pirates estimated to be roving the world's seas (Rediker 255). By the time Branwell Brontë was writing, the historic 'golden age of piracy' had passed.[11]

Unlike the other kingdoms that make up the Brontës' Glass Town Confederacy, Angria shares its name with a pirate. Wellington's Land, Parry's and Ross's Lands are named after military heroes and famous explorers.[12] In contrast, Angria is the Anglicized name both of a famous family of Indian pirates and of the pirate kingdom founded by Kanhoji Angrey (often spelled Connagee Angria in English accounts) in the late seventeenth century. Located about 30 miles south of Bombay (Mumbai), Angrey's kingdom consisted of a series of fortified islands along the Indian coast. Although contemporary accounts differ somewhat from more recent scholarship, by the beginning of the eighteenth century Kanhoji Angrey had amassed enough naval power to establish an independent state that controlled the waters south of Bombay down the Konkan (at that time referred to as the Deccan), the western part of the Indian peninsular ruled by the Hindu Marathas (Malgonkar 4).[13] In Johnson's *General History of the Robberies and Murders of the Most Notorious Pyrates*, 'Angria' is described as 'a famous Indian Pyrate, of considerable Strength and Territories, that gives continual Disturbance to the *European* (and especially the *English*) Trade' (124). The seriousness of the threat afforded by Angria to the

---

[11]   Rediker suggests that 1726 marked the end of the great era of piracy, as does Hans Turley, who dates the Golden Age from 1695 to 1725 (3).

[12]   The kingdoms were named for after Duke of Wellington and the famous arctic explorers Admirals William Edward Parry and John Ross, whose polar expeditions and attempts to find a Northwest Passage were reported in newspapers and monthlies such as *Blackwood's Edinburgh Magazine* in the early nineteenth century.

[13]   For contemporary accounts, see J. Cooke, *An Authentick and Faithful History of that Arch-Pyrate Tulagee Angria* (London: printed for J. Cooke, 1756) and *The Arabian Pirate; or Authentic History and Fighting Adventures of Tulagee Angria. With an Account of his Predecessors, the Angrias, who carried on their depredations in the East Indies for upwards of Forty Years* (Newcastle: printed by G. Angus [1795]).

influential British East India Company was made manifest when the governor of Bombay, Charles Boone, published a proclamation of war against him in 1718. Three years later, and as reported in Johnson's *History*, Boone initiated several unsuccessful attempts to demolish the 'pirate's kingdom of forts' (672).[14] It was not until 1756 that the Angrian Empire finally fell to the combined British naval forces and ground troops led by Admiral Charles Watson and Colonel Robert Clive respectively at Gheria, Angria's stronghold.

Kanhoji Angrey presented a very real threat to the British and other European powers during the 40 or more years that he ruled over the western coastline of the subcontinent. He not only hurt the European powers financially by taking their ships as prizes and by interrupting trade for nearly half a century, but according to one biographer, the British alone spent vast amounts each year on defensive measures against Angria. As Malgonkar has described:

> To neutralize the man they chose to call a pirate, the British spent every year a sum equivalent to a million pounds at today's value. They dug a ditch around the town in Bombay as a protection against him, and then they erected a wall behind the ditch. They even joined hands with their bitterest rivals, the Portuguese, in an effort to destroy him … If, however, in the first years of the eighteenth century, any of the foreign powers along the coat of Konkan had been asked to nominate a common enemy, none of them could have picked out either the Moghuls or the Maratha. Their answer would have been the same: Kanhoji Angrey! (7)

Angria's 'continual Disturbance' of the European trade earned him a place as a pirate in contemporary accounts written by Clement Downing, Johnson and others. Although the British referred to him as a pirate, more recent scholarship has shown that Kanhoji Angrey was actually an admiral in the Maratha navy.[15] Eighteenth- and nineteenth-century Europeans saw things differently, however, pointing once again to the mutability of the term 'pirate'. Reading about Angrey, Branwell Brontë, who uses the same spelling for 'Angria' as Johnson, would have learned of his piratical behaviour against the East India Company and altercations with the British Navy, not his feats as a Maratha admiral (Collins xviii).

Over the 15 years or so that Branwell's Angrian writing spans, Percy the pirate, usually referred to as Rougue, figures prominently in the manuscripts (Alexander *Early Writings* 199). Formally known as the Earl of Northangerland, and later

---

[14]   Johnson writes that 'The attempt of the British fleet to attack Gheria in Sept. 1720 ended in dismal failure, as did the attack the following spring on Angria's stronghold at Kolaba' (672 n.12).

[15]   For a comparison of contemporaneous and twentieth-century historical takes on Kanhoji Angria and the British East India Company, see Cooke and Defoe referred to above; Clement Downing, *A History of the Indian Wars* (Lahore: Al-Birundi, 1978) versus Manohar Malgonkar, *Kanhoji Angrey, Maratha Admiral* (London: Asia Publishing House, 1959) and John Keay, *The Honorable Company* (New York: Macmillan, 1991).

as Viscount Elrington – a title he captures whilst pirating – the roguish figure of Alexander Percy rages throughout the manuscripts against all authority on land and on sea. Branwell Brontë's pirate features in the poetry, travel narratives, biography and society pages of the Angrian Saga. In the poetry written about and/or by Rougue, the pirate is portrayed as a fairly standard Byronic hero, a young man who runs off to sea to escape his own deeds and memories. Rougue's incomplete fictional biography, written by an Angrian neighbour and local historian, connects the early years of the pirate with the growth of the new nation, suggesting that they share mutual struggles and triumphs. By comparison, in the travel narratives 'published' in the Glass Town equivalent of society pages, encounters with the pirate are made public by an English tourist, providing a glimpse of the pirate in his native habitat, as seen through the eyes of a non-Angrian outsider. Two incidents in particular that enable a better understanding of the piratical figure and its use in the manuscripts are the 'confession' scene reproduced above and the events surrounding his capitulation, where Rougue publicly professes an end to his piratical career.

Percy, Branwell's pirate, and the imaginary new rogue nation of Angria, rise (and fall) together. As his 'biographer' relates, Rougue's infamous career begins with a teenage elopement, when he commits a kind of marital piracy with the slightly older but equally rebellious Augusta Segovia. Thus, at a relatively young age Rougue challenges both parental authority and social institutions. Upon discovery of the marriage, Rougue's father, 'Old Rougue', exiles his son to the Angrian university on the Philosopher's Isle. This pattern of rebellion and exile becomes the general theme of Rougue's life. At university, Rougue leads a short-lived student rebellion resulting in his expulsion. Returning home, he discovers his wife is conspiring to kill his father. Rougue carries out the plot and speeds his inheritance of his father's estate. Rougue's first wife is murdered by potential blackmailers, while his second wife dies of consumption. At this stage in the narrative, Rougue becomes a flag officer in the Glass Town military, appearing during land wars as an army general, and there are allusions to his time on the sea as an admiral in the navy (a transition between military services made possible in the imaginary kingdom). Like many eighteenth-century seafaring professionals, at some point during his naval career Rougue turns pirate.[16]

The pirate poetry composed by and about Rougue and his sea life simultaneously celebrates his freedom from authority and conveys his dejection following the loss of his first two wives.[17] The verses composed aboard his ship,

---

[16]   '[R]egardless of their methods, pirates necessarily came from seafaring employment, whether the merchant service, the navy, or privateering' (Rediker, *Between the Devil* 260).

[17]   Poems of pure mourning, also written during Alexander Percy's pirate years, include 'Sleep Mourner Sleep!' in which Rougue describes himself in his grief in a line that echoes Percy Shelley's 'Ode to Autumn': 'I feel and say that I am cast / From Hope and peace and power and pride / A withered leaf on Autums [sic] blast / A shattered wreck on Oceans tide (64–8).

the *Rover*, reflect the recurring themes of his life, the driving desires to escape from mental suffering and economic crisis. Reminiscent of Lord Byron's 'Childe Harold's Pilgrimage', *Don Juan* and 'The Giaour,' Rougue's verses in 'An Hours Musings on the Atlantic' contrast the innocence imbued in his earliest childhood memories of the ocean with the need, born of his adult disillusionment with the world, to use the sea as an antidote for grief. The pirate's recollection of how '... when I was a little child / With what a burst of pleasure wild / I gazed upon the sea' (115–16) replaces the resolve, expressed earlier in the poem, to '... turn my forehead to the blast / And gaze upon the sea / That chainless boundless restless waste / Which shines so gloriously' (24–7). His desire to use the ocean as an antidote to emotional suffering is in keeping with what Rediker describes as the 'wanderlust and romantic introspection' inherent in 'the romantic obsession of the sea' that emerged in nineteenth-century novels and travelogues (4).[18] The pirate uses the challenge posed in pitting himself against 'the blast' and nature's other violent elements, as well as against all non-piratical humanity, as an escape from painful memories. The piratical life also offers an escape from authority when the ocean becomes both 'That only Lethe for the past / Or Freedom for the free!' (28–9). As a pirate, Percy becomes Freedom's champion. The entire world was the pirate's enemy and his freedom resided in his choice of career. Unlike a buccaneer or privateer who attacked only the ships of nations with which his government was at war, the pirate acted as an independent agent, and therefore became the enemy of all (Turley 29–36). Although 'An Hours Musings on the Atlantic' ends on a sorrowful note, with Rougue lamenting the death of Mary, his second wife, the final stanzas sharply contrast with the elation in piratical freedom expressed earlier in the poem:[19]

> See the billows round me now
> Dash against my cleaving prow
> Far and wide they sweep away
> Oer [sic] the rough and roaring sea
> By heaven! my heart beat high to day
> Lord of such a realm to be
> Monarch of the fierce and free! (9–15)

---

[18] Towards the sea there was a Romantic 'obsession witnessed in later characters like Herman Melville's Ishmael in *Moby Dick*, who turns to a life at sea to escape his own depression, "a damp, drizzly November in soul"' (quoted in Rediker, *Between the Devil* 4). Rediker sees this romantic use of the idea of sea life in sharp contrast, as he has shown, to the reality of a seaman's life, as only part of the equation in which seamen had to collaborate against both nature and a captain who represented merchant and royal powers, a near-dictator in a strict class hierarchy on board ship.

[19] The poem is subtitled 'Composed off Norway – by Alexander Percy 1818'.

Among the piratical 'fierce and free' Rougue, captain of the *Rover*, revels in being 'Lord of such a realm' even as he mourns his personal loss. Rougue has much in common with the Byronic-Satanic-Napoleonic hero-figure described in Byron's *Lara*:

> In him inexplicably mix'd appeared
> Much to be loved and hated, sought and feared;
> Opinion varying o'er his hidden lot,
> In praise or railing ne'er his name forgot. (289–92)

Rougue shares with the hero of *Lara* 'a vital scorn of all / As if the worst had fall'n which could befall' (313–14), and in the pirate's poetry glimpses of the Byronic antihero's dichotomous nature emerge as Rougue attempts to embody both elation and despair, to celebrate and mourn simultaneously. The duality of the Angrian pirate, whose deeds, like those of the real pirates, are celebrated in literature even as history condemns them as thieves, is mirrored in the pride and anxiety surrounding the increasing power of the new nation.

In Byron's works a hero like Don Juan functions on two levels: he is at once an exporter of Britishness and of nationalism; and, as an exile, he critiques the culture to which he is opposed. In Branwell Brontë's writing the connection between the hero and the nation, where the protagonist is a symbol of national character, is more pronounced than in Byron's verse. The poem 'Northangerland's Name', by Rougue's fellow Angrian and revolutionary, Captain Henry Hastings, sets up, and is perhaps the best example in the Angrian Saga of, the tie between the individual and the emerging nation-state. Establishing this relationship solidifies the connection between piracy and the insurgent nation. Hastings, a young Angrian soldier and author, celebrates Rougue's fame as a pirate and his place in history. Here, the pirate is not only freedom's champion, but his deeds are admired by the figures of History and Freedom.

As she holds 'the pencil of fate' over her manuscript, at Freedom's urging, History 'thought of the "Rover" unconquered and free / Her noble Northangerlands Empire and Home' (10–11), and determines to inscribe his place alongside that of Angria's king, Zamorna. In the process, the poem conflates the pirate and the king, and the pirate and the creation of the kingdom. From 'the hours of that ocean' (13) to Africa, Rougue's 'historical' place is chronicled as 'a pirate ... unconquered in heart and as glorious in form!' (15–16) and co-founder of 'that Empire so bright and divine' (21). The 40-line poem establishes the connection between Rougue as remembered pirate and as nation-builder. After the Romantic tradition, the individual is celebrated; in the ode to Northangerland, Rougue becomes not only the hero of the piece but also the model for the nation. His very roguery and rebelliousness are deemed admirable characteristics of the new nation-state, in which individual freedoms and national independence are paramount. Described as 'He whose bidding has roused up a land / From midnight to morning to life from the tomb' (25–6), the pirate is a Christ-like figure, a 'Saviour' whose rebellious nature defies the political equivalent of death, the lack of individual freedom and democracy, and who raises the nation like Lazarus from the tomb. It is a celebration of the piratical nature triumphant. It is also a celebration of Rougue's republicanism, for in the poem it is the figure of Freedom who takes Rougue as 'my Saviour' (35) and justifies History's entry for him 'high on the top of her column of Fame' (39).

In addition to the poetry, several Angrian narratives focus on Rougue, further documenting his piracy and his relationship to the fledgling nation. The multi-volume travel narrative written by the Angrian tourist James Bellingham, 'Letters of an Englishman to his Freind [sic] in London', contains one such account of Rougue. 'Published' by the Glass Town press, Bellingham's letters are probably modelled on James McQueen's 'Letters from Africa', a series about British attempts to colonize the Ashanti lands near the Niger River delta. McQueen's 'Letters' appeared sporadically in *Blackwood's Edinburgh Magazine* between December 1826 and February 1832, years when the young Brontës were devouring the magazine. Offering an outsider's observations of the new African nation and its people, 'Letters of an Englishman' affords a glimpse of Rougue as he seizes control of the capital during the civil war. Bellingham is taken hostage and very nearly executed for his royalist sympathies by Rougue.

Following the uprising's failure, Rougue disappears from Glass Town society for several years. During this time he roves far and wide over the seas. He resurfaces in 'The Pirate', the first comprehensive story in Branwell Brontë's manuscripts featuring Rougue as hero (Neufeldt *Works* I.240 n.2). The story opens when Bellingham, despite his initial, unpleasant encounter with the pirate, visits the newly opened office of 'Rogue Sdeath and Co.' While Rougue appears as a more or less traditional Romantic Byronic antihero in the poetry about his time at sea, in 'The Pirate' he is no longer a pirate poet, but a pirate posing as a merchant. Rougue's occupation of the seemingly contradictory positions of tradesman and outlaw of Angrian society is made possible by the kingdom's carnivalesque landscape. His position allows him to overthrow and subvert the existing hierarchies of state and law while aggrandizing his own, individual identity. Such positional contradictions allow the pirate to undermine both the stereotype of the successful tradesman as model citizen in a nation of shopkeepers and the popular image of the pirate as a common enemy.

Ironically, the story that provides the most complete description of Rougue's piratical business includes both a boastful admission and a public renunciation of piracy. During an initial interview with Bellingham, Rougue alludes to the source of his newfound wealth, virtually confessing his piracy:

> Well Friend I have taken you see to the navy since you last saw me why man I've been on my voyages ha! Ive turned Merchant you see no not so I am an Admiral. But Ive not hit it yet Im more I'm Rougue I Im all three Im Three in one you know ha. dont you? (*Works* 241)

Rougue mocks Christian belief when he substitutes Navy Admiral, Merchant and the unnamed, but real, employment of pirate. He is his own 'holy trinity' of capitalism as he asserts, 'I'm Rougue I Im all three Im Three in one you know' for the holy trinity: god the father, son and holy ghost. A self-proclaimed atheist, Rougue's religion is republicanism. And it is republicanism, hand in hand with unscrupulous capitalism, that forms the connection between Rougue the pirate and, in a later incarnation, Rougue the politician.

In the interview with Bellingham, his would-be banker, the pirate evokes the premise behind the spiritual union – a litany that Branwell Brontë, the son of a curate, would have known very well – only to replace it with an economic nexus in which he paradoxically plays a three-in-one position by asserting simultaneously his self-identity as 'Rougue' and 'all three'. In the context of the story this makes sense; Rougue makes his confession to Bellingham, whose money he would like to 'invest' in his company, instead of to a clergyman. His speech, punctuated with its repeated 'ha's' and unconventional syntax, includes theatrical body language – 'he took a long pull from a flagon of claret', 'he fixed his eyes upon me', 'laying his hand on his forehead', 'drinking again largely' – that breaks up the one-sided dialogue and creates a visual image of a swashbuckling pirate. Rougue's rant proposes and then denies any tension between the economic and the spiritual. Rather than being distraught over this quandary, Rougue is amused by his situation as 'a man whose wealth was in danger of being lessened by the very means he used to get wealth'. He offers up a guiltless confession to the banker, meanwhile urging him to invest in Rogue Sdeath and Co.: 'look my man if youve money and want it in safe hands (here he took a long pull from a flagon of claret) I say if youve money and love it let me have a hand on it and it'll stick to you for ever' (*Works* I.241).

The lack of regard for grammatical convention is typical of Branwell Brontë's writing about the imaginary kingdoms of Glass Town and Angria. In the carnivalesque context, the informality of the writing symbolizes disrespect, lending to Rougue's speech an air of stream of consciousness, vulgarity, piracy and even roguishness bordering on dementia. Without naming what exactly he is – Rougue names instead the socially acceptable, admissible roles of 'pitiful land Louping Merchant' or a navy 'Admiral' – he nonetheless confesses he is a pirate. The pirate, as he is labelled in the title of the story, broaches this otherwise unspoken socio-economic position in terms of a highly ironic and simultaneously spiritual and existential crisis in which his 'wealth was in danger of being lessened by the very means he used to get wealth'. His physical state reflects his anxiety over this philosophical catch-22. Looking as though he is about to 'fall into some fit', Rougue admits to being 'a Perfect wreck' caught in the vicious circle of his own rationale: 'I could'nt keep body and soul together if it wasn't for this Body and soul did I say. Fool who in the name of nonsense ever heard of two things separating that were never together?' (Winnifrith 14: 172).

Occupying contrary positions of merchant and pirate, hero and thief, public citizen and outlaw, Rougue shares the same ambiguous space with historic 'pirates' like Kanhoji Angrey and privateers including Woodes Rodgers or Drake.

His position as both economic outlaw and first-generation Angrian places him in the crux of an imperial cash nexus: capitalism in the name of colonization, which he expresses in the terms of a transcendental dilemma he discounts as 'nonsense'. Although repudiated, the very denial draws attention to the problem. In 'The Pirate' and other narratives featuring Rougue, the connection between the character and the geography of an imaginary Africa extend this dilemma beyond the individual level to a question of the morals of colonialism and nation-building, even as the hero of the saga moves from pirate to politician to stay abreast of developments in the imaginary world.

The events in the subsequent chapters of 'The Pirate' recount Rougue's transition from pirate to peer and from outlaw to politician. Acts of piracy enable his transformation. Rougue and his company stand accused of piracy by the Glass Town Admiralty, headed by the fictional Duke of Wellington, who is also king of the imaginary Wellington's Land. Suspecting that Rougue is behind 'a number of armed Vessels carrying scarlet colours … recently infesting these Seas [the harbours and rivers along the west coast of Africa] and committing the most violent and wanton aggressions upon the vessels carrying the Flags of this Nation as also upon those of France Parrys Ross's and my own [Wellington's Land]', the Admiralty serves up 'a writ calling upon Alexander Rougue to present himself to morrow before the court of the Admiralty to clear up some aspersion[s] which at present rest upon his character' (*Works* I.243). Although Rougue and company never come to trial, there are several indications, in addition to the title of the story and Rougue's confession to Bellingham, of his involvement in piratical activities. The reference to Rougue, Sdeath and Co. carrying 'scarlet colours' is one sign. According to historian Charles Grey, when hoisted, the red or 'bloody' flag used by pirates signified that no quarter was to be given to resistance.[20] The use of the red flag preceded that of the Jolly Roger, which is now more commonly associated with piracy, and continued even after the Jolly Roger was widely adopted. The name of Rougue's company may also be another allusion to its piratical nature. The firm bears the names of its partners, Rougue and S'Death, the nickname of Robert King, an old rascal who acts as Rougue's surrogate father throughout the

---

[20]   'Pirates also occasionally used red or "bloody" flags' (Rediker 279 n.78). Charles Grey also notes, 'For those who have been accustomed to consider the Black Flag with the skull and cross-bones, the invariable ensign of the pirates from a very early period, it will come as a surprise to learn that so far from this being the case, this flag was only used in the last two decades of the Golden Age of piracy, i.e. from 1700–1722. Even then it was not universal. The earlier pirates all fought under their national colours, to which was added a red Flag, denoting no quarter if resistance were offered. Even when the black flag came in, the national colours were occasionally used in conjunction with it and the red flag. The first mention of the Jolly Roger occurs in the year 1700 when it was shown by the French pirate Emanuel Wynne, who fought an indecisive action with H.M.S. *Poole* off the Island of St. Jago' (17). See also Hans Turley, *Rum, Sodomy, and the Lash: Piracy, Sexuality, and Masculine Identity* (New York: New York University P, 1999), p. 3.

narrative. Usually read as a pun on the oath, 'God's Death', King's nickname and his given name when taken together suggest the pirate flag's other sobriquet, 'King Death'. Finally, Rougue's name and that of his ship are both words associated with piracy. Like his historical predecessors, the pirate in the Angrian Saga is a rogue who constantly sets himself at odds with authority. The very name of the protagonist is another label for a vagrant and rascal and frequently associated with pirates. It could also be a sign of Branwell's familiarity with pirate lore, for according to an analysis of pirate ship names conducted by Marcus Rediker, 'Rover' or 'Ranger' was an extremely common name for pirate vessels, second only to names with 'Revenge' in them (269).[21]

The event that officially ends Rougue's 16-year piratical career is a whirlwind marriage, a token captivity romance with underlying class and economic motivations. Aboard the *Rover*, Rougue captures his final and perhaps biggest prize, Lady Zenobia Elrington, 'the bonniest lass in the Glasstown' (*Works* I.249), when the *Rover* captures her ship. Rougue proposes a union, convincing Zenobia to become his third wife, so that she, and her title, become part of the pirate's booty. Like many of Defoe's criminal main characters, including Moll Flanders and the pirate Captain Singleton, Rougue's public reformation comes about with the realization of wealth. In keeping with the pirate tradition of accepting single men only, Rougue renounces piracy upon his marriage (Rediker 265).[22] Eighteenth-century pirates were often offered a reprieve by the English government if they swore to end their piracy. In similar fashion Rougue is granted a pardon by the rulers of Glass Town on the condition that he compensate them fully for their losses and leave off his pirating ways. Rougue takes the pardon, but when he uses his newly obtained social status to secure a place in parliament, the political arena becomes for Rougue another forum for piracy.

Now formally known as Lord Elrington, but still very much a rogue, Alexander Percy engages in a new form of piracy, convincing, through a combination of verbal eloquence and the threat of blackmail, the Glass Town parliament and its four kings to create Angria, a new country where his son-in-law and sometimes archenemy Zamorna would be king. Yet Rougue no sooner assumes his post as prime minister than he begins initiating yet another rebellion, a republican revolution in which he attempts to overthrow the very government he is instrumental in forming. Rougue's rebellion, like the civil war he once waged in Glass Town, ultimately fails. Exiled to an island off the African coast, Rougue receives a fitting punishment for both

---

21   Rediker offers an analysis of the names of 44 pirate ships and found that the most popular name, which referenced 'revenge' was used by seven ships. The second most common name was *Ranger* or *Rover*, 'suggesting mobility and perhaps, as discussed subsequently, a watchfulness over the way captains treated their sailors' (269).

22   Rediker states that: 'Wives and children were rarely mentioned in the records of trials of pirates, and pirate vessels, to forestall desertion, often would "Take no Married Man"' (*Between the Devil* 260–61).

a pirate and a politician.[23] Among pirates and other seamen, such exile was a common sentence for crew members who transgressed a ship's articles. Like the famous Alexander Selkirk, unruly sailors were often marooned or made 'Governor of an island' (Rediker 265). Rougue survives his exile, though, and by the end of the manuscripts has negotiated the terms of his return to Angria.

A first-generation Angrian, and in many respects the first citizen of Angria, Rougue's life parallels the birth and rise of the new nation. Rougue's transitions from pirate to poet to politician allow him to adapt to the changing political and economic scenes in the imaginary world as, America-like, it grows from a colonial outpost to a powerful, independent nation. Just as the pirate is transformed into the prime minister in the new government, the new nation is transformed from a lawless territory to a nation with laws and the means, such as the Glass Town Admiralty, to enforce them. Yet even as the original confederacy becomes more powerful and seemingly less open to adventurers seeking their fortunes, Rougue's ascension to the aristocracy occurs as a direct result of, and a reward for, his criminal activities. It is the establishment of trade that allows Rougue's piracy of the Glass Town merchants to take place. Likewise, it is the establishment of a parliament, of a democratic format within the monarchical political structure of the Glass Town Confederacy, that creates the space in which Rougue wages his debates. The parliament provides a more structured forum for rebellion and a place for Rougue to argue for the formation of a new republic.

Rougue spends 16 years plundering at sea. His behaviour on land is equally piratical and reprehensible; he maintains his roguish image by keeping 'bad' company, inciting numerous rebellions against first the Glass Town and later the Angrian governments, and seducing both the unmarried and married high society women of Angria – all the while drinking and swearing profusely, as befitting a pirate (Rediker 166, 278). As the Angrian story progresses, Percy's military prowess, marriage and political machinations earn him the titles of General Northangerland, Viscount Elrington and Prime Minister of Angria. Like the new nation, he must adapt economically and politically to a changing atmosphere. Rougue is always a rogue, though, and this label follows him through the manuscripts. Regardless of his elevated political and social trappings, Percy remains a pirate.

Branwell's use of the pirate figure is key to understanding the complexities of the Angrian text. As a pirate, Rougue embodies some of the more problematic aspects of imperialism and colonization. Expressed in his own words, the inability to 'keep body and soul together' is symptomatic of the kind of growing pains felt by an emerging empire, be it Britain or the imaginary Angria.[24] While the

---

[23] In 1821, shortly before the Brontës began their sagas of imaginary kingdoms, Napoleon died in exile on St Helena, a small island 1,200 miles off the west coast of Africa, and which is now one of the last remaining relics of British colonialism.

[24] Significantly, the Angria stories are written after the trial of Warren Hastings (1788–1794) and the parliamentary inquiry into Robert Clive (1772–1773), who co-led the force that finally defeated the real Angria. Clive was called to account for his actions and

historical pirate Angria was terrorizing the East India Company and costing the British large sums of money in the Indian Ocean, pirates were busy establishing their hold on Africa. After George I commissioned Woodes Rogers to clear the pirates out of the Bahama Islands in 1718, the displaced outlaws relocated to the islands and inlets of Africa. Pirates plagued Africa from 1691 onwards and, by 1718, Madagascar served as both a repository for booty and a pirate settlement. The west coast of Africa was also used as a layover for pirates, who unloaded their spoils near the mouth of the Sierra Leone River (Rediker 257), just north of where the imaginary kingdom of Angria would have been. Africa had thus become one of the last strongholds of pirates, and it is not so surprising that pirates from the not-so-distant past made their way into the imaginary kingdom of Branwell Brontë (Terry 127).[25]

Eventually, pirating poems from the Angrian manuscripts, Branwell Brontë began publishing some of his verses in Yorkshire newspapers (*Poems* xliii).[26] The first poem appeared in the *Halifax Guardian* on 5 June 1841 (*Poems* xlv). All save one of the nineteen total poems published before Branwell Brontë's death in 1848 appeared under the pseudonym 'Northangerland', the name of the earldom of his pirate, Alexander Percy, otherwise known as Rougue. Thus, through the use of the pirate, simultaneously evoking contempt, sympathy and admiration for his antihero, Branwell Bronte's imaginary kingdom of Angria becomes a space for interrogating free trade economics, the political institution of the monarchy and, through them, cultural imperialism.

---

the wealth he obtained in India. Misgivings regarding certain aspects of imperialism were being entertained in Britain, and these same issues are reflected in the Angrian world and the existential crisis of its piratical protagonist.

[25]   In her early writings Charlotte Brontë mentions the household taking several papers as well as reading *Blackwood's Magazine*: 'We see the John Bull it is a High Tory very violent[:] Mr Driver Lends us it as Likewise Blackwoods Magazine the most able periodical there is' (*Charlotte Brontë: Juvenilia, 1829–1835*. Ed. Juliet Barker (London: Penguin, 1996), pp. 2–3).

[26]   Brontë, Patrick Branwell. *The Poems of Patrick Branwell Brontë*. Ed. Victor A. Neufeldt (New York: Garland Publishing, 1990).

Chapter 4

Ho! For China: Piratical Incursions, Free Trade Imperialism and Modern Chinese History, c. 1832–1834[1]

Ting Man Tsao

China's domestic output had far surpassed Europe's until the nineteenth century when the British colonizers arrived in China. The British therefore had to grow opium in India in exchange for Chinese products. From the contemporary Chinese perspective, those pirates and opium dealers who came to the China coast were no different from the Japanese sea-robbers who had haunted the Chinese coastal areas a few centuries before. ... Should the Chinese of the time call the pirates and opium traders who brought with them syphilis and drugs 'emissaries of civilization'?

Kuang Xinnian[2]

In the history of Sino-British relations, the early 1830s was a period of remarkable change. In 1834, an Act of English parliament abolished the British East India Company's (EIC) century-old monopoly over the China trade and opened this commerce to 'all British subjects', thus beginning the 'free-trade' era. However, the British public's first taste of free trade with China predated this official abolition of the EIC's charter by two years. In 1832, defying both the EIC's longstanding pacific China policy and Qing law,[3] Charles Marjoribanks, president of the EIC's Canton Factory, sent Hugh Hamilton Lindsay (an EIC supercargo) and Charles Gutzlaff (a Prussian missionary) on a secret mission to the forbidden

[1] This work was supported in part by a grant from The City University of New York PSC-CUNY Research Award Program. The chapter grew out of my dissertation 'Representing China to the British Public in the Age of Free Trade, c. 1833–1844', State University of New York at Stony Brook, 2000. The chapter benefited from comments by Nancy Berke, Remi Castonguay and Heidi Johnsen of the Interdepartmental Faculty Scholarly Writing Group of LaGuardia Community College.
[2] All excerpts and quotations from Chinese sources such as this epigraph are my translations.
[3] Before China was defeated by Britain in the Opium War and forced to open five ports to British subjects for 'mercantile pursuits' in 1842, the Qing government strictly confined the activities of foreign traders within a small designated area called the Factories by the Canton River, forbidding any foreigner from setting foot on Chinese soil beyond it.

coast of the Middle Kingdom 'to ascertain how far the northern ports … may be gradually opened to British commerce' (*Ship Amherst* 3).[4] The voyagers loaded a private ship, *Lord Amherst*, with English products, disguised themselves, landed in several forbidden ports, distributed Chinese tracts about 'the English character' and religion, and clashed with the Qing authorities trying to drive them away.

Upon their return, Lindsay and Gutzlaff lost no time in publicizing their so-called 'success' in 'befriending' the 'hospitable' Chinese people and frustrating the local authorities' attempts to block their entrance. In their published accounts of the voyage, the European men write of themselves as if they were piratical heroes, defiantly barging into the defenceless coast of China and audaciously exploring a potentially boundless emporium and missionary field into which few Europeans had ever ventured. Their travel narratives became instantly popular and sparked off a 'free-trade mania' in political, commercial and religious circles in Britain and the United States.[5] These publications even impressed John Barrow, who had gone on the 1792 Macartney mission (the first British embassy ever to China) and had published groundbreaking works on this empire.[6] Barrow conceded that the adventurers' accounts exhibited, 'in a style beyond all our previous conceptions' ('Free Trade' 449), the utter weakness of the Qing authorities and their maritime defences. The importance of Barrow's statement cannot be overstated because this renowned 'China hand', together with other members of the Macartney mission, had once shaped 'all [of Britain's] previous conceptions' (449) of China by publishing influential narratives of the embassy.

How should we account for the emergence and popularity of piratical figures at this historic juncture of Sino-British relations that saw the decline of the EIC's influence and the rise of free-trade interests? Histories written for generations of modern Chinese people have provided a painful but straightforward answer. Lindsay and Gutzlaff's voyage was a planned reconnaissance which provided later British imperialists with an accurate knowledge of Qing China's longstanding military and naval weaknesses (Nan 2). As such, the incursion is seen as a precursor to the endless list of British 'piratical' and 'predatory' crimes against the Chinese

---

[4]   All references are to page numbers in the original edition, not to reprint page numbers.

[5]   For an historical examination of the reception of Lindsay and Gutzlaff's travel books among not only British but also Chinese audiences from the 1830s to the present, see my article: Ting Man Tsao, 'A Reading of Readings: English Travel Books, Audiences, and Modern Chinese History, c.1832 to the Present', *Asian Crossings: Travel Writing on China, Japan and South East Asia* (Hong Kong: Hong Kong UP, 2008), 47–70.

[6]   John Barrow, *Travels in China* (London: T. Cadell and W. Davies, 1804); *Some Account of the Public Life and a Selection from the Unpublished Writings of the Earl of Macartney*, 2 vols (London: T. Cadell and W. Davies, 1807).

people during and after the Opium War, a historic war that led to the 'opening' of China to western imperialism.[7]

The epigraph at the beginning of this chapter is a typical example of how Chinese historical narratives represent different forms of western imperialism during the long nineteenth century as 'piracy'. The 'pirate' is sweepingly and ahistorically used as a synonym for many an enemy or invader of China. The 'pirate' and the 'opium dealer' represent, interchangeably, the British 'who came to the China coast'. The nineteenth-century British 'pirates' are seen as 'no different from the Japanese sea-robbers who had haunted the Chinese coastal areas', despite a gap of several centuries and, with it, incomparable historical contexts. In the epigraph, as in some other Chinese historical accounts, the British 'pirate' personifies, rather economically, the lawlessness, greed, ferocity and promiscuity of western imperialists and colonizers.

Representing 'piracy' as a series of 'predatory' crimes against China over a centuries-long span, these Chinese histories, however, fail to capture its specificity as *historical* activities that served different, not necessarily compatible, functions for Britain's mobile and multiple imperial projects. Historically speaking, piracy did have close connections with Britain's and other European nations' commercial expansion in Asia since the sixteenth century. However, according to Robert Antony, by the late seventeenth century, as Qing China strengthened its maritime control and as 'Western merchants began putting pressure on their home governments to suppress freebooting, and officials responded by passing stiff new anti-piracy laws and by building navies to protect their merchant ships on the oceans[,] European piracy soon waned in Asia and around the world' (36–7). Not insignificantly, during the nineteenth century not only did Britain continue its own anti-piracy policy in Chinese waters, it also helped the weakening Qing government suppress local pirates.[8]

It is against the backdrop of the British government's anti-piracy imperial policy that this chapter seeks to recover the historical specificity of the rise of piratical adventurism in the early 1830s from overgeneralization and even misrepresentation in modern Chinese history. I will illuminate the connections between the emergence of the British piratical hero and the rise of free-trade imperialism by situating the popularity of Lindsay and Gutzlaff's travel accounts in the history of shifting British representations of China. To do so is to go beyond

---

[7]   The first Chinese historian who linked Lindsay and Gutzlaff's voyage with the Opium War was Zhang Dechang, 'Hu Xia Mi huo chuan lai Hua jing guo ji qi ying xiang' [The voyage of Hu Xai Mi's cargo ship to China and its impact], *Zhongguo jin dai jing ji shi yan jiu ji kan* [*Studies in Modern Economic History of China*] 1.1 (1932): 60–79, reprinted in *Zhongguo she hui jing ji shi ji kan* [*Studies in Social and Economic History of China*] (Xianggang: Long men shu dian, 1968), juan 1.

[8]   Grace Fox, *British Admirals and Chinese Pirates: 1832–1869* (London: Kegan Paul, Trench, Trubner & Co., 1940); John C. Dalrymple Hay, *The Suppression of Piracy in the China Sea, 1849* (London: Edward Stanford, 1889).

seeing Lindsay and Gutzlaff's incursion as the precursor to Britain's 'piratical' aggressions against Qing China during and after the Opium War. I will, instead, historicize the voyage as an occasion initiating a major shift from one genre of representing China to the British middle-class reading public toward another. By appropriating the masterless, defiant, valiant and enterprising image of the pirate, a popular cultural icon, Lindsay and Gutzlaff created a new subject-centred, interactive genre beyond the British public's 'previous conceptions' of China during the monopoly-free trade transition to replace the outdated objective, distanced genre of the decades-old embassy literature published by Barrow and his ambassadorial cronies. Accounts of the intruders' 'buccaneering or piratical enterprise' ('British Connexion' 127) dramatized the bulk of the arguments by the up-and-coming free-trade interests, from Manchester to Canton, against the EIC's China-trade monopoly in an easily recognizable and hence repeatable genre. These stories could embody what the decades-old embassy literature could no longer represent, namely an increasingly hawkish spirit shared by the British middle class of forcing open China to private enterprises, both commercial and religious.

The historical significance of the incursion thus lies less in the 'piratical' and 'predatory' crimes that Lindsay and Gutzlaff committed on the China coast than Chinese scholars have led their audience to believe. More historically important are the new meanings and conceptions that Lindsay and Gutzlaff's writing about the incursion generated for the contemporary British middle class, who had a stake in the London money markets affected by the prices of tea imported from China and the export of Indian-grown opium to the Middle Kingdom. For these avid readers, the publications of Lindsay and Gutzlaff's 'buccaneering or piratical enterprise' provided a fresh perspective to rethink Britain's China policy as the EIC's China-trade monopoly was counting its days.

Macartney Embassy Narratives

To understand the new perspective offered by Lindsay and Gutzlaff's piratical adventures, a brief analysis of Britain's 'previous conceptions' of China shaped by the Macartney embassy accounts is in order. These narratives, in the main, offered late eighteenth and early nineteenth-century readers a 'team' approach to encountering China and the Chinese, one that by and large frowned upon the kind of masterless independence, valour and defiance that characterize the pirates in romantic literature such as Lord Byron's *The Corsair* (Gerassi-Navarro 1–2). As such, the 'team' approach was in line with the contemporary monopolistic trading system, in which the EIC or the company's interests were more or less identified with the country's interests (Greenberg 2), and under which the country traders'[9]

---

[9]   The country traders were private merchants who were engaged in the 'country trade'. The term 'country trade' referred to the private trade between one eastern port and

individual rights to trade were regulated, limited and even sacrificed for the sake of the 'collective good' of the company and the country.

Among all the publications of the embassy, George Staunton's account was the most bureaucratically toned and, exactly because of this quality, the most popular and respected. To build up an aura of bureaucracy, Staunton adopts a detached, third-person perspective ('they') identified with the embassy as the official organ representing the whole country. From such a vantage, he manages to narrate an ostensibly impersonal account, effacing himself as an individual and wiping from the narrative any of his personal experiences and feelings. It is from this collective and objective point of view that the narrator concentrates on delineating one 'natural' scene or 'native' setting after another as though they naturally presented themselves to his 'innocent' eye:

> Every thing being ready, the Embassy pursued their journey towards Canton. On their route they perceived stages upon the sloping sides of hills, in which were cultivated pulse, grain, yams, sweet potatoes, onions, carrots, turnips, and other culinary vegetables. Upon the top of the mountain was a reservoir to catch rain water, which was conveyed thence, by channels, to irrigate these cultivated terraces. (410)

The narrator is equally detached when describing the Chinese people:

> The collecting of compost for the land is, with [the embassy], an object of the greatest attention; in which business are employed old and young, incapable of any other kind of labour. They rummage every street, road, jakes-pots, river, and canal; and also pick up with their hands, in baskets, the ordure of animals, an offal of every kind which can answer the purpose of manure. (410–11)

Conspicuously absent from the above text, as in other descriptions of the 'natives', are interactions of any sort – verbal or physical – between Staunton's team and the Chinese people. In their separate realms, the British are always observing and the Chinese people are always being observed, thus leaving little ground for personal or commercial reciprocity. This distanced observation created the impression that the Chinese people were indistinguishable from their leaders. For the embassy writers, the Chinese who were 'almost under the entire dominion of their government' (Barrow, *Travels* 359) lacked human 'spontaneity' (Marshall and Williams 144) and were as 'jealous' and suspicious as their leaders.

Staunton's objective narrator is comparable to the 'landscanning, self-effacing producer of information' (Pratt 78) in eighteenth- and nineteenth-century European travel literature on Africa and South America. According to Mary Louise Pratt, this

---

another, over which the EIC did not keep its monopoly. This information is based on Peter Ward Fay, *The Opium War: 1840–1842* (1975; New York: Norton, 1976) 18.

kind of objective narrator constitutes 'the panoptic apparatuses of the bureaucratic state' (78) embodying state-controlled imperial projects such as territorial expansion, colonization and military intervention. In the historical context of British imperialism in China, the embassy writers' distanced observation of the Chinese land and people upheld the values of the EIC's monopoly practices. It served to valorize the 'team', the larger mercantile bureaucracy, over the individual Briton, the country trader. Not too subtly, it legitimized bureaucratic regulation and control of the China trade while frowning upon the country traders' desire for the kind of masterless independence, associated with the piratical icon in fiction and history, to enter the boundless Chinese emporium and conduct free, unfettered trade with a largely 'jealous' population.

The strategy of distance also structured the ways the embassy writers narrated their diplomatic interactions with the Qing emperor and officials, and served to support the nation's submissive China policy that the EIC favoured in protecting its exclusive trading system. Consider the most memorable diplomatic encounter of the mission, Macartney's historic meeting with the Emperor of China, in Barrow's *Some Account of the Public Life and a Selection from the Unpublished Writing of the Earl of Macartney*.[10] Macartney, at first, presents a series of arresting images of the Qing palace:

> The materials and distribution of the furniture within [the palace] at once displayed grandeur and elegance. The tapestry, the curtains, the carpets, the lanterns, the fringes, the tassels were disposed with such harmony, the colours so artfully varied, and the light and shades so judiciously managed, that the whole assemblage filled the eye with delight, and diffused over the mind a pleasing serenity and repose undisturbed by glitter or affected embellishments. (Barrow, *Some Account* 2: 260–61)

The ambassador then concludes his impression of Qing splendour: 'The commanding feature of the ceremony was that calm dignity, that sober pomp of Asiatic greatness, which *European refinements have not yet attained*' (261, emphasis added). How did Macartney deal with such 'Asiatic greatness', which was superior to the European counterpart? After a short distraction, the ambassador struck back by figuratively removing himself from the immediate surroundings of Qing 'grandeur and elegance':

> Thus have I seen 'King Solomon in all his glory'. I use the expression, as the scene recalled perfectly in my memory a puppet show of that name which I recollect to have seen in my childhood, and made so strong an impression of

---

10   My analysis of this historic meeting is indebted to James L. Hevia, *Cherishing Men from Afar: Qing Guest Ritual and the Macartney Embassy of 1793* (Durham, NC: Duke UP, 1995) 105–8. My differences from his interpretation will be shown in the rest of this paragraph.

my mind that I thought it a true representation of the highest pitch of human greatness and felicity. (261)

According to James Hevia, the ambassador, '[a]ssaulted by "disturbing" sensory evidence of oriental splendor', had to escape and resort to 'an idealized childhood' for the purpose of saving his 'objectifying gaze' (107–8). By comparing the Emperor of China with a puppet show seen by children, Macartney could, of course, belittle the former and thereby empower himself *vis-à-vis* the Chinese Other. Yet, the very association of a childhood memory in a narrative of one of the most serious diplomatic encounters in British history shows that the ambassador, though given instructions to demand national equality as the first priority, still abided by the EIC's conservative, 'acquiescent' China policy, and refrained from a more aggressive diplomacy. The plenipotentiary's rather circuitous counter of the 'pompous' Chinese Other was a far cry from the intrepidity and daredevilry of piratical legends such as the Queen's Pirate, Francis Drake, in facing Britain's enemies.[11]

Lindsay's New Narrative

By 1830, Britain's political climate, which had previously favoured the EIC's China-trade monopoly, had changed. As Peter Ward Fay states, 'Monopoly in politics, in religion, in almost everything, was [after the 1832 Reform Bill] the object of widespread public suspicion' (58).[12] The British middle-class public no longer took for granted the old assumption that the company and the country had compatible interests. In fact, the country traders and the manufacturers had been bombarding them with newspapers and pamphlets carrying the opposite messages that the China-trade charter had been hurting the nation's economy, and that the government's conservative China policy needed an overhaul.[13] Although the Macartney embassy books still found themselves in subscription libraries and private collections, providing 'useful knowledge' about the Middle Kingdom to the reader, their 'team' approach had become obsolete, failing to represent the post-Reform public sentiment that China should be opened to private enterprise.

It is Lindsay and Gutzlaff's 1833–34 publications that superseded the embassy literature and filled the narrative void in English travel writing by offering a revolutionary approach to imagining China and the Chinese, an approach that went beyond Britain's 'previous conceptions' of the Celestial Empire. Although the EIC's

---

[11] For a recent reappraisal of Drake, see Harry Kelsey, *Sir Francis Drake: The Queen's Pirate* (New Haven, CT: Yale UP, 1998).

[12] For a historical survey of the rise of free trade imperialism, see Bernard Semmel, *The Rise of Free Trade Imperialism: Classical Political Economy, the Empire of Free Trade and Imperialism, 1750–1850* (Cambridge: Cambridge UP, 1970).

[13] See Greenberg 175–84.

Canton Factory sponsored their voyage, what Lindsay and Gutzlaff emphasized in their accounts were not their 'services' for the company, but their individualism, independence, defiance and audacity. These were seafaring qualities commonly associated with the popular piratical hero in early British imperial history and literature. However, for the early nineteenth-century middle-class reader, Lindsay and Gutzlaff were still distinguishable from 'the evil pirate' or 'Sea-Monsters' depicted by earlier writers like Daniel Defoe, Cotton Mather and Jonathan Swift.[14] For all their defiant and illegal actions on the China coast, Lindsay and Gutzlaff did not associate themselves in any way with the most hateful crimes by which the old pirates had earned their notoriety, namely treason and perverse violence. On the contrary, the two adventurers exhibited in their piratical individualism the defining trait of the middle class with which their nineteenth-century audience could readily identify – the spirit of *laissez-faire* and enterprising opportunism. It was their piratical yet respectably middle-class qualities that set Lindsay and Gutzlaff apart from earlier European travellers/writers to/on China.

In the case of Lindsay, as the EIC's supercargo, he submitted his 'Report of Proceedings on a Voyage to the Northern Ports of China' to the Company's Court of Directors in London. Considered public record, the 'Report' was first published as part of the parliamentary paper titled *Ship Amherst* in 1833.[15] Though reporting to the EIC's Court of Directors in London, Lindsay in *Ship Amherst* presented himself not as the Honourable Company's 'servant' but as an independent hero who abided more by his instincts than by the EIC's instructions; who interacted with the 'natives' in defiance of the Qing authorities' interdictions; and who challenged the Qing local governments every step of his way. Displaying little formality and impersonality of the typical 'blue-book' paper, Lindsay's 'Report' gave rise to a pirate-like adventurer with fuller individuality and richer self-expression than such contemporary seafaring heroes as the midshipmen in Captain Frederick Marryat's popular novels, which focused more on actions than the actors themselves.[16]

Unlike Staunton, who effaced himself in his account, Lindsay made himself the hero of his 'Report': the initiator of all his actions taken during the voyage; the observer of all that happened around him; and, politically speaking, the one

---

[14]   Joel H. Baer, "The Complicated Plot of Piracy': Aspects of English Criminal Law and the Image of the Pirate in Defoe', *Studies in Eighteenth-Century Culture*, vol. 14, ed. O.M. Brack, Jr (Madison: U of Wisconsin P for American Society for Eighteenth-Century Studies, 1985), 11–17.

[15]   *Ship Amherst* was so popular that it was later commercially republished: [Hugh Hamilton Lindsay, and Charles Gutzlaff], *Report of Proceedings on a Voyage to the Northern Ports of China in the Ship Lord Amherst*, second edition (London: B. Fellowes, 1834). All references to Lindsay's 'Report' are to the parliamentary paper, *Ship Amherst*.

[16]   Patrick Brantlinger, *Rule of Darkness: British Literature and Imperialism, 1830–1914* (Ithaca, NY: Cornell UP, 1988), 47–70. Frederick Marryat's contemporary novels include: *The Naval Officer, or, Scenes and Adventures in the Life of Frank Mildmay* (1829), *The King's Own* (1830) and *Peter Simple* (1833).

wholly responsible for all his 'buccaneering or piratical' actions in defiance of the EIC's court and the Qing government. The following excerpt exemplifies his self-writing:

> The result of our constant intercourse with the natives of China ... had impressed so strongly *on my mind* the prospective advantages which would be derived by disseminating a little correct information respecting our countrymen among a people who manifest so ready a will to cultivate our friendship, that after *mature reflection* of several days, *I have determined to take on myself the responsibility* of distributing copies of that pamphlet on English character, written by Mr. Marjoribanks, which gives much useful information in a plain intelligible style. (*Ship Amherst* 26, emphasis added)[17]

Although he could easily have done so, Lindsay did not defend his distribution of the tract, considered impolitic and improper by his superiors, by resorting to the authority of the pamphlet's author, Charles Marjoribanks, who had been president of the Select Committee of Supercargoes at the Company's Canton Factory and had years of experience in Chinese affairs. Nor did Lindsay give his explanation from a third-person point of view comparable to Staunton's in order to make his role in the distribution less obvious. Rather, he emphasizes in the 'Report' *himself*, *his* experience of interacting with the Chinese, *his* 'mind' and 'mature reflection' as the sole rationale on which he decides on the distribution. What stands out in the above rhetoric is the individual, who relies on his own sensorium and who claims total responsibility for whatever course he determines to pursue. Pushed to the background in this account are the EIC, the crew and Britain's old 'China hands' as well. What Lindsay displayed was the spirit of masterless freedom to explore 'our empire' in the East – a spirit shared by contemporary fictional pirates like those in Bryon's *The Corsair* as they venture over 'the glad waters of the dark blue sea' with their 'boundless' thoughts and 'free' souls (1.1–2).Unlike the Byronic corsairs, however, Lindsay did not create a solitary, melancholic empire in the Orient. For all his masterless independence in narrating his 'buccaneering or piratical' incursion, Lindsay did not exhibit any of the antisocial traits that had defined the most notorious pirates in earlier British history and literature. On the contrary, his autonomous 'mind' and 'reflection' enabled Lindsay to explore anew more fruitful and more 'respectable' ways of interacting with the Chinese than the cold observation model set by the earlier embassy writers such as Staunton. Regardless of being deemed rash and unlawful by the EIC, the adventurer's exploration nonetheless found what many British gentlemen merchants had longed

---

[17] I found and published the original manuscript of this pamphlet by Charles Marjoribanks, titled 'Brief Account of the English Character': Ting Man Tsao, 'Representing "Great England" to Qing China in the Age of Free Trade Imperialism: The Circulation of A Tract by Charles Marjoribanks on the China Coast', *Political Matters*, ed. David E. Latané, Jr. Special issue of *Victorians Institute Journal* 33 (2005): 178–95.

to hear: the European stranger could initiate a 'reciprocal' relationship with the Chinese along the northern coast of China, a relationship that was believed to be conducive to free trade not only at Canton but also beyond. The following passage about the crew's arrival in Chongming (originally known as 'Tsung-ming'), quoted and praised by such contemporary periodicals as the *Westminster Review*,[18] is exemplary of Lindsay's interactive narrative:

> After walking about three miles, *gathering companions like a snow-ball*, we arrived at the town ... We saw apricots in abundance in the fruit stalls, and purchased some ... Having walked through the town, about half a mile long, *attended by a great concourse of people*, and looked into various shops and houses, we returned as we came. The *friendly demeanour of these simple people*, who now for the first time in their lives beheld a European, surpassed anything we had hitherto witnessed; and there being no mandarin in the place, no artificial check was placed to *the natural friendly impulse of their hearts*. Having observed that the apricot pleased us, *numbers came to us* offering the finest they could select. On all sides we were requested to bestow a copy of the pamphlet, of which we distributed about 20, and *a crowd was immediately formed round the possessor to read it*. On our return, *we were escorted by at least 300 people of all ages*, many of whom offered and begged us to accept presents of fish and vegetables, and anxiously expressed a hope that we would return another day. ... On returning, *the country people from all quarters had gathered to see us pass*, and by the time we reached our boat, at least *600 people were assembled*, and *all seemed to vie which should be the most kind and friendly*. (*Ship Amherst* 82, emphasis added)

This passage creates – borrowing Mary Louise Pratt's term for a comparable type of colonial encounter – 'the mystique of reciprocity' (69). In contrast with Staunton's non-interactive narrative, in which the British and the Chinese exist in separate realms, Lindsay's narrative presents every British movement in tandem with a responsive, friendly and hospitable inter/action on the part of the Chinese. As the crew arrives, 'companions like a snow-ball' gather. After the crew buys and tastes some apricots, 'numbers' come to offer 'the finest they could select'. As if to vindicate his 'impolicy and impropriety' of distributing the Chinese tracts, Lindsay recounts that Gutzlaff and he actually 'were requested' by an enthusiastic crowd to give out copies of their pamphlet, and that 'a crowd was immediately formed round the possessor to read it'. Significantly, the Chinese do not receive the tracts without reciprocating; when the crew returns, more and more people 'offered and begged us to accept presents of fish and vegetables', and 'all seemed to vie which should be most kind and friendly'.

---

[18]   See [John Crawfurd], 'Voyage of Ship *Amherst*', *Westminster Review* 20 (1834): 33.

In recounting these lively human exchanges, the first-person narrator syntactically mixes the British ('I', 'we' and 'Mr Gutzlaff') with the Chinese ('companions', 'numbers', 'a crowd', 'the country people' etc.) in harmonious ways. The use of parallel participial clauses to delineate the two groups' interactions is a case in point. Consider the following two sentences from the above excerpt: 1) 'After walking about three miles, gathering companions like a snow-ball, we arrived at the town.'; 2) 'Having walked through the town, … attended by a great concourse of people, and looked into various shops and houses, we returned as we came.' In both sentences, though apparently 'we' (the English crew) are the subject and the natives are the object, the insertion of the participial clauses – 'gathering companions like a snow-ball' and 'attended by a great concourse of people' – at once delays the appearance of the subject (who were 'walking'?) and smoothly places the Chinese object in the midst of the subject's actions. Sometimes, the narrator fuses the British and the Chinese to such an extent as to create a semantic confusion: 'On returning, the country people from all quarters had gathered to see us pass, and by the time we reached our boat, at least 600 people were assembled …' Who were (the subject of) 'returning'? The English 'we' or 'the country people'? Confusion of this kind belies not the narrator's grammar of standard nineteenth-century English but his consuming desire to narrate a highly interactive encounter between the British and the Chinese.

Alarming was this narration of Chinese 'reciprocity' to the EIC and its supporters. Lindsay's 'free intercourse' with the natives was adding fuel to the already aggressive campaign by the country traders for opening the China trade to private enterprise and extending British commerce to the forbidden ports north of Canton. Since reciprocity was the rationale of international trade,[19] and since the Macartney embassy and the ensuing British diplomatic efforts had failed time and again to bring the Qing government into a 'mutually acceptable' commercial relationship according to 'the law of nations', the 'kind' and 'friendly' Chinese people in the northern ports became the *raison d'etre* of British commerce there. Although the best Chinese 'reciprocity' that Lindsay's narrative could offer was limited to non-commercial, 'innocent' interactions such as the ones cited above, and although Lindsay himself admitted that commercially speaking his voyage was a partial failure, free-trade lobbyists such as John Crawfurd showed no hesitation in declaring in the *Westminster Review*, 'The people are able and willing to trade' ('Voyage of the *Ship Amherst*' 37). In no ambiguous language, the *Eclectic Review* saw the discovery of the 'friendly' Chinese character as a breakthrough in 'opening' China: '[The voyage] places the character of the natives altogether in a new light, and opens to us the most cheering prospect as to the possibility of wholly breaking down the partition wall which has for ages separated from civilized society a fourth portion of the human race' ('Voyage' 332). Echoing one another, the liberal periodicals and newspapers swelled the chorus of *laissez-faire*.

---

[19]   For a brief discussion of Marx's understanding of 'reciprocity', see Pratt 84–5.

To the pro-monopoly interests, if Lindsay's narration of Chinese 'reciprocity' was startling, the fact that such a discovery was made at all possible by the adventurer's 'piratical', less than lawful expedition was ominous. For the 'discovery' of a 'respectable' and mutually beneficial way of relating to the Chinese did more than just vindicate Lindsay's one-time 'buccaneering or piratical enterprise' and embarrass the EIC (after all Lindsay was the Honourable Company's 'servant'). It could, worst of all, unleash the 'free-trade mania' that had already been fermenting among the increasingly unruly British and American traders whose blatant trafficking of opium on the southern coast was prodding the Qing court's nerves. In the *Quarterly Review*, Barrow's criticism of Lindsay reflected how the supporters of the monopoly status quo feared the ominous effects of the adventurer's imprudent incursion on Britain–China relations. From Barrow's perspective, what was most troubling about Lindsay's book was the dangerous examples that it held out, such as 'successful resistance to lawful authority' and 'stirring up the *people* against their rulers' ([Barrow], 'Free Trade' 448). For '[s]uch an example will be but too readily followed by some of the uncontrolled free-traders' ([Barrow], 'Free Trade' 448). As Barrow further explained, despite Lindsay's admission of the expedition's commercial shortcoming, and despite the EIC's condemnation of the misguided mission, 'the successful daring of this young man ... will find its admirers and imitators' ([Barrow], 'Free Trade' 449). It would 'very probably', the old 'China hand' forewarned, involve Britain in 'a collision with the Chinese' ([Barrow], 'Free Trade' 449).

Barrow's grave warning was not groundless. Although the country traders and their lobbyists had long advocated a more hard-line China policy, they fell short of any concrete illustration of what it would entail exactly and how it would achieve 'an equal footing' with the historically arrogant Celestial Empire. This lack of specifics or convincing examples on the part of *laissez-faire* advocates had hampered their campaign for an overhaul of Whitehall's China diplomacy because any drastic change, the public was cautioned, might turn China into 'a second India' (Graham 407).[20] It was by putting on the cloak of a determined, quick-witted buccaneer that Lindsay provided the reader with a concrete example of what a firm, uncompromising China policy should be, and how it could finally do justice to the honour of an English gentleman conducting business in the Middle Kingdom.

At Shanghai, for instance, while presenting a petition to the 'taoutae', a local mandarin, Lindsay refused to stand according to Qing customs, demanding that he and Gutzlaff be seated if the mandarins were seated. The request was denied because, as the officials explained, seating was allowed only for mandarins when they were communicating business 'of a public nature' (*Ship Amherst* 76).

---

[20]   Gerald S. Graham, *The China Station: War and Diplomacy, 1830–1860* (Oxford: Clarendon/Oxford UP, 1978): 'Britain must never risk the consequences that would follow the acquisition of a second India, in "a fit of absence of mind"' (407).

Determined to be more adamant than the previous British embassies, Lindsay continued to argue:

> I am no mandarin; but my petition, if favourably received, and the request it contains is complied with, it may be called of a public nature; and it is not on my account I object to stand in the presence of your mandarins so much as on account of the high respectability of my country. (*Ship Amherst* 76)

After a prolonged debate, arrangements were made for both parties to stand to meet each other. Yet upon 'seeing no symptoms of any of [the mandarins] rising to receive [him]' Lindsay stormed out of the hall and expressed his 'indignation at the paltry artifice which had been played on [him and Gutzlaff]' (*Ship Amherst* 76). Lindsay's insistence reflected the sentiment expressed by many country traders who found the Chinese customs of treating 'foreign devils' humiliating and demanded that commercial and diplomatic communications be conducted on 'an equal footing'. In his 'Report', Lindsay showed what the free traders wanted to hear – a firm stand on diplomatic 'equality' did work: 'Such are Chinese mandarins all over the empire. Compliance begets insolence; opposition and defiance produces civility and friendly professions' (*Ship Amherst* 78). Whereas it was easy to strike up 'friendship' with the Chinese people, it was through 'a show of force' that 'friendly professions' from the mandarins could be obtained. Historically, then, Britain's shift toward the gunboat policy with Qing China began not with any formal decision of the Foreign Office, but with Lindsay's heroic determination against England's arrogant and 'jealous' enemy – a heroism that had historically turned notorious buccaneers such as Henry Morgan into national legends.[21]

Gutzlaff's Dual-Purpose Narrative

As a young, ambitious trader, Lindsay convinced the British public of the necessity to resort to 'buccaneering or piratical' means to fight for the respectable free-trade cause in China. For Gutzlaff, however, the case that he had to make to Britain was more complicated. Working as an 'individual' missionary unaffiliated with any missionary society, Gutzlaff needed to show that to accomplish the nobler goals of evangelizing China, the missionary had to embark on 'the fatal road of combining missionary work with political and economic interests' (Schlyter, *Karl Gützlaff* 293–4),[22] employing religiously and even morally questionable methods

---

[21] The legend of Henry Morgan continued in the early nineteenth century. See such publications as *The Extraordinary Adventures and Daring Exploits of Captain Henry Morgan, a Notorious Pirate* (London: G. Martin, 1813).

[22] For a comprehensive discussion of Gutzlaff as an 'individual' missionary, see Herman Schlyter, *Der China-Missionar Karl Gützlaff und seine Heimatbasis* ([Lund, Sweden]: C.W.K. Gleerup, 1976).

of spreading the Word of God. Gutzlaff's *Journal of Three Voyages along the Coast of China* (hereafter *Journal*)[23] – devoted to his mission with Lindsay and his two other equally problematic journeys – glorified his missionary adventures, while at the same time exposing the darker aspects of his operations such as cooperation with the opium traffickers and 'going native'.

For all its potentially controversial contents, the *Journal* nonetheless succeeded in promoting Gutzlaff's 'fatal road' of extending the Christian mission to China on risky 'piratical' voyages. Published in London and New York, and running four editions, the *Journal* won more widespread popularity than Lindsay's 'Report'. The book was enthusiastically reviewed not only by such prestigious general periodicals as the *Westminster Review* but also, more importantly, by the organs of major missionary societies such as the *Missionary Register* of the Church Missionary Society and the *Evangelical Magazine* of the London Missionary Society. Echoing one another, reviewers praised Gutzlaff as an 'active, enterprising, and intelligent adventurer' ([Crawfurd], 'Chinese Empire and Trade' 221) and 'a wonderful man, a heroic Christian, and a zealous philanthropist' (qtd. in Schlyter, *Der China-Missionar* 28) as well. Such a high-profile reception indicated that many influential spokesmen for the religious and political circles condoned Gutzlaff's 'piratical' missionary enterprise and urged 'the churches of Christendom' 'to emulate that spirit [of the commercial world] for more important ends!' ('Gutzlaff's *Three Voyages*' 391).

To lure the respectable middle-class readership into embracing his 'fatal road' of combining the Christian mission with the 'buccaneering or piratical enterprise', Gutzlaff created a self-image more appealing than Lindsay's. To be sure, Gutzlaff, as a seafaring hero, did exhibit some pirate-like characteristics in common with Lindsay, such as individualism, independence, defiance and audacity. However, to elevate his otherwise purely 'buccaneering or piratical' voyages to the status of missionary pilgrimage, Gutzlaff cloaked his *Journal* with an aura that Lindsay's free-trade oriented 'Report' lacked, namely the aura of spirituality.

It was this aura of spirituality that helped Gutzlaff win public sympathy for his dangerously unconventional missionary methods, one of which was 'going native' and plunging into the seafaring underworld of Southeast Asia, dominated by villainous sailors, treacherous plotters, dishonest merchants, opium smokers and traffickers, gamblers, prostitutes and idol-worshippers. Consider the missionary's delineation of his complete Sinicization in his first voyage that took place before his mission with Lindsay. At that time, Gutzlaff was reduced to the nadir of his life. Just before embarking on his first ever trip to China, he had lost his wife and fallen very ill. Feeble and depressed, he was further confined to the abject environment of a Chinese junk – 'a hole, only large enough for a person to lie down in, and to receive a small box' – and surrounded by six Chinese passengers, who disgusted

---

[23]   All references are to the third edition of Charles Gutzlaff's *Journal of Three Voyages along the Coast of China in 1831, 1832, & 1833*, intro. by W. Ellis, published in 1840. The first and second editions were published in 1834.

him one way or another by their 'opium-smoking', 'villainy', 'deceitfulness' and 'idolatry' (Gutzlaff 90–91).

It was at this most vulnerable moment of his life that the following self-portrait of the missionary, widely cited by contemporary periodicals such as the *Eclectic Review*, became all the more moving:

> When I embarked, though in a very feeble state of body, I cherished the hope that God in his mercy would restore me again to health, if it were his good pleasure to employ in his service a being so unworthy as myself – the least, doubtless, of all my fellow-labourers in the Chinese mission. ... Long before leaving Siam I became a naturalized subject of the celestial empire, by adoption into the clan or family of Kwo, from the Tung-an district in Fuhkeen [Fujiang]. I took, also, the name Shih-lee, – wore, occasionally, the Chinese dress, – and was recognised (by those among whom I lived) as a member of the great nation. *Now*, I had to conform entirely to the customs of the Chinese, and even to dispense with the use of European books. I gladly met all their propositions, being only anxious to prepare myself for death; and was joyful in the hope of acceptance before God, by the mediatorial office of Jesus Christ. My wish to depart from this life was very fervent, yet I had a sincere desire of becoming subservient to the cause of the Redeemer among the Chinese; and only on this account I prayed to God for the prolongation of my life. (Gutzlaff 92)

Unlike Lindsay and the embassy writers, who had to address one way or another the bureaucracy with which they were affiliated, the 'individual' missionary adopted a much more solipsistic, spiritual voice, speaking only to God, himself and the reader. In his struggle between the suicidal wish to escape pain by death on the one hand, and the evangelical hope of serving God in the salvation of countless Chinese pagans on the other, the missionary wrote of himself as the most self-renouncing European ever found in China. Determined to prolong his life only for the Chinese, Gutzlaff makes the ultimate sacrifice, his Europeanness – that which sets him apart from 'barbarians' – by Sinicizing himself. Such a move is a far cry from the embassy writers' distanced observation of the Chinese.

The protestant missionary's deepest moment of evangelical martyrdom was also his most solitary, non-reciprocal moment. Even though he interacted with other passengers, such interactions almost always ended up in his condemnations of their vices. The lone missionary reached out only to be turned back by the unredeemable paganism of others. Though incurring the risks of 'going native' in the perilous maritime underworld of Southeast Asia, his one-of-a-kind missionary style won Gutzlaff more public respect than the embassy writers and Lindsay. As the *Eclectic Review* wrote, 'What pompous and costly embassies, what mercantile intercourse and commercial treaties have failed to effect, it is probably reserved for the humble and noiseless labours of the self-denying Missionary to accomplish' ('Gutzlaff's *Three Voyages*' 391). Although it was touching, spirituality narrated in a purely solipsistic voice could at best create a romantic empire similar to the one constructed by the Byronic pirate hero in *The Corsair*. For all its literary appeal, this sort of 'lonely' empire was out of place in the political discourses of Britain–China relations. In fact, Gutzlaff's missionary-cum-free-trade imperial vision was, like Lindsay's *laissez-faire* imaginary, dependent on narrating a reciprocal relationship with the Chinese – a 'friendly' relationship that necessitated the European voyagers' illegal incursions into the forbidden Chinese ports and their 'buccaneering or piratical' activities there. Therefore, after the solipsistic episode discussed above, the *Journal* shifted to a reciprocal narrative. Recall Lindsay's Chongming episode cited above and see how differently the missionary describes the incursion into the city:

> We bent our walk towards Ho-chin[24] ... and found it *interesting* and *pleasant* to pass through such *richly-cultivated* fields. At first, the natives were much *astonished* at our *sudden* appearance, having never seen an European; but they soon became *familiar* and *friendly*, because we distributed books among them *freely*. ... At first, they hesitated to receive them; but, on glancing at the contents, the people became *clamorous* for more. ... We scarcely anywhere experienced such friendship as among these islanders, all of them seeming very *anxious* to oblige us, and prove that the Chinese character is exempt from misanthropy. ... The concourse of people was so *great* that we could scarcely pass through the streets; but there was no rudeness, and they rather seemed *interested* to shew us everything *worthy* [of] our attention. (Gutzlaff 217–18, emphasis added)

Compared with Lindsay's, Gutzlaff's narrative voice had a keener sensitivity, adding a deeper psychological dimension to the encounter with the locals. While Lindsay creates a dynamic scene of interactions through a frequent use of action verbs, Gutzlaff produces an exquisite description of exchanges by dint of adjectives (see the italicized words). Adjectives, which tend to slow down the inter/actions, nonetheless enrich them with perceptions ('interesting', 'pleasant'), emotional responses ('very anxious') and evaluations ('richly-cultivated', 'worthy'). Employing an abundance of adjectival markers of his sensorium, the sensitive narrator internalizes the 'friendly' encounter, narrating almost every inter/action in terms of his psychological and moral responses. This narrative practice matches the supposed spirituality of evangelizing the Chinese through the illegal distribution of religious and moral pamphlets. Lindsay's narrative voice is quite different. Capable of drawing necessary political inferences from the exteriority of the 'friendly' encounter (which is enough to prove commerce can be extended), he is content with it and refrains from probing any further.

Reciprocity in Lindsay, as we recall, justified and intensified the 'free-trade mania' among the British, particularly the 'uncontrolled free traders'. In Gutzlaff, reciprocity legitimized and fuelled something grander still – the dual 'mania'

---

[24] 'Ho-chin' probably refers to the town now known as Hezhen Xinkai, located in the middle of Chongming.

of forcing open China to British commerce *and* 'the individual enterprise' of 'preaching the gospel to the heathen' and 'saving souls' ('Gutzlaff's *Journal*' 608, 610), regardless of the piratical means it took to accomplish both enterprises. Reviewing Gutzlaff's narrative for the pious British and American readerships, the *Quarterly Christian Spectator*,[25] for instance, had no qualms in praising the missionary's audacity as though he were a pirate hero: 'Of dauntless courage and indomitable fortitude, like a true soldier of the cross, his motto seems to be, "victory or death"' ('Gutzlaff's *Journal*' 593). Nor did the periodical hesitate to highlight Gutzlaff's fruitful connections with the commercial interests, commending him for exhibiting 'the energy and sound discretion of an accomplished man of business' ('Gutzlaff's *Journal*' 593). The Christian magazine was completely confident in 'the utility of [Gutzlaff's] enterprise' because 'both the medicines and books dealt out by Mr. G., were accepted joyfully' ('Gutzlaff's *Journal*' 600)[26] and because the Chinese themselves confessed, 'How gladly ... would we, if permitted, cultivate amicable intercourse with you!' ('Gutzlaff's *Journal*' 601). In light of such enthusiastic reception of Gutzlaff among the natives, the *Quarterly Christian Spectator* appealed to both the religious and the mercantile circles to follow the missionary's example to realize 'the power of individual enterprise' ('Gutzlaff's *Journal*' 610):

> Parents will deem it a privilege to have sons properly educated, and willing to go forth as their representatives to preach the gospel to every creature. ... Merchants will load their ships with the scriptures; yea, go themselves too, to aid in their distribution. ('Gutzlaff's *Journal*' 611)

One would be hard pressed to find in another discussion of Britain–China relations during the monopoly-free trade transition an ampler justification of Gutzlaff's daredevil 'piratical' missionary style than this fervent call for joining the evangelical and the *laissez-faire* causes.

Conclusions

It remains to draw some conclusions from Lindsay and Gutzlaff's 'buccaneering or piratical enterprise' to rethink European piracy and imperialism in modern Chinese history. The piratical seafarers' accounts and their unquestioned receptions among contemporary British middle-class readers throw into question the Chinese 'patriotic' historical narrative, which represents British imperialism merely as

---

[25] This polemical Christian periodical was published in New Haven, Connecticut. It was sold in London as well.

[26] For a historical examination of the reception of the tracts distributed by Gutzlaff among the Chinese and the Qing authorities, see pp. 184–6 of my article 'Representing "Great England"'.

a laundry list of 'predatory crimes' against Qing China during the nineteenth century. As I have shown in this chapter, in an era in which the British government adopted an anti-piracy policy, the significance of Lindsay and Gutzlaff's voyage lies less in their 'piratical' aggressions against the people and the authorities along the China coast than in the powerful images and perceptions that these actions generated for Britain's middle-class audience – images and perceptions that involved these readers in their nation's transition from monopoly to free trade in the China diplomacy. By co-opting the characteristics of the pirate, a popular icon, such as independence, defiance, valiance and opportunism, Lindsay and Gutzlaff's accounts provided concrete (and entertaining) examples of how 'the individual enterprise' – both commercial and religious – could successfully break open the historically secluded Middle Kingdom, fuelling as much the 'free-trade mania' as the missionary craze among the political, mercantile and religious circles in Britain. The adventurers' individualistic, interactive accounts superseded the older narratives published by embassy writers as the dominant genre of relating to China and the Chinese among the British. The new view of a 'friendly' Chinese population justified not only the piratical means to penetrate the empire, but also the gunboat policy against a government that was too 'tyrannical' and 'jealous' to welcome British 'friendship'.

Though illuminating, the intersections between piratical voyages, the meanings they created, and the larger shifts in Britain's China policy have unfortunately been missed by generations of Chinese scholars, who were too quick to seize the moral high ground and condemn Lindsay and Gutzlaff as pioneers of British imperialist piracy, poisoning their nation with opium, robbing treasures, killing the innocent and exploiting China's health and wealth. Based on this moral high ground, Chinese historical narratives of imperialist piracy have expediently constructed a monolithic victim – i.e. modern China, falling prey to another monolith, British 'piratical' and 'predatory' imperialism during the long nineteenth century. However, this 'patriotic' critique of imperialism becomes problematic now that the world has been increasingly globalized, and when even China has eagerly joined the World Trade Organization. For this irresistible globalization has brought about new significance of 'piracy', undermining China's traditional moral ground.

As China's representatives who had participated in international copyright and other negotiations lamented, when their country was accused of being 'a kingdom of piracy', they felt very indignant. The negotiators would recall almost instinctively the familiar history of European powers' 'piratical crimes' against China, resulting in the loss of thousands of national treasures to museums in the very nations that now charge China with 'piracy' – Britain, France and the United States. Nevertheless, as the representatives were aware, they could hardly trumpet this painful chapter of modern Chinese history to defend their country on the negotiation table in this age of information when the dominant meaning of 'piracy' has, as Andrew Knighton, Sean Grass and Kate Mattacks remind us, changed to 'theft of intellectual property' (Wu). It is a great historical irony that the word 'piracy', once used expediently to denounce western aggression and thereby to assert a sense of national moral superiority, has returned to haunt China, reducing it to 'a lawless nation of thieves'. Caught between their memory of nineteenth-century free-trade imperialism and the current globalization, the Chinese negotiators found themselves in a semantic predicament originating from the historical fluidity of the term 'piracy'. Without an understanding of 'piracy' as a *historical* activity that generated and still generates different meanings for the world powers' mobile imperial projects, we cannot even begin to address the semantic predicament faced not only by the Chinese representatives but also by people concerned about the lasting legacy of imperialism.

Chapter 5

The Wreck of the *Corsair*: Piracy, Political Economy and American Publishing

Andrew Lyndon Knighton

> Our sailing orders are simple: – Overhaul every craft on the literary seas – ransack her lading –take out of her what is valuable, and send her on her voyage
>
> *Corsair*, 'The Quarter Deck', 1

Such was the declaration with which the *Corsair* was launched, in March of 1839. The weekly gazette of literature and the arts, headed by 'Captain' T.O. Porter and 'First Mate' Nathaniel Parker Willis, published 52 issues before folding in the following year. During its short run, the *Corsair* endeavoured to fuse editorial opportunism with political protest against the absence of international copyright law; its strategy was the unabashed appropriation of the works of European writers, including Balzac, Bulwer and Dickens, for publication under its own stateside banner.[1] Drifting upon the unregulated seas of transatlantic literary exchange, the *Corsair* mobilized and modified the conventions of pirate mythology to intervene in debates surrounding the relationship of intellectual property to the market and the meaning of antebellum authorship. Its brand of piracy posited a set of unrealized possibilities for American literature that in many ways anticipated the economic exigencies of today: it celebrated circulation over creation, transience over tradition and the cynical over the romantic. The *Corsair*'s staging of these various economic, literary and ethical tensions would ultimately lead to its undoing; from its wreckage, however, we might recover insights that challenge

---

[1]   In addition to its pirated copy, the *Corsair* frequently published pro-copyright screeds drawing attention to its dubious ethics. Its prospectus explains: 'It is their [the editors'] design to present as amusing a periodical as can be made from the current wit, humor, and literature of the time: to collect the spirit not only of English, but of French and German belles letters … to picture the age in its literature and fashion, its eccentricities and amusements … . As the piratical law of copy-right secures to them, free of expense, the labors of BULWER and BOZ, SCRIBE and BALZAC, with the whole army of foreign writers, they cannot at present (consistently with the pocket wisdom so well understood by American Publishers) offer anything for American productions. Their critical department, however, will be always on the alert for native literature, and to the best of their ability they will keep a running guage [*sic*] of the merits of compatriot authors' ('Prospectus of the *Corsair*' 16).

conventional understandings of both piracy and the dynamics of nascent industrial capitalism.

The forced fellow-feeling of its 'Carriers' Address' captures much of its spirit:

> Now break the bottle o'er the bow!
> Three cheers! The craft is christened now!
> Let thunder rend the air!
> Three cheers for Captain, Mate and Crew!
> Three cheers for all their friends so true!
> And three for the CORSAIR! ('Carriers' Address' 683)

However, the address takes a sinister turn when the *Corsair* is depicted overtaking a foreign literary craft – significantly, that of Charles Dickens, who would later become one of the more visible advocates for an extension of international copyright protection. The *Boz* is 'bound for fame', and, buoyed by the recent success of *The Pickwick Papers* and *Oliver Twist*, is freighted with a 'cargo' attractive to American pirates. It proves no match for the legal but crass piracy of the *Corsair* and its bloodthirsty crew:

> 'Lay to! – your cargo first we claim!'
> What! Without purchase? Oh, for shame!
> Consider first, with care,
> The midnight lamp – the cost of mind –
> The pleasure which I give mankind.
> 'We can't, to those our laws are blind.' ('Carriers' Address' 683)

The address thus articulates – while hiding behind – a notorious and wilful blind spot in the American copyright law of 1790 regarding the copyright protection accorded to foreign authors. The provision explicitly designates that:

> [N]othing in this act shall be construed to extend to prohibit the importation or vending, reprinting, or publishing within the United States, of any map, chart, book or books, written, printed, or published by any person not a citizen of the United States, in foreign parts or places without the jurisdiction of the United States. (qtd. in McGill 80)

This apparent wink at literary piracy left a turbulent wake, and international copyright law was a consistently contentious issue in both the United States and in England. In the States, adjustments to the law doubled its domestic term in 1831 (to 28 years); from 1837 to 1842, Kentucky Senator Henry Clay repeatedly and unsuccessfully introduced to Congress bills extending further the protections of authorship (Barnes 71). Despite such efforts, the United States would only bow to an international copyright agreement half a century later, in 1891. Meanwhile, the most heated debate on the copyright issue, and one closely monitored by the editors of the *Corsair*, took place in England. There, a bill featuring 'rudimentary international protection' (Seville 238) was introduced in 1837 by Sarjeant Thomas Noon Talfourd, a celebrated advocate of copyright reform in England. The initial failure of Talfourd's bill inaugurated 10 subsequent attempts on his part to pass an extended copyright law, culminating in 1842 with a mealy-mouthed compromise shorn of its international language and much else.[2]

A first generation of English copyright advocates, comprising the likes of Wordsworth and Southey, staked their claims to a market still chiefly regarded as domestic: having built for themselves an audience, they sought an extension of the term during which their works would be protected (and the classification of the heirs of Scott and Coleridge in this camp testifies to its posthumous import). But a second generation emerged in the late 1830s and 1840s, chafing at the unauthorized reproduction of English works across the Atlantic, and lamenting the lost profit and prestige resulting from pervasive piracy there (Feather 149). Though a few American publishers did remit some modicum of compensation to British authors, the widespread practice was piratical, occasioning the *Corsair*'s sympathies for Boz, who 'feels his sufferings keen'.

> For still we steal his choicest store,
> That merchant's very eyes before,
> Nor make the slightest fuss;
> And yet – which grieves us much to think –
> The price of half a tent of ink
> He never had from us. ('Carriers' Address' 683)

As stateside copyright advocates pointed out, such literary poaching undermined American authors as well, by creating little incentive for publishers to compensate them for original (and domestically copyright-protected) works, when top-notch efforts by elite British authors were freely available. That this was enabled by the absence of international protections in the 1790 copyright law was precisely what the *Corsair* sought to emphasize, in both its rhetorical flamboyance and its very title – it unambiguously labelled as 'piracy' what the copyright law sanctioned as legal 'vending, reprinting, or publishing' of foreign works. Yet, the *Corsair*'s position is hardly without its ambiguities, as it simultaneously embraced and critiqued the lawlessness of the international literary seas, inveighing against the absence of copyright protection, all the while illustrating its protest by pushing the unregulated literary market to its extreme. Its piratical conceit was swathed in diverting wordplay and general literary mischief – long the strong suits of the 'dandy-editor' Willis – exemplified in the over-the-top personae of its staff (including such characters as the second mate, a claret-swilling Frenchman

---

[2] For a frugal account of British copyright history since the early eighteenth century, see Seville 3–6.

named 'Monsieur Moquetoi', and the third mate and translator from German, 'Herr Hinkspiller') and in recurring features such as 'Extracts from the Log' and 'Plunderings by the Way', which narrativized the business of American publishing as a version of piratical conquest.[3]

At the same time, the *Corsair*'s editors presented themselves as thoughtful advocates for legislative action on behalf of proprietorial authorship, in alignment with those, like Talfourd, who argued for the extension of copyright protections. Somewhat ironically, Talfourd's influential pro-copyright address of 27 February 1849 so resonated with the professed aims of Porter and Willis that it, too, was poached for the pages of the *Corsair* ('Sargeant Talfourd's Speech' 54). Similar treatment was granted to an excerpt from Dickens, complaining of the damage wrought when an impostor takes credit:

> [A]s author, with the honourable distinction annexed, of having perpetrated a hundred other outrages of the same description. Now, show me the distinction between such pilfering as this, and picking a man's pocket in the street: unless, indeed, it be, that the legislature has a regard for pocket-handkerchiefs, and leaves men's brains, except when they are knocked out by violence, to take care of themselves. (*Corsair* 303)

Though aimed at unauthorized stage adaptations, Dickens's complaint could hardly be better tailored to fit Willis and Porter and their piratical project. The two were the first to explore the potential of such newspaper reprints, setting the precedent for similar reprint vehicles such as *Brother Jonathan* and the *New World*, which were launched in July and October 1839, respectively. So great was the scale and impact of their literary poaching that Meredith McGill has dignified the practice, in the title of her recent study, as epoch-making: 'the culture of reprinting'. Taking advantage of not only the free accessibility of foreign texts, but also of conducive postal rates and a voracious national appetite for steady reading, such reprint vehicles eventually issued entire novels as 'extras' in folio and quarto formats, beginning in 1841. These 'mammoths' earned their name for their remarkable size (used to exploit postal loopholes about what constituted a 'newspaper'), the astonishing standard being set by the *New World*'s 'Christmas Leviathan' of 1841, which measured over six feet by four feet. The *New World* boasted of having issued in this fashion some 35 complete works in 1843; such reprint literature was available so cheaply that, in John Feather's estimate, the same price would have bought only two of the works in their original editions in London (14).

The *New World* was hardly bashful about promoting its reprinting strategy, which it saw as heralding:

> [A] new era in ... Popular Literature, which deserves the patronage and support of every friend of cheap reading throughout our extended country – and from

---

[3]   The title of the latter feature rather indulgently 'plunders' Willis's own successful volume of European travel writings, *Pencillings by the Way*, published in London in 1835.

the unparalleled cheapness of our republications, we see no reason why at least one hundred thousand copies of each popular new work may not be issued and circulated among the millions of readers which the United States contain. ('Another Extra Double New World' 322)

The competition between the *New World* and what it called its 'stupid contemporary', *Brother Jonathan*, was fierce, and resulted in an ever-accelerating race to expeditiously reprint whatever arrived by transatlantic steamer. In some cases this piracy was quite literal, as ships were boarded by agents of the magazines even before docking, such that copies of new releases might be issued in just hours (Ashby 29). Suffering more than anyone from such frenzied poaching was Dickens – his *American Notes* travelogue was available in a reprint edition a mere 17 hours after its arrival on a Sunday in November 1842. In a day's time, some 24,000 reprint copies were issued; by the week's end, four American versions were available in runs totalling an amazing 60,000 copies (Ashby 29; Houtchens 23).

Unlike the subsequent mammoths – whose editors rarely missed an opportunity to intervene in the copyright disputes on the side of free trade and against authorial rights – the *Corsair* danced delicately around the issue, brassily demanding an international copyright law at precisely the same time that it exploited its absence. In part, its own swashbuckling self-promotion as a reliable advocate of authors' rights may be responsible for the underestimation of its role in the reprint economy by contemporary literary historians (an underestimation that only aggravates the conventional neglect of N.P. Willis generally).[4] An odd passage from Lawrence H. Houtchens's dated but telling account of a pro-copyright petition circulated by Washington Irving illustrates the success of the *Corsair*'s pro-copyright smokescreen. Arguing that 'the curious anomaly in the fact that several signers of Irving's petition were or had been connected with thieving journals deserves some comment', Houtchens nevertheless goes on to bluntly declare that 'Nathaniel P. Willis may be passed over. From March 16, 1839 to March 7, 1840, he had helped to edit the *Corsair*, which was a vigorous proponent of international copyright' (24).

If we refrain from merely passing over Willis and the odd paradoxes of his *Corsair*, we are forced to challenge a set of assumptions about literary practice under capitalism, namely, the prevailing tendency to see authorial proprietorship

---

[4]   Only in very recent years has Willis been admitted as a deserving subject of serious literary study. Despite being among the most widely read and highly paid writers in the antebellum United States, the trivial or topical nature of his essays and sketches, not to mention his grating public personality, have repelled critics. Notable exceptions to this are Thomas A. Baker's recent critical biography of Willis, *Sentiment and Celebrity: Nathaniel Parker Willis and the Trials of Literary Fame* (New York and Oxford: Oxford UP, 1999), as well as Sandra Tomc's important piece, 'An Idle Industry: Nathaniel Parker Willis and the Workings of Literary Leisure'. *American Quarterly* 49 (December 1997): 780–805.

as a necessary epiphenomenon of the rise of the capitalist literary market and the ideological primacy of the 'work'.[5] As we will see, reading an historical continuity in this respect is unsustainable in the light of the nineteenth-century American context, where the persistent reluctance of legal and legislative opinion to extend legal and economic protections to intellectual production contributed to what Michael Newbury has suggestively described as the 'tremendously unstable, fluid, half-formed, and multiply-signified idea' (203) of antebellum authorship.

Furthermore, the resistance to copyright was not merely a nigglesome hurdle to be cleared en route to American literature's maturation, but rather, for many, a sign that American literature had achieved its maturity in the culture of reprinting. With the idea of authorship itself so keenly in doubt, our attachment to the model of the author-as-proprietor – seemingly so compatible with both our conventional critiques of bourgeois individualism and the fetish character of commodities – risks naturalizing the eventual establishment of international copyright as the inevitable modern telos of a linear and continuous historical trajectory. Such a position furthermore reproduces the very bourgeois individualism it seeks to understand, heralding as the singular achievement of modern subjectivity the construction of an authorship for which there could be no alternative. This approach, as David Saunders argues, means that:

> The law of copyright loses its positivity and becomes the pliant tool of a general movement of consciousness. Complex but contingent relations between highly specified forms of legal and aesthetic personality are collapsed into the expression of a successful (or a failed) advance toward the future completion of this movement in the synthesis that fulfills the dialectic. (97)

The lesson of the *Corsair* for such scholarship, then, may be regarded as twofold. On one hand, the editorial agenda of Willis and Porter – however disingenuously – clumsily sunders the question of copyright from that of authorship, a difficult task that forces the *Corsair* to hover in the zone of historical contradiction that the publication itself helpfully makes visible. However, the *Corsair* furthermore reveals the notion of authorship to be overdetermined; it unveils the 'author-function' as a product of power relations that far outstrip both Romantic conceptions of genius and the author-as-proprietor model reproduced by ideology critique. The *Corsair* not only counteracts such notions of authorship, but in its transparent contradictions reveals some of the anxieties undergirding both American literature and American capitalism just prior to mid-century – especially in the 'grieving' for the author that so strains its own 'Carriers' Address', and the palpable fears produced by an encounter with texts that behave as if they were radically unstable.

---

[5] For a brief overview of major texts in this critical discussion – from Michel Foucault to Mark Rose to Martha Woodmansee and beyond – see Saint-Amour, Paul K. *The Copyrights: Intellectual Property and the Literary Imagination* (Ithaca: Cornell UP, 2003), 10–12.

At Sea

The editors regret to note that, of the *Corsair*'s 'Carriers' Address', they have been able to print only 'those portions which seem to us most spirited and most descriptive of the *piratical* enterprises in which our craft has been employed' (683). In all, the address seems calculated to instil in the reader the sensory effects of the pirate's ship, but instead of conveying the tense strain of the mainsail lines, it is instead the strain of the *Corsair*'s central metaphor that is most palpable (does Boz *really* suffer 'like [a] new-skin'd eel'?). What is at stake in this play-acting, and why is the sea the setting for a drama that is, essentially and avowedly, one of political economy?

We might approach an answer by way of Willis, whose buoyant personality lent the *Corsair* most of its initial flair, and who had long experienced a kind of metaphorical kinship with water, that element which he felt best reflected the famous fluidity, mobility and fungibility of his literary personality. Just as his editorial writing scrambled from issue to issue and from celebrity to celebrity, his own personality was chameleon-like, readily shaped to suit whatever character could best work to his advantage – diplomat, journalist, poet, socialite, romancier or pirate. Professing to 'detest water in small quantities', Willis nevertheless lionized its sublime qualities in his writing on landscape, gushing that 'it is, by much, the belle in the family of elements … water! Soft, pure, graceful water! There is no shape into which you can throw her that she does not seem lovelier than before' (Sherman and Willis, *Trenton Falls* 52). Elsewhere, he directed his readers to 'sit back in your chair, and let me babble! I like just to pull the spigot out of my discretion, and let myself run' (Willis, *Dashes* 24). His contemporaries frequently resorted to the water metaphor when discussing him, as did the editor, Rufus Griswold ('The stream of thought and feeling in him is like the bubbling outspring of a natural fountain, which flows forth with gayety and freedom, if it flows at all' (qtd. in Richards, 'Idlewild' 166)) as well as the poet James Russell Lowell, who, in his 'Fable for Critics' suggests that Willis's prose 'winds along with a blithe, gurgling error', and when 'free and unlaced … runs like a stream with a musical waste, / And gurgles along with the liquidest sweep; – 'T is not deep as a river, but who'd have it deep?' Lowell's poem culminates with the famous and widely quoted description of Willis the socialite as 'the topmost bright bubble on the wave of the town' (131).

Mobilized in the *Corsair*, these tropes of fluidity and liquidity not only invoke the changing status of literary celebrity, but also articulate an emerging response to the transformation of value – both literary and economic – under way in the years leading up to the middle of the century. This transformation, as Cesare Casarino has demonstrated, had significant ramifications for the 'political economy of the sea' (4) and the literature concerned with it. The consolidation of industrial capital on the western shores of the Atlantic meant that the factory eclipsed the sea as the central arena associated with economic value. The sea, however – and especially its borderlessness, its indifference to taming by man – is pressed into cultural service in new ways, and one of these is as the antithesis to conventional understandings of property. Since Locke, the idea of proprietorship had been founded in the land, which, with the application of labour, could be improved, cultivated and parcelled in the pursuit of economic values. This metaphor was repeatedly pressed into service by the likes of Edmund Burke, to provide a common-law explanation of the workings of literary creation; even so immaterial a notion as that of 'genius' could be made tangible through metaphors of inheritance and landed property, metaphors that made land the model for all kinds of possession (Newlyn 271).

The conceit of the *Corsair*, however, proposes that the urgent questions regarding property are no longer those of the common law and its earth-bound traditions, but rather those pertaining to the sea – with its fluidity, its transience and its statelessness. This is but one manifestation of a similar argument that circulates more widely, and often more explicitly, in the unstable milieu preceding international copyright. Consider, for example, the introductory pages of James Morgan's *Law of Literature*:

> Property may exist in whatever is CAPABLE OF OCCUPATION; the surface of the globe, and everything upon it which it is possible to occupy, is, therefore, a legitimate subject of property. That surface itself, consisting of solid earth, or rock, or mould, or shifting sands, may be divided up into parcels and become the property of individuals, together with such sheets of portions of water as are included in the boundaries thereof. *But the ocean cannot be occupied. No boundaries other than its own can ever be given to it. No limits or marks of proprietorship can ever be fixed or impressed upon its surface.* (1: 1–2, emphasis added)

The sea, then, is that arena in which possession becomes a problem. Its vast borderlessness and its propensity to spill over any man-made demarcations remove it from the jurisdiction of property. As such, it becomes the object of nostalgia and utopian projection, a reserve from the striated disciplinarity of industrial time and space and the bewitching proprietorship over alienated labour enjoyed by the capitalist. This can only occur because the sea at this juncture is tending toward economic marginality – less a wellspring of value and more an anachronism. Casarino has remarked that this transition is responsible for a shift of emphasis in many of the sea narratives that emerge at mid-century: the heroic individuals of Romantic portrayals as well as the exoticized destinations appropriate to the picaresque are complemented or supplanted by narratives sited on the sea itself (9). There, the ship is projected as a heterotopic enclosure in which the manifold contradictions of emergent capitalist modernity are visible. We thus must remark a signal shift: Lord Byron's 'Corsair' (clearly an influence on the later piratical magazine) is a man; Willis's *Corsair* is a ship. The meaning of piracy undergoes a transition, from an emblem of romantic unity to one of modern paradox.

In Morgan's estimation, the figurative importance of the sea does not end there. Crucially, he pushes his discussion of property, land and sea even further, into an analogy that brings us back to the unstable idea of authorship. Can ideas, sentiments and expressions – in short, the work of literary genius – can they be property? In answer, he notes that all of the above 'are clothed in language … which appears to be as much the common highway of the thoughts, as the ocean is the common highway of the commerce of nations' (Morgan 1: 2). On that common highway – the shared social space in which language and property alike may elude the certainties of ownership – the *Corsair* discovered an ideal harmony between its economic interests and its literary personality. At sea, amidst the fluidity of both authorial identity and economic proprietorship, there momentarily flourished a vision of American literature governed by the ideology of what might be called 'republicationism'.

Republicationism

The stage was set for this controversial episode in the history of American intellectual property by the 1834 case of *Wheaton versus Peters*.[6] A dispute about the opposing rights of two Supreme Court reporters to publish their own accounts of the court's decisions, *Wheaton versus Peters* emphasized the interests of textual dissemination over the property rights of individuals. In contrast to the fumbling Lockean paradigms of Wheaton's attorneys (who essentially argued for the intrinsic originality of Wheaton's production), Peters's lawyers strategically flattered the court by arguing for the imperative utility of widespread dissemination of its own decisions, while crucially redefining 'the court reports in question from material objects that can be owned to something like pure circulation' (McGill 51).[7] The court ruled that at the point of publication the 'author' relinquishes any common-law right to the text as property, and is thereafter protected only by the fungible dictates of statute. In consequence, the court established a different standard of protection for the author's private manuscript than for any printed copies that might subsequently circulate. Thus was established a central pillar of the republican apologia for the rampant republication that would, in the subsequent decade, radically recast American literature as a 'culture of reprinting'.

The American embracing of the widespread circulation and dissemination of literary and journalistic works also prominently featured a strong nationalist

---

[6]   A full account of the case is not necessary or possible here, though it is exceedingly interesting. See McGill's *American Literature and the Culture of Reprinting, 1834–1853* (Philadelphia: U of Pennsylvania P, 2003), 51ff.

[7]   Christopher Hill, in his influential description of Captain Mission's Madagascar pirate community, makes specific remark of the fact that there 'the laws were printed and dispersed among the people ("for they had some printers and letter-founders among them")' (164), an arrangement completely compatible in spirit with the disseminatory ideology of American republicanism.

emphasis on the specific literary identity of the United States.[8] The mammoth *New World*, for example, promised 'to place the perusal of every valuable book which may be issued in the power of the entire reading public of America' ('Another Extra Double' 322), a populist vision wedded to that of overcoming the perceived exclusivity and stasis of English social hierarchies. Trumpeting its 'great literary revolution', the *New World* elsewhere described its 'truly democratic' motivations as 'utterly subversive of that intellectual aristocracy which has hitherto controlled the energies of the nation' (qtd. in Barnes 15). Putting an even finer point on it, the paper credited English literary production to:

> [H]er wealthy aristocracy, enjoying the leisure and means to store their minds and cultivate their powers, without being forced, as are most of the writers in this country, either to write hurriedly for bread, or to make writing much the secondary occupation of time saved from money-getting employments. ('Remarks' 173)

Recoiling from the excesses of the British literary elite, republican advocacy of reprinting celebrated the labours of those Americans who facilitated the widespread circulation of knowledge – publishers, printers and even pirates – but not authors, whose monopoly rights to literature were thought to erect an obstacle to the freedoms of enlightenment, centralizing intellectual power in the hands of an undesirable literary elite. In contrast to such ill-gotten privilege, the American (re-)printer became a cherished figure of reprint culture, an industrious and yeomanly agent in the dispersion of knowledge (and, as a group, printers were responsible for many self-interested petitions to Congress in opposition to international copyright). Republication advocates made the compelling argument that American authors (the ostensible beneficiaries of international copyright) need not try to match the productions of their English counterparts, for the quality of American literature is defined by populist priorities and an entirely different market structure. It would be the popularization and democratization – not the production – of knowledge that constituted the true task of American literature.

For both sides in the emerging dispute, the question of dissemination was couched in the language of fluidity. The stability of European precedents – where

---

8   Such advocacy of dissemination was not, however, only typical of the American copyright dispute. The English debates too witnessed a proliferation of anti-copyright petitions and opinions – not only from publishers and printers opposed to more expensive books, or free marketers wedded to the ideological idea that a book was a simple economic good like any other – but also from Utilitarians, radical opponents of taxing knowledge and organizations like the Society for the Promotion of Christian Knowledge and the Society for the Diffusion of Useful Knowledge. See Catherine Seville, *Literary Copyright Reform in Early Victorian England: The Framing of the 1842 Copyright Act* (Cambridge: Cambridge UP, 1999), 21–4.

'policy seeks to make literature and literary institutions the pillars of monarchical government' ('Memorial' 323) – is contrasted with the 'fructifying streams' of American enlightenment, which, as Ohio Senator Benjamin Ruggles wrote, must be allowed to run freely (494: 5). Unsurprisingly, copyright advocates saw these streams of knowledge somewhat differently, decrying a 'general flood of pamphlets' that 'settles down, at its leisure, into a dark, slimy, universal pond' (Bryant et al. 11). The future of American literature lay suspended between these two visions: on the one hand the transcendent structures of European monarchy, and on the other, the wager placed by 'republicationism' on a pure circulation, figured in the horizontality and fluidity of water.

General Circulation

To invoke circulation during the unstable economic years around 1840 is to unambiguously invoke the flow of money: Dickens's *American Notes for General Circulation* – a text which he rightly assumed would be a hot property for American reprint pirates – packed into its titular pun an implied commentary on the relationship between journalistic and monetary circulation. Piracy, it has been memorably said, 'was a business', the practice of which in the antebellum ambit fused notions of literary and monetary circulation amidst a changing political economy of the sea. Nadal suggests in his contribution to the collection *Bandits at Sea* that corsairing is 'a phenomenon that is peculiar to a crisis economy' (128), and certainly the extreme economic turbulence prevailing during the tenure of the *Corsair* and its sister pirate ships suggests that we may extend his observation on crisis to the literary field. Not only did questions of international property transfer and ownership remain completely unresolved, but banking and monetary policy struggled with a cycle of recession inaugurated by the rash of wildcat bank failures in the late 1830s. A period of currency speculation that would only be slowed with the founding of the national bank and the establishment of a unified currency in 1863 saw the issuance of millions of dollars of suspect 'American notes' that in many cases held only bogus value. These conditions of crisis rendered mysterious the relationship of economic value to its monetary equivalents, provoking a period of rampant speculation and abstract exploitation, and galvanizing the pirate newspapers to highlight both their cheapness and their kinship with these freely circulating monetary tokens.[9]

---

[9] Nathaniel Parker Willis would himself experiment with the resonances between journalistic and monetary circulation during his co-editorship of the short-lived *Dollar Magazine*, in 1841. The *Dollar* was an offshoot of *Brother Jonathan*, and proclaimed its desire to attain 'the character of STANDARD CURRENCY' and to serve as 'LEGAL TENDER in the world of literature' (*Dollar Magazine* 1 (Dec. 1841): 384). Carrying on the discourse of dissemination we have been observing, the *Dollar* half-cheekily demanded that 'This Magazine – meant for the people – already nearly universal, must circulate on

Arguing that sheer cheapness facilitated the free circulation that was the very principle of democratic society, the *New World*, for instance, claimed that it could print extras of pirated novels 'at so low a price, (never to exceed twenty-five cents for any one entire work) as to place the perusal of every valuable book which may be issued in the power of the entire reading public of America' ('Another Extra Double' 322). Furthermore, such cheapness was promoted as the optimal means of breaking down those hindrances which would impede free circulation. In response to those who argued that the reprint culture emphasized subpar works, the *New World* rejoined that 'The best remedy that can be devised for the evil is by giving every facility to the dissemination of better works – that is, by making them as cheap as possible; not by throwing obstacles between them and the mass of the people' ('Remarks' 173).

Piracy, as piracy, must be chiefly concerned with streamlining precisely this task of delivery, for, as Starkey notes, 'piracy is a service industry, a business concerned with the transport and distribution, rather than the production, of commodities' (108). Literary piracy broke with Romanticism in its indifference toward interiority and creation as the site of production for literary value; it similarly refused the sovereignty of consumption that would later hypostatize the act of reading. The pirate navigates between these poles of production and consumption, deftly situating value – both economic and literary – at the moment of the heist. All of the creativity the literary pirate can muster is dedicated to speeding the flow of knowledge, entertainment and information, to overcoming every artificial barrier – whether class privilege, geography or tradition – to the complete and total flow of often undifferentiated content at the greatest imaginable velocity.

Such conditions are recognizable to us today; they are those of a highly advanced capitalism that has devised myriad means to profitably exploit such flows. And though in the middle of the nineteenth century such conditions were only episodic (for they could only at great risk of instability be made lucrative), they nevertheless produced in these pirates affective traits highly suited to a global and total capitalist economy. Starkey notes how piracy must develop the most exploitative possible response to 'particular, often short-term conditions' (109) – in short, the pirate must be flexible, mobile and cunning, constantly innovating and finding new ways to capitalize on turbulent conditions.[10] As in a fully global economy, the innovation

---

the widest and most central plane of sympathy of intelligence' (*Dollar Magazine* 1 (Aug. 1841): 225).

[10]   Some of the parallels between this condition and that of the contemporary moment may be teased out by consulting Paolo Virno's 'The Ambivalence of Disenchantment', *Radical Thought in Italy*. Ed. Paolo Virno and Michael Hardt. Trans. Michael Turits (Minneapolis: U of Minnesota P, 1996): 13–34, especially the passages in which he defines postmodernity by the tactical skills that typify both opportunism and radicalism: 'habituation to uninterrupted and nonteleological change, reflexes tested by a chain of perceptive shocks, a strong sense of the contingent and the aleatory, a nondeterministic mentality ... These are the qualities that have been elevated to an authentic productive

of this pirate economy was deployed to overcome the spatial distances separating markets, but also, and importantly, to obliterate temporal hindrances to circulation. Piracy is an anticipation of totalizing circulation, emerging prior to the system's ability to translate such unregulated flows into value.

The debate over copyright reveals how this form of intellectual property is nothing other than a temporal restriction on circulation, an obstacle to the total and complete dissemination of texts at maximum velocity. With the myth of perpetual copyright having been punctured by *Wheaton versus Peters* (in the US) and the landmark case of *Donaldson versus Beckett* (in England), the copyright term's most arbitrary and artificial underpinnings were made transparent; its protections are the constructed right of a constructed persona – the author. From the standpoint of 'republicationism', such artifices obstruct the realization of literature, and thus the *New World* would inveigh against copyright, noting not only that 'literature wants no such protection as that law would give', but also that by pressuring prices upward, restricting the general accessibility of better authors and creating incentives for English publishers themselves to enter the American market (at the expense of American workers), the effect would be 'to *retard the now rapid progress* of American literature' ('Remarks' 173, emphasis added).

Two somewhat surprising conclusions loom. Initially, the case of literary pirates provokes us to reevaluate some of the romantic connotations that have long accrued to piracy. Thus, I have accentuated – instead of the communitarian ethic or the erotics of the ship – the piratical traits of economic flexibility, cunning, and mobility on the uncharted economic seas. Most fundamentally, it is the equation of piratical banditry with exteriority and resistance to capitalist social relations that cannot be sustained here: to stress the way that pirates 'directly challenged the ways of the society from which they excepted themselves', standing in 'defiant contradistinction to the ways of the world', as Rediker does (139–40, 146), is inadvertently to repress piracy's historical anticipation of late capitalism's dissolution of borders between states, of definitions of property and of the intangibility of the monetary economy. The pirate, in this instance, is not chiefly a rebel against the state and its capitalist protectors, but rather represents the most advanced form of capitalism in a nascent stage of its tendential expansion and consolidation.

The implications of this account for authorship are consequently also intriguing. We have seen already how piratical publishing practice trivialized the romantic bond between author and text as property, esteeming instead the moment of circulation and dissemination as the nexus of economic and literary value. It

---

force' (15). Consider also Gilles Deleuze's description of the economic character of modern 'control' societies in 'Postscript on Control Societies', *Negotiations*. Trans. Martin Joughin (New York: Columbia UP, 1995): 177–82, which are 'no longer directed toward production but toward products, that is, toward sales and markets. Thus [contemporary capitalism is] essentially dispersive ... Control is short-term and rapidly shifting, but at the same time continuous and unbounded' (181).

is not merely that the understanding of authorship – and the copyrights that are theorized as constitutive of it – was simply unstable during this period, only to be shored up as further copyright protection cemented the modern, capitalistic economic relationship between the author and the work. Instead, my study suggests that copyright and its stabilization of authorship actually worked *against* the tendencies of capital, serving as an internal restraint on the pure circulation of literary and economic values toward which capitalism strains. In contrast to our expectations, we find that, structurally speaking, capitalism does not care a lick about *authors*. Far from constituting the foundation of capitalist literary value, copyright functioned at its birth as a limitation or curb, a humanistic restraint upon the crises potentially unleashed by general circulation.

Epilogue: The Wreck of the *Corsair*

Like its piratical brethren, the *Corsair* would fatally flounder amidst the very turbulence that initially enabled it to exist. The endeavour apparently proved too much for Willis's shaky sea legs, and he departed for England a few months after its launch, ostensibly to dispatch a series of letters sharing with the American reader matters of topical interest abroad. Comically, the reports of this voyage reveal just how ridiculous was the pirate conceit of Willis's magazine in the first place. Captain Porter describes 'Mr. Willis's First Letter from England' to be a declaration of Willis's

> happiness in again setting foot on terra firma. His most welcome letter will speak
> for itself; but in justice to Mr. Willis we will take the liberty of saying that, when
> on the ocean, it is his misfortune to be constantly ill with sea sickness and mostly
> confined to his berth, which readily accounts for his refraining to enter into any
> detail of the events of the voyage. ('Mr. Willis's First Letter' 265)

Willis himself would avow that 'the sea is a dreary vacuity, in which he, perhaps, who was ever well upon it, can find material for thought. But for one, I will sell at sixpence a month, all copyhold upon so much of my life as is destined "to the deep, the blue, the black"' (265). Once safely settled ashore, Willis would be revived, rediscovering the 'humanity, killed in me invariably by salt water'. But his contributions to the *Corsair* thereafter would wane, and the once-punchy little magazine gradually surrendered its spirit, a fact seemingly not lost on Captain T.O. Porter, whose laments for his lost first mate became increasingly plaintive as weeks roll by with no word from Willis. ('The failure of recent advices from our correspondent and ally in England, is entirely attributable to the successive disappointments in the sailing of the British Steamships on the day advertised ... . We have felt it our duty to make this explanation, to prevent the impression getting abroad that any thing had occurred to prevent our associate from continuing his interesting 'Jottings' 825)). By its 51st number, a gruesome fate for the *Corsair* seemed imminent; a column given over to the topic of 'General Bankrupt Law' tellingly confesses that 'distress is stalking over the land, crushing the energies of those embarked in the various departments of industry' ('General Bankrupt Law' 809). And the tone of the final issue is apparently forecast in its lead items: two poems, one titled 'Resignation' and another 'Hope – The Ever Springing', along with Edward Mayhew's 'A Tale of the Morgue' (*Corsair* 818–20).[11]

While its last number makes no overt mention of the magazine's ultimate collapse, one senses that its piratical posture has reached a dead end in the short fictional sketch that graces the magazine's final pages. The sketch is entitled 'The Life-Boat', and it commemorates 'the moment … for all hands to quit the ship'. The ill winds of piratical publishing, once having speeded the *Corsair*'s enterprise, now blew mercilessly upon the vessel dispatched to rescue its distressed crew:

> All were now on board the airy messenger; and as her canoe-like form neared the haven, three cheers from their countrymen on the pier gave recognition of their success; which grateful greeting had feeble response on the wings of the blast. Ten minutes after the abandonment of the vessel, she parted on the reef; and the same surf which bore her rescued crew to land, drifted portions of the wreck upon the beach. ('Life-Boat' 831)

---

[11] The other pirate magazines would meet similar, if postponed, fates. In 1841, Horace Greeley had lamented that 'the great beasts murder me in the way of circulation', but soon the mammoth reprinters succumbed to the extremely competitive conditions they had helped to foment. Their decline (*Brother Jonathan* sank in 1843) was accelerated when reliable publishing giants like *Harper's*, enjoying favourable economies of scale, began dumping huge runs of their own content into the channels of circulation. That, combined with the closing of postal service loopholes and the reemergence of general prosperity after 1843 (which created demand for more upmarket publications) rendered the mammoths extinct (Barnes 17).

Chapter 6

Female Pirates and Nationalism in Nineteenth-Century American Popular Fiction

Katherine Anderson

Imagine finishing an American pamphlet novel – say, *The Land Pirate, or The Wild Girl of the Beach* – in 1847. The sensational plot has left you hungry for more and conveniently, there at the back of the book, the publishers include a catalogue of other stories 'Just Published!' for you to peruse. Readers eager for more pirate lore may be tempted by *The Witch of the Wave* and *The Sea Serpent; or, Queen of the Coral Cave*, while those dreaming of frontier adventure may look for *Corilia, or the Indian Enchantress; A Romance of the Pacific* or *The Trapper's Daughter, A Tale of Oregon*.[1] As these titles suggest, intrepid, cross-dressing heroines, largely forgotten today, were a common feature of American popular fiction in the second half of the nineteenth century. On one hand, as Henry Nash Smith argues in his classic study *Virgin Land*, these heroines, who appeared in the mid-1840s and became increasingly common from that time through the 1870s, were in some ways products of their harsh, new-world environment.[2] On the other hand, the creators of these figures are likely to have drawn inspiration from a rich European popular tradition, which includes not only familiar characters from Shakespeare and Defoe, but also numerous narratives of cross-dressed women working as sailors or soldiers in the seventeenth, eighteenth and nineteenth centuries.

Dianne Dugaw's comprehensive study of the 'woman warrior' type in English ballads of 1650–1850 points to the centrality of the intrepid heroine in the popular imagination, while Rudolf M. Dekker and Lotte C. van de Pol's archival study, unearthing nearly 100 cases of sailors and soldiers in the Dutch and English armies who were discovered to be women, reveals how closely the trope is

---

[1]   These examples are taken from the catalogue inside the back cover of Benjamin Barker's *Land Pirate; or, The Wild Girl of the Beach* (Boston: Gleason's, 1847).

[2]   See Chapter X, 'The Dime Novel Heroine', in Smith's *Virgin Land: The American West as Myth and Symbol* (Cambridge, MA: Harvard UP, 1970). Smith offers an exhaustive examination of the development and nuances of the daring heroine as a type, yet does not address the significance of her sudden appearance and proliferation between the 1840s and the 1870s. He suggests only that she and her male counterpart both indicate a decline in the moral and social significance of popular American fiction in these years.

grounded in historical fact. Women who had fought as men were the subjects of popular biographies as well as songs. Robert Walker's *The Female Soldier*, for example, recounts the adventures of Hannah Snell, who served in the English army from 1747 to 1750 under the name James Gray, then revealed her sex and was nonetheless honourably discharged, even receiving a military pension. First published in 1750, new editions of the tale appeared through the early 1800s. *The Female Review* (1797) tells the story of Deborah Sampson, who fought in the American Revolutionary War.[3] By far the most notorious women who lived and fought as men are, however, the pirates Mary Read and Anne Bonny, who were tried along with the rest of their crew in Provincetown, Jamaica, in 1721. Their sensational exploits earned them their own chapter, and prominent illustrations, in the renowned *General History of the Robberies and Murders of the Most Notorious Pyrates* (1724), often attributed to Defoe, although Charles Johnson is another contender for its authorship. Today, their legend lives on in popular forms ranging from movies and comic strips to board games and action figures.[4]

Despite the broad spectrum of possible sources for the American dime novel heroine, however, she had few counterparts in contemporary British or Continental fiction. By the nineteenth century, the golden age of Atlantic piracy was long past and women were no longer enlisting as men with the frequency, or the notoriety, with which they had done up until around 1800. Yet the cross-dressed heroine emerged with prominence in the American mid-nineteenth century, nearly 100 years after her European heyday. To examine the new-world resurgence of this

---

[3]   The commercial success of books such as *The Female Soldier* and *The Female Review* inspired spin-offs which claimed to be true and were taken as such. *The Female Marine* (1816), for example, purports to be the first-person account of Louisa Baker, alias Lucy Brewer, a young woman who flees her family and seeks refuge in a Boston brothel after having been impregnated by a seducer, and then escapes prostitution by disguising herself as a man and enlisting in the War of 1812. Interestingly, while the fictional Louisa Baker cites the real-life case of Deborah Sampson as her inspiration to live as a man, real-life female soldier Sarah Emma Edmonds claims, in her autobiographical account of her service in the American Civil War (*Nurse and Spy in the Union Army*, 1865), to have got the idea from reading *Fanny Campbell*.

[4]   Many more recent works discuss Read and Bonny, too, including studies on Atlantic piracy (such as David Cordingly's *Under the Black Flag: The Romance and the Reality of Life Among the Pirates* (NY: Random House, 1995), C.R. Pennell's *Bandits at Sea: A Pirates Reader* (NY: New York UP, 2001), Marcus Rediker's *Villains of All Nations: Atlantic Pirates in the Golden Age* (Boston: Beacon Press, 2004) and Robert Ritchie's *Captain Kidd and the War Against the Pirates* (Cambridge, MA: Harvard UP, 1986)); books on women who lived and/or fought as men (including Julie Wheelwright's *Amazons and Military Maids: Women Who Dressed As Men in the Pursuit of Life, Liberty and Happiness* (Boston and London: Pandora, 1989)); and books focusing specifically on women pirates (including Jo Stanley's *Bold in Her Breeches: Women Pirates Across the Ages* (San Francisco and London: Pandora, 1995), Ulrike Klausman et al's *Women Pirates and the Politics of the Jolly Roger* (New York: Black Rose Books, 1997)).

figure, I turn to the best-selling pulp novelette, *Fanny Campbell, Female Pirate Captain: A Tale of the Revolution* and its eponymous heroine, the formidable foremother of the American type.

Signed with the seafaring pseudonym of Lieutenant Murray, *Fanny Campbell* was published serially in 1844 and in book form the following year. Remarkably, the book sold a hundred thousand copies within a few months – and kept selling, remaining in print until the 1870s (Benson 35).[5] The material form of the pamphlet novel – hardly more sturdy than a newspaper – indicates its short life-expectancy, yet this story of a female pirate captain enjoyed such popularity that it circulated continuously for 30 years. *Fanny Campbell*'s initial success led its author, Bostonian Marturin Murray Ballou, to co-found with Frederick Gleason what would quickly become the United States' largest publishing plant. The pair launched a story paper, which also proved wildly successful, and began hammering out cheap pamphlet novels, including *The Female Land Pirate*. Soon, fighting female heroines had become a stock part of their formula, but *Fanny Campbell* was the first of these and also the most successful of its class. Significantly, the decades during which *Fanny* (and its myriad spin-offs) continued to sell coincided with an era of intense US expansion, fuelled by the ideology of manifest destiny. That the novel circulated throughout these years – an extraordinary achievement for a dime novel – suggests that it held an unusually strong appeal for the popular fiction readership of a young nation fast becoming an empire.

This chapter examines how the subversion of novelistic conventions in *Fanny Campbell* allowed readers to envision a proto-national past in service of contemporary expansionist, or imperialist, ideology. By imaginatively mapping the Revolutionary moment – in which a barely viable entity fends for its right to nationhood against powerful old-world empires – on to the mid-century present – in which the US was competing with those empires to secure its hemispheric status – the novel evacuates historical discourse, failing to account for change in terms of human agency. The cross-dressed female pirate, with her implicitly inferior physical strength, embodies this refusal of change, symbolizing a nation that will never reach maturity (conceived of as manhood). A 'gentle hearted girl' (*FC* 56) inside a fierce costume, the female pirate carries a far greater allegorical significance than her male counterpart could; this sword-bearer for US interests seems not a bloodthirsty outlaw but a 'soft conqueror' – one for whom might alone could not possibly guarantee victories, which thus appear underwritten by right.

---

[5]   *Fanny Campbell*'s success was to some degree part of an industry-wide publishing boom, facilitated, as I will discuss below, by new technologies in printing and distribution: 'between 1820 and 1850, the value of all books produced and sold in the United States increased fivefold, from \$2.5 to \$12.5 million' (Benson 37). See *The Female Marine and Related Works: Narratives of Cross-Dressing and Urban Vice in America's Early Republic*. Ed. Daniel A. Cohen (Amherst: U of Massachusetts P, 1997). The mechanics of her entry into the American imagination, however, do not account for her ongoing appeal.

While I shall focus on Fanny Campbell, I remain mindful of her dual status as an exceptional figure in a unique text, and as an exemplary instance of several broad trends. This popular story warrants our interest not so much for its strictly literary value – even its author called it a 'desultory and hastily written tale' (*FC* 96) and an 'ill-spun yarn' (99), going so far as to thank the reader 'for the great patience that has carried [him] through to these [final] lines' (99) – as for what George Orwell called the 'semi-sociological' significance of boys' weeklies in the late 1930s. Like those cheap periodicals, Ballou and Gleason's stories 'only exist[ed] because there [was] a definite demand for them', and can therefore be understood as a 'guide to popular taste', which was, moreover, 'probably the best indication of what the … people really [felt] and [thought]' (Orwell 62). At the same time, *Fanny Campbell* stands out from its class for the incomparable hold of its protagonist on the popular imagination – both in the nineteenth century, as the work's extraordinarily long print life testifies, and in the present, when her name is invoked by scholars as frequently as it appears in juvenile literature. However, those who evoke Fanny Campbell have rarely read her tale (which is indeed relatively hard to come by) and some have even mistaken her for an historical figure.[6] Here, I shall situate *Fanny Campbell* in the tradition of woman warrior narratives, while elucidating the specific intersection of the intrepid heroine, the pirate novel and the national historical tale.

Empty History and Expansionist Ideology

While Fanny Campbell is the only female pirate heroine of an historical novel to have come to my attention, a vast number of nineteenth-century historical narratives starred male pirates. Focusing on Spanish-American texts, Nina Gerassi-Navarro, for example, has shown that the ways in which a number of authors portrayed pirates to invoke history depended on the concept of national identity they wished

---

[6]   David S. Reynolds and Julie Wheelwright both take up *Fanny Campbell*, the former (in *Beneath the American Renaissance: The Subversive Imagination in the Age of Emerson and Melville* (New York: Alfred A. Knopf, 1988)) to place her story in a class of subversive and lurid popular fiction (an inaccurate description), and the latter (in *Amazons and Military Maids*, see note 4) to discuss the heroine's influence on nineteenth-century women readers who took inspiration in Fanny's example (but using only the book's cover image and secondary sources). Others have encountered Fanny's story but not its fictional source. Fanny swashbuckled her way into F.O. Steele's recent nonfiction book, *Pirates: A Brief Anthology of Thirteen Notorious Female Pirates* (Bloomington, IN: iUniverse, 2007). Maritime historian Linda Grant De Pauw's account of an historical Fanny, in her study *Seafaring Women* (1982), is probably the most oft-cited source of confusion. The misunderstanding predates De Pauw's work, though. In a footnote to a recent essay, for example, Lizabeth Paravasini-Gebert quotes from Edward Rowe Snow's account of Fanny's real exploits in his 1953 *True Tales of Pirates and their Gold* (New York: Dodd Mead, 1957). Fanny also has her own entry in a 1968 *Biography Index*.

to deploy. Observing that Benedict Anderson's model of 'imagined communities' does not account for nations which had taken shape along lines previously drawn by the Spanish crown rather than as a result of locally inflected nationalisms united through a vernacular print culture, Gerassi-Navarro highlights the struggle writers faced when 'set[ting] out to create national legends and myths' in which they could formulate 'a unified vision of their past' (3–4). Thus, unlike Walter Scott, whose focus on universal conflicts 'Lukàcs so emphatically praised' (Gerassi-Navarro 119), Spanish-American authors attempted through historical narrative to define themselves; the ambivalent pirate figure – alternately representing freedom, desperation or rapaciousness – embodied their difficulties in coming to terms with their own pasts.

Ballou, too, was concerned with the local. While I would hardly go so far as the critic who, in 1933, overzealously credited Ballou with the establishment of an autochthonous American popular literary tradition – a 'vast step in art and culture in the United States' for which he deserved 'a monument, next to [Walt] Whitman' (Admari 127) – both his fiction and his publishing ventures demonstrate an interest in writing and selling what he understood as the story of the American experience. Ballou is best understood as both an innovator and an imitator, however, for he owes a significant debt to Scott. By the time Ballou was writing, Scott had inspired followers throughout Europe and the Americas – including those whom Gerassi-Navarro discusses, Alessandro Manzoni in Italy and James Fenimore Cooper in the US. Interestingly, it was to Scott, and not to Cooper's native example, that Ballou turned for the inspiration for his first novel, *Fanny Campbell*.

Fanny Campbell's opening scene so closely resembles that of Scott's *The Pirate* (1822) that one wonders whether Ballou consciously pastiched it. In both texts, historical time is introduced by a narrator, who looks down from the vantage point of a coastal cliff, surveying the place where the story's events unfolded many years before. In Scott, the changes time has wrought are manifest: 'the vestiges only' of one character's house 'can be discerned with difficulty' (Scott *Pirate* 14). The narrative, as though growing out of this observation, will mitigate this sense of loss by infusing imaginative life back into the ruins. As Scott so eloquently explains in the final chapter of *Waverley*, he wrote historical novels precisely because things change: but by 'preserving some idea of the ancient manners of which [he] ha[d] witnessed the almost total extinction' (Scott *Waverley* 340), narrative could help readers understand and accommodate social change. Ballou, by contrast, subverts this familiar narrative sense of history, insisting instead on the degree to which things remain the same. Rather than offering a means of accounting for change, the historical mode in *Fanny Campbell* remains strangely hollow, invoking the form but not the substance of history:

> There lived at the very base of High Rock about seventy years ago, a few families of the real Puritanical stock, forming a little community of themselves. … The neighborhood, resembled in every particular, save that it was far less

> extensive, the present town of Swampscot, ... and whose inhabitants, a hardy
> and industrious people, are absolutely to this day 'fishermen all.' (*FC* 10)

Ballou seems to want it both ways, first evoking the 'little community' as
though it has disappeared like Scott's, when, instead, it has but grown a little, and
thus remained like itself 'in every particular' (*FC* 10). Admitting to no change
in kind, and only a slight change in degree, between colonial times and the mid-
century, national present, *Fanny Campbell* is an historical novel that paradoxically
denies history.

The changelessness visible to the narrator in the opening scene of Ballou's
novel is replicated at the level of the plot, which, despite its sensational elements,
is driven by Fanny's desire to restore her fiancé to his anticipated role in their
common future. Love and ambition first spur the male lead, William Lovell, to
sail for the West Indies, in search of the 'pecuniary competency' (*FC* 11) that
will allow him to marry, only he does not return as he had intended. After two
years, Fanny finally gets word that William has been jailed in Havana: his ship was
attacked by pirates and he was forced to join their crew; then, staggering ashore in
Havana after attempting to escape off Cuba, he was immediately incarcerated by
the Spanish authorities there. At this news, Fanny decides to rescue him. Disguising
herself as a male officer, she ships as second mate on a British merchant vessel
bound for the Caribbean, intending to stir up a mutiny and hijack the vessel to
Havana. She succeeds, rescuing her fiancé from one imperial oppressor, while
helping the United Colonies, now at war, in their struggle with another. Returning
to Boston in command of not one but three British ships, she learns that in her
absence Boston has fallen to the Colonists. Her potentially criminal conduct at sea
thus fortuitously coincides with rebellion on land.

Seen as patriotic rather than piratical, Fanny – or rather the mysterious male
captain she impersonates – is credited with having initiated, albeit unwittingly,
maritime hostilities against the British, and with founding, albeit with stolen ships,
the new nation's navy. Fanny's cross-dressed, mutinous jailbreak mission and the
two naval victories she scores en route are thus portrayed as incidental effects
of her romantic motives, such that the literally revolutionary elements of the
plot find themselves subsumed by the novel's ultimately conservative, domestic
agenda.[7] Although the narrative begins with a colony and ends with a nation,
the text's emphasis on stasis downplays the transition from independence to the

---

[7]   Pursuing love or lost love is a motive frequently offered in accounts of women
sailors and soldiers. *The Female Soldier* claims that Hannah Snell joined the army in order
to track down a lover who had abandoned her. Anne Bonny allegedly cross-dressed and ran
from her father's house in Charleston, South Carolina, in order to follow her sailor lover
and avoid marrying the man to whom her father had betrothed her. Scholars interested in
gender and sexuality are quick to point at out that the love motive normalizes an otherwise
aberrant choice and may not be historically accurate. Some working-class women chose
the hard life of disguise and military service because they found themselves unable (or

republican narrative present. As a result, the novel celebrates the earliest moments of American national consciousness to the rapidly growing pulp readership of an imperial power, as though that readership still comprised a pre-national or barely post-colonial society.[8] In the three decades when *Fanny Campbell* was widely available, the United States more than doubled in size by acquiring land, through wars and purchase, from France, Britain, Spain and Mexico. It at first seems unlikely that the historical fantasy propagated by the novel could maintain its wide appeal throughout a period of such radical change. However, the text's empty historical discourse reflects expansionist ideology, which similarly admitted to changes in degree but not in kind.

Like Ballou's portrayal of Swampscot, the discourse of national growth held that the country was merely getting a little bigger, eliding the conflicts and negotiations that were resulting in continual redrawings of the map. Expansionists claimed that it was in fact the 'manifest destiny' of the United States to grow as it would, unhampered by the competing territorial claims and economic interests of European nations. Growth was perceived as an organic process, occurring not only of itself and without encouragement, but even in spite of others' attempts to stop or even shape it. The concept of manifest destiny, then, did not so much utterly deny change as fail to understand it in a causal framework.

The phrase 'manifest destiny', which became common shorthand for the rhetoric of expansion, first appeared in a newspaper editorial in July 1845, as Texas was being admitted to the Union. Although politicians had rejected just a year earlier the idea of including Texas, the moment suddenly seemed ripe for growth, as the editorialist explains:

> Why, were other reasons wanting, in favor of now elevating this question of the reception of Texas into the Union, out of the lower region of our past party dissensions, up to its proper level of a high and broad nationality, it surely is to be found, found abundantly, in the manner in which other nations have undertaken to intrude themselves into it, between us and the proper parties to the case, in a spirit of hostile interference against us, for the avowed object of thwarting our policy and hampering our power, limiting our greatness and checking the fulfillment of our manifest destiny to overspread the continent allotted by providence for the free development of our yearly multiplying millions. (qtd. in Weinberg 112)[9]

---

unwilling) to earn a living otherwise. And women of all classes appear to have chosen to live as men in order to live with the *women* they loved.

   [8]   I use the term 'post-colonial' to describe the United States in the late eighteenth century, following Stuart Hall's proposal in 'When Was the 'Post-Colonial'?: Thinking at the Limit'. *The Post-Colonial Question: Common Skies, Divided Horizons*. Eds Iain Chambers and Lidia Curti (New York and London: Routledge, 1996): 242–60.

   [9]   Weinberg quotes this editorial, originally titled 'Annexation', from the *United States Magazine and Democratic Review* (see 500 n53). Williams et al. quote the same text,

Quickly losing sight of the Texas question to make vast, grandiose statements regarding the nation's limitless rights, the writer anticipates the rate of expansion in the breathless pace of his prose. As in the single sentence quoted here – whose final stop can be long staved off by the ad hoc addition of clause after clause – the potential for growth seems infinite.

Expansion appears not only limitless, occurring regardless of others' attempts to 'thwart', 'hamper', 'limit' or 'check' it, but at once ineluctable and natural. The editorialist goes on to predict that a growing population of Americans in then-Mexican California would, like Texas, 'necessarily become independent' and later incorporated into the United States:

> without agency of our government, without responsibility of our people – in the
> natural flow of events, the spontaneous working of principles, and the adaptation
> of the tendencies and wants of the human race to the elemental circumstances in
> the midst of which they find themselves placed. (qtd. in Williams et al. 526)

The terms 'spontaneous', 'adaptation' and 'elemental' evoke a natural process, one unsurprisingly paired with denials of 'agency' and 'responsibility' – as though it were absurd to think that the country could control its own growth any more than a person might. Thus, the editorialist's contradictory portrayal of vast growth without vast change recalls Ballou's reworking of Scott to refuse, rather than account for, both the transformative power of history and, further, man's role in effecting historical change. In *Fanny Campbell*, the telescoping of present into past compounds manifest destiny's denial of responsibility regarding change, as the dual significance of the novel's Caribbean setting reveals.

It is in the Caribbean that Fanny (as Captain Channing) first gains control of the British brig aboard which she left Massachusetts. As she raises the flag of the United Colonies on her newly acquired mast, the narrator hails the country's first maritime victory, suggesting that replacing a British flag with that of the rebels signifies the Colonies' assertion of nationhood against Britain. Locating this victory far from North American shores, however, suggests an additional, extra-national significance, such as the mid-nineteenth-century commercial rivalry between the United States and Britain in that region:

> This was the earliest if not the very first capture upon the high seas so far from
> our own country by the humble but victorious flag of the Colonies. ... The pine
> tree flag had never before floated in the seas of the West Indies and Captain
> Channing's hand was the first to give it to the breeze and fight under its folds in
> these seas of perpetual summer (36).

---

excerpting for a slightly different emphasis, from the New York *Morning News* (526). The unsigned piece was the handiwork of journalist and *Review* editor John L. O'Sullivan. See Robert Sampson, *John L. O'Sullivan and His Times* (Kent, OH: Kent State UP, 2003).

Indeed, a fledgling nation would have no reason to claim military victories 'so far from [its] own country'; despite insistence on the flag's 'humble' significance, this phrase belies the statement of imperial strength here couched in nationalist terms.

In the 1840s–1870s, in addition to vying with Britain for access to Caribbean markets, the US was responding to British pressure in the Northeast and Northwest by negotiating trade agreements and by formalizing lines on maps in Maine and Oregon. Thus, as Reginald C. Stuart has shown, enthusiasm for a self-evident model of expansion was contradicted by the reality of ongoing competition with Britain.[10] The novel's unsympathetic portrayal of the mother country encourages an American readership to imagine the David-and-Goliath scenario of Revolutionary times, as though Britain's looming new-world presence threatened the nation's very viability. Rather than portraying the US as a young empire jockeying for a position in hemispheric affairs, the novel echoes manifest destiny rhetoric by portraying Britain's stake there as stymieing the US's 'natural' growth.

The Caribbean setting allows Ballou to stage his national tale on an international stage, involving not only Britain but also Spain. The fact that Fanny rescues William from a specifically Cuban jail probably alludes to contemporary American interest in the island. Around the mid-century, some US politicians were advocating 'annexing' Cuba as a slave state in order to add weight to their side of the sectional cause (Stuart 81–95) – a scenario that would result in Cuba becoming a US possession rather than a Spanish one.[11] *Fanny Campbell* covers over the obvious connection between Spain and the US (both empires with eyes on Cuba) by somewhat dishonestly suggesting that the United Colonies provide a model for Cuba, which might, like the US, soon overthrow the colonial government to achieve independence. Mention of Britain's brief control of Cuba, which occurred in 1760 and lasted less than a year, disproportionately emphasizes its short, shared history with the Colonies. Portraying Cuba as 'in the hands of the Spaniards now, from whom the British took it awhile ago, but have given it back again' (*FC* 22)

---

[10]   See Stuart's Chapter 4, 'Manifest Destiny and Provincial Boundaries'.

[11]   Intense American interest in Cuban affairs must have been a key factor in Ballou's decision to travel there shortly before writing *Fanny Campbell*. From notes made in the early 1840s, he compiled and published in 1854 his first of two books on the island. The dramatic opening of *History of Cuba; or, Notes of Traveller in the Tropics. Being a Political, Historical, and Statistical Account of the Island, from its First Discovery to the Present Time* (Boston: Phillips, Sampson and Company; J.C. Derby; and Lippincott, Grambo & Company, 1854) draws a more implicit parallel than the novel between the US and Cuba:

The remarkable degree of interest expressed on all sides, at the present time, relative to the island of Cuba, has led the author of the following pages to place together in this form a series of notes from his journal … . So critically is the island now situated, in a political point of view, that ere this book shall have passed through an edition, it may be no longer a dependency of Spain, or may have become the theatre of scenes to which its former convulsions shall bear no parallel. (5)

further contrasts the 'natural' nationhood of the US (and perhaps, someday, Cuba) with the arbitrary, unjust governance of these interchangeable imperial powers.

The parallels drawn in *Fanny Campbell* between Cuba and the United States indeed reflect a political discourse that was current through the 1830s but was fast becoming obsolete when the novel was published. While Cuba would not achieve independence until 1898, several mainland Spanish American republics did so in the 1820s and 1830s. President James Monroe (1817–25), understanding the independence movements to the South as inspired by the example of the US as Ballou would later suggest regarding Cuba, spoke in support of them in an 1823 speech to Congress. Monroe gestured towards defending new free states from future meddling on the part of old-world imperial entities, significantly *without* tacking on a programme for US expansion: '[t]he American continents, by the free and independent condition which they have assumed and maintain, are henceforth not to be considered as subjects for future colonization by any European powers' (qtd. in Williams et al. 333). By contrast, the administration of President James Polk (1844–49), was motivated to find a juridical precedent for expansionism, and reinterpreted Monroe's speech, reading the refusal to tolerate European interference in American interests as favouring the United States' own territorial and commercial expansion in the Americas. A speech which had conceived of the US and Spanish American republics as like-minded new-world democracies, together founded on anti-imperialist principles, was thus pressed into service as a justification for the US to assume what the Polk administration saw as its true status in the hemisphere. The Monroe Doctrine, as it has since become known, therefore became a foundational text of manifest destiny.[12] *Fanny Campbell* conflates both meanings of this political theory, as Fanny rescues William from an unjust Spanish colonial administration while, at the same time, theatrically chalking up American military victories far from the US. The novel's unusual heroine – not only a pirate, but a captain and a female – chimerically encapsulates this contradictory rhetoric.

---

[12]   The bombastic rhetoric of some precluded any limit to how far the mysterious forces of manifest destiny could enlarge the nation. In *The Foundations of the American Empire: William Henry Seward and U.S. Foreign Policy* (Ithaca, NY: Cornell UP, 1973), Ernest N. Paolino conveys an extreme example of such an attitude by quoting from speeches made by American statesman William H. Seward, an influential policymaker who held public office from the 1830s to the 1870s. Seward claimed he could see prospects for expansion in almost every direction:

> [s]peaking at St. Paul, Minnesota, in 1860, he addressed a friendly word of encouragement to the Canadians, and advised them that it was 'very well you are building states to be hereafter admitted into the American union.' He called attention to the Russians in the Pacific Northwest and assured his listeners that those settlements 'will yet become outposts of the United States.' Looking southward, Seward hazarded the opinion that the capital of the United States would, in the not too far distant future, be situated somewhere in Mexico. (8).

What figure could more aptly embody the strangely agent-less qualities of expansionist ideology than a Revolutionary-era female pirate? Although Fanny comes across as a national heroine, her exploits merely coincide with the national interest; after all, pirates, by definition, operate independently of a government's agency. Moreover, as a *female* pirate, Fanny represents a threatened victim merely seeking to defend, or fulfil, her natural, inherent rights. Cross-dressed as Captain Channing, Fanny symbolizes a vulnerable yet victorious soft conqueror, at once colonized victim and (absent) imperial perpetrator.

The Female Pirate as an Allegory for Expansion

As Marcus Rediker has shown, piracy was a briefly practised profession, attracting sailors, for a few years at most, from the military in times of peace, and from the merchant marine in protest against overly harsh conditions. Privateers, officially designated by government-issued licences, might provisionally turn pirate when their vessel's official status had expired.[13] Because pirates *become* pirates through shifting political and economic contingencies, an accusation of piracy depends first on one's perspective; the criminality of piratical acts is relative. For Fanny, acting during the transition of legal authority from one government to another, the question of perspective bears a double importance. Fanny's deeds may have constituted piracy in the Boston she left, in which 'St. George's flag floated from the topmasts of a dozen men of war, which lay at anchor in the harbor, and floated from a number of lofty points in the town' (*FC* 27), but not in the Boston to which she returns, where she sees the same previously unknown flag she had raised on her own stolen mast: 'the King's fleet had sailed, and the American flag floated from the town' (*FC* 77). The text sensationally raises the possibility that Fanny's actions might be criminal, only to dismiss the question of her guilt:

> Some fears were entertained by Fanny and her family, touching upon the captures she had made, inasmuch as strictly speaking she had laid herself liable to the charge of piracy! and Fanny, in the eyes of the law, was actually a *Female*

---

   [13]   See Chapter 3 of Rediker's *Villians of all Nations: Atlantic Pirates in the Golden Age* (Boston: Beacon Press, 2004). Most pirate histories address at some point the question of why one would become a pirate. See also David Cordingly, *Under the Black Flag*; Hans Turley, *Rum, Sodomy, and the Lash: Piracy, Sexuality, and Masculine Identity* (New York: New York UP, 1999); Capt. Charles Johnson [Daniel Defoe?], *A General History of the Robberies and Murders of the Most Notorious Pyrates*. 1724. Ed. Manuel Schonhorn (Columbia: U of South Carolina P, 1972); Michel Le Bris, *D'Or, de rêves et de sang: l'épopée de la flibuste, 1494–1588* (Paris: Hachette, 2001); Ulrike Klausman et al., *Women Pirates and the Politics of the Jolly Roger*. Trans. Tyler Austin (China Sea) and Nicholas Levis (New York: Black Rose Books, 1997).

Pirate Captain! But there were none to prosecute such a charge, and if there had been, Captain Channing could no where be found. (*FC* 79)

The double absence evoked here – of a prosecuting juridical entity and of a responsible party who could be charged – associates Channing with the US government, while denying the potential for agency in both.

Interestingly, though, if a flesh-and-blood Fanny had in fact captured British ships at the moment the fictional Fanny does, she would have been acting during the transition of judicial power – after the British had retreated from Boston and before the still-unrecognized government of the United Colonies had passed laws regarding privateering on its behalf. Not until 25 November 1775 did the Continental Congress pass a resolution acknowledging that some colonists had already begun 'fitting out armed vessels and ships of force' while henceforth forbidding them to do so without letters of marque: 'That no master or commander of any vessel shall be intitled to cruize for, or make prize of any vessel or cargo before he shall have obtained a commission from the Congress, or from such person or persons as shall be for that purpose appointed in some one of the United Colonies' ('Journal' 1132). In other words, the new government had not yet outlawed the unauthorized raiding of British ships; as a result, the story's most outrageous crimes are exonerated by their coincidence with the moment when legal authority was in limbo. As one whose conduct could be considered criminal only under laws that no longer apply or which do not yet apply, the pirate captain can be simultaneously hailed as a national hero and distanced from the nation as a juridical entity. The actions of a cross-dressed pirate captain whom readers know to be female, moreover, seem that much less likely to serve a primarily political objective.

The provisional aspect of piratical status is especially true for Captain Channing, who exists only so long as Fanny masquerades to assume that role. As Dianne Dugaw has shown, cross-dressing is a distinctive feature of all narratives of female sailors and soldiers: '[n]ot only does the woman's adventure depend entirely upon [cross-dressing], but the masquerade functions throughout the narrative as a transforming element – the pivotal signifier' (Dugaw 9). In *Fanny Campbell*, masquerade introduces an element of play which ensures that Channing, as sword-bearer for the national cause, may continue winning facile combats against imperial straw-men while symbolically refusing the nation's own increasingly imperial aspirations. Readers' knowledge of the woman's body inside the costume lends Channing an allegorical quality, detracting from the literal significance of Fanny's actions by amplifying their symbolic value. In general, as Louise Jarvis observes in her review of Druett's *She Captains: Heroines and Hellions of the Sea*, our investment in women's 'underdog' status prevents us from reading women's violence literally:

[although] there is no reason to empathize with Bonnie more than Clyde ..., Druett's hellions are redemptive heroines because they are outsiders not only among women but among miscreant men. As a result, their actions, their very grisliness, read like insurrections against a repressive society, and not simply as crimes. They are underdogs, even when wielding the bigger sword. (15)

Battle after battle, readers continue to perceive Fanny as an underdog by remaining aware that Channing's fierce piratical endeavours are enabled by sartorial trappings, underneath which lies only an intrepid but ultimately vulnerable girl and her suitably limited romantic ambition. Cross-dressing combines with the novel's telescoped sense of time to convey Fanny's 'bigger sword' as merely part of the costume – hardly a tool of expansion, it seems really no more than a glittering stage prop.

Unlike the iconic Bonnie Parker, however, Fanny significantly fights not alongside but *instead of* a male counterpart. William's inactivity corresponds to the imagined passivity of the American people regarding their nation's building an empire, while Fanny, in the role of Channing, seems to channel the guiltless forces of manifest destiny. It is Fanny who orchestrates William's passage from boyhood to manhood; only through her actions does he eventually achieve the material security he initially sought. On his first venture, without her aid, William failed utterly. Captured and forced to labour in a pirate crew, he spent nearly 18 months in miserable servitude before managing to escape, and did so only to be taken captive by someone else. Another six months elapsed before he stood trial in Havana; lacking the language skills to defend himself adequately, he landed summarily back in his cell. Imprisoned first by one group and then another, this son of the nation seems ill-suited for commercial or political acquisitions of any kind. The regretful exclamation William utters at hearing of all Fanny's adventures en route to rescue him – 'And all this time I have been lying idle and inactive in a Spanish prison!' (47) – seems to express both the wish that he could have protected her from such dangers and a claim of innocence regarding the crimes she has committed as Channing. William's comment emphasizes that things happen in the novel not because of his efforts, but in spite of his inertia. He embodies the effortlessly occurring national plan, while Fanny, wielding Channing's sword, serves as its symbolic handmaiden.

William's passive transition into manhood encapsulates the advent of nationhood as portrayed in the mid-century expansionist climate to the extent that a metaphor of human growth can describe both processes: '[t]he bond was severed; the child sprang at once to the estate of manhood and to all its responsibilities and cares; but it was under the divine guardianship of the spirit of peace and the especial guidance of Freedom herself; with such patrons [he] was sure to prosper' (*FC* 81). As was the case with the novel's falsely historical discourse, discussed above, *Fanny Campbell* does not deny change so much as deny responsibility for change; William's arrival at maturity, and that of the nation, can be admitted if the 'responsibilities' and 'cares' arising from that change remain in the hands of vaguely named forces. Responsibility is consistently denied or transferred elsewhere, a factor that contributes to the resemblance between the pseudo-historical space of *Fanny Campbell* and Barrie's Neverland. What Marjorie Garber has argued regarding *Peter Pan* – that the role of Peter is always played by a woman precisely because a woman 'will never grow up to be a man' and thus never compromise Neverland's premise of eternal boyhood (168) – holds true for Channing, too. While William does enter manhood, he does so only with Channing's assistance; as for Channing, the fact that he is played by a woman leads mid-nineteenth-century readers to imagine the United States as perpetually post-colonial, not on its way to achieving maturity as a nation.

I have suggested that the allegorical quality of Channing's actions derives from readers' knowledge of the female body within the costume, while also claiming that the masquerade in effect does away with Fanny's material, sexed body, allowing her to represent abstract concepts such as 'the spirit of peace' and 'Freedom' (*FC* 81). The answer to this apparent contradiction lies in the third of the title's operative words, '*Captain*'. It is important to keep in mind that a triple masquerade, involving not only cross-dressing but also performing a high maritime rank and claiming a yet-unrecognized national affiliation, comprises the significance of the Channing figure. After all, 'to transvest' means simply 'to disguise' (*OED*) and Fanny manipulates flags and clothing to masquerade in all three of these regards. While Fanny's cross-dressing places her in a large historical and narrative cohort of similar heroines, the assumed rank of Captain sets her apart within this tradition. Narratives of women living as men typically draw a substantial portion of their dramatic tension from the threat of being discovered – or rather uncovered – but rank obviates such threats for Fanny.

In most narratives of women sailors and soldiers, including those of historic cross-dressers Mary Read and Hannah Snell, economic desperation informs the initial decision to live as a man. Under those conditions, as part of the ill-fed and ill-paid lowest ranks (whether on land or at sea), their lives are characterized by promiscuously shared spaces, making the success of their disguises all the more incredible. These narratives notch up the tension by manipulating this potential for revelatory discovery. Sooner or later, the typical cross-dressed heroine will either be forced to reveal her sexed body (if wounded, for instance) or choose to do so intentionally, often by baring her breasts – fiercely, to a scorned adversary, or coyly, to a desired lover. As Lizabeth Paravasini-Gebert has shown regarding accounts of Mary Read, for example, the 'unveiling of her breasts ... was always in the guise of a "confession" that would eventually lead to marriage and the possibility of assuming her true identity' (8). More importantly, such unveilings affect key epistemological shifts by selectively divulging readers' knowledge of the disguise to characters. These instances constitute 'confessions' because they air the character's (and readers') secret within the diegetic space, heightening the drama by making the sexed body a potential source of plot conflicts.

In the narrative space of Fanny's commandeered *Dolphin*, rank protects Fanny by conditioning her relationship to the crew in visual and spatial terms. As second mate and later captain, Channing is exempt from the close quarters and collective labour shared by the crew. The crew has little reason or occasion to stare at their captain and, appropriately, the narration includes few visual images of him. When they do look at Channing, the signs that indicate rank, instantly read by any sailor, detract attention from possibly revelatory but more nuanced signs of sexual difference. In a rare descriptive glance, for example, the narration remains focused on the quality and neatness of the sailor's dress and arms, all signs of rank:

> He soon made his appearance from the cabin, dressed in white pants and a becoming frock coat. About his waist was tied a heavy silk sash, into which was thrust a pair of boarding pistols, and at his side hung a light but serviceable cutlass. He wore a graceful velvet cap upon his head and looked the honest manly sailor that he was. (*FC* 43)

The type of clothing, and the arrangement of clothes and weapons, constitute an impression of manliness without reference to any quality of the body within the clothes, such as stature or even stance. If the crew seldom *sees* its Captain, however, they often *hear* him, as their job is to follow verbal orders; thus few visual references to Channing are compensated by frequent allusions to the quality of his voice.

The crew's acknowledgement of Channing's authority derives more from the pleasing sound of his voice and the perceived fairness of his orders than from his appearance: 'for although his orders were given in a prompt and decided tone, and implicit obedience was exacted, yet was his voice musical and kind, and his orders were almost anticipated by the promptitude of the willing crew, who soon came to love him for the generous consideration he evinced for their good and that of the vessel' (*FC* 27). Repeated references to Channing's 'low, musical' voice (28, 41, 42, 56) are concentrated during battle scenes, when the sailors, busily operating cannon, would reasonably be least likely to look at their commander. The diversion of descriptive attention from Fanny's physique to Channing's voice has a dematerializing effect; heightening the sense of 'agent-lessness' in her victories on behalf of the rebelling Colonies, it contributes to her allegorical significance in the expansionist mid-century. *Fanny Campbell* does invoke the potential display of the female body, however, once William has been rescued and recognizes his liberator as his fiancée. His presence aboard ship allows for a hybrid narrative perspective, which accounts for both his awareness of Fanny's sexed body and the crew's lack of suspicion.

As Fanny sets course for home, having accomplished her purpose, the narrative contrasts William's visual register with the crew's understanding, still portrayed in terms of the captain's voice. Narration focalized through William makes him seem cognizant of that distinction, as he reassures himself of Fanny's safety by listening to her speech – that is, by perceiving her as the crew does: 'now that he knew the secret of her disguise he feared that it might be disclosed at any moment. But there was nothing wanting; she was perfect even in all the minutiae of sea parlance' (49). William's double awareness is most clear when all aboard witness Fanny's determining whether to execute a British mutineer:

> It was a scene of strange and peculiar interest. There stood that huge Hercules of a man before that gentle hearted girl to be adjudged to death. Her deep soul

seemed to be reading the prisoner's inmost thoughts through the blue of her beautiful eye. Her voice did not tremble, her hand was firm, and she was a man at heart. The woman feeling which was so lately called into action in her breast, was banished, and nothing save stern justice might be expected to come out those lips which displayed at that moment a decision of purpose and character which Lovell had never remarked there before. (56)

The decisive expression on Fanny's 'lips' is 'displayed' to William alone; the others perceive 'stern justice', in the steadiness of her voice. Highlighting Fanny's inferior physical strength evokes the nation as colonized victim, while the authority the clement 'girl' wields, arising from right and not might, reinforces her status as soft conqueror. Ultimately, her body, although referenced by William's gazing on her 'lips', reveals itself only as the source of an abstract concept, justice. When one fond sailor wonders aloud whether the Captain is 'a saint and no man at all', the salient question shifts from one of gender (whether Channing is really a man or a woman in disguise) to whether the Captain, so like a sword-wielding angel, is even human. As much as gender, rank proves a key aspect of Fanny's masquerade that defines her in terms of manifest destiny rhetoric.

Once Fanny is safely home, she again turns her attention to her engagement with William, which inspired the whole adventure. Their marriage marks Fanny's entrance into domestic life. Her career as Channing behind her, Fanny's allegorical significance accordingly diminishes; within the more closely delimited domestic sphere, she rematerializes as a wife and mother. The fact that Fanny and William return home, marry and establish a household together reinforces the novel's refusal of an American imperial consciousness by reiterating the text's denial of change.

Itinerant Domesticity: Boats and Books

In the several genres whose codes are present in *Fanny Campbell* – not only historical romance but also sentimental fiction and travel narrative – marriages commonly signify the resolution of the plot's tensions. In historical fiction, marriage can function as a social strategy for accommodating change, as in Edward Waverley's marriage to Rose Bradwardine, to take another example from Scott. In travel narratives, as Katie Trumpener and Mary Louise Pratt have demonstrated, marriages can indicate compromise with, or submission to, an imperial power. Trumpener offers examples of Unionist travel tales in which an English traveller in Scotland or Ireland ends up marrying his or her native guide. Pratt discusses marriage as an arrangement that codifies in sentimental terms colonial subjugation to an imperial power, and then conveniently dissolves when European explorers return home. Fanny Campbell's union with William Lovell, by contrast, signifies neither compromise nor submission, nor even revolution, but rather conservation. William, like Fanny, is of the 'few families of the real Puritanical stock, forming a little community of themselves' in Swampscot, a man not only from her own neighbourhood, but from her own house. The Lovells and Campbells occupy together 'one spacious and comfortable cottage', the two fathers 'sailed a staunch fishing craft together' and 'it was the honest hope and promise of the parents that the children when arrived at a proper age should be married to each other' (11). Once husband and wife rather than merely neighbours, Fanny and William will continue to share a house and a boat, so that their union only perpetuates their families' arrangement. Lastly, the wedding's placement in the text, occurring closer to the middle than the end, emphasizes its dissociation from the novel's dénouement. Instead of resolving conflict and difference, Fanny and William's marriage elides them.

The absent conflict is that of mid-century expansion, which the couple's union denies through its being predicated on the idea of return – to their original plan, to their native village, to their parents' house. Fanny and William's adventures did lead them to challenge two other imperial powers but, since they did so only to secure a domestic future for themselves, their adventures do not appear connected to any American imperial design. As an emblem of this homecoming, their household – quite the opposite of the outwardly turned focus of expansion – functions as a microcosm for the nation still understood at mid-century in post-colonial terms. The couple's return to sea, however, soon complicates this picture.

After lucrative privateering throughout the remainder of the war, the scene of Fanny and William's 'domestic enjoyments' (81) shifts from Swampscot to a yacht, on which they live for long stretches. Although Fanny and William's national feeling at first seems derived from their attachment to a particular location, domestic space in the novel is conceived as more ideological than geographical. The ocean comes to symbolize not a means of transportation, but an (American) domestic space, where the couple feel *as if* at home, at once '[tasting] the excitement of a life at sea' and '[dwelling] upon its breast *as a home*' (18, emphasis added). It is also at sea, 'far out of sight of land' (93), that Fanny has the family-founding experience of childbirth. If travel narratives usually posit a 'there' and a 'here', allowing the manners and customs of a foreign place to be described through comparison to the familiar ones of home, Fanny and William sail in and out of the United States, yet feel everywhere at home; as a result, every place can be imagined *as*, rather than in contrast to, the nation. By unmooring national space from geographical place, Fanny and William's itinerant household evokes the possibility that any place could be that of American national feeling. This is not simply an image of nation shrunken to a single household, but an image of a household inscribing its national – 'domestic' – feeling all over the world.

Admittedly, to some degree maritime domesticity within the novel simply reflects the contemporary practice by which captains' wives and children would sometimes accompany them on long voyages, allowing families to live together aboard ship.[14] While these journeys did not result in territorial acquisition, they did carry out cultural work by combining a specifically American domesticity with lives that carried Americans far outside the national borders. By land, of course, journeys did result in space being claimed for the nation, as covered wagon trains transferred whole communities to lands either only recently, or not even quite yet, part of the country. Further, as the newspaper editorial quoted above obliquely acknowledges, official United States territorial acquisition during the 1830s and 1840s had actually followed Americans having settled in the acquired areas for reasons independent of the American government, such that communities of Americans purposely living outside the United States had already seen the national boundaries swell to include them.[15] The potential ideological impact of Fanny and William's displacements becomes clearer when placed in a broader historical context of people, ideas and boundaries on the move. Metaphorically, national feeling outside the nation would seem manifestly destined to bring the national boundaries to encompass the feeling. Surely, then, Fanny and William's wandering domestic space, mapping American feeling in places not (yet) American, constitutes something of an imperial gesture.

Fanny Campbell's occluded imperialism seems all the more sinister for its exclusive focus on geographical acquisitiveness, as though the places to be acquired were empty. Like the newspaper editorial quoted above, the novel does not imagine peoples in these places, nor does it strategize as to how to accommodate or acculturate them. As much as the country might grow, Fanny and William seem almost to be the only people in it – or even beyond it, for that matter. With the exception of a few (drunk or lascivious) British sailors and a few (sleeping) Spanish prison guards, the Lovells travel, in war and in peace, from Boston all over the Caribbean, to North Africa and Europe, meeting no one. The

---

[14]   Maritime historian Joan Druett gathers from the 'nearly eighty female whaling journals that survive in various archives' that 'hundreds of wives ... accompanied their husbands to sea' ('Introduction'. *'She Was A Sister Sailor': The Whaling Journals of Mary Brewster, 1845–1851*. Ed. Joan Druett (Mystic, CT: Mystic Seaport Museum, 1992): p. viii.). See also Druett's *Hen Frigates: Wives of Merchant Captains Under Sail*, which draws on archives pertaining to sea-dwelling families from New England, Australia, Hong Kong and elsewhere, as well as Herndon, and Creighton and Norling.

[15]   Such was the case of Americans drawn to settle in Mexican Texas by land grants from the Mexican government, or of American Mormons who had purposely expatriated themselves to the (Mexican) Utah wilderness to avoid further persecution. Americans had been attracted to settle in Texas by land grants from the newly independent Mexican government in the 1820s. Soon this incentive created an area within Mexico but mainly populated by Americans, who fought for independence from Mexico, declaring themselves a Republic and immediately requesting annexation by the United States in 1836. But internal differences over whether to admit Texas as a slave state postponed its actual absorption into the Union for nine years, until 1845. Similarly, Mormons settled in Mexican Utah in the 1830s, only to see the United States gain control of the territory in 1848, following the Mexican–American War.

novel's settings – port cities and maritime trade routes – might evoke what Pratt has called 'contact zones', spaces in which 'transculturation' takes place through a complex set of interactions among indigenous peoples, Creoles and imperial and colonial subjects who mutually influence one another. However, in contrast to the cosmopolitan crew Ishmael calls messmates in *Moby Dick*, for example, in Ballou's novel these spaces have been purged of their historic, ethnic and cultural complexity. No mention is made of Africans or African-Americans, erasing the historic presence of sailors of African descent as documented by Linebaugh and Rediker. Native Americans, further, are relegated to a pre-national past, as when one sailor situates a yarn of a wronged Indian maiden in the past tense of his own boyhood. By the Revolutionary present of his story-telling, only a spectral trace remains of the maiden and her people: 'on any clear moonlit night the form of the Indian girl is seen at midnight upon that lofty rock' (*FC* 67). In this light, Fanny and William's floating home becomes a rather uncomfortable microcosm; as they travel, there is as little sense of visiting something as there is of having visitors in their mobile domestic sphere.

In describing Fanny and William's attitudes towards their seagoing home as 'itinerant domesticity', I am adapting Janet C. Myers' term 'portable domesticity', which she coined to describe the enabling role English literature played in British emigrants' establishing domestic lives in Australia. Analysing archival sources and domestic fiction set in the Australian bush, Myers argues that English literature – specifically the domestic novel – provided a portable conceptual model which aided emigrants in establishing a sense of home, in the same manner as the furniture and personal objects that emigrants brought were meant to do. Whereas the characters and historic emigrants Myers discusses transfer domestic norms from one place to another within the British Empire, Ballou's characters carry their values as they roam the world in a floating house – imagining as home places not already conceived as part of their nation. Further, the easily portable format of flimsy duodecimo pamphlet novels such as *Fanny Campbell*, combined with the geographic range over which these little books were distributed, and the likelihood of their having changed hands from reader to reader, suggests that the books themselves may have traced haphazard itineraries that resemble those of the mobile characters within them. Myers notes that one emigrant character in an Australian domestic novel bolsters her courage in a challenging new environment by repeating to herself her favourite poetry, which she calls her 'household treasures" (Myers, 58), an observation which calls attention to the dual nature of books, both material objects and sources for cultural mores that live in the minds of a readership. The ideological mapping that takes place within the narrative space of *Fanny Campbell* was arguably mirrored in the 1840s–1870s by the thousands upon thousands of pulp novelettes circulating within and beyond the nation; within the Revolutionary-era narrative and in the mid-century US world of its readers, itinerant boats and books traced an American 'domesticity' in foreign places.

While I have been focusing on *Fanny Campbell*, it is only by placing this single tale in the context of other similar novels, published by Gleason's as well as by competing pulp outfits, that we can begin to understand the full potential of their cultural impact. Ballou and his partner Gleason innovated an unprecedented distribution network for the cheap products of their Boston-based United States Publishing Company by exploiting a combination of coastal and inland water routes, along with the growing transcontinental rail and post systems (Benson 36). The lists of distributors included at the backs of the books document this system's growth: an 1847 novelette mentions distributors in New York, Buffalo, Philadelphia, Cincinnati, Baltimore, New Orleans, Louisville, Detroit and St Louis; a similar list in an 1849 novelette adds a San Francisco agent and, further, announces that the titles could be purchased 'at all of the Periodical Depots, and of News Agents in any part of the United States and the Canadas' (Ballou *Belle of Madrid* 94). Strikingly, the books may have gone further once purchased than they had when they made the long journey from the printing house to their point of sale. Sold for about a dime at train stations and in towns with significant boat traffic (whether by river or sea), these little books – curled into a pocket, tucked under an arm, rapidly read and passed along – would have met a fairly mobile readership.

Seeing the list of distributors inside the back cover, directly facing the last page of the story, highlights the disjunction between the rapidly changing US with its transcontinental rail, and the quaint, local-seeming national space which the text encourages readers to imagine. *Fanny Campbell* ends with the narrator urging readers to visit the Lovells' still-standing house (where the pair spent their old age, after returning from the sea) and, significantly, to do so the old-fashioned way:

> If you [visit the Lovell estate], eschew the rail-road, take a horse and vehicle, and be your own master; go where you will, and return when you will. ... The deuce take all rail-roads, I say, where romance is concerned; for while one is exercised by some very fine feeling, he may awake from his lethargy and find that the cars have ... gone off and left him. (*FC* 90)

Without having to worry about the timetables of the modern rail infrastructure, readers can give themselves over entirely to the 'very fine feeling' of historical fantasy which *Fanny Campbell* encourages readers to entertain. As a sign of real change, the railway inconveniences the narrator through its incongruence with the novel's empty historical discourse; it is in this sense that the rail system is incompatible with 'romance'.

The injunction to 'eschew the railroad' seems doubly dubious given that publishers relied on those very tracks not only to distribute their printed products, but also to receive pulp manuscripts penned in the nation's frontiers by nomadic authors. Although Ballou himself was based in Boston throughout the 1840s and 1850s, the manuscripts of many tales he published with Gleason were actually written by Americans living outside the United States. Popular fiction authors were an errant bunch: some, like Ballou, travelled for health or pleasure, whereas others travelled from economic necessity, moonlighting as pulp authors as they laboured in the emerging empire's margins as soldiers, sailors or in other such frontier-skirting, nomadic lines of work (Benson 33).[16] Thus, the nation's margins functioned as both source and destination of these tales as authors and readers alike imagined a growing nation without imagining their participation in its growth, or understanding growth in terms of historical change.

Fanny Campbell, Female Pirate Captain was a keystone text in this contradictory imaginative project, as its heroine conquered softly on two fronts. In terms of her piratical endeavours as Captain Channing, Fanny translates to an allegorical register the violence of expansion, incarnating the ideology of manifest destiny by means of the evacuation of agency she enables. In terms of her stint as oceangoing wife, she cultivates an extra-national sense of a specifically American homeliness, re-enacted among a readership spread within and beyond the nation.

---

[16]   Interestingly, Ballou even devotes a long passage of *Fanny* to praising sailors as sources of great stories – compliments all the more humorous considering he signed the novel 'Lieutenant Murray':

> Thus the inhabitants of the forecastle, seldom possessing books, are thrown much upon their own resources for amusement during such time as they mind their own. Story-telling is a very natural as well as fascinating mode of amusement; and this they universally adopt, on all occasions. I have sometimes heard landsmen remark that the nicely told stories put in print as coming from seamen while spinning a yarn to their messmates, were all moonshine; that foremast men could not talk like that. This is a mistake – the constant habit renders them very perfect, and I have listened through a whole watch to as well a told story from the crew of a merchantship, as I have ever read; told too with a degree of refinement entirely unlooked for. (*FC* 64)

John Sutherland has found evidence regarding British novelists suggesting similar trends. By studying the bio-bibliographic information of nearly 900 novelists, he uncovered a large number of author-sailors. 'Sea captains in the 1830s, for instance, were recruited in large numbers into the profession .... Clearly, peace, half-pay, and the national nostalgia for the Great Victorious War all played a part. But so too did the training and discipline of the officer's life at sea' (263). See Sutherland's 'The Victorian Novelists: Who Were They?' *The Book History Reader*. Eds David Finklestein and Alastair McCleery (New York and London: Routledge, 2003): 259–68.

Chapter 7

Mutiny on the *Orion*: The Legacy of the *Hermione* Mutiny and the Politics of Nonviolent Protest in Elizabeth Gaskell's *North and South*

Deborah Denenholz Morse

Just before midnight on 21 September 1797, a violent mutiny broke out on HMS *Hermione*, at anchor in the West Indies.[1] The mutiny is still the 'bloodiest uprising ever to take place in the British Navy' (Jeans 168). The mutineers butchered the tyrannical captain, Hugh Pigot,[2] and killed nine other officers, including a boy, a midshipman named Smith. Pigot had held violent sway over the *Hermione*'s crew for two years; the final acts of cruelty that instigated the sailors' rebellion were Pigot's threats that he would flog whichever of the crew came down last from the rigging. In their haste not to be flogged, three young sailors fell to their deaths. Pigot allegedly scoffed at their corpses lying on the deck, and commanded that the sailors' bodies be unceremoniously thrown into the sea. The sailors responded later that same day by brutally hacking Pigot and his officers to death with swords and hatchets. Even officers who had acted fairly to the mutineers

---

[1]   Dudley Pope, in *The Black Ship* (London: Weidenfeld & Nicolson, 1963; New York: Henry Holt & Company, 1998), devotes an entire riveting book to the horrific events on the *Hermione*. See also Richard Woodman, *A Brief History of Mutiny* (New York: Carroll & Graf, 2005) for a detailed analysis of this event. Woodman's book has two chapters devoted to the *Hermione* mutiny. *The Oxford Companion to Ships and the Sea*, edited by Peter Kemp (Oxford: Oxford UP, 1976): 386 gives a succinct narrative of the event.

[2]   For the character of Pigot, see not only Pope and Woodman, but also the nineteenth-century account by William James, *The Naval History of Great Britain*, vol. II (London: Richard Bentley, 1837): 'he has been described to us by those who knew him well, as one of the most cruel and oppressive captains belonging to the British navy' (103). Pope states that 'only rarely did a captain become so warped that he became an irresponsible tyrant; and this book is a study of one particular case, the worst in the whole history of the Royal Navy' (16). G.J. Marcus, in *A Naval History of England: The Formative Centuries* (Boston and Toronto: Little, Brown and Company, 1961), gives Pigot as an example of naval captain who was 'a sadistic tyrant' (391).

were slaughtered, despite their desperate entreaties for mercy.[3] The mutineers then sailed the *Hermione* to the Spanish Main and handed her over to the Spaniards, France's ally in England's war against Napoleon. In the 10 years following the mutiny, 33 of the mutineers were hunted down or gave themselves up, and 24 were hanged at the yardarm by the Royal Navy. More than 100 of the 'Hermiones' escaped retribution, however, and 'with changed names and silent prayers no one would recognize them, found their way into U.S. warships and were serving there during the pre-1815 years' (McKee 255).[4] The *Hermione* was recaptured in October 1799 in a daring raid by HMS *Surprise* under Captain Sir Edward Hamilton. After the *Hermione* mutiny, as Christopher McKee states, the spectre of mutiny was more horrifying, 'the bloody phantasm of the *Hermione* close to the surface of the collective memory':

> Certain, too, it is that the *Hermione* mutiny – swift, brutal, bloody, vengeful – and not the much more famous British mutinies at Spithead and Nore in 1797 captured the imagination of both quarterdeck and lower deck in the U.S. Navy. When the word mutiny was used, the image released, genielike, was of that ultimate revolt: murder of the officers and seizure of the ship. (255)

In her Condition-of-England novel *North and South*, Elizabeth Gaskell reimagines this violent mutiny in the dramatic sub-plot that tells of the 'passionate' (108) mutineer Lieutenant Frederick Hale, brother to the novel's heroine, Margaret. Margaret Hale in the main plot of *North and South*, like her sailor brother Frederick, involves herself in disputes between oppressed workers and those in authority over them. Unlike Frederick, however, Margaret does not support violent insurrection, but rather models a nonviolent politics of resistance amidst mob fury. Through her story, the politics of tolerance and nonviolent protest evolve against a backdrop of the real bloodshed of the *Hermione* mutiny, the unstated but implicit violence of the fictional *Orion* mutiny and the strikers' angry riot.[5]

---

[3]   Perhaps the case of Third Lieutenant Foreshaw, whom Midshipman Casey, a witness to the mutiny, called 'a good humane young man', is the saddest. Foreshaw begged for his life in the name of his wife and three children, but was viciously attacked and thrown overboard – twice. The first time Foreshaw hit the mizzen chain-wales. The second time he was tossed into the sea – after exclaiming, 'Good God men, what have I done to harm you that I should be treated in this manner?' See Pope, 158–67 and Woodman, 130–31.

[4]   See McKee, Chapter 22, 'The *Hermione* Phobia', 255–68.

[5]   Any discussion of tolerance in *North and South* must acknowledge the germinal work of John Lucas, 'Mrs. Gaskell and Brotherhood', in *Tradition and Tolerance in Nineteenth-Century Fiction: Critical Essays on Some English and American Novels*. Eds David Howard, John Lucas and John Goode (London: Routledge & Kegan Paul, 1966): 161–74.

Although a few Gaskell scholars have recognized the significance of Frederick's role in the novel, no critic has connected it to the historical *Hermione* mutiny.[6] This is all the more surprising when one considers that Gaskell was intensely interested in English history and often set her works in the past, whether during the English Civil War and its aftermath, as with the novellas *Lois the Witch* and *Morton Hall*; during the French Revolution, as in the novella *The Grey Woman* and the story 'My French Master'; or during the Napoleonic Wars, as in her novel *Sylvia's Lovers*. Gaskell would have been familiar with the *Hermione* mutiny, which occurred in this last period, in the tumultuous 1790s, when fear of invasion from Napoleon was pervasive in England. The *Hermione* mutiny is, as Dean King has noted, 'one of the defining events of men at sea during the Napoleonic wars' (10).

Frederick Hale opposes the tyranny of one cruel man against many powerless sailors during a mutiny on HMS *Orion* that resonates with the details of the historical *Hermione* rebellion. (Indeed, *Orion* seems to echo *Hermione*.) Yet as details about his impetuous, passionate character are revealed throughout the novel, the wisdom of his actions comes into question, and he appears as perhaps more reckless than heroic. In his letters to his mother, which Margaret silently reads in Mrs Hale's sickroom, the tale of the *Orion* mutiny unfolds:

> Margaret slowly read the letter, half illegible through the fading of the ink. It might be – it probably was – a statement of Captain Reid's imperiousness in trifles, very much exaggerated by the narrator, who had written it while fresh and warm from the scene of altercation. Some sailors being aloft in the main-topsail rigging, the Captain had ordered them to race down, threatening the hindmost with the cat-of-nine-tails. He who was farthest on the spar, feeling the impossibility of passing his companions, and yet passionately dreading the disgrace of the flogging, threw himself desperately down to catch a rope considerably lower, failed, and fell senseless on deck. He only survived for a few hours afterwards, and the indignation of the ship's crew was at boiling point when young Hale wrote. (107)

Frederick's subjective, written testimony is uncertain evidence in more senses than one, necessitating Margaret's interpretation of the barely legible faded ink,

---

[6] See especially Patricia Ingham, 'Introduction'. *North and South*. London and New York: Penguin, 1995; Felicia Bonaparte, *The Gypsy-Bachelor of Manchester: The Life of Mrs. Gaskell's Demon*. Charlottesville: U of Virginia P, 1992; and Jennifer Uglow, *Elizabeth Gaskell: A Habit of Stories*. London: Faber & Faber, 1993. Rosemarie Bodenheimer preceded all of these interpretations with her short, insightful discussion of the Frederick sub-plot in relation to 'the dangers of Thornton's authoritarian position'. See '*North and South*: A Permanent State of Change'. *Victorian Fiction* (now *Victorian Literature*) 34.3 (December 1979): 281–301. Reprinted in *Elizabeth Gaskell, North and South*. Ed. Alan Shelston. A Norton Critical Edition (New York and London: W.W. Norton & Company, 2005): 531.

years after his letter was penned: 'It might be – it probably was … .' The 'wicked newspaper' in which the Hales first read the public view of the event is another kind of evidence, another mediation. Mrs Hale recalls that her husband was in so much anguish that he 'began to shake and cry in a strange muffled, groaning voice'; she tells Margaret that she rejected the newspaper's judgement of Frederick as 'a traitor of the blackest dye' and 'tore it up to little bits – I tore it – Oh! I believe, Margaret, I tore it with my teeth' (109). After listening to her mother recall the animal pain she has suffered, Margaret still believes in Frederick's moral imperative to lead the mutiny: 'Loyalty and obedience to wisdom and justice are fine; but it is still finer to defy arbitrary power, unjustly and cruelly used – not on behalf of ourselves, but on behalf of others more helpless' (109).

Yet the narrator's portrayal of what is most likely Margaret's consciousness while reading the letter casts doubts upon Frederick's emotional state during the writing of the letter, and perhaps upon his judgement during the mutiny itself: 'It might be – it probably was – a statement of Captain Reid's imperiousness in trifles, very much exaggerated by the narrator, who had written it while fresh and warm from the scene of altercation.' Moreover, Mrs Hale's allusion even in this conversation to Frederick as 'such a fine fellow, only perhaps rather too passionate' (108) places doubt in the reader's mind about Frederick's wisdom in leading a mutiny that results in so many deaths among the rebelling sailors. Some of the mutineers are taken, court-martialled and hanged from the yardarm of the ironically named *Amicia*; the court 'in condemning them to death, said they had suffered themselves to be led astray from their duty by their superior officers (109). Frederick, however, is not caught, and he spends several years in South America before travelling to Cadiz. Although neither Mrs Hale nor Margaret condemns Frederick for this dark punishment to others in the mutiny while he survives, certainly the implication is that he has some responsibility for these sailors' deaths. The story that Margaret relates of Frederick, 'one of the earliest things I can remember' (251), in which he wanted the sweetness of stolen apples more than the plenty in the Hales's own Helstone orchard, perhaps also suggests a flaw in Frederick's character, a sense of adventure coupled with an urge toward transgression that is figured almost as a biblical Fall.

Margaret's role in the workers' riot, in contrast, is an effort to prevent violence and death. She tries to protect the hunger-crazed millworkers from the police *and* the millowner, Thornton, who defies their fury alone. Margaret is injured when she shields Thornton from the mob even as she exhorts him to listen to the people's grievances and demands. Ultimately, Margaret searches for a different paradigm for master–worker relations and is able deeply to influence Thornton, the man who loves her, both through her ideas and through her inheritance, which she uses to fund Thornton's more humane cotton mill. Thus private, sexual politics impinge upon Thornton's public decisions. He changes his thinking and his actions toward his factory 'hands' as he learns to treat them as full human beings, to break bread with them in the new workers' eating-hall, and to help nurture and educate even the rioter Boucher's children.

Gaskell uses the historical mutiny on the *Hermione* to explore the politics of power and authority not only on British ships, but also in the British ship of state, in relations between the masters and men in the cotton mills of Milton-Northern (Manchester), and between individuals. As Leonard V. Smith states, 'Mutinies are interesting as historical phenomena, perhaps, because they bring such localized concerns so abruptly and quixotically up against all the attributes of modern state power' (523–4). Through the recollection of the *Hermione* mutiny, Gaskell also approaches issues of violence in labour relations, most dramatically in the scene of the strikers' riot. Gaskell's historical memory of the brutal consequences for both loyal officers and mutinous sailors on the *Hermione* informs her understanding of the rebellion against tyranny – and the destructive aftermath of violence. It also informs the construction of an alternative politics of tolerance in which authority is wielded responsibly and violent confrontation is replaced by nonviolent reconciliation.

In Gaskell's transformed mutiny plot, at no point is Frederick overtly condemned, although, as I have suggested, his actions are implicitly questioned. The idealistic Margaret, her principled clergyman father and her distraught mother all believe in Frederick. He is considered as unfortunate rather than criminal even by the dispassionate, worldly London solicitor Henry Lennox, who takes up Frederick's case in the hope that Margaret will be grateful to him and will smile upon his marriage suit. Only the unrelenting state – England – is not willing to exonerate Frederick. He finds that an English court-martial is, in his words, 'a court where authority weighs nine-tenths in the balance, and evidence forms only the other tenth' (253–4). Thus, Frederick leaves England forever, exiled from a seemingly unjust country to Spain, a land of succor, where he finds an exotic, beautiful wife and begins a successful career as a merchant. Ultimately, he embraces the Catholic religion, further separating himself from the nation of his birth:

> Frederick had written to Margaret a pretty vehement letter, containing his renunciation of England as his country; he wished he could unnative himself, and declared that he would not take his pardon if it were offered him, nor live in the country if he had permission to do so. (335)

Frederick is not – like the majority of the leaders of the historical *Hermione* rebellion – relentlessly pursued and hanged as punishment for his part in a mutiny on a British naval vessel. Whatever his responsibility in the *Orion* mutiny may have been, Gaskell does not punish Frederick with death or imprisonment – or even with poverty or unhappiness. Ultimately, Frederick is able to see his dying mother, to get free of his persecutor Leonards (who dies an ignominious death, for which Frederick has some responsibility), to create a family with Delores, a devoted Spanish woman whom he passionately loves, and to establish a prosperous career. Although Frederick Hale will live out his life in exile, he is not only ultimately reconciled to that fate, but he also renounces the country that has treated him with what he considers to be fierce injustice. Unlike that most famous of officer mutineers – Acting Lieutenant of HMS *Bounty*, Fletcher Christian, whose later history is that of an outlaw who went 'native' on the uncharted Pitcairn Island[7] – the expectation is that Frederick Hale will live a normal, unthreatened upper middle-class life outside England, comfortable in his embrace of the foreign – with his Delores, his Catholicism, his Spanish family and career. Yet Gaskell writes Frederick out of the novel – and out of England. His brand of impetuous, dangerously violent leadership is not England's future, but an echo of England's bloody history of mutiny.

To look at *North and South* through the historical lens of the *Hermione* mutiny is of course to give greater prominence to the character of Frederick in the novel, and to the relationship between Frederick and Margaret, brother and sister. Among Gaskell critics, Patsy Stoneman and Patricia Ingham have most strongly emphasized the significance of Frederick's role in the novel in shaping Margaret's plot. Stoneman comments: 'The most forceful and extensive of these parallel situations concerns Frederick Hale, whose justified naval mutiny provides an analogy, more acceptable to middle-class readers with its Robin Hood air of chivalry, for the mutiny of mill-workers' (123). Ingham too decides that 'it is through affinity with Frederick (whom she closely resembles physically) that [Margaret] develops a model for dissent' (Ingham xi). However, a more viable 'model for dissent' would be the nonviolent mutiny[8] that occurred at Spithead in

---

[7]   The history of Fletcher Christian after the famous *Bounty* mutiny is disputed, although most accounts state that he was murdered on Pitcairn Island on 20 September 1793. (See the British Museum website, http://www.britishmuseum.org/explore/highlights/ highlight_objects/aoa/b/barkcloth_made_by_fletcher_chr.aspx.) Richard Woodman (*A Brief History of Mutiny*. New York: Carroll & Graf, 2005), however, insists that when the sole surviving mutineer on Pitcairn, John Adams, related the mutineers' history in 1825 (the year of Adams's pardon) to Captain Beechey of HMS *Blossom*, Christian's end 'remained specifically unaccounted for – and will remain so forever' (95). There are over 2,000 books, articles and films on the *Bounty* mutiny, of which perhaps the best known are Nordhoff and Hall's 1932 Bounty Trilogy (*Mutiny on the Bounty, Men Against the Sea* and *Pitcairn's Island*); the 1935 Frank Lloyd film adaptation of the first two books of the Trilogy, which starred Clark Gable as Fletcher Christian and Charles Laughton as Captain Bligh; and the 1962 film version, directed by Lewis Milestone and based on Nordhoff and Hall, starring Marlon Brando as Fletcher Christian and Trevor Howard as Captain Bligh.

[8]   There was one incident at Spithead in which three seamen were killed and several wounded when delegates came aboard HMS *London*. According to Eugene L. Rasor in *Reform in the Royal Navy* (Hamden, CT: Archon Books, 1976), 'misunderstanding, delay, and lack of communication caused the incident' (154). Valentine Joyce, one of the leaders of the Spithead mutiny, 'restored order' (154). Among Rasor's many sources are three of the seminal histories: George Ernest Manwaring and Bonamy Dobree, *Floating Republic* (New York: Harcourt Brace, 1935; London: Geoffrey Bles, 1935); Michael Arthur Lewis, *Spithead* (London: Allen & Unwin, 1972); and James Dugan, *The Great Mutiny* (New York: New American Library, 1967).

1797, the same year as the *Hermione* mutiny, in which the British Channel Fleet argued for and won concessions from the Admiralty.[9] As Frank Mabee notes,

> The rational discourse of Spithead begins a process of reshaping the public view of British sailors and redefining mutiny as a form of political protest, as a mode through which to conduct a collective labour strike. (134)[10]

However, Gaskell chooses instead for Frederick's story to echo the events of the violent *Hermione* mutiny, not the nonviolent mutiny at Spithead. I would contend that the 'parallel' between Frederick's actions in the *Orion* mutiny and Margaret's actions in the millworkers' riot is more troubled than either Stoneman's or Ingham's arguments acknowledge, largely because of the backdrop of the historical *Hermione* mutiny. Once that bloody insurrection is viewed as a precursor to the novel's dramatic events of rebellion both onboard ship and in the streets of Milton-Northern, the mood of the novel darkens considerably, and the knowledge of past violence influences the depiction of both the mutiny on the *Orion* and the millworkers' strike in *North and South*. The implicit insertion of this fearful historical event into the memories of her readers may in fact be a part of what Hilary Schor calls in another, very different context 'Gaskell's critique of the *form* of the industrial novel' (144).

For Gaskell herself, the sibling bond between brother and sister is a deeply emotional connection. In her own life, Gaskell's much older sailor brother, John Stevenson – the only living sibling from her father's first marriage – disappeared on a voyage to India and was never heard of again. As Jenny Uglow tells us: 'That winter John vanished from her life ... She never wrote or talked about this loss ... But the figure of the sailor in peril moves through her fiction with the power of a recurring dream ...' (53). Other Gaskell biographers and scholars, most notably Winifred Gérin and Felicia Bonaparte, have also commented upon this sudden absence in Gaskell's life and how it must have influenced the creation of the many returning sailor figures in her fiction, from the irreverent, charming Will Wilson in *Mary Barton* and dashing Peter in *Cranford* to the uxorious husband and despairing suicide, Frank Wilson, in *The Manchester Marriage* and the sexy, glamorous harpooner Charley Kinraid in *Sylvia's Lovers*. Bonaparte states, 'Always the sailors of her fiction are enormously appealing' (30) – and other than in *The Manchester Marriage*, this is true. Bonaparte goes farthest in her speculations on the effects of John Stevenson's vanishing without a trace when she writes of

---

[9]   See Woodman, Chapter 6, and Manwaring, Lewis and Dugan for more complete histories.

[10]   The mutinies at Spithead, the fleet anchorage between Portsmouth and the Isle of Wight, and the Nore, the fleet anchorage in the Thames estuary, are together known as 'The Great Mutiny'. The mutiny at the Nore 'exemplified irrationality, disruption, and violence on both sides', according to Rasor (63). (See note 8 above.) The mutiny at the Nore resulted in 'over 400 courtsmartial' and 29 executions (64).

Gaskell's need to create a male daemon to live out not only her own adventurous side, but also to embody the dead brother's lost male experience; Bonaparte argues that in *North and South*, Frederick 'is Margaret's daemonic self' (173). Bonaparte even goes so far as to declare that 'Frederick's mutinous rebellion is Margaret's demon acted out' (175).

While Bonaparte's assertions are provocative, even the more modest parallel that Ingham makes between the brother's actions in the *Orion* mutiny and the sister's role in the workers' riot is certainly vexed. This is because of Gaskell's insistence upon comparing the brother and sister – and in finding the sister to be, ultimately, the stronger and more admirable figure. While Frederick must perpetrate violence in an armed insurrection in order to halt what seems to be brutal tyranny, Margaret is able to embody Christ's self-sacrifice; she averts violence aimed at others by taking a blow upon herself. Margaret is both doubled with her flamboyant, courageous older brother – whom she resembles – and distinguished from his possible excess of passion. This narrative strategy is important to articulating the politics of protest in *North and South*. Further, as Rosemarie Bodenheimer has argued: 'None of the painful paradoxes and consequences of Frederick's shipboard mutiny is avoided in the brief treatment of that subplot' (536). As his letter and even his mother's assessment of his character suggests, Frederick might have been reckless or at least precipitate as well as brave and selfless; we are left in uncertainty. During his secret visit to Milton, he advises Margaret: 'My precept is, "Do something, my sister, do good if you can; but, at any rate, do something."' As a theory for domestic use, Margaret finds that although she 'thought Frederick's theory rather a rough one at first, she saw how he worked it out into continual production of kindness in fact' (245). Although we are meant to admire Frederick as his loving and beloved younger sister does, we can still hear the voice of the restless man who may have acted decisively and bravely without enough forethought for all contingencies – including the deaths of many more sailors than the poor man who fell from the masts.

Frederick is also compared to Margaret's romantic interest and eventual husband, the industrialist John Thornton. Thornton is a dark, forceful and passionate Milton-Northern factory owner who learns from Margaret during the course of the novel about the incremental process of reconciliation between social classes. His reformed politics of tolerance is in the ascendant at the close of *North and South*, when he proposes to Margaret, who is now an heiress whose money will fund his new factory and his enlightened policies toward his workers. Together, Margaret and Thornton model a politics of reconciliation within England that displaces the politics of confrontation. While Frederick's cause is viewed sympathetically throughout the narrative and his exile is a terrible personal loss to Margaret – 'he is lost to me, and I am so lonely' (373) – his bold actions on behalf of English sailors on an English ship are not viewed as a paradigm for resistance to oppression experienced on English soil. Thornton and Margaret displace Frederick, and they remain in England – and in communal relation to their workers. Margaret prevents bloodshed at the workers' riot, when she helps to disperse the crowds before the police arrive with their guns. Unlike Frederick, Margaret is not responsible in any way for the deaths of other human beings. Thornton's role, as one of the masters of the working men, is more compromised in this regard: his unbending will before his reformation under Margaret's tutelage could be cited as contributing to the desperate suicide of the rioter Boucher, who is shunned by both masters and union men. Thornton's response to this tragedy is to help educate Boucher's orphaned children and to give a job to the union worker Nicholas Higgins so that Higgins can support the children as well.

Frederick, who has become a merchant in Spain, is in something of a parallel situation to Thornton as master and manufacturer. This is somewhat ironic, as Frederick looks down upon Thornton as a man engaged in commerce. Margaret has been told that one of the 'shopmen' has come to the house. Although she declared at Helstone that 'I don't like shoppy people' (20), Margaret's evolving sense of social class and of the character of a gentleman since her Northern sojourn contrasts with her brother's Southern sense of class distinctions. Margaret says:

> 'I fancied you meant some one of a different class, not a gentleman; someone come on an errand.'
> 'He looked like someone of that kind,' said Frederick, carelessly. 'I took him for a shopman, and he turns out a manufacturer.'
>
> Margaret was silent. She remembered how at first, before she knew his character, she had spoken, and thought of him just as Frederick was doing. It was but a natural impression that was made upon him, and yet she was a little annoyed by it. She was unwilling to speak; she wanted to make Frederick understand what kind of person Mr. Thornton was – but she was tongue-tied. (252)

There is no sense that Frederick will institute reforms into his father-in-law's business in the aftermath of his actions on the *Orion* sailors' behalf, as Thornton eventually does in his own mill. Indeed, his embrace of Catholicism (although that is apparently his wife's and her mother's religion, rather than her father's) in combination with his acceptance of a position in his wife's father's business, the 'extensive' Spanish Barbour and Company, may suggest that Frederick is now more complicit in entrenched patriarchal authority in his adopted country. The models for dissent in *North and South* are not the *Orion* mutiny Ingham cites, but instead Margaret's brave shielding of the beleaguered Thornton as he faces the mob during the strikers' riot and Margaret's egalitarian friendships with Bessy and Nicholas Higgins in the working-class community, to both of which I will return later in this chapter.

The mystery of Frederick Hale is introduced early on in the novel in conjunction with Mr Hale's crisis of faith, as Margaret wildly surmises about the reasons for her father's dejected spirits:

What could he mean? It was all the worse for being so mysterious. The aspect of piteous distress on his face, almost as imploring a merciful and kind judgement from his child, gave her a sudden sickening. Could he have become implicated in anything Frederick had done? Frederick was an outlaw. Had her father, out of a natural love for his son, connived at any –

'Oh! What is it? Do speak, papa! Tell me all! Why can you no longer be a clergyman? Surely, if the bishop were told all we know about Frederick, and the hard, unjust – '
    'It is nothing about Frederick ...' (35)

Yet of course, Mr Hale's decision to become a Dissenter has much in common with the situation of his mutineer son, although the decision is not overtly 'about Frederick'. Both father and son act on principle – even if the son seems to have acted rashly – and both Mr Hale and Frederick will become exiles, Mr Hale to the North of England and Frederick to Cadiz. Mr Hale cannot 'make a fresh declaration of conformity to the Liturgy at my institution' (37). Frederick cannot witness the brutal injustice on the ship *Orion*, and cannot conform to the Navy's institutional hierarchy of authority. Both father and son will suffer much for their principled rebellions. However, just before his death, reflecting upon his wife's long sickbed and his own crisis of conscience, Mr Hale states that 'even if I could have foreseen that cruellest martyrdom of suffering, through the sufferings of one whom I loved, I would have done just the same as far as that step of openly leaving the Church went' (340–41) Frederick too will defend his actions in his letters to his parents, although – as we have seen – those 'ocean letters' betray the son's natural hot-headedness as much as they might reveal his courage.

Frederick's history is the dark secret of the Hale family, the germ of the illness to which Mrs Hale will eventually succumb. It is a significant element in the sense of loss that Terence Wright argues is pervasive in the novel:

North and South is a book full of pain – not the pangs of hunger, as in *Mary Barton*, but the pain of stress and disturbance, of pangs of conscience and sexual torment. It is also the pain of loss, particularly for the heroine, and indeed it seems surprising on reflection that a happy ending could be retrieved from such unpropitious material. Those who are not suffering are the exceptions ... (105)[11]

---

[11]   Although Wright does not mention the Bible in relation to his argument, in fact the Book of Job is invoked early in the novel, at the close of Chapter 6, when the Hales have left Helstone and must stay for a night in London: 'London life is too whirling and full to admit of even an hour of that deep silence of feeling which the friends of Job showed, when "they sat with him on the ground seven days and seven nights, and none spake a word unto him; for they saw that his grief was very great"'. (58)

Margaret is conscious of her parents' suffering over her brother. She knows part of her brother's history but feels restraint about burdening her parents with her desire for knowledge of him; she is an only child who knows she has an outlaw brother:

> On such evenings Margaret was apt to stop talking rather abruptly, and listen to the drip-drip of the rain upon the leads of the little bow-window. Once or twice Margaret found herself mechanically counting the repetition of the monotonous sound, while she wondered if she might venture to put a question on a subject very near to her heart, and ask where Frederick was now; what he was doing; how long it was since they had heard from him. But a consciousness that her mother's delicate health, and positive dislike to Helstone, all dated from the time of the mutiny in which Frederick had been engaged, – the full account of which Margaret had never heard, and which now seemed doomed to be buried in sad oblivion, – made her pause and turn away from the subject each time she approached it … Frederick was always spoken of, in the rare times when he was mentioned, as 'Poor Frederick'. His room was kept exactly as he had left it. (21–2)

In the dreary quiet of the Helstone vicarage, Margaret has been discussing her London life at her Aunt Shaw's on Harley Street, when she longs to talk about the secret subject that is generally silenced in the household: the lost son and brother and his public disgrace. Not only does Margaret have an 'outlaw' brother, but she also has a brother who is nearly worshipped in this family, whose room is kept as a shrine of remembrance, and of forlorn hope for his return. Frederick is forever a boy, while Margaret has daily witnessing to her maturation. Perhaps this is a part of Margaret's distress early in the novel, just subsequent to the scene quoted above, when Lennox, the London solicitor, proposes marriage to her: 'Margaret felt guilty and ashamed of having grown so much into a woman as to be thought of in marriage' (34).

In Frederick's long absence, Margaret has taken on the role of authority in the household that would normally have gone to a grown son. Indeed, her father asks her to break the news to his wife of his religious crisis and the consequent demise in the family's fortunes: 'Would you dislike breaking it to her very much, Margaret?' (38). The tentative father's abdication of authority necessitates that the daughter be more forceful, particularly in view of the invalid Mrs Hale. When Mr Hale tries to figure out how his family will be supported without his vicar's salary to live on and vicarage to live in, he suggests that they might need to send Frederick less money:

> 'Yes, I suppose we have about a hundred and seventy pounds a year of our own. Seventy of that has always gone to Frederick, since he has been abroad. I don't know if he wants it all,' he continued in a hesitating manner. 'He must have some pay for serving with the Spanish army.'

'Frederick must not suffer,' said Margaret, decidedly; 'in a foreign country; so unjustly treated by his own.' (39)

Yet the suffering that Frederick's actions in the mutiny have caused is dwelt upon in the novel. Mrs Hale in particular is agonized about her son's exile. She recalls that Fred was, as she tells Margaret, 'much prettier than you were' and that he was 'born with the gift of winning hearts' (200). The suffering mother tells her daughter of her dreams – that 'I dream of him in some stormy sea, with great, clear, glass-green walls of waves on either side his ship, but far higher than her very masts, curling over her with that cruel, terrible white foam, like some gigantic crested serpent' (106). Frederick's 'yellow, sea-stained letters, with the peculiar fragrance ocean letters have' are kept in a 'little japan cabinet' like the precious relics they are. Her dearest wish is that she will see her exiled son again before she dies, and the night he arrives, which he spends at her bedside, is her final night on earth. She can rest now that she has once again seen that her beloved son is well.

It is surely not a coincidence that Margaret's realization of her love for Thornton coincides with her brother's visit to Milton to see Mrs Hale on her deathbed. Margaret perceives that her brother is now a man and she can therefore more fully accept that she is a woman, no more a girl than Frederick is still a boy. She reflects upon his visit and its aftermath at Outwood Station, the very name of which suggests the margin between the town and its more primitive environs; it is in this indeterminate space and departure point for an outlaw that she lies to protect Frederick, who will be tried and likely hanged if he is discovered in England. Frederick tells his father and sister:

I've a good mind to face it out, and stand my trial. If I could only pick up my evidence! I cannot endure the thought of being in the power of such a blackguard as Leonards. I could almost have enjoyed – in other circumstances – this stolen visit: it has had all the charm which the Frenchwoman attributed to forbidden pleasures. (251)

Frederick's comment about the attraction of the 'forbidden fruit' may signal the restlessness and impetuosity in his nature that makes his role in the mutiny ambiguous. It may also suggest his fallenness and state of exile from England. As Margaret comments, 'One of the earliest things I can remember ... is your being in some great disgrace for stealing apples ... some one had told you that stolen fruit tasted sweetest' (251).

The climactic scene involving Frederick occurs at Outwood Station. Margaret tells a lie for her mutineer brother in order to protect him from the 'rascal' Leonards, of whom Frederick says that 'a worse sailor was never on board ship – nor a much worse man either' (250). The brother and sister are followed to the station by the disreputable man, where 'a man in the dress of a railway porter started forward; a bad-looking man, who seemed to have drunk himself into a state of brutality, although his senses were in perfect order' (259). The despicable

Leonards becomes a kind of representative of English law-as-persecution, since he is willing to bring Frederick to 'justice'. Margaret is the witness to this struggle, which is a literal 'wrestling':

> In an instant – how, Margaret did not see, for everything danced before her eyes – but by some sleight of wrestling, Frederick had tripped him up, and he fell from the height of three or four feet, which the platform was elevated above the space of soft ground, by the side of the railroad. There he lay. (259)

Possibly Gaskell's choice in depicting Frederick's role in Leonards's death as ambiguous reflects the uncertain part Frederick played in the mutiny. The question of responsibility for both actions is murky at best. Was Frederick reckless or brave in the mutiny? Was his tripping of Leonards self-defence or manslaughter? Nevertheless, the novel's view of English law as falling short of a true system of justice is buttressed by Frederick's ensuing problems in the attempt to reopen his case, his resultant sense of hopelessness and his decision to leave England forever.

Against the repercussions of the *Orion* mutiny and Frederick's uncertain role in that event, the politics of nonviolent tolerance and reconciliation are worked out between Thornton and Margaret. The strikers' riot is the scene in which Thornton and Margaret oppose one another's politics most overtly. Thornton, exigent master that he is at this mid-point of the novel, has called the police to handle the strikers, who are threatening the Irish 'knobsticks' whom he has hired to take their places in the factory. Thornton goes down to face the workers at Margaret's behest:

> 'Mr. Thornton,' said Margaret, shaking all over with her passion, 'go down this instant, if you are not a coward. Go down and face them like a man. Save these poor strangers, whom you have decoyed here. Speak to your workmen as if they were human beings. Speak to them kindly. Don't let the soldiers come in and cut down poor creatures who are driven mad. ' (175)

Thornton of course takes up her challenge to his manhood. But he is facing the 'savage satisfaction' of the hunger-crazed mob. Margaret longs for Thornton to speak to the workers 'man to man', but the mob is like 'a troop of animals'. Margaret 'tore her bonnet off' – symbolic that she relinquishes a conventionally feminine role at this point in the scene. She 'had lifted the great iron bar of the door with an imperious force – had thrown the door open wide – and was there, in face of that angry sea of men, her eyes smiting them with flaming arrows of reproach' (176). The 'imperious force' with which Margaret lifts the 'great iron bar' also signals a kind of unconventional strength in this woman, a strength that is physical as well as moral. Margaret is depicted in biblical language, 'smiting' the rioters with 'flaming arrows of reproach', most like the Archangel Michael – or like Christ himself.

Margaret's beseeching words articulate a politics of nonviolence: 'Oh, do not use violence! He is one man, and you are many' (176). She watches the 'savage lads, with their love of cruel excitement' take off their clogs in preparation to fling them at Thornton, who 'might be smitten down, – he whom she had urged and goaded to come to this perilous place. She only thought how she could save him. She threw her arms around him; she made her body into a shield from the fierce people beyond' (177). Finally, she herself is struck as she protects Thornton from the mob: Her words echo those of Christ on the Cross:

> 'For God's sake! Do not damage your cause by this violence. You do not know what you are doing.' ...
>   A sharp pebble flew by her, grazing forehead and cheek, and drawing a blinding sheet of light before her eyes. She lay like one dead on Mr. Thornton's shoulder. Then he unfolded his arms, and held her encircled in one for an instant. ... They were watching, open-eyed and open-mouthed, the thread of dark-red blood which wakened them up from their trance of passion. (177)

In the momentary Pieta that Margaret forms with Thornton lies the embodiment of Margaret's – and Gaskell's – politics of nonviolence.[12] Margaret acts out the role of Christ's sacrifice and takes on his stigmata and crown of thorns in the 'thread of dark-red blood' on her forehead.[13] She is successful in averting the disaster that would surely have ensued if she had not intervened: either Thornton's murder, the slaughter of the workers by the police, or both. Unlike her brother Frederick, Margaret is responsible for saving lives, not for leading men into an action that ends with their being hanged.

Margaret takes personal responsibility in another context as well, with her friendship with the intelligent, articulate millworker Nicholas Higgins and his daughter Bessy, fatally ill with a lung disease contracted because of the 'fluff' in her lungs from the carding room in which she worked as a child. As Susan Morgan argues:

> We see the basic choices clearly in *North and South*, in the contrast between the workers' strikes and riots and Margaret Hale's friendship with Bessy and Nicholas Higgins. That friendship, linking Higgins to Mr. Thornton, may have been the beginning of more factory reforms in Manchester than all the strikes and riots and political votes. (97)

---

[12]   See pp. 48 and 64 of Deborah Denenholz Morse's 'Stitching Repentance, Sewing Rebellion: Seamstresses and Fallen Women in Elizabeth Gaskell's Fiction' in *Keeping the Victorian House: A Collection of Essays.* Ed. Vanessa D. Dickerson (New York and London: Garland, 1995): 27–73, for a discussion of Gaskell's symbolic use of the Pieta.

[13]   See Wright for a different emphasis: 'Her challenge to him to go downstairs is a sexual challenge, and her taking of the blow is a sexual reconciliation, marked by blood and wounding' ('We Are Not Angels' 112).

It is this vision of community that inspires Thornton's and Nicholas Higgins's eating-hall experiment. Thornton at first has a plan for the hall, but he accepts Nicholas's amended worker-run project. Mr Bell, Mr Hale's old Oxford friend, comments: 'Nothing like the act of eating for equalizing men' (354). His words suggest the Eucharist as well as the recognition of our common human hunger – and Gaskell's intention of imbuing the common dinner of master with men with a sense of the sacred.[14]

In the final scene of the novel, Margaret, now the inheritor of Mr Bell's fortune, lends her money to Thornton to recoup the fortunes of Marlborough Mills – and thus not only Thornton's livelihood, but also that of his former workers. Although it is the mutineer Frederick who is Mr Bell's godchild, it seems fitting that this Milton man turned Oxford don should bequeath his fortune to his old friend Mr Hale's reformist daughter Margaret rather than to his rebellious godson Frederick. In Gaskell's novel, she suggests that empathy, self-sacrifice and a willingness to compromise might lead to greater peace between masters and men. It is the zeal and commitment of Margaret Hale and John Thornton to find common ground with English workers that might transform Milton – and England – into a more egalitarian, tolerant, and nonviolent place.

Frederick Hale's movement in the novel seems to be a progression from fiery mutineer to content, wealthy, middle-class merchant in a foreign land. He is not severely punished for his role in defying naval authority, as were many of the historical 'Hermiones' – and indeed, many of the leaders of much less violent mutinies.[15] Tantalizingly, we never know what Frederick really did during his ship's mutiny, since all of the evidence Gaskell provides in the novel is mediated. The mutiny on the *Orion* remains a haunting memory when the reader closes *North and South* – as the knowledge of the historical *Hermione* mutiny darkened English naval history. In both events, the response to tyranny was violence, and that bloody tumult was answered in turn with the harsh retribution of hanging at the yardarm.

---

[14] Margaret Markwick, in reading this chapter, particularly emphasized the significance of Bell's words. I would like to thank not only Margaret, but also Anca Vlasopolos, Deborah Robbins and Grace Moore for their perceptive reading of my work.

[15] Perhaps the history of Richard Parker, the leader of the Nore mutiny, is the best example here. Parker was hanged on HMS *Sandwich* on the morning of 30 June after the confederacy of ships involved in the mutiny dissolved. Twenty-eight of his fellow mutineers were also hanged.

Chapter 8

Acts of Piracy: *Black Ey'd Susan*, Theatrical Publishing and the Victorian Stage

Kate Mattacks

On 4 December 1853, celebrated actor and manager Benjamin Webster appeared at the Adelphi as the villainous adventurer Carlos in the spectacular nautical melodrama *The Thirst of Gold, or the Lost Ship and the Wild Flower of Mexico*. This lengthy play, lasting over three-and-a-half hours, allowed Webster to represent all the variant forms of piracy, from thief, mutineer, profiteer and adventurer, to identity fraudster. For Carlos begins by stealing a treasure map showing the location of gold deposits in California, incites mutiny to commandeer the ship, plunders foreign wealth and finally assumes an ancient family name to reconstruct himself as the Mexican nobleman, the Marquis Del Monte.

Reviews of Webster's performance were brief and perfunctory, with *The Era* referring to him as 'excellent' and *Lloyd's Newspaper* praising his 'greatest power' without further elaboration.[1] Rather, the interest of the 'excitement-loving audience of the Adelphi' had been captured by the central spectacle in which the mutineers set the captain and his family adrift on a sea of ice.[2] Occupying the whole of the stage, the sheet of ice then proceeds to break up, leaving the captain's child orphaned on the last stable iceberg as the tableau of Act II. The technical aspects of this scene required a large tank to hold the volume of water and specific machinery below stage to part the two plates, moving the mountains of ice through the gap into the stage below. Explosives were used to mask the mechanics of the scenery shifts, as the child is dramatically left on the remaining fragment. The sheer creative invention necessitated by this scene indicates how sensation and melodramas furthered technological innovation, often ensuring the play's success at the expense of a deeper encounter with its thematic issues.

The temporal displacement of the play's action back to the 1700s allowed the work to avoid potential censorship in its display of concerns over both the lack of domestic protection owing to the forces deployed in the Crimean War and the rising tensions in India over Britain's own piratical plundering of its resources which led to

---

[1]   See *The Era*, Sunday 11 December 1853, Issue 794 and *Lloyd's Weekly Newspaper*, Sunday 11 December 1853, Issue 577.

[2]   See *The Era*, Sunday 11 December 1853, Issue 794. *The Illustrated London News* capitalized upon the interest in the scene, carrying a full plate illustrating the scene in the issue for 17 December 1853.

the Indian Mutiny just three years later (see Chapter 9 for Garrett Ziegler's extended discussion of the revolt).[3] However, the issue of piracy and the consequences of the illicit profits remained central to the public's perception of *The Thirst of Gold, or the Lost Ship and the Wild Flower of Mexico*. For Webster had not only played the pirate on stage, but more significantly had committed an act of dramatic piracy in taking the play from D'Ennery and Dugué's *La Prière des Naufragés* (1847), which he had seen at the Ambigu-Comique on 20 October 1853.

The case of *The Thirst of Gold* illustrates the implicit connection between the pirate, the actor and the playwright. For, like Carlos the adventurer, Webster profited materially from piracy through the play's successful six-month run – the antecedents of the crime returned to undo him.[4] After the final curtain of the play's unlicensed première, Webster publicly acknowledged the aid of a French playwright whom he announced 'did not wish his name mentioned'.[5] However, both the authoritative *Era* and the *Examiner* published full details of the source, enabling other theatres to commission their own 'translations' to capitalize on the fame of the Adelphi's sensational melodrama.[6] A matter of weeks later, three further versions of the play appeared: Edward Stirling's *A Struggle for Gold, or, A Mother's Prayer and the Adventurer of Mexico* at the City of London on 23 January; *The Search for Gold, or Greenleaf and Redberry* at the Standard Theatre on 26 January; and *The Struggle for Gold and the Orphan of the Frozen Sea* at the Marylebone Theatre on 20 February 1854.[7] Indeed, the problem of piracy was not confined to the domestic arena, as acting tours and the telegraph functioned in much the same way as the Internet does today in allowing the illicit trade of information between continents.[8]

---

[3]   An article in *Reynold's Newspaper* entitled 'British Tyranny in India' interestingly refers to the British 'thirst for gold' which was to precipitate the Indian Mutiny. See *Reynold's Newspaper*, Sunday 7 September 1856, Issue 317.

[4]   The play ran until June 1854, and was revived for one night only as Madame Celeste's benefit on 7 June 1854.

[5]   See the *Morning Chronicle*, Tuesday 6 December 1853, Issue 27130. Interestingly, the play's original manuscript was sent by Webster directly from Paris to the Lord Chamberlain's Office to obtain a licence for a performance at the Soho Theatre a day after it premièred at the Adelphi. See MS Lord Chamberlain's Collection 5299 at the British Library. The title was also re-registered as *The Prayer in the Storm, or, The Thirst for Gold, or, The Lost Ship and the Wild Flower of Mexico* in 1874.

[6]   See *The Era*, Sunday 11 December 1853, Issue 794, and *The Examiner*, Saturday 10 December 1853, Issue 2393.

[7]   The play at the Standard Theatre was originally entitled *The Gold Finders of Australia, or, Greenleaf and Redberry* and was relicensed with additional scenes, adding 'The Sea of Ice' to the title. See MS Lord Chamberlain's Collection 52945H at the British Library. The latter two plays were not attributed.

[8]   See Catherine Seville, *The Internationalism of Copyright Law: Books, Buccaneers and the Black Flag in the Nineteenth Century* (Cambridge: Cambridge UP, 2006)

Webster's practice of translating plays without attribution or payment was consistent with a theatrical culture grounded in forms of piracy that ranged from direct plagiarism to the dynamics of the performative mode that relied on impersonation and the creative input of numerous theatre personnel. Here, the figure of the pirate becomes the locus of an extended debate on theatrical creativity and the business practices created by the specific cultural conditions of the Victorian period. In an era that saw significant changes in copyright law, the rise of the printed Acting Edition and the advent of royalty payments to playwrights, images of piracy on stage articulated the theatre's response to a shifting legal framework that challenged their rights to material. Indeed, it is no coincidence that the most popular nautical dramas, such as Douglas Jerrold's *Black Ey'd Susan; or, All in the Downs!* (1829) and Edward Fitzball's *The Mutiny at the Nore* (1830) and *The Flying Dutchman* (1826),[9] were written at a time of heightened tensions surrounding copyright and piracy that precipitated the 1833 Dramatic Copyright Act and the founding of the Dramatic Authors' Society.

This chapter explores the connection between the stage pirate and the traditions of dramatic piracy that pervaded the Victorian theatre, arguing that the figure of the pirate came to represent both the material conditions of theatre practitioners and the threat of piracy from publishers. Webster was further disenfranchised from his version of *La Prière des Naufragés* when an independent translation, later attributed to T.W. Robertson, appeared as the Lacy Acting Edition of *The Sea of Ice; or, the Prayer of the Wrecked, and the Gold-Seeker of Mexico* in 1854.[10] Under the Dramatic Copyright Act of 1833, Webster owned the performance rights to his adaptation for a limited period, but in printing a specially commissioned version, Thomas Hailes Lacy had created an edition that enjoyed the protection of Talfourd's Literary Copyright Act of 1842 without the need to purchase the Adelphi promptscript. The business of theatrical publishing indicated the schism between creative possession and legal copyright assignments, further compounded by the multiplicity of influences from actor to stage manager that resisted the notion of a single author's moral right of ownership. As a result, a new piratical figure emerged, as Andrew Knighton has noted – namely that of the publisher as profiteer. Through the surviving business papers of T.H. Lacy and his Acting Edition of Douglas Jerrold's *Black Ey'd Susan*, I will demonstrate how nautical drama offered the playwright an arena in which to debate the state's role in regulating dramatic piracy. Through the central figure of William, Jerrold

---

[9]   Edward Fitzball's *The Mutiny At the Nore. A Nautical Drama* (1830) was published by T.H. Lacy in vol. 78 (c. 1868) and *The Flying Dutchman; or, the Phantom Ship. A Nautical Drama* (1826) appeared in vol. 71. (c.1867). These are available from the Victorian Plays Project at http://victorian.worc.ac.uk Lacy's two-act version of *Black Ey'd Susan* was reprinted in volume 23.

[10]   This appears in Lacy Acting Editions, vol. 13 and is available at the Victorian Plays Project, http://victorian.worc.ac.uk. The play has been attributed by the British Library as having been included in his complete works.

articulates his position as a writer beset by the specific cultural conditions that allowed Lacy to publish a variant, pirate text.

Framed by Talfourd's 1842 Literary Copyright Act and the Berne Convention of 1886, T.H, Lacy's publishing career provides a unique insight into the illicit trade of mid-Victorian plays. His printed edition of *Black Ey'd Susan* in 1855 is a prime example of the challenge of reconstructing copyright assigns that were proved by fragmentary receipts or bypassed through personal connections. As a former actor, theatre manager, playgoer and playwright, Lacy had built up a close network of peers and bought manuscripts directly from prominent figures within the Dramatic Authors' Society – such as Mark Lemon, Henry Byron, J.B. Buckstone, Boucicault and the Morton brothers – despite accusations that his fees for provincial performances were designed to undercut the Society's.

When he began trading in 1848, Lacy's initial portfolio was based upon the purchase of the stock of Cumberland's Minor Theatre and John Duncombe's business, but by 1873 he had published 100 volumes of Lacy's List containing over 1,500 plays, ranging from melodramas and historical dramas to farces, burlesques and sketches. In addition, his catalogue advertises a wealth of contextual material, including memoirs, costume books, make-up, printed scenery, handbooks and specialized genres such as sensation dramas, charades and Ethiopian dramas.[11] Lacy's standardized texts included stage directions, costumes, original cast lists and playbill details, anticipating Jacky Bratton's intertheatrical method of reading Victorian drama.[12] Often taken from promptscripts rather than original manuscripts, Lacy's editions sought to become the authoritative, prescriptive text for theatre practitioners, an act that arguably went against the performative ethos of a creative, evolving form. The detailed stage directions and prefaces also attracted

---

[11]   A further four supplementary volumes of plays are lodged at the British Library, containing many plays which did not appear in his 100-volume set. This is likely to have been a preservation issue on the part of the British Library, as neither Birmingham Central Library nor the V&A Theatre Museum has supplementary volumes. It is unclear as to why certain plays were not included in Lacy's List. Colin H. Hazlewood's adaptation of M.E. Braddon's novel *Lady Audley's Secret* (1863) appears in a supplementary volume, yet Suter's version did not; and it was Suter's version that caused Braddon's publishers to successfully sue Lacy. It may be that the supplementary plays were less lucrative in terms of performance rights. Hazlewood's contracts with Lacy often stipulate that the original commissioners would own performance rights and that he would retain provincial rights. In the case of *Lady Audley's Secret*, the performance was free by the author's permission. Lacy's *Classified Index to Two Hundred Female Costumes, Dramatic, Historical and National* (London: T.H. Lacy, 1865) and *Classified Index to Two Hundred Male Costumes Dramatic, Historical and National* (London: T.H. Lacy, 1865) have been digitized by the University of Georgia, http://fax.libs.uga.edu/GT513xL32/ldcmenu.html. Copies of the catalogue are bound in with the plays at the British Library, but have been removed by Birmingham.

[12]   Jacky Bratton, *New Readings in Theatre History* (Cambridge: Cambridge UP, 2003).

a readership keen to experience the theatrical from within the respectability of the home, and to capitalize on this market Lacy sold plays in volumes for readers and collectors.

Lacy's success, however, brought a certain, not undeserved, notoriety. The entry in the *Oxford Dictionary of National Biography* typically portrays him as a profiteer with a 'cavalier attitude to copyright', who often 'assumed copyright without authority' (Stephens) and, initially, his edition of *Black Ey'd Susan* would appear to support his piratical reputation. For there is no copyright assign for the play within his business papers, and despite the fragmentary nature of early receipts, Lacy carefully pasted them into his ledger to locate them as legal evidence in the event of a copyright infringement against his assigns. The assumption that Duncombe's rights to the first edition (printed in 1829) were automatically transferred to Lacy when he purchased the stock is undermined by the existence of John Dick's Acting Edition that predates Lacy's.[13] Dicks' edition is essentially a reprint of Duncombe's first edition, suggesting that the initial copyright assigns were transferred to Lacy's rival, Dicks, significantly leaving Lacy's List without the most popular nautical melodrama of the century.[14] However, from the outset of his career Lacy was highly aware of how to manipulate copyright law to both his advantage and that of the playwright. For Dicks' small typeface, poor paper quality and double-column format was highly unsuitable for use by a professional actor, and Lacy sought to relaunch Jerrold's text into the marketplace through a more accessible edition.[15]

Lacy's version of *Black Ey'd Susan* problematically appears soon after its republication in volume 8 of Jerrold's complete works in 1854, indicating Lacy's adept reworking of copyright laws to avoid prosecution.[16] Appearing after the 1842 Copyright Act, the publisher Bradbury and Evans may have held the copyright assigns to the text, although many playwrights, including John Maddison Morton,

---

[13]   Jerrold's *Black Ey'd Susan* (1829) was reprinted by John Dicks as No. 230 of Dicks' Plays. These were undated but were numbered sequentially in a similar way to Lacy's editions. The British Library dates his edition of Thomas Holcroft's *Deaf and Dumb; or, The Orphan Protected* (1809), No. 263 as being published in 1871; but given that Dicks' run numbered over 1,000 plays by the time of his death in 1881, this seems as little late given that it was also bound with J.R. Planché's *A Cabinet Question* of 1845.

[14]   Dicks' playtext changes only a few words, the most notable of which is Crosstree's final speech of Act II, Sc. I: 'I know it is wrong, but I will see her – and come what may, I must and will possess her'. This is modified to 'I know it is wrong, but I will see her – and come what may, I must and will have her' in Dicks' edition to emphasize the sexual threat faced by Susan.

[15]   Interestingly the typeface changes according to the dramatist. Mark Lemon's popular comedies are printed in the largest and most user-friendly typeface.

[16]   See Douglas Jerrold, *The Writings of Douglas Jerrold. Volume 8: Comedies and Dramas* (London: Bradbury and Evans, 1854).

withheld the right to publish a complete set of works for themselves.[17] Whoever the copyright holder was, Lacy's awareness of the precedent set by printed works was clear. Pasted in the front cover of his first Assignments book is his handwritten extract of the Act for handy reference:

> 5 + 6 Vir . 45. enacts that after the passing of the Act (1st of July 1842)
> the author and his assigns shall have copyright for the term
> of the authors life and seven years after his death or if these
> seven years expire before the end of the forty two years from
> the time of publication then for such period of forty two years
> for books *previously* published in which copyright still substistra [sic]
> at the time of *the passing of the act* the copyright shall be
> confirmed for the full term provided in the cases of books
> thereafter *wholly or in part* to a person [sic] *other than the author*
> 'who shall have acquired it for other consideration than
> that of natural love and affection' In these excepted cases
> the author or his personal representations and the proprietor
> of the copyright may again before the expiration of the subsisting
> term to accept the benefits of the Act and now on a minute
> of such an agreement being entered in a book of registry deeds
> to be kept at Stationers Hall the copyright is to be
> confirmed as in other cases for the authors [sic] life and
> seven years after his death or for forty two years from
> the time of publication and will be property of the person
> or persons specified in the minute [...] the copyright of
> a book published after the authors [sic] death is to endure for
> forty two years from the time of publication and to belong
> to the proprietor of the manuscript from which it is
> first published and his assigns. (Lacy 'Assignments Book 1')

Despite its appearance prior to the 1842 Copyright Act, re-registration for *Black Ey'd Susan* was not in point of law necessary for plays published within the author's lifetime, as the case of *Lacy v. Rhys* had publicly proved.[18]

---

[17]   Morton only allowed Lacy to print 1,000 copies of the melodrama *The Writing on the Wall* (1852), requesting a further £5 for any subsequent editions, and retained the right to publish the play in any future complete edition of his works. He was paid £15 initially. This melodrama was jointly authored with his brother Thomas Morton and was printed in vol.7 of Lacy's Acting Editions. The existence of detailed receipts that gave playwrights a second payment upon another edition may well have fuelled Lacy's impetus to produce a series of volumes that comprised unaltered copies, as these were not technically new editions at all.

[18]   Lacy successfully sued Horton Rhys for staging Thomas Egerton Wilks' *Roll of the Drum* at Sadler's Wells without his permission. As Lacy owned the copyright assigns

Instead of obtaining the permissions from Jerrold's publisher, Lacy relied on his connections with the family to create a new, variant text. His catalogue reveals a long-standing arrangement with both Douglas Jerrold and his eldest son, W. Blanchard Jerrold, to publish their works, as Lacy continued to add Jerrold's titles to his list until he sold the business to Samuel French.[19] The nature of Lacy's regard for Jerrold can be measured in his printing of a lengthy preface for the Acting Edition of *Nell Gwynne* (1833), which considerably reduced his profit margin in terms of paper usage alone. Lacy's direct attribution of the play to Jerrold signals a legitimate business relationship based upon mutual respect, in direct contrast with Lacy's piratical acts concerning *Uncle Tom's Cabin* (1853) and *The Corsican Brothers* (1850). Here Lacy adapted or retranslated his own versions of these highly successful plays in order to avoid copyright fees.[20] Having located his edition of *The Corsican Brothers* outside the jurisdiction of English copyright law through the claim of translating it from the original source, Lacy exploited its vagaries and turned profiteer by asserting his full ownership of performance and print copyright.[21]

Lacy's ownership of his Acting Edition of *Black Ey'd Susan* is, however, less clear. No contract for either the adaptation or the corresponding performance rights has survived, and the edition predates Lacy's introduction of a typed contract to fully clarify ownership of London and provincial performance rights.[22] Although Lacy's edition did not vary significantly enough from the original to warrant the need for a new licence from the Lord Chamberlain's Office, the lack of any paperwork concerning *Black Ey'd Susan* is distinctly problematic. Given that the edition became the standard acting text for theatre professionals until the turn of the century, its absence from the ledgers suggests that partial rights may have been

---

by purchasing them from Wilks' estate, the technicality of re-registration was deemed unnecessary by the judge who found in Lacy's favour. See *The Times*, 18 April 1863: 13. The case is discussed in some detail in Ronan Deazley, *Rethinking Copyright: History, Theory, Language* (Cheltenham: Edward Elgar, 2006).

[19]   Lacy published a total of 19 Jerrold Snr's plays, including *The Rent Day* (1852), *The Mutiny at the Nore* (1830) and *The Painter of Ghent* (1836). See the Victorian Plays Project at http://victorian.worc.ac.uk.

[20]   See Anon., *Uncle Tom's Cabin* (1853) in vol. 12 of Lacy's edition; and M.M.E. Grange and X de Montepin (trans.), *Les Frères Corses; or, The Corsican Brothers* (1850) in vol. 6. A receipt for £5 from Henry B. Addison for *Uncle Tom's Cabin* is dated 24 October 1860 in Samuel French Archive 81/2366, Box 1, Assignments Book 1, f.269.

[21]   His business records contain the licence from the Lord Chamberlain's Office for the first performance of *The Corsican Brothers* for February 1852 at the Royal Princess's Theatre in London. Interestingly the licence is dated April 1852, over two months after the first performance. See Samuel French Archive, 81/2366 Box 1, Assignments Book 3, f.111.

[22]   C. Hazlewood's contracts with Lacy often stipulate that the original commissioners would own performance rights and that he would retain provincial rights. In the case of *Lady Audley's Secret* (1863) the performance was free by the author's permission.

retained by Jerrold's family following his death in 1857, since Samuel French's later catalogues include the play as available.[23] Prominent playwrights were certainly in a stronger position to place conditions upon Lacy reprints and assigns. Indeed, W.S. Gilbert stipulated that Lacy could publish an old score 'on the understanding that the drama shall always be kept in print and obtainable on reasonable demand' (Lacy 'Assignments Books 2' f.10).[24] Any further payments made to Jerrold would at least have begun to address the impoverishment of dramatic authors under the fixed payment system. Douglas Jerrold was paid only £60 for the first manuscript of *Black Ey'd Susan*, in comparison to the £60,000 made by its star actor, T.P. Cooke.[25] Indeed, Cooke's iconographic status can be measured through later Lacy Acting Editions, where stage directions were abbreviated to the theatrical shorthand of 'cuts a nautical caper à la T.P. Cooke'.[26]

What emerges through Lacy's edition of *Black Ey'd Susan* is a positive experience of theatrical publishing. Despite Daniel Barrett's contention that playwrights avoided printing because of a fear of piracy, Lacy's later publishing practice reflected a shift towards 'copyright as a recognition of cultural worth and not a commodity' (Seville 6). While Lacy's lucrative act of publishing a second version of *Black Ey'd Susan* sits uneasily with his support of Jerrold as the creator of an iconographic Victorian text, the edition formed a space where the continuing rights of the author and the image of theatrical publishing could be debated.

The 1855 edition of *Black Ey'd Susan* retains the basic plot of the original, but makes significant revisions to both the structure and the text. As Jerrold was writing up until his death, it is possible that he made the revisions to adapt the play for a new generation of theatregoers. The discourse on piracy, legitimacy and nationality remained central, as the virtuous Susan is faced with a series of threats located in the figures of her landlord uncle, a pirate and a captain of the British navy. Her profiteering uncle, Doggrass, colludes with the pirate Captain Hatchet to evict her, leaving her open to seduction. The timely return of her husband, the sailor William, averts disaster and the traditional pirates are duly caught and punished.

The moral boundaries between piracy and legitimacy in the play become blurred when William is forced to again defend Susan from his superior officer's drunken advances. In defending marital and moral values, the hero William is

---

[23]   Numerous playbills indicate that Lacy's two-act edition was used in practice. See for example the playbill for the Gaiety Theatre, London for Saturday 25 May 1878, located in the Mander and Mitcheson Collection, http://sirsi3.tcm.ac.uk/Archimages/3803.JPG.

[24]   Receipt from W.S. Gilbert for £10 for an unnamed 'old score' dated 22 October 1869.

[25]   See Michael R. Booth, *The Theatre in the Victorian Age*. Cambridge: Cambridge UP, 1991: 144–5, and Alan Fischler, 'Drama'. 1999. *A Companion to Victorian Literature and Culture*. Ed. Herbert Tucker (Oxford: Blackwell, 2005), 341.

[26]   For example see Charles Selby, *Pirates of Putney*, Lacy Acting Editions, vol. 60, Act I, Sc. i, p. 3.

recast as a mutineer and his court martial occupies the final scenes. He is saved from execution by the timely appearance of his discharge papers that predate the attack, but the play's initial concerns with the fragile definitions of piracy and mutiny remain unresolved. Lacy's Acting Edition restructured the play from three acts to two, and rebranded the play as a 'nautical and domestic drama' to appeal to the rising demand for domestic drama epitomized by Boucicault's *The Colleen Bawn* (1860). The omission of the finale for Act I, in which Lieutenant Pike disarms Hatchet's pirate crew, allows the first two acts to be joined, whilst the third act remains unchanged to form Act II of Lacy's edition.

This reconstruction of the play indicates the influence of publishing practice as piracy on a number of levels. The simple revision of acts created a variant text that could be differentiated enough from the original to avoid copyright issues and subsequent prosecution. The removal of the scene in which Lieutenant Pike, disguised as a French officer, infiltrates the smuggler's cave and overpowers the pirates with the aid of the *Skylark*'s crew indicates a revised attitude to the notion of dramatic piracy, in terms of both publishing codes of conduct and audience demographics.[27] An increasing demand for domestic drama created by rising numbers of middle-class theatregoers was gradually supplanting the early nautical drama's blend of patriotism and moral melodrama aimed at largely working-class audiences. Here Lacy's printed edition records the adaptability of theatrical genres, if not the performative moment itself, allowing Jerrold to retrospectively reconsider his thematic concerns over dramatic piracy after both the 1833 and 1842 Copyright Acts. For the smuggler's act of aiding a French prisoner of war to escape is highly suggestive of the connections between the dramatic piracy of French drama and the destruction of quality English drama. Here the anti-patriotic act of admitting a Frenchman into the pirate gang reflects Jerrold's personal campaign to invigorate the health of English drama through a rigorous reform of the fixed payment system.

Jerrold believed that a lack of financial recognition for original works underpinned the practice of plagiarism, leading to his prominence in the Dramatic Authors' Society that sought to claim payments for performance rights. Jerrold's convictions were clearly shared by many, as the prolific dramatist William T. Moncrieff called for a collective uprising of dramatists against the practices of piracy, albeit paradoxically from within a preface to a pirated version of Mélesville and Duveyrier's vaudeville *La Meunière de Marly*,[28] entitled *The Mistress of the Mill* (1849):

---

[27]   This is Act I, Sc. v of Duncombe and Dicks' Acting Editions. Duncombe's edition of *Black Ey'd Susan* was reprinted in George Rowell (ed.), *Nineteenth-Century Plays* (Oxford: Oxford UP, 1953).

[28]   Mélesville was the pseudonym of Ann Honoré and this drama was itself a later version of Scribe and Mélesville's 1821 opera comique *La Meunière*. At the première of Moncrieff's *The Mistress of the Mill* at Sadler's Wells on 17 October 1849 he was immediately accused of plagiarism. Edward Morton claimed the piece to be a direct copy

If the dramatic purveyors of our day [...] would agree *never to touch a French piece at all*, but trust to their own *native talent* – thrice would I hail such a determination. It would be the first step towards restoring our lost drama; it would rid us of the wretched crew of vampires and pretenders that have too long fattened on the very life's blood of our dramatic resources. (6)

Moncrieff's analogy of the dramatist to the pirate 'crew' resonates with the tension between financial necessity and a sense of patriotism. Couched in the language of gothicism, dramatic piracy represented a vampiric presence that endangered the healthy body of the nation's drama, threatening to fragment the English cultural identity. That Jerrold removes the scene in which the treacherous pirates are captured suggests a tacit acknowledgement that dramatic piracy was far more difficult to contain than the 1833 and 1842 Copyright Acts had allowed for.

In response to the legal developments in copyright and the deregulation of the theatres, the 1855 edition of *Black Ey'd Susan* reassessed the nautical genre's association with issues of legality and censorship. Before the 1843 Theatre Regulation Act, only the two patent theatres at Drury Lane and Covent Garden were permitted to stage the 'legitimate' drama that was comprised almost exclusively of the spoken word. In advancing technological innovation through the demands of spectacular scenes such as shipwrecks, icebergs and arctic weather, the early nautical drama offered 'to the patent theatres royal a way of drawing upon "illegitimate" spectacular effects and to the minors access to a form made "legitimate" by its inclusion on the major stages' (Cox 172–3). The sensational representation of the ship on stage is key here, as it functioned as a metaphor for the theatre. Similarly built of wood, the ship's crew is analogous with a theatre company as the sailors' sea shanties and traditional dances equate them with performance artists, while the carpenter's highly valued skills maintained the medium on which their living depended.

The ship's movement between nations paralleled the piratical trade in foreign plays that was particularly prevalent in the smaller theatres built across the water of the Thames, outside the jurisdiction of the London officials. At sea, the ship functioned as a self-regulating state outside English legal jurisdiction that allowed the crew to evaluate their own conduct through a combination of naval law and the sailor's own moral codes of honour. These values were embodied in the tale of Tom Gunnel's encounter with St Domingo Billy the shark. Retold by the hero, William, the story concerned the brave act of Tom Gunnel, who not only rescues a Caribbean child from the jaws of a shark, but in killing the legendary monster profits from the contents of its stomach in the form of 10 years' worth of watches, tobacco boxes, three telescopes and an admiral's hat (Jerrold, Lacy I.vi 26–7). The appropriation of stolen goods is justified in Lacy's edition by the survival of

---

of his play *The Windmill* (1842) and threatened legal proceedings against Phelps and Greenwood, the lessees of the theatre. In a further twist, Lacy also reprinted Morton's play in 1868 in Lacy's Acting Editions vol. 71.

the child, as Dicks and Duncombe's edition recounts the gory image of a child's corpse alongside that of the shark (Jerrold, Oxford UP II.iii 28).

While the oral traditions of the sailor are preserved, the play's use of songs and ballads becomes distinctly more problematic for Jerrold in the wake of the new copyright laws. Sailor Seaweed's full rendition of 'Sweet William's Farewell to Black Ey'd Susan' had formerly legitimated the drama for the stage through its inclusion of musical material (Jerrold, Lacy I.vi 24–5). The ballad's evocation of patriotism and domestic fidelity measured by William's address to Susan before he embarks on naval duties formed the central tenet of Jerrold's representation of William as the mythic hero of the play. Prefiguring his defence of Susan against his own captain, the ballad's representation invests the figure of William with an idealized, specifically 'English' cultural identity. As the figurative embodiment of moral tenacity and patriotic loyalty, William ensured the mass appeal of both T.P. Cooke's representation and Jerrold's play. However, in an era marked by its debate on the difficulty in distinguishing between influence, heritage and piracy, the ballad served to remind Jerrold of the popular literary reputation he had openly traded upon.[29]

In an attempt to reduce the possible charges of literary piracy, Lacy's edition of *Black Ey'd Susan* only reprints the first two and last stanzas of John Gay's poem.[30] While this may reflect Dicks' footnote that only the first two verses were sung in representation, stage managers and actors were at liberty to adapt performances to suit the exigencies of time or audience demand (Jerrold, Dicks II.ii 9). Given the complex renegotiation of Jerrold's discourse on domestic piracy that follows, Lacy's revisions signify a change in William's role to reflect a new agenda. William's function as the locus for debates on the definition of piracy and legitimacy is catalysed by his actions in defending his wife that recast him as a mutineer. The wounding of Captain Crosstree is the finale of the penultimate act in both editions, but the later 1855 Lacy edition marks a significant diversion in terms of sympathy and intended purpose. Through the stage directions and illustrations from both Dicks' and Lacy's Acting Editions, it is possible to partially reconstruct the variant dynamics of the scene. Indeed, despite the shifting nature of the performative mode, the playscripts reveal unequivocally opposed visions of William's culpability.

While the variant frontispieces suggest the ways in which William's act was represented on stage, their composition forms direct evidence of how the two publishers commissioned illustrations to market the play for different audiences. William's crime is the pivotal moment in redefining the boundaries between

---

[29]   For the popularity of *Black Ey'd Susan* see Louis James, 'Was Jerrold's *Black Ey'd Susan* More Popular than Wordsworth's *Lucy*?' in David Bradby (ed.), *Performance and Politics in Popular Drama: Aspects of Popular Entertainment in Theatre, Film and Television 1800–1976* (Cambridge: Cambridge UP, 1980), 3–16.

[30]   This enormously popular ballad was John Gay's 1720 poem, often wrongly attributed to Henry Carey, set to music by Richard Leveridge in c. 1800.

piracy and legitimacy; Dicks frames William within the moral framework of melodrama, whereas Lacy's picture creates a complex interplay between modes of representation.

As Figure 8.1 shows, Dicks' illustration is inscribed with Crosstree's line 'I deserve my fate', and pictures Susan clinging to William as both recoil from the prostrate captain (Jerrold, Dicks II.ii 10). Susan's hair and clothes are dishevelled and highly suggestive of the nature of the attack by Crosstree, who appears as a dark figure on the ground. William's gestures are indicative of surprise and shock, and his raised left hand pointing towards heaven cancels the threat of the cutlass still held in his right. In line with the genre, this tableau is formed in front of a seascape, with the ships reminding the audience of the connection between the men.

The text upholds the representation of William as the victim of circumstance. Believing Susan to be at the mercy of 'buccaneers', William strikes her attacker, whose *'back is towards him'* (Jerrold, Dicks II.ii 11). Crosstree's admission of guilt precedes the final tableau in which *'William turns away horror-struck, Susan falls on her knees, the sailors bend over the Captain'* (Jerrold, Dicks II.ii 11). Here Susan's figure embodies the melodramatic codes of the heroine in distress, while William's reaction of horror undercuts his subsequent status as a mutineer. In direct contrast, Lacy's frontispiece, engraved by Findlay (Figure 8.2), pictures William in a defiant pose, with his hand positioned to prevent any further attack. The sword lies on the floor, but his pose is demonstrably aggressive, while his left hand is held back to protect Susan. Her figure is retranslated into a slightly shocked gentlewoman in full costume, including bonnet, who according to the script, *'rushes up to William'* (Jerrold, Lacy II.vi 29). Lacy's illustration is framed by domestic references – from respectable clothing and the house in the background, to the social gathering around the main tableau – reflecting the transition from the nautical genre of the first act to the domestic drama of the second, as promised by the new subtitle.

William's active, demonstrative pose is further emphasized by the costume and stage position of Crosstree, for the captain is facing William in full military dress and would be instantly recognizable as his superior officer. If, as Victor Emeljanow asserts in his chapter, the representation of the pirate signified a 'complex discourse of performance conventions' that included stage impersonation and costume, then the full naval uniforms of Crosstree and William would appear to visually undercut both Crosstree as a 'buccaneer' and William as a 'mutineer' in the traditional sense. This pictorial scene indicates a schism between word and image to problematize a reading of piratical traits based upon visual representation alone. Rather, it questions the theatrical form of representation that fails to visually articulate the domestic piracy of Crosstree and William for a less discerning audience. Lacy's edition relocates the tension of the drama in the interplay between the images of domestic piracy represented by Crosstree's appropriative act of Susan as object and William's defence of personal rather than national domestic values. The debate over the validity of theatrical representation as a method of legitimating

Cross.—"I DESERVE MY FATE.*"—Act 2, scene 3.*

Figure 8.1   Frontispiece to Dicks' Acting Edition of *Black Ey'd Susan*

moral codes of conduct becomes evident in Lacy's additional material. Jerrold's revisions crucially omit Crosstree's line 'I deserve my fate', underpinning the translation of William from victim of circumstance to the defiant aggressor of the illustration. Specific stage directions concerning William's gestures and stage presence before the tableau are markedly absent, allowing the actor and stage manager to reinterpret the dynamics of the scene.

Lacy, however, adds a description below the frontispiece, which does not appear in the play text. Prefiguring the playscript, Lacy anticipates the absence of stage directions and includes the words '*strikes the Captain down, upon discovering who* [sic] *he had wounded, drops his cutlas* [sic] *with astonishment*'.[31] These words create a discrepancy between the gestural figuring of William in the picture above; but ironically they also highlight the piratical heritage of *Black Ey'd Susan*. Indeed, Lacy's illustration was taken from Duncombe's edition,

---

[31]   It is unclear as to the source of the sword. In Act I, Sc. v, p. 22 of Lacy's edition, Lieutenant Pike gives William the pirate Captain Hatchet's belt as a trophy. If this was the source, then the act of stabbing Susan's second attacker with the weapon of the first has a deeper significance.

Figure 8.2   Frontispiece to Lacy's 1855 Edition of *Black Ey'd Susan*

visually indicating that Jerrold's play itself had become an iconographic symbol of a theatrical tradition inextricably grounded in piracy.

Jerrold's recognition of the play's piratical antecedents and of his own complicity in the development of such a culture was depicted through the final court martial and execution scenes. William's trial, or rather his lack of legal redress, focuses on the disjuncture between the domestic values of state and subject, symbolized by Lacy's removal of the gesture of William embracing the union jack before approaching the scaffold. In all versions, William is forced to admit a guilty plea under a system that disallowed any mitigating circumstances. Here the 'honesty of a sailor' (Jerrold, Lacy II.ii 33) is juxtaposed with the 'half tack of a lawyer' who sails in 'Beelzebub's ship, the Law!' (Jerrold, Lacy I.iv 17). The state-sanctioned authority of the admiral is further undermined by his commencement of the hearing without the two key witnesses, Susan and Crosstree. Lacy's 1885 edition further supports the reading of the hearing as a formality through the repositioning of the admiral's decision before even the sailor's testimonies. William's defence of the eponymous black-eyed Susan represents the position of the playwright beset by the material conditions of the theatre before the 1833 and 1842 Copyright Acts, as he struggles to fight the domestic piracy of publishers and adaptors who assumed the protection of the law.

The setting crucially shifts the jurisdiction of the trial from state to theatre, for both the court martial and execution scene take place on the ship, which acts as a metaphor for theatrical milieu. William's figure signifies the moral authority of the theatre, as Quid testifies that he 'plays the fiddle like an angel' (Jerrold, Lacy II.ii 34). State control is limited to the symbol of the Union Jack above the admiral's chair rather than above the ship. Despite William's admission of guilt, his narrative recasts him as the melodramatic hero defending 'the sweet craft', Susan 'battling with a pirate', and it is theatrical convention that prevents his execution (Jerrold, Lacy II.ii 35). The appearance of Crosstree and the discharge papers that predate the assumed act of mutiny averts his death in accordance with the moral melodramatic framework expected by the audience; yet this is partially tempered by the state's control over the ending as the Lord Chamberlain's Office forbade the representation of execution scenes (Davis 12). However, the discharge on a legal technicality was heavily suggestive of the way in which Lacy manipulated the vagaries of English copyright law to reprint *Black Ey'd Susan*. The court martial scene effectively serves as a critique of the validity of copyright as a regulatory tool against piracy.

What the publishing context and material playscripts of *Black Ey'd Susan* have revealed is that the figure of the pirate on the Victorian stage became the centre of the debate on dramatic piracy and copyright legitimacy. The nautical drama provided an arena in which Jerrold could assess the state's role in defining and controlling illegitimacy through legal reform. The variant 1855 edition allowed Jerrold and his publisher T.H. Lacy to respond to the advances in copyright law made by the 1833 Dramatic Copyright Act and the 1842 Literary Copyright Act. What emerges is a complex discourse on the creative dynamics of piracy, renegotiating the figure of the pirate as the embodiment of the theatrical condition.

Chapter 9

The Perils of Empire:
Dickens, Collins and the Indian Mutiny

Garrett Ziegler

Nine months after news of the 1857 massacre of English women and children at Cawnpore had begun trickling back to England, *Household Words,* the journal conducted by Charles Dickens, published an account of the execution of captured Indian rebels. The prisoners were mounted to the open barrels of artillery pieces and blown from cannon under the watchful eyes of English troops, newspapermen and not a few natives. In a piece entitled 'Blown Away!' *Household Words* writer George Craig recorded the events, describing the guns 'enveloped in thick white clouds of smoke, through the white wreaths of which little particles of crimson color were falling, thick as snow-flakes' (350). The bits of crimson, of course, were the remains of the sepoys, turned, by the might of British justice, 'into atoms'. The lingering account given of these proceedings, coupled with the lack of any real deliberation as to their morality, make it clear that, for Dickens and his writers, as well as for many other British men and women in the winter of 1857–58, there was little to feel for Indians but relish in their sufferings.

Having begun in May 1857, the Sepoy Rebellion, known in England as the Indian Mutiny, was largely under control by Christmas, although it took almost two years to fully suppress the shockwaves of insurrection across India. Though pockets of resistance lingered on for months, the focus shifted from containment to vengeance: a common vow heard that year was to have 'blood for blood, not drop for drop, but barrels and barrels … for every drop of [British] blood' (qtd. in Hibbert 212). Dickens did not take long to chime in, calling for the complete destruction of the Indian race in a now-infamous and oft-cited letter to his friend Angela Burdett Coutts:

> And I wish I were Commander in Chief in India. The first thing I would do to strike that Oriental race with amazement … should be to proclaim to them, in their language, that I considered my holding that appointment by the leave of God, to mean that I should do my utmost to exterminate the Race upon whom the stain of the late cruelties rested; and that I begged them to do me the favour to observe that I was there for that purpose and no other, and was now proceeding,

with all convenient dispatch and merciful swiftness of execution, to blot it out of mankind and raze it off the face of the Earth. (*Letters* 8:459)[1]

Dickens, we must remember, was by no means exceptional in espousing such views, as William Oddie and others have pointed out.[2] Dickens, however, held the public ear, which made his anger much more influential than that of many of his contemporaries; his role as editor of *Household Words* was such that his 'pool of writers ... became extensions of his own pen' as Hyungji Park has noted (103). Nothing appeared on the pages of Dickens's journal that had not first passed under his own scrutinizing eye, as he would later remark in *All the Year Round*: 'The statements and opinions of this Journal generally, are, of course, to be received as the statements and opinions of its Conductor' (qtd. in Park 102).[3]

Dickens's assurance that the ideas expressed in his magazines were in accordance with his own, however, was undermined by one of his closest friends and contributors. Wilkie Collins, who joined Dickens's staff at *Household Words* in September 1856, chafed against the anonymity and impotence engendered by Dickens's editorial practices and took on the appointment only in exchange for guaranteed serialization of his next novel in the journal.[4] Collins's difference of opinion with Dickens was not limited to publishing practice; his mentor's vitriolic reaction to the events of the Mutiny was met with considerable calm from Collins. Dickens's literary response to the events in India, apart from writing pugnacious letters, was to enlist Collins to help him draft a special story for the 1857 Christmas edition of *Household Words* to commemorate, 'without any vulgar catchpenny connexion or application, some of the best qualities of the English character that have been shewn in India' (*Letters* 8:482–3). The story the two crafted together, 'The Perils of Certain English Prisoners, and their Treasure in Women, Children, Silver, and Jewels' ('Perils'), has become a landmark in imperial literature, being, as Patrick Brantlinger notes, the first fictional response to the Mutiny.[5] While 'Perils' is fairly transparent in its relationship to the Mutiny, the Indians whom Dickens was so eager to eradicate from the earth are not mentioned at all. Instead, the villains of the story are pirates. This substitution, while it ensured Dickens's goal of avoiding 'any vulgar catchpenny connexion' to the actual events in India,

---

[1]   See also Dickens, 'To Emile de la Rue, 23 October 1857', *Letters* 8: 473.

[2]   See also Christopher Hibbert and Laura Peters.

[3]   *All the Year Round*, 26 December 1863, p. 419; see also Catherine Peters, *The King of Inventors: A Life of Wilkie Collins* (Princeton, NJ: Princeton UP, 1991): 123.

[4]   See Catherine Peters, 167–8; see also Nuel Pharr Davis's *The Life of Wilkie Collins* (Urbana: U of Illinois P, 1956): 190–91 and Kenneth Robinson's *Wilkie Collins: A Biography* (New York: Macmillan, 1952): 103–5.

[5]   See Brantlinger's *Rule of Darkness: British Literature and Imperialism, 1830–1914* (Ithaca and London: Cornell UP, 1988): 206–8. For a recent and comprehensive discussion of the place of the Mutiny in British culture, see Gautum Chakravarty's *The Indian Mutiny and the British Imagination* Cambridge: Cambridge UP, 2005).

also, for reasons that will become clear, allowed for the possibility that Dickens's anger would be blunted, as the characteristics of the mutinying Indians could not so easily be equated with the moral and sexual ambiguities embodied in pirates.

Divided into three sections, the story is noteworthy in Dickens scholarship for the first and third pieces, penned by Dickens, which reflect his animosity towards 'natives' and his jingoistic view of British imperialism. The Collins section, however, is decidedly more ambiguous and, as I will show, actually undermines the imperial ideologies and anxieties present in the Dickens pieces by blunting and obscuring the aims of British imperial power in the months following the Indian uprising. Previous critics, including Lillian Nayder, have noted the ambiguities of Collins's text, but none have given it the full treatment it deserves, especially in connection to Dickens's framing work.[6] Consideration of the events of the Mutiny and the subsequent post-Mutiny imperial anxieties is essential for an understanding of the oppositional forces present in the text, as these events deeply inform the response of both writers.

Rebellion, Rape, Response

The immediate cause of the uprising that became the Indian Mutiny was the rumour that cartridges for the Enfield rifle, the standard weapon of the British Indian Army, were greased with pork or beef fat, thus rendering them unacceptable to either Muslim or Hindu troops. But, as Benjamin Disraeli stated, 'the decline and fall of empires are not affairs of greased cartridges. Such results are occasioned by adequate causes, and by an accumulation of adequate causes' (qtd. in Pionke 112).[7] These 'adequate causes' were numerous and complex, including both internal disputes about caste and precedence, and rising nationalist sentiment on the part of Bengalis in response to British expansion. Also, as Edward Said has pointed out, the army officer staff was made up almost entirely of British troops, creating a unilateral distribution of power that served as a microcosm for the presence of the British in India: 'The causes of the Mutiny,' Said writes, 'were constitutive to British imperialism itself' (*Culture and Imperialism* 143).

---

[6] See Lillian Nayder, 'Robinson Crusoe and Friday in Victorian Britain: "Discipline", "Dialogue", and Collins's Critique of Empire in *The Moonstone*' *Dickens Studies Annual* 21 (1992): 213–31. Nayder has written extensively on the relationship between Collins and Dickens, and on 'Perils' specifically. Her scholarship is extremely valuable and voluminous on the subject, and every effort will be made to preserve the distinctions between her multiple and sometimes overlapping works.

[7] Speech before the House of Commons, 27 July 1857. Discussion of the causes of the Mutiny is indebted to Pionke and Hibbert. One of the major motivating factors of the Mutiny was the British seizure of property in the provincial Oudh kingdom. The branch of the Bengal infantry that initiated the Mutiny in May was made up largely of Oudh landholders.

The British response to the Mutiny was complicated by distance and misinformation. The initial reaction was to blame the government, citing the mismanaged Crimean War as foretelling the disastrous consequences of bureaucracy in India. Dickens himself, though never hesitating to blame the 'low, treacherous, murderous, tigerous' Indians, stringently criticized British governors, who made little attempt to understand Indian cultural politics: 'Why did they know nothing of the Hindoo character? Why? Do you ask why? Because it was the system to know nothing of anything; and to believe that England, while doing nothing, was doing everything' (*Letters* 8:472–3). Criticism of government ignorance and ineptitude became, however, criticism of government leniency and inaction as news, rumours, gossip and outright lies came drifting back to England in the hot, bloody summer. What arrived was almost unspeakable. '[Children were] put alive into boxes and set fire to – others were spitted on bayonets and twisted round in the air, and to make the tortures more exquisite all this was done in the presence of the mothers who were compelled to look on ... in a state of nudity' (qtd. in Hibbert 213).[8] This was just one of the horrifying stories surrounding the massacre of some 200 hostages, mostly women and children, under orders from rebel leader Nana Sahib in the town of Cawnpore. News of this massacre cemented British anti-Indian sentiment; the death sites were preserved exactly how British troops found them, replete with locks of bloody hair stuck to the walls and blood-stained palm prints on the floor, as a reminder of the nature of the enemy. Stories of dismembered corpses, slave auctions, publicly raped women and forced cannibalism sprang up instantly. The appalling nature of these crimes generated a new way of viewing and governing the empire. Out went the possibility of creating miniature liberal Britains across the globe; in came an insistence on racial difference, a binary opposition between civilization and barbarism, which created, as Laura Peters has demonstrated, a new 'mode of colonial control' (115–17), one that reasserted British power through public display and management.[9] Post-Mutiny British rule in India required, as Bernard Cohn has pointed out, 'a brutal demonstration' of British power, as well as 'the establishment of a myth of the superiority of the British character over that of the disloyal Indians' (178–9). Britain was no longer in the business of cultivating India, as the distance between the two cultures was now perceived as unbridgeable; people who could commit such heinous actions were fit only to be ruled.

Commissioners investigating the crimes, however, found no evidence of any atrocities beyond murder on the part of the Indians. The widespread rumours of the abduction and rape of British women boiled down to a single attestable occurrence,

---

[8]   My discussion of the incidents at Cawnpore is indebted to Hibbert.

[9]   One of the more immediate consequences of the Mutiny was that the British government dissolved the (mis)managing East India Company, asserting Crown rule over India in 1858.

and that woman married her abductor.[10] Even bellicose British historian G.O. Trevelyan noted that the English women of Cawnpore 'died without apprehension of dishonour' (145–6). The British army, press and public would hear none of this, and when Indian Governor-General Earl Canning called for an end to 'needless bloodshed', he was lambasted in the press, earning the nickname 'Clemency Canning' overnight (Maclagan 135–8). Dickens himself noted, 'a greater mistake was never committed in the world, than this wretched Lord Canning's maudlin proclamation about mercy' (*Letters* 8:473). He need not have vexed himself, as the British military response was to meet perceived atrocities with real ones. Mass hangings, cannon executions and crucifixions greeted the captured Indians, few of whom saw anything resembling a trial. At Cawnpore, Indian prisoners were forced to lick the blood off floors and walls – while being lashed – before being led away to hangings. Though there were some British citizens – Disraeli, for instance – who spoke out against the barbarism of the British army, their voices were drowned out in the roar of bloodlust.

At the centre of this maelstrom was an unspeakable crime, an atrocity that was hinted at only by innuendo and silence: the rape of British women. Appearing in the press as 'deeds too foul to mention' and as 'crimes worse than murder', sexual violence became the focal point of imperial power, 'appealing to heaven for vengeance' (qtd. in Hibbert 214). As Jenny Sharpe has pointed out, 'a discourse of rape' developed, articulated by letters, press accounts and rumours, but maintaining always 'a single, unrepresentable center' (33). Rape became a locus for anxieties about threats to Victorian domesticity, and called for a powerful response. Continuing the work of Sharpe, Nancy Paxton has shown that this discourse of rape 'emerged at a particular crisis point in the British rule of India and performed specific ideological work' (6); namely, it opened a space in which British power could affix and expand, legitimating itself, both in the empire and at home. Any doubt that the British were just in their rule of Indians was erased by the unutterable treatment of British women at native hands. In December 1857, rape had become the unspoken Evil, empire had become the impetus for murder, and Collins and Dickens published their story.

Dickens, Collins, 'Perils'

'Perils' is a thinly veiled account of the Mutiny. Dickens's initial narrative depicts a dispirited British marine, Gill Davis, arriving at an island known as Silver-Store, near present-day Nicaragua, with a company of men who are to relieve the

---

10   This woman, alternately known as Margaret Frances Wheeler and Ulrica Wheeler, was the daughter of the British commander at Cawnpore, General Hugh Wheeler, who had himself married an Indian woman. General Wheeler died in the siege. See Paxton, 'Mobilizing Chivalry: Rape in British Novels about the Indian Uprising of 1857'. *Victorian Studies* 36.1 (Autumn 1992): 5–30, especially 8, and Chakravarty, 202 n16.

British colony there and take the silver that the colonists have been mining back to England. The colony, however, is under threat from vicious local pirates 'on a pillaging and murdering expedition' (188). Through the duplicity of ostensibly friendly 'sambo' Christian George King, a party of British soldiers and sailors is lured away, leaving Davis and a handful of men to protect the women and children. They are attacked by the pirates and taken hostage, though not before a good number of the innocents fall beneath the aggressors' swords. Collins's middle section tells of the captives' march through the forest to the ruined palace of a vanished civilization, where they are then held prisoner. Under Collins's direction, the pirates are less concerned with murdering and pillaging and considerably more interested in singing, lying about and refurbishing their palace. Collins concludes his piece with a daring nighttime escape by the colonists, who drug the pirates and float down a nearby river to freedom. In the third and final narrative, Dickens has the wayward colonists discovered by the previously duped British sailing party. King is found, shot and hanged; the treasure in silver and jewels – what the pirates were after in the first place – is restored to British hands; Gill's burgeoning love interest, Miss Maryon, is married to the noble and brave Captain Carton; and Gill lives out his days in the marines, with Lady Carton as his benefactress.

Though the driving force behind the story was Dickens, it was Collins's idea to remove the story to Central America, replace mutinying Indians with a nationless band of pirates, and make treasure the motive for the attack, suggesting that from the beginning, Collins was attenuating Dickens's praise of the British and criticism of the Indians.[11] The switch from traitorous Indians to mercenary pirates is crucial, since it turns the enemy into a particularly flamboyant variant of the common thief, thereby evacuating much of the sexual danger associated with the mutineers. As Hans Turley has argued, there is an 'implicit link between homoeroticism and piracy' (29), one that reins in the threat presented to the honour of British women. Moreover, Collins's decision to transform the Indians into pirates also silences the nationalist tenor of Dickens's response to the Mutiny. The fact that pirates are by their very nature extra-national – in 'Perils' we are told that 'there were Malays among them, Dutch, Maltese, Greeks, Sambos, Negroes, and Convict Englishmen from the West India Islands … some Portuguese, too, and a few Spaniards' (199–200) – means that the rhetoric of ethno-national conflict deployed in response to the Mutiny is unavailable here. India is a nation and thus can be conquered and ruled; pirates can only be defeated. By transforming the sepoys into pirates, Collins has made it impossible for British power to function in the way Dickens and others desired. The tension between the two writers' formal styles – Dickens's sections are largely devoted to character development, while

---

[11]   See Catherine Peters, 182, and Kenneth Robinson, 117–18. Dickens, it should be noted, did the legwork on this new setting for the story, writing to Henry Morley in October of 1857 to ask for information about any British colonial activity in the Americas. Dickens wrote to Morley, 'I wish to avoid India itself; but I want to shadow out in what I do, the bravery of our ladies in India' (*Letters* 8:468–9).

Collins focuses on plot and scene – is homologous with the political tensions at work in the text. Dickens makes use of the ideologies and anxieties surrounding the Mutiny, especially those about rape and British ineptitude and leniency, in organizing post-Mutiny British power, while Collins works to undercut these and offers a critique of the imperial project. Dickens situates post-Mutiny power on essentialized otherness, circumscribing Indians within their perceived barbarism and therefore manifesting British power in overdetermining forms. Operating through the discourse of rape, Dickens highlights the natives' uncivilized nature and indicts English bureaucracy for its failure to recognize this savagery and deal with it accordingly. Collins, on the other hand, disrupts Dickens's ideological work, undermining, ridiculing and collapsing the post-Mutiny reorganization of imperial power. Collins's section is a centrifugal force in the text, disunifying the authorized and centralized systems of power articulated by Dickens. By evacuating racial panic, removing the threat to sexual purity and Victorian domesticity, reasserting the value of intellectual government and critiquing the exploitive policies of empire, Collins attempts to implode the text, to dissolve its authoritative ideological labour.

Patrick Brantlinger has argued that the texts that arose from the Mutiny are homogenous in their strident orientalism and vicious nationalism, in their transformation of the British presence in India from a liberal humanizing force into a distributor of unilateral power for no end other than empire. Mutiny texts, he claims, 'display extreme forms of extropunitive projection, the racist pattern of blaming the victim expressed in terms of an absolute polarization of good and evil, innocence and guilt, justice and injustice, moral restraint and sexual depravity, civilization and barbarism' (200). In contrast, I will show that Collins's section of the text is a repudiation of precisely those characteristics of literary accounts of the Mutiny that Brantlinger describes. Conflicting responses to the Mutiny are not absent from imaginative representations as Brantlinger claims, but rather they are localized in the very first fictional version of the uprising to appear in Britain. Collins, as we will see, enacts an oppositional political and humanist criticism of the British handling and representation of the Mutiny within the confines of Dickens's energetic nationalist production of a newly minted, post-liberal empire.

Dickens and the Empire

From the outset of his narrative, Dickens makes apparent the operations of imperial power on 'native' land: The ship Gill arrives on – the *Christopher Columbus* – invokes the long history of European exploration and subsequent colonization of indigenous peoples. The false hybridity of joint British–native rule is elicited immediately upon Gill's arrival on the island by his meditation on the flag flying above the colonial outpost: '[The] South American Flag and the Union Jack, flying from the same staff, where the little English colony could all come together, if they saw occasion' (179). The operative word in this description, of course, is 'if', and as Laura Peters has shown, physical space within the colony is anything but heterogeneous, segmented even to the point of enumeration:

> '[A]bout thirty Englishmen of various degrees,' said the young lady, 'form the
> little colony now on the Island. I don't count the sailors, for they don't belong to
> us. Nor the soldiers,' she gave us a gracious smile when she spoke of soldiers,
> 'for the same reason.'
> 'Nor the Sambos, ma'am,' said I.
> 'No.' (180)

At a party held later in the evening, Gill sees 'all the inhabitants then upon the Island, without any exception' (185) except, of course, for the natives, who are conspicuously absent from the festivities. We are told that both 'friendly Indians' and 'Sambos' populate the area (177), and even that they are 'trustworthy' (180), but apart from Christian George King we see little evidence of their presence. Collins's decision to transform the villains from Indians to pirates has left Dickens in strange straits. The 'natives' remain the target of his animosity, but the threat in the story comes from the pirates. Thus, the most he can do with regard to the natives is have Gill urge one of his fellow soldiers, 'for the love [of] all who were dear to him, to trust no Sambo' (195). The binary opposition between Britons and Indians that emerged in the rhetoric surrounding the Mutiny is here displaced on to the pirates, who become so different that they are no longer human: 'They broke over [the wall] like swarms of devils – they were, really and truly, more devils than men' (200). Their conduct is overtly contrasted to the noble, brave and calm English character, which 'will bear [their] bodies to wherever duty calls' (192). When the pirates attack, the British remain stoical before their task, 'as cool as if [they] were waiting for a play to begin' (198). Though the pirates are not Indians, the essential otherness that Dickens is committed to leads him to emphasize their racial characteristics, identifying the origins of the pirates – one is 'a sort of wild Portuguese demon', for instance (200) – even though it is unclear how one could tell a Portuguese pirate from a Spanish one by sight alone (they all speak English and are under the same black flag) during a nighttime raid. The fact that pirates are, as I noted above, extra-national, and that these pirates in particular count Englishmen among their numbers does not stop Dickens from attempting to imbue them with radical racial otherness.

Dickens does have one native on whom he can foist racial otherness, of course: Christian George King, the native 'sambo' whom the British believe 'would die for us' (180). With his obsequious posturing, King has earned English trust. Indeed, he even wins Gill's 'infantine and sweetly beautiful' (187) admiration through his hard work to salvage the *Christopher Columbus*, pulling it up on the beach before it sinks into the sea. King's treachery, however, turns out to validate Gill's initial response to him, which was to kick him 'over the side, without exactly knowing why, except that it was the right thing to do' (178). It is only when King's duplicity becomes known that Gill is able to see that he is 'a double-dyed traitor, and a most infernal villain' (193). Much like the Indians rounded up at Cawnpore, King is ultimately reduced to an 'animal', shot by the British and left hanging to a tree, 'with the red sun making a kind of dead sunset on his black face' (254).

The difference between the English and their enemies is powerful enough to supersede all other oppositional forces. Gender lines, for instance, become blurred when faced with overpowering racial opposition. The women under Gill's care are 'as unflinching as the best of tried soldiers' (197) in battle, loading British guns and fighting off the pirates themselves. Similarly, Gill's initial distaste for the leisurely life of the colonists is forgotten amidst the fight, replaced by an overwhelming sense of Englishness. Even fellow soldier, Tom Packer – a man who has sworn revenge on the tyrannical Serjeant Drooce – comes to the latter's aid when under attack, filling Gill with 'inexpressible joy' (202). As both Eric Hobsbawm and Patrick Brantlinger have noted, imperialism functions to reorganize social distinctions in regard to a colonized other, thus defusing metropolitan social tension. Hobsbawm writes, 'imperialism encouraged the masses, and especially the potentially discontented, to identify with the imperial state and nation, and thus unconsciously to endow the social and political system represented by that state with justification and legitimacy' (70).[12] This identification operates in 'Perils', as Lillian Nayder has perceptively shown, as class distinctions are absorbed into the racial binary of imperialism, only to reappear when the characters leave the imperial lands.[13] Gill, after all, cannot marry Miss Maryon, 'I knew well that she was as high above my reach as the sky over my head' (255). The temporary eradication of class difference is thrown into relief by the fact that the real (rather than simply imagined or potential) threat faced by the colonists and the soldiers is, after all, an economic one. Piracy is above all else an economic crime, and part of its transgressive nature stems from the fact that the pirate ignores any economic order at all as he seeks his own ends, as Hans Turley has shown.[14] The presence of the pirates thus plunges the existing class order into chaos as all economic bets are off, and only once that threat is eliminated is order restored, as Gill notes upon the party's escape from the pirates: 'I said to myself, it was a very different kind of voyage now, from what it had been; and I fell into my proper place and station among my fellow-soldiers' (251). The imperial experience and the threats it encounters generate an overwhelming binary opposition of otherness, which economizes national power by limiting internal conflict; Gill and the other Englishmen congeal into a unified extension of British power despite their gender and class differences, but only so long as they are under threat.

The overdetermining dichotomy is most rigidly enforced by Gill's compatriot, Harry Charker, whom Gill characterizes as 'one of the best of men', and for whom every situation can be boiled down to oppositional forces: 'As soon as he had brought a thing round to what it was not, he was satisfied' (176). Dickens uses

---

[12] See also Brantlinger, 35.
[13] See Nayder, 'Class Consciousness' and Nayder, *Unequal Partners*, 100–28.
[14] See Turley, 41–2.

Charker to initiate his criticism of the bureaucratic governing powers in India that have allowed the Mutiny to develop through excessive reliance on intellectual consideration:

> [H]e had always one most excellent idea in his mind. That was, Duty. Upon my soul, I don't believe, though I admire learning beyond everything, that he could have got a better idea out of all the books in the world, if he had learnt them every word, and been the cleverest of scholars. (176)

Charker makes no plans, draws no resolutions, deliberates over nothing: he simply acts, rushing into battle without a moment's hesitation, eventually accepting even his own death heroically, without vacillation (199).

Gill's purported admiration of erudition is inverted by Dickens into a criticism of imperial intellectualism: the men who save the colony are the dutiful, uneducated soldiers like Charker and Gill, in contrast to the resident bureaucrat, Commissioner Pordage, a 'stiff-jointed, high-nosed old gentleman ... of a very yellow complexion' (183) – a parody of 'Clemency Canning'. Mocking Canning's clemency resolution, Dickens has the effete Pordage, always attended by the even more effete Mr Kitten, perpetually requesting pen and paper so that he may write up reports, documents and acts. When confronted with the pirate onslaught, Pordage has to be hustled to safety by Gill and the other soldiers, and afterwards he tries to write a proclamation asking the Pirates to lay down their arms (196). Pordage stands in for the entire pre-Mutiny system of governance in British India as Dickens saw it; flaccid, overwrought, indecisive and overeducated in all the wrong ways, he is the type of man who nearly lost Britain the empire, who, as Dickens said, 'knew nothing of the Hindoo character' (*Letters* 8:472–3); knew nothing, one supposes, of the distinct and irreducible otherness and inferiority of the Indians or their pirate surrogates. Dickens's use of Pordage to criticize imperial bureaucracy and inaction dovetails most tellingly with his invocation of the discourse of rape as an ideological pole from which British power can operate.

Rape is unspeakable and almost unimaginable – 'Those villains had done such deeds in those seas as never can be told in writing, and can scarcely be so much as thought of' (194), Gill tells us about the pirates – and the spectre of it drives the actions of the noble British soldiers, who are bound by duty to do anything they can to protect the sanctity of their women. Commensurate with Sharpe's ideas about the signification of silence in the rape discourse, never once is rape mentioned. Instead we see the soldiers motivating themselves with allusions to the violation of domestic purity: 'The word among our men is "Women and children!"' (194). The dutiful Charker goes to his certain death because he cannot bear the thought of female endangerment: '"Look at these ladies and children, sir!" says Charker. "I'd sooner *light myself,* than not try any chance to save them." We gave him a Hurrah!' (198). Upon receiving misinformation from King that there are pirates on the island, a scouting party sets out to meet them. Before doing so, however, there occurs a very long exchange between Captain Carton and Pordage that is worth examining in some detail as it exemplifies the constellation of the major post-Mutiny imperial ideologies and anxieties expressed by Dickens:

> 'Sir,' says Commissioner Pordage, 'I trust there is going to be no unnecessary cruelty committed?'
>
> 'Sir,' returns the officer, 'I trust not.'
>
> 'That is not enough, sir,' cries Commissioner Pordage, getting wroth. 'Captain Carton, I give you notice. Government requires you to treat the enemy with great delicacy, consideration, clemency and forebearance.'
>
> 'Sir,' says Captain Carton, 'I am an English Officer, commanding English Men, and I hope I am not likely to disappoint the Government's just expectations. But, I presume you know that these villains under their black flag have despoiled our countrymen of their property, burnt their homes, barbarously murdered them and their little children, and worse than murdered their wives and daughters?'
>
> 'Perhaps I do, Captain Carton,' answers Pordage, waving his hand, with dignity; 'perhaps I do not. It is not customary, sir, for Government to commit itself.'
>
> 'It matters very little, Mr Pordage, whether or no. Believing that I hold my commission by the allowance of God, and not that I have received it direct from the Devil, I shall certainly use it, with all avoidance of unnecessary suffering and with all merciful swiftness of execution, to exterminate these people from the face of the earth. Let me recommend you to go home, sir, and to keep out of the night air. (190–91)

Carton's Englishness precludes him from challenging Pordage's authority, but it simultaneously impels him to avenge his countrymen. Clemency, then, is irrelevant next to the commands of nationality. Dickens's criticism of bureaucratic government is made blatant here, as the absurd Pordage refuses to even admit knowledge of commonly known facts. Just as the stories about Indian atrocities during the Mutiny were accepted by most as beyond doubt, there is no room for questioning Carton's tales of piratical murder and pillaging: Pordage's is the closest to an oppositional voice we hear, and Dickens makes it clear that anything he says must be untrue. Most importantly, however, Dickens introduces the rape of British women as the motivating force behind violent retribution; in the litany of crimes committed by the pirates, rape is worse, even, than infanticide. Pirates are outlaws, of course, and a major part of the danger they represent is sexual – they were not imagined to abide by the rules and conventions that governed ordinary conduct between the sexes, and their inherent masculinity makes it easy to imagine them as sexual predators. Rape generates such a panic among the British that Miss Maryon asks Gill to kill her if the pirates try to capture her: 'And if you cannot save me from the pirates, living, you will save me, dead. Tell me so' (196). As Dickens ends his narrative, the Pirate Captain has rounded up all of the women into his own boat, draping the pall of imminent rape across the page as he hands the tale over to Collins (203). The threat the pirates represent is real and deeply felt by Dickens;

they embody sexual danger, economic chaos and radical racial otherness, and the only just response to such people is to be rid of them.

Collins and the Empire

Collins's first move upon beginning his narrative is to dissolve the discourse of rape that Dickens invokes, replacing it with an equally unspeakable, piratical act – sodomy.[15] Collins displaces the Pirate Captain's sexual predation by queering him; any threat to British women is negated by the Pirate Captain's implied homosexuality: Not only is the 'little, active, weazen' Captain 'dressed in the brightest colours and the finest clothes', but he actually out-feminizes the women: 'When the dance was given at the Island, I saw no such lace on any lady's dress there as I saw on his cravat and ruffles' (204). The Pirate Captain's flamboyant dress, excessive jewellery and accented shawl are topped off by a violent mark of feminization, 'a blue scar running all across' his cheek, an emasculating gash which renders him ostensibly emasculated: 'Judging by appearances, [he was] the very last man I should have picked out as likely to fill a place of power among any body of men' (204). This is in contrast to Dickens's version of the pirate, who knocks Gill to the ground with his cutlass (202–3). Much like Dickens's Uriah Heep, there is an air of masturbatory unease around the Pirate Captain, who is perpetually stuffing 'his hands in his pockets, smoking a cigar' (204). In a moment charged with both the Pirate Captain's femininity and an air of sexual servitude on the part of his men, the delicate leader writes a hostage letter to the misdirected party of soldiers:

> 'Something to write on,' says the Pirate Captain. 'What? Ha! why not a broad nigger back?'
>
> He pointed with the end of his cigar to one of the Sambos. The man was pulled forward, and set down on his knees with his shoulders rounded. The Pirate Captain laid the paper on them, and took a dip of ink – then suddenly turned up his snub-nose with a look of disgust, and, removing the paper again, took from his pocket a fine cambric handkerchief edged with lace, smelt at the scent on it, and afterwards laid it delicately over the Sambo's shoulders. (205)

This suggestion of homoerotic relations between the Pirate Captain and his men, indicated by both the Captain's phallic appraisal of the 'sambo' and the

---

[15]   The connections between piracy and sodomy are explored at length in the context of seventeenth- and eighteenth-century writing in Turley's *Rum, Sodomy, and the Lash*. While Turley is particularly interested in the representation of pirates as ambiguous heroes – which very much does not occur in 'Perils', where there is no admiration for the pirates at all – his point that there are strong parallels between 'the piratical subject and the sodomitical subject' is certainly tenable here (41).

latter's assumption of submission, rapidly extends to the English men, whom the Pirate Captain decrees will remain alive for unspecified purposes: 'They [the captives] will be taken up the country, with fourteen men prisoners (whose lives the Buccaniers have private reasons of their own for preserving)' (207). This induces a moment of homosexual panic on Gill's part: 'I wondered then, as I had wondered once or twice already, what those private reasons might be, which he had mentioned in his written paper, for sparing the lives of us male prisoners. I hoped he would refer to them now – but I was disappointed' (212). Both the essential characteristic of the discourse of rape – the unmentionable nature of the crime itself – and the sexual ambivalence associated with pirates allow Collins to redirect the anxiety of heterosexual rape and thus to dampen the motivation that so ignited Captain Carton in Dickens's initial section. If it is men these pirates are after, instead of women, then Carton's belief that the Englishmen are obligated 'to exterminate these people from the face of the earth' (191) is no longer so compelling.

The homoerotics of captivity override the terror implicit in the discourse of rape to such an extent that the trip from settlement into the forest becomes, for the British at least, comic. The Pirate Captain's ridiculously effeminate habits become the topic of conversation for the soldiers:

> 'I can stand a good deal,' whispers Tom Packer to me, looking hard at the [Pirate Captain's] guitar; 'but con-found me, Davis, if it's not a trifle too much to be taken prisoner by such a fellow as that!'
> The Pirate Captain lights another cigar.
> 'March!' says he, with a screech like a cat, and a flourish with his sword, of the sort that a stage-player would give at the head of a mock army. (213)

Later, when the Pirate Captain, decked out 'in a languishing attitude, with a nosegay in the bosom of his waistcoat', begins to play his guitar, Gill has to restrain the men from openly laughing at him (215). Although the Pirate Captain may be holding the thread of the Britons' lives, they cannot take him seriously, for his tendency to 'thumb his nose at any conventions' (40), as Hans Turley says of the pirate, is so great that he is reduced to a sexually ambiguous comic figure. The Pirate Captain has become a sort of exaggerated dandy, so caught up in his own pleasures that other men cease to recognize him as one of their own. Even the men of the pirate gang begin to take on decidedly un-masculine characteristics, as Collins discusses them lounging among flowers, not only linking them with femininity but pointing out the ridiculousness of the situation:

> It was a sight not easily described, to see niggers, savages, and Pirates, hideous, filthy, and ferocious to the last degree to look at, squatting about grimly upon a natural carpet of beauty, of the sort that is painted in pictures with pretty fairies dancing on it. (215).

Gone, then, are the intimations of rape, not merely ignored, but replaced and negated by the comic homosexualization of the supposed attackers. The discourse of rape that Dickens created has become de-articulated, collapsed by Collins to the point where all vestiges of terror are gone, a farce put in their place. The very ambiguity that made the pirates dangerous in Dickens's eyes – they might not observe the rules of sexual propriety regarding women – is taken by Collins to an extreme end. So sexually ambiguous are these pirates that they are not any threat at all to the women, Collins suggests – being pirates – they are perhaps more interested in the men.

The displacement of terror – the replacement of its objects and subjects – becomes a key element in Collins's critique of Dickens's narrative and the imperial ideologies it represents. Quickly it is apparent that the captives will not be treated poorly: the Pirate Captain orders them to be freed from their restraints, gives them good meat and sends his own men into the thick woods to gather water. From the outset of the march, the captives are joking with one another, as well as laying the grounds for future emotional bonds: As Short, one of the sailors, carries a young girl along the way, Collins narrates, "'I expect you'll marry me, my darling, when you grow up," says he, in his oily, joking voice. And the poor child, in her innocence, laid her weary head down on his shoulder, and gravely and faithfully promised that she would' (214). Camaraderie extends even to the pirates; Gill experiences a transcendent moment when the party lays down to sleep at night, seeing them all – captives and pirates alike – under the same blanket sky:

> Our sleeping arrangements, though we had not a single civilized comfort, were, thanks to the flowers, simple and easy enough. For the first time in their lives, the women and children laid down together, with the sky for a roof, and the kind earth for a bed. We men shook ourselves down, as well as we could, all around them; and the Pirates, relieving guard regularly, ranged themselves outside of all. In that tropical climate, and at that hot time, the night was only pleasantly cool. The bubbling of the stream, and, now and then, the course of the breeze through the flowers, was all we heard. (216)

As the party moves ever deeper into the forest, the nights become increasingly loud and frightening, with crashing trees and howling winds as the backdrop for sleep. Fear and anxiety link the captives with the pirates, just as the warm night held them contentedly together earlier: 'The children shuddered with fear; even the Pirate Captain forgot, for the first time, to jingle his eternal guitar' (217). The forest Collins describes is a racial nepenthe, eliding the division between the pirates and their captives, and thus counteracting Brantlinger's claim that the 'reductive, racist fantasy patterns' of Mutiny writings 'shape a literature antithetical to sympathy' (222). When the party finally emerges into a clearing, Collins reduces the severity of their captivity by reminding readers of the prisoners' essential, irrevocable freedom: 'Prisoners as we were, there was a feeling of freedom on stepping into the light again, and on looking up, without interruption, into the clear blue heaven, from which no human creature can keep any other human creature' (219). The post-Mutiny racial essentializing that Dickens enacts is unwound: binaries blur, oppositions break down, terror is ejected and peaceful and unifying emotions flow together as the captives and pirates enter the lost city of a past empire.

Just as Dickens's use of the discourse of rape and essentialism is undermined by Collins, so too is his criticism of imperial bureaucracy and intellectualism. Pordage, whom Dickens has such great sport in ridiculing, continues to make outrageous statements at the tip of Collins's pen, but does so in a markedly different way. The shock of the encounter with the pirates, Collins tells us, leaves Pordage insane, therefore unaccountable and incomprehensible:

> What with the fright he had suffered, the danger he had gone through, and the bewilderment of finding himself torn away from his safe Government moorings, his poor unfortunate brains seemed to be as completely disposed as his Diplomatic coat. He was perfectly harmless and quiet, but also perfectly light-headed –as anybody could discover who looked at his dazed eyes or listened to his maundering talk. (210)

No longer the threat to Englishness that he was just before the party set out to find the pirates, Collins's Pordage is 'perfectly harmless', a babbling invalid who needs constant care and reassurance. By having the pirates reduce Pordage to insanity, Collins absolves him of responsibility and makes it apparent to the reader that his bizarre speech is not to be taken seriously. Tellingly, in the final section of 'Perils', Dickens restores Pordage to sanity but continues to have him issue proclamations, protests, and documents, thus reviving his earlier critique of the effete and useless bureaucrat (251). Pordage, Dickens tells us, received 'great compliments at home for his conduct on these trying occasions', but dies of the same cowardice that plagued him on the island – 'yellow jaundice' (251).

Collins's counter-critique of Dickens's take on imperial leadership and policy takes more overt form with respect to Mr Kitten, who is the unlikely hero of Collins's narrative, showing the other prisoners how to draw a sleep-inducing narcotic out of a plant in order to drug the pirates and make their escape (232–4). The clear-headed Kitten, one of 'the sharpest of our fellow-prisoners' (231) in Collins's narrative, is returned by Dickens in the final section to the role of glorified secretary to Commissioner Pordage (251). Perhaps the most overt criticism of imperial policies on Collins's part occurs when a group of the captives are taken into the forest to cut down trees for thatching on the roofs of the ruined buildings in the ancient city. Here Collins throws the racial politics of imperial labour exploitation into high relief, as the native, Christian George King, gets to oversee the work of the colonizers:

> Christian George King tumbled himself down on the grass, and kicked up his ugly heels in convulsions of delight.
> 'Oh, golly, golly, golly!' says he. 'You dam English do work, and Christian George King look on. Yup, Sojeer! whack at them tree!' (229)

Though Collins does not see this reversal as a good thing, it nevertheless has the effect of reminding readers of the fundamentally exploitative nature of empire and shows that while Collins's labour was for hire, his politics were not. His substitution of the pirate plot for the actual affairs of the Mutiny, coupled with his representations of the pirates themselves and their effects on British men and women, enabled him to challenge and even undermine the feelings and politics that led Dickens to propose the story in the first place. By making shrewd use of the morally and sexually ambiguous nature of pirates and piracy, Collins was able to reduce the threat that they – and thus their Indian counterparts – represented to British interests and actual Britons. The moral ambiguities of piracy, of course, are not all that different from the moral ambiguities of empire, and while Collins was unable to turn the tables so far that the connection between the plunder of the colonists and the plunder of the pirates became overt, he was able to eradicate some of the difference and distance that Dickens had put between the two parties. Unfortunately, British resistance to the imperial project like the kind offered by Collins was in short supply in the decades following the Mutiny, and the naturalization of imperialism that occurred in subsequent years reveals by contrast the few thinkers who had the foresight to wonder who the pirates in this story really were.

Chapter 10

Pirates for Boys: Masculinity and Degeneracy in R.M. Ballantyne's Adventure Novels

Grace Moore

'I would not give tuppence for a man of books, if he had nothing else in him.' (28)
'I say, Jack, you're a Briton – the best fellow I ever met in my life!' (29)
R.M. Ballantyne, The Coral Island (1857)

By the middle of the nineteenth century, the pirate had largely become, for British readers, a mythological figure. While piracy might be a threat to imperial traders on distant waters, it was no longer regarded as a serious danger to British shores. It is curious, then, that as real-life piracy was, if not in decline, then at least less visible, the number of fictional pirates increased markedly. The pirate became the subject of sentimental nostalgia and by the end of the century it was almost de rigueur for pirates to feature somewhere in the boys' adventure story. This omnipresence may, of course, be partially explained by the popularity of the Byronic corsair that Deborah Lutz outlines in Chapter 2, but the cursing, brawling pirates of the stories for boys were often a world away from Byron's brooding, sensitive intellectual.

One of the most influential writers of the story for boys, R.M. Ballantyne, wrote a number of novels featuring pirates and, as Stuart Hannabuss points out, his prolific output made him 'a considerable influence on boys, young men and men' (54) of the latter half of the nineteenth century. The pirate occupies a curious position in Ballantyne's writing and, focusing on *The Coral Island* (1857) and *The Madman and the Pirate* (1883), this chapter will examine his role in narratives that were closely aligned with the moulding of young men's characters and the drive for imperial conquest.[1] In particular, I shall focus on representations of the pirate as

---

[1]   Ballantyne's pirates were an important source for Robert Louis Stevenson, as he registers in his address to the 'Hesitating Purchaser' that appears at the beginning of *Treasure Island* (1883), in which he locates his pirates (and himself) as part of a broader literary tradition:

>   If studious youth no longer crave,
>   His ancient appetite forgot,
>   Kingston, or Ballantyne the brave,

degenerate, along with depictions of men who were only half-heartedly committed to a life of buccaneering. Unswayed by portraits of the pirate as a glamorous bohemian, Ballantyne viewed him as an unruly threat to the moral order. I shall therefore argue that, writing against the grain, he deployed his ungainly pirates as a warning to young male readers of the dangers of succumbing to baser instincts and a reminder of the need for rigid moral standards at all times.

R.M. Ballantyne was in many ways a pioneering figure in the transformation of the adventure story from a penny dreadful to the type of volume routinely awarded as a school prize for good conduct.[2] Ballantyne's biographer, Eric Quayle, has remarked that 'for the first time in the annals of English juvenile literature, youngsters were able to identify themselves with the heroes of the tales they were reading' (37); thus adventure stories were frequently deployed to exemplify desirable traits of the young English male and to cultivate them in young, impressionable readers. Patrick Howarth has argued that so popular were Ballantyne's novels that they formed an 'effective counterweight' (37) to the notorious penny blood crime stories and I would extend this suggestion to argue that they also worked to counter the romanticization of the pirate. Although Quayle overstates the case, in that he seems to suggest that Ballantyne single-handedly drew the youth of England back from the abyss, he is right to highlight Ballantyne's part in helping the colonial adventure to achieve respectability, along with its role in shaping the minds of a new generation of imperial pioneers. Readers were drawn to tales of nautical adventures and piracy, but through careful narrative direction, they would be brought to reject the amorality of the charismatic pirate villains in favour of the diligent, principled behaviour of Ballantyne's youthful Christians.

Kevin Carpenter has drawn attention to the complexity of the pirate's role in Victorian adventure narratives, noting a shift in the 'island story' around the 1850s. Publishers of juvenile fiction sought to assert their respectability, moving away from celebrating the pirate's swashbuckling adventures and marginalizing him as a villain rather than a hero. As Carpenter notes, 'It became increasingly difficult, in view of the severe criticisms levelled at the "penny dreadful" around mid-century, to justify stories wound round the escapades of thorough villains'

Or Cooper of the wood and wave:
So be it, also! And may I
And all my pirates share the grave
Where these and their creations lie! (7)

[2]   For a discussion of books as prizes in the late nineteenth century see Gillian Avery 'The Manly Boy, 1800–1914' in Gillian Avery, *Childhood's Pattern: A Study of the Heroes and Heroines of Children's Fiction 1770–1950* (London: Hodder and Stoughton, 1975). As Avery notes, Ballantyne's works were a firm favourite of Charlotte M. Yonge, who listed them in her *What Books to Give and What to Lend*, along with *Robinson Crusoe* and *Treasure Island*.

(74). Nevertheless, the pirate was a popular feature and while his role needed to be curbed, there was no reason to banish him altogether. As Carpenter puts it:

> There had to be other ways of getting round the problem of introducing pirates as characters, but not encouraging glamorization of their lives. Perhaps all the old props could be retained if the pirate were no longer the *main* character. The boy-hero, well-established in juvenile fiction by then, could pit his daring against the pirate-villain and come off with flying colours. (75).

The pirate was therefore reinvented for the Victorians, just as the fictional criminal had been at the beginning of the nineteenth century to showcase the skills of the detective, and Ballantyne played a key role in this reshaping. Like the criminal, the pirate could remain part of the narrative, but only on sufferance, as an exemplar of the debauchery spurned by the truly heroic boy who was always ready to pit his physical and intellectual prowess against the depraved sea dog.[3]

Ballantyne's views on boyhood as a type of trial or test of character are well known and he is frequently aligned with writers like Thomas Hughes, Henry Newbolt and Charles Kingsley, known for their fervent advocacy of muscular Christianity. He believed firmly that boys should be educated to become responsible citizens and that fiction should play an important part in helping to form the well-rounded upholder of British imperial values. As Hannabuss notes, adventure stories for boys became part of an emerging 'tradition of self-help and self-improvement' and Ballantyne devised a tried and true formula that shaped all of his adventure narratives and their youthful, but manly, protagonists:

> [T]he central narrative thread was the episodic and often picaresque adventure of a tenderfoot hero, whose manly courage and good moral sense, coupled with much coincidence and occasional authorial intervention, took him safely through a series of adventures, usually pitted against overtly characterised enemies, usually assisted by obviously good men like missionaries and whimsical (and, by modern standards racist or paternalistic) caricatures of Irish, black or other personalities. (55)[4]

---

[3]   The movement to a capitalist economy had seen the demise of lovable rogues like Moll Flanders, Dick Turpin and Robin Hood, and a growing emphasis on the detective as a hero able to solve puzzles and restore order within an increasingly chaotic society. See, for instance, Stephen Knight, *Crime Fiction 1800–2000: Detection, Death, Diversity* (Basingstoke: Palgrave, 2004).

[4]   Notwithstanding his use of stereotypes that leave the modern-day reader feeling less than comfortable, Ballantyne's views on race are, as I shall discuss later in this chapter, much more complicated than Hannabuss suggests here; and mixed in with his gruesome depictions of South Sea island cannibalism are denunciations of slavery and attacks on white traders who patronize or exploit 'native' peoples.

While the format may have been comfortingly predictable to the nineteenth-century boy reader, Ballantyne viewed these physical and mental challenges as an essential mode of developing heroism and bravery, and generally strengthening the masculine character. As the narrator of *The Gorilla Hunters* (1861) famously expresses it:

> I also reflected, and not without a feeling of shame, on my want of nerve, and was deeply impressed with the importance of boys being inured from childhood to trifling risks and light dangers of every possible description, such as tumbling into ponds and off trees, etcetera, in order to strengthen their nervous system. I do not, of course, mean to say that boys ought deliberately to tumble into ponds or climb trees until they fall off; but they ought not to avoid the risk of such mishaps. They ought to encounter such risks and many others perpetually. They ought to practise leaping off heights into deep water. They ought never to hesitate to cross a stream on a narrow unsafe plank *for fear of a ducking.* They ought never to decline to climb up a tree to pull fruit merely because there is a *possibility* of their falling off and breaking their necks. I firmly believe that boys were intended to encounter all kinds of risks, in order to prepare them to meet and grapple with the risks and dangers incident to man's career with cool, cautious self-possession – a self-possession founded on experimental knowledge of the character and powers of their own spirits and muscles. (42)[5]

Ballantyne tried to live his own life in the manner of one of his boy heroes, spending his early adult years in Canada as an employee of the Hudson's Bay Company and enduring the physical hardship of life on the frontier. These experiences were, of course, to feed into his depictions of young men developing 'character' in response to physical and emotional challenges; and, as Patrick Howarth has commented, Ballantyne was deeply committed to verisimilitude and exposed himself to a number of the challenges endured by his characters:

> In order to ensure that his treatment of the subject was authentic he stayed aboard a lightvessel for seven days, during which he was continually seasick, and later he had a fortnight of seasickness aboard a trawler when preparing to write a book about the work of the Mission to Deep Sea Fisherman. (44)

For Ballantyne, then, authenticity was essential and his ability to withstand the types of challenges he meted out to his boy heroes was bound up with his sense of authorial integrity. Ballantyne's boys did not only undergo physical ordeals, however; their adventures also involved resisting temptation and often

---

[5]   The narrator goes on to suggest that girls should also be trained to take risks and to respond positively to danger, although the suggestion that they may be exposed to burning crinolines points to trials that may be more closely aligned with the domestic.

these character tests took the form of inducements to abandon English values and standards of 'civilization'. As Bruce Haley has noted,

> [T]he world of the adventure story is so vast and variable, so impossible to grasp as a whole, that a young man must provision himself with self-cultivated values and talents before he enters it. Physically and morally he is on his own, and, since the highest morality is quick action, to a large extent his physical health becomes his moral health. (160)

This interplay between physical and moral vigour is crucial to the development of character in Ballantyne's world and, importantly, it is antithetical to the slovenly conduct and appearance of the pirates who appear in so many of his works. While not always the most obviously dangerous figures in the novels, the pirates frequently signify European civilization gone wrong and as such, they are figures to be feared.

Ballantyne draws heavily on discourses of degeneration in his descriptions of pirates.[6] The pirate captain who kidnaps Ralph in *The Coral Island* is described as 'a white man – that is to say, he was a man of European blood, though his face, from long exposure to the weather, was deeply bronzed' (148); and in detailing his captor's appearance, Ralph dwells on the hybridity of his dress, with his Greek skull cap, heavy silk shawl and visible weaponry. The rest of the band of brigands have their villainy stamped upon their countenances with their 'shaggy beards and scowling brows' and 'mean, rascally expression(s)' (149). Equally, Redford – who becomes first mate to the unfortunate mutineer, Richard Rosco, in *The Madman and the Pirate* – is notable for his 'coarse nature', 'laxity in discipline' (14) and generally unprepossessing demeanour. Thus, these pirates may have begun life as Europeans, but their sunburned faces, curious dress and blatantly evil aspects point to a degeneracy that the boy heroes must work hard to avoid.[7]

---

[6] Although Max Nordau did not publish his lengthy study of degeneracy until 1892, the concept was a familiar one to the mid-Victorians, as is evidenced by debates stimulated by the publication of *On the Origin of Species*. In 1861, for instance, *The Lancet* published a sequence of letters responding to an article on 'The Degeneration of Race' and although most of the debate revolves around inbreeding, it demonstrates a growing concern with atavism, latency and the role that genetics plays in determining character. Jenny Bourne Taylor has written of the role that sensation fiction played in stimulating debates about degeneracy in the 1860s (Jenny Bourne Taylor, *In the Secret Theatre of Home: Wilkie Collins, Sensation Narrative and Nineteenth-Century Psychology* (London: Routledge, 1988)), while Andrew Maunder's essay on Ellen Wood, '"Step-children of Nature": *East Lynne* and the Spectre of Female Degeneracy, 1860–1861' (*Victorian Crime, Madness and Sensation*. Eds Andrew Maunder and Grace Moore (Aldershot and Burlington, VT: Ashgate, 2004), 59–72), offers a useful survey of the 'panic' surrounding discourses of degeneracy.

[7] The pirate captain is remarkable only insofar as he displays a slight physical superiority to his unpleasant crew, otherwise he too is represented in terms that point to his

While the story of three boys cast adrift to fend for themselves on a coral island paradise is well known, *The Madman and the Pirate* is less widely read, but revisits a number of concerns from the earlier novel, presenting a pirate with much more psychological depth than the swaggering villains of *The Coral Island*. Against a backdrop of missionary activity and the conversion of 'natives', Antonio Zeppa and his son Orlando board a ship without feeling entirely certain of the captain's integrity.[8] Before long, the ill-tempered captain is overthrown by the hasty behaviour of Rosco, the first mate, who finds himself transformed into a pirate through his rash conduct. Unable to control his crew, Rosco believes that Orlando has been killed, having been thrown overboard by the unruly pirates. On hearing the news, Zeppa instantly falls into a state of 'mania' and is left to fend for himself on a remote island, vowing death to Rosco should they ever meet again. A strong swimmer, Orlando does not in fact die, but is saved by a 'savage'. He is eventually reunited with his father, who has degenerated both physically and mentally, but who is restored to health on seeing his son once again. Through a series of coincidences, Rosco is also involved in this reunion, having grown increasingly doubtful of his suitability for a pirate life and placed himself in exile. Zeppa rescues Rosco from a hostile group of islanders who have tried to burn him at the stake. The terror of the burning purges Rosco, who is subsequently referred to by the narrator as an 'ex-pirate', and we learn that 'the ruin of his body had been the saving of his soul' (120).[9] Having been sworn enemies, pirate

---

descent from civilized values:

> Although the captain was the tallest and most powerful man in the ship, he did not strikingly excel many of his men in this respect; and the only difference that an ordinary observer would have noticed was a certain degree of open candour, straightforward daring, in the bold, ferocious expression of his face, which rendered him less repulsive than his low-browed associates, but did not by any means induce the belief that he was a hero. This look was, however, the indication of that spirit which gave him the pre-eminence among the crew of desperadoes who called him captain. He was a lion-like villain, totally devoid of personal fear, and utterly reckless of consequences, and therefore a terror to his men, who individually hated him, but unitedly felt it to be to their advantage to have him at their head. (151)

[8]　Ballantyne's *The Pirate City* (1874) also involves characters boarding a vessel yet harbouring doubts about its captain's trustworthiness. Evil though these pirates are, they spend little time on the water, and most of the narrative takes place in the politically turbulent city of Algiers. This curious story attacks slavery through depicting enslaved Europeans, and also involves a positive portrait of a Jew, whose kindness and resourcefulness forces the characters to abandon their prejudices. The depictions of the Muslim 'pirates', however, are less enlightened and for the most part tap into contemporary stereotypes surrounding Eastern despotism.

[9]　It is a curious irony that having renounced piracy, Rosco takes on the appearance of a pirate since his legs must be amputated after he has been rescued. He ends the story hobbling about on a pair of wooden legs.

and madman are reconciled to each other and the novel ends in a celebration of community and godliness that is characteristic of the strong Christian inflection to all of Ballantyne's novels.

For the characters in *The Coral Island*, survival is inextricably bound to a strong work ethic and rigorous discipline, and idleness is associated with decline. In spite of the island's seductions, the castaway boys conform to the Robinsonade tradition, developing building projects for themselves and mapping the island. Ralph, the narrator, offers regular interjections for the reader on the value of hard work and particularly admires a colony of penguins for their 'regularity and order' (121). When the boys encounter a group of 'savages' they are represented as strikingly other; and while they are appalled by the scenes of murder and cannibalism that they witness, there is no danger that they will be enticed into 'going native' in the manner of later characters like Joseph Conrad's Mr Kurtz. The less aggressive members of 'native' tribes are presented as candidates for conversion to Christianity and by the narrative's close the 'good' natives have burned their idols and converted to Christianity, while the boys prepare to return to 'dear old England!' (245).

The boys of *The Coral Island* may not actively contemplate joining the South Sea islanders and adopting their customs, yet their interactions with the novel's true villains, the band of pirates who appear mid-way through the narrative, present a more ambiguous danger. Joseph Bristow has suggested parallels between Ralph, Jack and Peterkin and the pirates who threaten their island retreat, arguing that 'This island story ... allows the boys to get as close as possible to being both pirates (defiant, daring, individualistic) and savages (survivors taming nature) but without turning into them. Both of these contemptible groups are, metaphorically speaking, the boys' "countrymen"' (107). Patrick Brantlinger usefully extends this idea, reminding us that in 'imperial Gothic white men do not always rise to the top – just as they often sink into savagedom, cowardice, or exotic torpor' (239). Bristow's alignment of the pirates with the 'savages' is important in terms of the steps that Ballantyne takes to render them 'other'. I would argue, though, that while the islanders, for the most part, show the potential to develop once they are exposed to European influences, the pirates reveal the true depths to which men can plummet if they resist the order and discipline espoused by the boys.[10] Bristow goes on to assert that 'Pirates are those men who have degenerated from Western models of civilized behaviour and yet ... the boy heroes bear strong resemblances to them' (107).[11] Nevertheless, I would suggest that Ballantyne sets

---

[10]   As Bloody Bill notes, 'we find that whenever the savages take up with Christianity they always give over their cannibalism and are safe to be trusted'. Showing his own distance from civilization, he continues, 'I never cared for Christianity myself ... and I don't well know what it means; but a man with half an eye can see what it does for those black critters' (*The Coral Island* 166).

[11]   Indeed, so strong is the resemblance between the boys and the pirates and the boys and the 'savages' for some readers that William Golding was to use Ballantyne's story as the basis for his horrific 1954 novel *Lord of the Flies*.

up these overlaps so that his characters may ultimately resist the temptations of the pirate life. In short, the pirates are part of the test to which his young heroes must submit in order to prove their true mettle as English gentlemen by rejecting crime and debauchery.

The islanders in *The Madman and the Pirate* bear a remarkable resemblance to those of *The Coral Island*, although while Ralph is happy to bandy around the term 'savage', the omniscient narrator of the later novel is rather more reserved in his use of the word. As in *The Coral Island*, some islanders are represented as irredeemably 'savage', while others covert to Christianity at various stages of the action. Ballantyne's position on race and 'savagery' in *The Madman and the Pirate* is less totalizing, however, and in one memorable scene an islander missionary takes issue with a pompous English captain's classification of native peoples: "'They are not savages," returned Waroonga quietly, "they are God's ignorant children. I have seen worse men than South sea islanders with white faces an' soft clothin' who had not the excuse of ignorance'" (82).

Indeed, the loyal, but unimaginatively named servant 'Ebony' dwells on the English captain's hypocrisy and takes great pleasure in forcing Rosco to evade capture and thus outwit the Queen's navy. Ebony takes several opportunities to rail against English justice and its failure to acknowledge that men can be reformed. As a consequence, the story is a curious amalgam of unthinking racial stereotypes and attempts to undercut readerly expectations regarding 'savages'. What is important, though, is that savagery is lifted out of its racial context and becomes a condition that human beings can choose to inhabit. Thus, by the end of the story the warring factions of islanders have made peace and the narrator reminds us that 'savages come to this condition sometimes – civilised nations never do!' (137). Like Rosco, they have elected to spurn savagery, but the same cannot be said for the pirates who sail away to continue their plundering and who are depicted as atavistic throwbacks, revealing the depths to which the white man can descend when he abandons civilized values.

While the South Sea islanders show man in what Ballantyne would have regarded as a less developed state than the European protagonists, they do not pose a real temptation to the characters in either story. The challenge that the boys must overcome is something much closer to home and, as such, it poses a much greater, but less apparent threat. Both *The Coral Island* and *The Pirate and the Madman* include major characters whose physical and mental vigour is open to question. Peterkin in *The Coral Island* is the weak link in the trio of boys, since he is much more attracted to a life of idleness than his two companions, who are remarkable for their 'unflagging energy' (61). He lacks vigour and tenacity, is described as 'dreadfully reckless' (117) and is frequently placed in danger because he is unable to swim. Younger than either Ralph or Jack, the 13-year-old Peterkin's character is less developed. Although he is easily impressed by his friends' capability, in the novel's early chapters he is constantly seeking to avoid hard work and his endless joking incurs Ralph's 'disapprobation' (97). While Ralph painstakingly outlines the way in which he forces himself to observe things in which he would otherwise have no interest, we learn that Peterkin 'could never let slip an opportunity to joke, however inopportune it might be' (97). Peterkin is so hopelessly impractical that Jack recommends leaving him behind to take care of a cat, while he and Ralph embark on a reconnaissance mission. When Jack declares 'I have been a great reader of books of travel and adventure all my life, and that has put me up to a good many things that you are, perhaps, not acquainted with', Peterkin responds by asserting that it is 'humbug', commenting 'I've seen a lot o' fellows that were always poring over books, and when they came to try to do anything, they were no better than baboons!' (27–8). Jack quietly points that his book-learning combined with practical skills has equipped him with the skills to survive on the island; but this is just one example of Peterkin's youthful exuberance, which is at odds with the strict order maintained by the other two boys. Peterkin's rejection of the type of improving literature penned by writers like his creator shows that he has much to learn about self-discipline and self-improvement; it also suggests that he has the potential to backslide.

Significantly, Peterkin's bravery is tested and confirmed when the pirates arrive on the island and he is forced to dive ten feet into a dark cavern. Retreating from men he fears even more than water, Peterkin is forced to trust in his companions and to literally take the plunge:

> [T]he stern gravity of his marble features, and the tension of his muscles satisfied us that he had fully made up his mind to go through with it. Just as the pirates gained the foot of the rocks … we bent over the sea, and plunged down together head foremost. Peterkin behaved like a hero. (145–6)

Jack compares the experience to being drowned and in this respect the scene is akin to a rebirth for Peterkin. It is not simply the pirates that he is escaping, but everything they stand for. When he leaps into the water, he reveals courage and a faith in his friends that is distinctly at odds with the savagery and selfishness of the pirate crew who are united only by self-interest. Through this single symbolic action he sheds the recklessness that Ballantyne associates with piracy and begins his journey towards a more responsible, Christian manhood.

The titular 'madman' of the later novel, Antonio Zeppa, retreats rapidly into an unstructured world of insanity and exile when he falsely believes his son Orlando to have been killed by pirates. Both of these characters reveal a weakness that is at odds with the rigid work ethic propounded by Ballantyne's narrators and both signal the potential for what by the end of the century would be termed 'degeneration'. Zeppa is mentally weak and, although a Christian, his faith is not strong enough to allow him to reconcile himself to God's will when he fears his son is dead. Rosco is hot-tempered and, although he rejects the bloodiest elements of the pirate life, he remains happy to plunder property as his men spread terror and mayhem. Once he leaves the pirate band it is significant that Rosco develops what is almost a co-dependency with Zeppa, suggesting that by the 1880s Ballantyne had come to equate piracy with insanity. The narrator of *The Madman and the Pirate* draws parallels between the two characters who give the novel its name, indicating that the hot-headed insanity that leads to piracy is not all that different from the mania in which Zeppa languishes after his 'loss'. Rosco thinks to himself 'If you and I were sane, we should not be here', although he does not articulate the feeling and expresses it only with a 'contemptuous curl of his lip' (29). Both characters experience moments when they wish to be dead and both have to re-learn their faith in a higher power. Nowhere is this spiritual need more apparent than in the scene where Rosco contemplates suicide:

> As he bent over the pool he saw his own distorted visage dimly reflected therein, and the thought occurred, – 'Why not end it all at once? Five minutes at the utmost and all will be over!' The pirate was a physically brave man beyond his fellows. He had the courage to carry the idea into effect but – 'after death the judgment!' Where had he heard these words? They were strange to him, but they were not new. (72)

Rosco's face may be distorted because it is reflected in the pool; however, on a figurative level the image reflects a spiritual fragmentation that is emphasized by the distinction between his physical bravery and emotional cowardice. His thoughts here mirror a number of scenes where Zeppa is simply unable to face Orlando's fate and moves between the greatest sorrow, mania and murderous impulses. Together, these two damaged characters point to the dangers of indolence and self-indulgence. As the story unfolds they also develop a co-dependency to the point that they become doubles, as Ballantyne involves them in one another's rehabilitation and uses them to explore degrees of degeneration.

Ballantyne frequently equates piracy with savagery in order to make his disdain for the pirates explicit.[12] When Ralph in *The Coral Island* recounts hiding in a cavern prepared in case of adversity, he comments, 'Little did we imagine that the first savages who would drive us into it would be white savages, perhaps our own countrymen' (146). Later, he describes the horror of being caught between two groups whose values differ wildly from his own:

> I was surrounded on all sides by human beings of the most dreadful character, to whom the shedding of blood was mere pastime. On shore were the natives, whose practices were so horrible that I could not think of them without shuddering. On board were none but men of the blackest dye, who, although not cannibals, were foul murderers, and more blameworthy even than the savages, inasmuch as they knew better. (180)

---

[12]   Ballantyne is certainly not alone in rendering his pirates a race apart. As Garrett Ziegler argues in Chapter 9, Wilkie Collins deliberately racialized the pirates in his chapter of *Perils of Certain English Prisoners* to downplay Dickens's more extreme pronouncements on 'natives'.

The reference to the pirates as 'men of the blackest dye' reveals them to be even more detestable than the 'savages' who know no better and who are open to the possibilities of redemption and conversion. Ralph's disapproval is so evident when he denounces the pirates that it seems to point to an unspoken fear of becoming one of them, or at the very least, it suggests that there are traces of the pirate buried deep within his soul, waiting to be released. Moreover, the pirate captain plays upon these fears when he announces to Ralph, 'Pirate Bill there was just such a fellow as you are, and he's now the biggest cut-throat of us all' (153), then later tries to recruit him as a 'sandalwood trader', pretending that he is not a pirate at all. The captain's attempts to enlist Ralph imply that he sees potential within the young man to be a terrifying buccaneer and indeed, part of Ralph's quest for the remainder of the narrative is to prove to himself that this is not the case.

Not all of Ballantyne's characters are strong-minded when faced with the temptations offered by piracy and some are more disposed to its libertine charms than others. The unruly first mate, Redford, in *The Madman and the Pirate* is explicitly compared to a savage when the narrator describes Rosco's inability to tame him:

> Upwards of three years of Rosco's rule had subdued Redford to the condition of a hypocritical and sly, but by no means a submissive, savage. One or two spurts at the commencement of their career had satisfied the mate, as well as the men, that the only way to overcome Rosco was to take his life; and as Redford had not sufficient courage, and the men no desire, to do that, they pursued their evil courses in comparative harmony. Nevertheless, the pirate captain knew well that the savage Redford was more acceptable to the pirates than himself so he determined to carry out intentions which had been simmering in his brain for some time, and rid the pirate crew of his presence. (63)

Importantly, it is a sign of Rosco's own deficiencies that he is unable to bring Redford to heel. Caught as he is between no longer being a respectable sailor, yet resisting the life of a fully fledged pirate, Rosco is presented as 'miserable and half-hearted' (63) and lacking strength of character. While Redford may be a much more whole-hearted, terrifying pirate, Rosco is also associated with savagery and battles between two sides of his personality for much of the drama. Throughout the novel Rosco is drawn to the 'natives' and frequently imagines abandoning life on the seas in favour of a less complicated island existence. The fact that he wishes to join the islanders paradoxically highlights both his atavistic leanings (he spurns European society) and his potential for redemption. Indeed, unlike his ghastly crew, he is troubled by his conscience and is known even to the British naval captain who wishes to pursue him to the death as an advocate of mercy. Ballantyne shows the pirates in different stages of decline as a way of signalling Rosco's potential to return to a respectable way of life. In so doing, he strips the true pirates of the glamour associated with their profession and shows Rosco wrestling with his conscience, apparently in mortal danger of succumbing to a life of depravity and violence as he is forced to compromise principle after principle. Indeed, it is only by physically removing himself from the crew that he is able to reassert his better qualities and avoid completely degenerating.

Rosco is, in many ways, a deeply unsatisfactory pirate, who exemplifies the dangers of being lulled into a degenerate life on the high seas, and he is what Kevin Carpenter would term a 'reluctant pirate' (76). Ballantyne seems to have been interested in men who give way to temptation and become buccaneers, only to be consumed by regrets, and his boy heroes often play an important role in bringing about their rehabilitation.[13] In *The Coral Island* the character 'Bloody Bill' shows how easily an essentially good man may slide into a life of piracy, only to regret it on his death-bed. Having shown flashes of sympathy and kindness towards Ralph that hint at his better nature, Bill finally admits his accidental piracy and weakness of character:

> Ralph, I've led a terrible life. I've been a sailor since I was a boy, and I've gone from bad to worse ever since I left my father's roof. I've been a pirate three years now. It is true I did not choose the trade, but I was inveigled aboard this schooner and kept here by force till I became reckless and at last joined them. Since that time my hand has been steeped in human blood again and again. Your young heart would grow cold if I – ; but why should I go on? 'Tis of no use, Ralph; my doom is fixed. (194)

Ralph speaks to Bill of redemption and forgiveness, repeating passages from the Bible to him, whilst single-handedly sailing the schooner they have escaped on through a storm that is clearly loaded with symbolism. As Ralph struggles against the wind, so Bill grapples with his faith. The energetic Ralph holds on in adversity and continues to handle the boat even when the decks are drenched. Bill, however, loses hold of the belaying-pin that has been steadying him and dies, having received a blow to the head. Figuratively, the storm functions as a test of spiritual endurance that mirrors the physical challenges that Ralph undergoes as he struggles to keep the vessel afloat. With Bill's death, Ralph is left alone on the seas, but steadies himself by adhering to a routine and reading Captain Cook's memoires until he is miraculously returned to the coral island.

Joseph Bristow has suggested that 'Bloody Bill is there, in part, to demonstrate that the lowest type of white man is infinitely more dignified that the Fijian ever could be' (105), but I would argue that this is not the case. Ballantyne sets up a number of scenes in which he contrasts the conduct of the pirates with that of the islanders, and the boys are always more shocked at the irredeemably dreadful

---

[13]   Carpenter notes that in many stories where pirates are redeemed it is often because the pirate is a long-lost parent or other relative (78). I would argue that Ballantyne too explores the 'blood tie', but only insofar as he examines shared atavistic traits that must be suppressed by heroes who must resist piracy's charms. Gasgoyne in *The Sandalwood Trader* (1865) is another of Ballantyne's 'reluctant pirates' who eventually converts to Christianity.

antics of the white men. Ralph ponders the aftermath of a scene in which the ruthless pirate captain has turned heavy artillery on a group of 500 or 600 islanders, expressing his horror at the 'frightful and wanton slaughter':

> 'And this,' thought I, gazing in horror at the captain, who with a quiet look of indifference, leaned upon the taffrail smoking a cigar and contemplating the fertile green islets as they passed like a lovely picture before our eyes – 'this is the man who favours the missionaries because they are useful to him and can tame the savages better than anyone else can do it!' Then I wondered in my mind whether it were possible for any missionary to tame *him*! (163)

Although not put to the test, it is safe to say that the pirate captain would prove immune to missionary activity and that his soul is irretrievably lost. Having made explicit the savagery that lurks within the pirate, Ballantyne has no further use for him. Thus, in both novels, those who show no inclination to reform simply disappear from the action and, while they are not punished, it is clear to the reader that their conduct is despicable and cannot be tolerated.

The pirate's role, then, is to alert both the boy heroes and boy readers to their own potential to 'reel back into the beast' (Tennyson, *Idylls of the King* l.125). To all appearances the pirate may seem attractive and exotic, but the boys need to learn that pirates are either figures of absolute evil, or they are tortured by doubts and anxieties. In short, they are at odds with English values and their overtures must be resisted. Ballantyne therefore takes pains to distinguish his heroes from those whose weakness has threatened their integrity. For instance, at no point during his escape from the 'island of the savages' (196) and his subsequent efforts to return to his friends does Ralph ever succumb to the doubt or the lack of moral fortitude that characterized the dead pirate. Once Bill dies, he is forgotten almost immediately, in spite of Ralph's compassion for him in his final hours. There is nothing piratical about the course Ralph steers back to the island, and the rigid structure he imposes on his days of lone sailing does not allow for any of the 'reckless' behaviour that brings about Bill's downfall. Allowing himself only three hours of rest each night and feeling 'anxious lest another squall should come' (197), Ralph denies himself even the slightest opportunity for indolence; and it is almost as though he is trying to exorcise Bill's memory through hard work and his battle against the elements. He will not allow himself to even contemplate anything other than a straight course and Ballantyne seems to invite his readers to interpret this rigidly straight sailing symbolically. Ralph's routine and discipline will, as always, be his saviours and he is in no danger of inadvertently sliding into piracy.

Ballantyne returns to the figure of the accidental pirate in *The Madman and the Pirate*. Like Gaskell's Frederick Hale, Rosco appears to become a mutineer and then a pirate in the heat of the moment. However, the narrator shows his degeneration to have been a gradual process that has almost crept up on him:

> Men do not reach the profoundest depths of wickedness at one bound. The descent is always graduated – for there are successive rounds to the ladder of sin – but it

is sometimes awfully sudden. When young Rosco left England he had committed only deeds which men are apt lightly to name the 'follies' of youth. These follies, however, had proved to be terrible leaks through which streams of corruption had flowed in upon his soul. Still, he had no thought of becoming a reckless or heartless man, and would have laughed to scorn any one who should have hinted that he would ever become an outlaw and a pirate. But oppression bore heavily on his hasty, ill-disciplined temper, and now the lowest round of the ladder had been reached. (11)

In spite of his descent, Rosco believes that he can still control his impulses and moderate the degree of his lawlessness, but even in his imagination he still needs to distinguish himself from his men and refuses to admit that he is a pirate. The fact that he had committed 'follies' prior to his departure from England signals that his descent has been a continuum and that giving way to an initial, apparently trivial, weakness has left him vulnerable to his emotions and to the committing of more heinous crimes. Importantly, he refuses to face up to what he has done, failing to take responsibility for his men's actions and believing that he can be a kind of compromise corsair:

Even in this extremity he did not utterly give way. He would not become an out-and-out pirate. He would merely go forth as a plunderer to revenge himself on the world which had used him so ill. He would rob – but he would not kill; except of course in self-defence, or when men refused to give up what he demanded. He would temper retributive justice with mercy, and would not suffer injury to women or children. In short, he would become a semi-honourable, high-minded sort of pirate, pursuing wealth without bloodshed! (11)

As Ballantyne shows, this path is an impossible one and Rosco lacks both control and respect. He must therefore make a choice, either to embrace his villainy or to repent his sins and begin anew.

The doctor and social critic Max Nordau distinguished in his 1892 work *Degeneration* between types of degenerates, suggesting that although some could be redeemed, others were doomed, and noting that 'these misguided ones we may hope to lead back to right paths' (551). While Redford and the pirate captain who kidnaps Ralph are clearly not open to the idea of reform, Ballantyne's interest lies in the pirate who can be reclaimed. These figures fulfil two roles in the novels: on the one hand they demonstrate how easily a weak character can lose sight of his duty as a Christian and fall prey to vice. On the other, particularly in Rosco's case, they show that it is never too late to repent. The accidental pirates therefore act as mid-points of degeneracy, warning impressionable boys against sliding into a life of violent sensuality and pointing to a shared atavistic proclivity that needed to be suppressed at all costs. Thus, while writers like Stevenson and Barrie continued the romanticization of the pirate initiated by Scott and Byron, Ballantyne worked against the tide to demonize him and to remind his readers that piracy and heroism would always be at odds with one another. For Ballantyne, the true boy hero would always be able to resist his inner pirate, weathering the storms of adolescence through self-discipline and moral strength and ignoring the allure of a misleadingly simple life of adventure.

Chapter 11

Piracy, Race and Domestic Peril in
Hard Cash

Sean Grass

With no parrots, peg legs or buried treasure to recommend it, Charles Reade's
Hard Cash (1863) is no conventional pirate story. On the contrary, it is a Victorian
sensation novel and contains all of the accoutrements typical of the genre: adultery,
crime, insanity, some mystery, an obsession with money and – as happens so often
with Reade – a graphic, even hysterical social exposé, in this case, of England's
private asylums and the dangerously pliable lunacy laws that delivered patients
into their clutches. But in Chapter VIII as sea-captain David Dodd sails back from
China bearing his life's savings (the novel's 'hard cash'), his ship is beset suddenly
and fiercely by pirates: a 'wild crew of yellow Malays, black chinless Papuans,
and bronzed Portuguese, [who] served their side guns, twelve-pounders, well and
with ferocious cries; [while] the white Britons … replied with loud undaunted
cheers, and deadly hail of grape' (164). This is the novel's only explicit rendering
of pirates, and it reads not only as a conflict between brutal marauders and valorous
tars but also as one drawn along clear racial lines. Piracy, the scene suggests, is
an explicitly racial peril, an outrage committed against 'white Britons' by dusky
savages at the limits of culture, a threat to English bodies and – perhaps more
important – the spoils of empire.

As I argue here, however, *Hard Cash* offers a more complex vision of piracy
than this, drawing upon literal and symbolic meanings of the term in order to
critique the financial depredation and gross rapacity of mid-Victorian England. In
this sense, its message about race and domestic peril revises the very function of
the pirate story, at least as that function was conceived by other Victorian writers.
Through ingenuity and steely British resolve, Dodd and his crew repel the pirates
who attack the *Agra*, and Dodd makes his way home to England with the £14,000
that will allow his daughter Julia to marry and his son Edward to continue his
studies at Oxford. But at home in the quiet English town of Barkington, Dodd falls
prey to more mercenary designs than any he encountered at sea. Wanting to secure
the money in the eminently reliable Bank of Barkington, Dodd realizes only too
late that its owner, Richard Hardie, has defrauded him, and he returns to the bank
to confront Hardie in a desperate attempt to retrieve his hard cash:

> 'My money! my money!' cried David fiercely: 'no more words, for I sha'n't
> listen to them: I know you now for what you are! a thief! I *saw* you put it into

> that safe: a liar is always a thief. You want to steal my children's money: I'll have
> your life first. My money, ye pirate, or I'll strangle you!' (261)

Dodd collapses at the end of the scene, awakens mentally enfeebled and spends
the balance of the novel convalescing in a private asylum. But his use of the word
'pirate' for Hardie is no act of incipient madness. It is a moment of especial clarity
and metaphorical meaning that ultimately underscores *Hard Cash*'s deeper thesis
about piracy: that it is neither a simple seafaring nor exotic racial crime, but rather
a domestic peril rooted in the financial and textual practices of mid-Victorian
England.

Such a thesis distinguishes Reade's novel from the several works that had
reinvigorated the pirate genre during the 1850s – particularly Charles Kingsley's
Westward Ho! (1855), Charles Dickens and Wilkie Collins's 'The Perils of Certain
English Prisoners' (1857) and R.M. Ballantyne's *The Coral Island* (1857) – since
these fictions, despite many differences, share in common a celebration of English
moral and social order. The pirates in Dickens and Collins's 'Perils' are radically
and racially other, the product of Dickens's venomous response to the Indian
Mutiny of 1857. While Kingsley and Ballantyne offer European pirates, they do
so only at a considerable remove: in Kingsley's case a temporal one to the reign
of Elizabeth I and in Ballantyne's a geographic one to the exotic setting of a desert
island (see Grace Moore's chapter for a more detailed discussion of Ballantyne
and piracy). All three works thus separate piracy from the comforts of home,
and Kingsley and Ballantyne rehearse the traditional figure of the white pirate
alienated profoundly (and mostly regretfully) from British moral and domestic
ideals. *Hard Cash*, however, engages deliberately with conditions at home rather
than abroad, locating the novel's piratical dangers within the commercial practices
of mid-Victorian England. Richard Hardie is not violent, nor does he fly the Jolly
Roger. Yet he remains – for all that he is white, respectable, and English – a pirate
of a distinctly modern kind. He plunders, defrauds, seduces and ruins. He disrupts
the legitimate flow of capital, and he copies and corrupts texts for mercenary gain.
He lives socially and sexually at the margins of morality and the law. The black,
bronze and yellow pirates who attack the *Agra*, then, may be the first and most
transparent iteration of the novel's concern with piracy, but they are neither the
most significant nor the most compelling. Instead, in its rendering of Hardie and
broader engagement with the commercial scandals and frauds of the 1840s and
1850s, *Hard Cash* makes the pirate story into a powerful critique of the civilized
rapacity of financial life in mid-Victorian England.

I

Despite *Hard Cash*'s predictable and racially charged presentation of pirates,
Reade's imaginative engagement with piracy was certainly far broader and ranged
across both literal and metaphorical applications of the term. Reade has fallen

into some obscurity now, but during the 1850s and 1860s he was a sensation novelist of the first rank, writing what he called 'matter of fact romance; that is … fiction built on truths' (*Hard Cash* 5) and drawing from current events to deliver a series of small shocks to Victorian readers.[1] He stopped at little when it came to sensationalizing and popularizing his fiction: abuses of prisoners at Birmingham Gaol, frauds involving British 'coffin-ships', lunacy law and problems inside private asylums, and cases of adultery and defrauded heirs all were grist for Reade's imaginative mill.[2] So it is no surprise that *Hard Cash*'s dark-skinned pirates and broader concern with race belong at least partly to a sensational agenda drawn from events of the day. Reade wrote *Hard Cash* against the backdrop of the Indian Mutiny and US Civil War – a circumstance that finds expression even before the pirate attack, in Ramgolam's and Vespasian's presence aboard the *Agra* – and he was not unwilling to capitalize on either event in his fiction.[3] Reade's pirates are rooted in specific contemporary matters, too, for at mid-century piracy remained a

---

[1]   As late as 1919 Walter Clarke Phillips still numbered Reade with Dickens and Wilkie Collins in the first rank of sensation novelists, and scholars still studied Reade frequently through the first half of the twentieth century. Besides Phillips's study, during the first half of the twentieth century John Coleman published *Charles Reade, as I Knew Him* (1903) and Malcolm Elwin published *Charles Reade, a Biography* (1931). In the United States alone, 20 dissertations and theses on Reade also appeared in 1900–1941. Even so, by 1943 Reade's reputation had declined so far that George Orwell asserted, 'it is unusual to meet anyone who has voluntarily read him' (2: 34).

[2]   Reade's first popular novel, *It Is Never Too Late to Mend* (1856), fictionalized the 1853 scandal at Birmingham Gaol, and *Foul Play* (1868) – which Reade co-authored with Dion Boucicault – exposed the horrors of British coffin-ships. *Hard Cash* (1863) and *A Terrible Temptation* (1871) both address the abuses associated with Victorian lunacy law. Many of his novels, including *Hard Cash*, deal at least indirectly with adultery and defrauded heirs.

[3]   By 1863 the public outrage and racial hysteria engendered in England by the Mutiny had given rise to several popular books and plays on the subject, and though Reade was an abolitionist and as such an admirer of Harriet Beecher Stowe, he was perhaps more impressed by the international success of *Uncle Tom's Cabin* (1852) than by the pathos and power of Stowe's attack on slavery. As Patrick Brantlinger points out in *Rule of Darkness*, '[i]nnumerable essays, sermons, novels, poems, and plays expressed a general racist and political hysteria' in the years just after the Indian Mutiny (202). One of the first was, as Garrett Ziegler discusses, Dickens and Collins's 1857 Christmas story 'The Perils of Certain English Prisoners', a thinly disguised retelling of events in India. In subsequent years the most popular texts were eyewitness accounts like Mrs J.A. Harris's *Lady's Diary of the Siege of Lucknow* (1858), Mowbray Thompson's *Story of Cawnpore* (1859) and the dozen or more different dramatic representations that appeared on the London stage. Hungry for commercial success, Reade certainly would have been impressed by such contemporary interest, just as he was impressed with Stowe's international success. He wrote *It Is Never Too Late to Mend*, according to Smith, partly with the intention of making it 'the *Uncle Tom's Cabin* of the British prisons' (32). See Elton Smith's *Charles Reade*. Boston: Twayne, 1976.

legitimate concern for England, particularly in the waters off the coasts of China and Malaysia. Earlier in the century, the Royal Navy had virtually eradicated piracy in the Atlantic Ocean and along the Barbary Coast, but the continued expansion of British trade to China exposed England's merchant fleet increasingly to piratical attacks like the one on the *Agra*. In 1848 the *Edinburgh Review* estimated that nearly 100,000 pirates roamed 'the eastern seas' and complained of the 'Malays, Illanuns, Balanini, Bajows, Sulus, Papuans, and other marauders who infest the Indian Archipelago' ('Art. III' 68–9). Over the next 15 years, dozens of articles on Chinese, Malay and other eastern pirates appeared in *The Times*, including a report on the death of Robert Burns, grandson of the poet, at the hands of Bornean pirates in 1852 and two stories on the attack against the merchant ship *North Star* in 1861.[4] In 1860 *The Cornhill* published an essay on Chinese pirates, as did Dickens's *All the Year Round*.[5] Together such reports kept eastern piracy before the public, reminding them of the perils of the growing empire and giving a sensational writer and opportunist like Reade excellent fodder for his fiction.[6]

Prior to the nineteenth century, however, piracy in England had only occasionally to do with race: more often it was a domestic crime, an act of treachery committed by British sailors against a British ship in tacit rebellion against the Crown. During the sixteenth century, England had cultivated a system of 'privateering' by which skilled ship captains worked essentially as independent contractors, hired by the Crown to harass the merchant ships and colonial exploits of England's two principal rivals, Spain and Portugal.[7] Such privateering continued through the seventeenth and eighteenth centuries as a way of buttressing the Royal Navy during times of conflict. But at the end of King William's War in 1697 and again after the War of the Spanish Succession in 1714, privateers who had been in the employ of the Crown were forced to seek other means of support. Some 5,500 British sailors turned pirate between 1697 and 1715 – resulting in the 'golden age'

---

[4]   The article on Burns appeared in a letter to the editor of *The Times* on 17 January 1852, 6d, while the articles on the attack against and seizure of the *North Star* appeared on 9 July 1861, 5b and 10 July 1861, 10e. Though each event certainly stirred contemporary interest, these articles are just three of more than 50 on such subjects to appear in *The Times* during the middle decades of the century.

[5]   See Elton Townsend's 'Chinese Pirates' in *The Cornhill* 2 (1860): 342–7, and 'Taking Pirate Junks' in *All the Year Round* 3 (1860): 178–80.

[6]   Winifred Hughes also asserts a strong affinity between *Hard Cash* and the early-Victorian popularity of nautical melodrama. The genre benefited from the nineteenth century's remarkable technical innovations in stagecraft, which allowed the staging of naval battles aboard real ships afloat in vast tanks of water. As Hughes writes, 'the seafaring episodes of *Hard Cash* – that incongruous jumble of shipwrecks, pirates, and sailor's hornpipes – make sense only in the once familiar context of nautical melodrama' (15). See Hughes, *The Maniac in the Cellar: Sensation Novels of the 1860s*. Princeton: Princeton UP, 1980.

[7]   For a fine overview of the origins of privateering, see Peter Earle's *The Pirate Wars* (New York: St Martin's, 2003), especially Chapter 2.

of piracy during the late 1710s – most of them having formerly been privateers (Rediker, 'The Pirate', 256). Turning on a domestic ship was enough to make a pirate, for it stripped a privateer of his natural legal and social ties to England. As Joel Baer puts it, pirates were left in the 'lonely and dangerous condition of being an enemy of all nations' (9), a status that Matthew Tindal described in 1694:

> *Hostis humani generis*, is neither a Definition, or as much as a Description of a Pirat, but a Rhetorical Invective to shew the Odiousness of that Crime. As a Man, who, tho he receives Protection from a Government, and has sworn to be true to it, yet acts against it as much as he dares, may be said to be an Enemy to all Governments, because he destroyeth … all those Ties and Bonds that unite People in a Civil Society under any Government. (qtd. in Baer 7–8)

Thus, the most notorious pirates of the day – Blackbeard, John Avery and William Kidd – were Englishmen whose lawlessness and outrageous brutality alienated them from British identity and domestic space. Pirates were willing generally to prey on any ship flying any flag, and the consequences of an attack could range from severed hands to severed heads, and from routine beatings and lashings to more creative punishments like 'blooding and sweating' and walking the plank.[8] Monstrous practices like these widened the gap between pirates and legitimate English citizens, just as they blurred the distinction between white Europeans and the savage racial others who, according to popular lore, lurked in the West Indies, off the west coast of Africa and along the Barbary Coast.

Yet violence was neither the principal aim nor the principal crime of most pirates; on the contrary, though pirates were clearly to be feared, they were troublesome particularly because they disrupted trade, plundered fortunes and otherwise preyed upon England's mercantile interests, forming a crude and – from the Crown's perspective – illegitimate analogue to the flow of wealth and goods between England and other parts of the globe. In *Captain Singleton* (1720), Daniel Defoe's narrator remarks that 'going upon the account' (169) was the common seafaring expression for turning pirate, the phrase having applied originally to the activities of merchant sailors who conducted clandestine and personally remunerative commerce in parallel with their ships' official transactions. At times, pirates inflicted violence even on the property aboard ships, 'descend[ing] into the holds … like "a Parcel of Furies," slashing boxes and bales of goods with their cutlasses, throwing valuable goods overboard, laughing uproariously as they did so' (Rediker, 'The Pirate' 246). More often, they functioned as a separate

---

[8]   Earle provides a sustained discussion of the typical cruelties pirates inflicted, including mutilations, decapitations and 'blooding and sweating', which involved pricking the captive repeatedly with a sail-needle across the buttocks, back and shoulders, then putting him in a sugar cask swarming with cockroaches and leaving him there to glut them with his blood (172–6). He also describes what may have been the first recorded instance of 'walking the plank', inflicted on the captain of *The Blessing* in 1822 (222).

economy, championing the interests of a different social order, inflicting losses on mercantile ships like so many Robin Hoods and punishing the merchants and captains who profited from the ill-treatment of their low-paid, poorly rationed crews (Rediker, 'The Pirate' 242). Many pirates of British fiction are cut from this same cloth of Englishness mingled with social subversion: Captain Singleton, Clement Cleveland, Long John Silver and even Captain Hook, who had been 'at a famous public school … its traditions still clung to him like garments' (Barrie 165).[9] Such fictions remind us that the pirate may have been feared and reviled, but he was also – even in Reade's day – a compelling, romantic personality, the swashbuckling English antihero of adventure stories and adolescent fictions. Thus, as Hans Turley argues, the fictional pirate is a complex figure, at once the rapacious enemy of all nations 'and the culturally revered … hypermasculine, transgressive, desiring subject' (7). He was also racially familiar, a liminal figure who bridged the gap between white Englishmen and exotic, barbarous others, and also between the legitimate and illegitimate economic spheres.

By the early part of the nineteenth century, the maritime depredations of the Barbary pirates, South American privateers and Greek insurgents against the Ottomans had begun to remake the imaginative relation between race and piracy in England.[10] But 'piracy' continued also to suggest more common thievery as well as seafaring crime and rapacity at home as well as rapacity abroad. According to the *Oxford English Dictionary*, 'piracy' and 'pirate' had by the 1700s already taken on their general modern association with the unlawful, sometimes forceful theft of property – an association that Defoe may have coined in 1707. Complaining in his *Review* about various kinds of commercial corruption, Defoe remarked:

---

[9]   Captain Singleton is the title character of a 1720 novel by Daniel Defoe; Sir Walter Scott features Clement Cleveland in *The Pirate* (1822); Long John Silver appears in Robert Louis Stevenson's *Treasure Island* (1883); and Captain Hook is Pan's familiar nemesis in J.M. Barrie's *Peter Pan* (1911).

[10]   In fact, the Barbary pirates had operated consistently in the Mediterranean Sea since the time of the Crusades, but by 1815–1816 British frustration on the subject had reached a very high pitch. Concluded in 1815, the Second Barbary War ended in bringing only a brief respite before piracy and other hostilities resumed, leaving a writer for the *Edinburgh Review* to complain in 1816: 'it is little less than incredible, that the civilized nations of Europe should so long have endured the piracy of those bloody and despicable Barbarians, who ravage the fairest coasts of its southern regions, and daily commit with impunity outrages, the least of which, if offered once in twenty years, by one great power to another, must have proved the cause of instant war' (450). See 'Art. IX – A Letter to a Member of Parliament, on the Slavery of the Christians at Algiers. By Walter Croker, Esq. of the Royal Navy. London, Stockdale, 1816'. *Edinburgh Review* 26 (1816): 449–57. For a fuller account of the privateers loosed on the Atlantic Ocean and West Indies by the rebellions in South America, see Earle (212–14) and Ralph Ward, *Pirates in History* (157). Earle also gives an account of the Greek pirates who operated against shipping of all nations during the Greek war for independence against the Ottoman Empire during the 1820s (225–6).

it would make a sad Chasm on the *Exchange* of *London*, if all the Pyrates should be taken away from among the Merchants there, whether we be understood to speak of your Litteral or Allegorical Pyrates; whether I should mean the Clandestine Trade Pyrates, who pyrate upon fair Trade at home; the Custom-stealing Pyrates, who pyrate upon the Government; the Owling Pyrates, who rob the Manufactures; [or] the privateering Pyrates, who rob by Law. (10: 425–6)

Such figurations of piracy were common enough by the mid-nineteenth century that in 1844 George Sydney Smythe wrote the story 'Social Piracy' for the *New Monthly Magazine*, centring it on the Hawke family's sharp eye for pecuniary gain and Mr Hawke's dubious employment with the Universal Providence Fire and Life Assurance Association. In an opening frame called 'On Land Pirates in General', the narrator remarks: 'There is a piracy not on the high seas, and many a Paul Jones, and many a Lambro, who never boarded a prize or drew a cutlass. ... In the spirit and morality of the piratical vocation, it makes no difference whatsoever whether it be prosecuted by water, or by land; on the waves of the Mediterranean, or in the squares of London' (1). By story's end the Hawkes have exhausted the generosity of their well-to-do cousins and the life assurance company has smashed, defrauding 50 widows of their property 'and the same number of too credulous and confiding spinsters' (362). Modern piracy, the story suggests, might be a nautical or terrestrial crime and is as likely to be committed by an unscrupulous London capitalist as by racial others at the far side of the world.

At mid-century, in fact, such crimes were very likely to be committed by ruined bankers and corrupt financiers like *Hard Cash*'s Hardie, whose financial depredations were drawn from contemporary scandals that Reade learned about while writing the novel. An obsessive researcher and deliberately documentary novelist, Reade studied the railway bubble of the 1840s while preparing to write, and his working notes contain a list of magazine and newspaper articles on banking, investing and fraud (Bankson 49, 56).[11] Altogether he compiled thousands of words of notes on such subjects, most of them intended to lend accuracy to his portrait of the novel's 'social pirate' (Bankson 288). While it is Dodd who calls Hardie a 'pirate', then, it is the narrator (with Reade's help) who draws the explicit connection between Hardie's local piracy and the larger realities of financial life in England. According to the narrator, Hardie is ruined by the railway bubble, which bankrupted thousands of investors and – as Parliamentary inquiries later showed – gave rise to 'an arsenal of fraudulent practices that made it ... impossible for investors to distinguish a legitimate company from one never

---

[11]   At the time of his death Reade left behind 36 volumes of massive notebooks that show the research he conducted for his novels, prompting E.G. Sutcliffe ('Charles Reade's Notebooks'. *Studies in Philology* 27 (1930): 164–211) to call him 'the earliest deliberately and thoroughly documentary novelist' (164) in English. A Baconian thinker who met with little early success as a novelist, Reade devised his 'great system' for writing documentary fiction in 1852, just before starting *It Is Never Too Late To Mend* (Sutcliffe, 198).

intended to survive' (Poovey 18). In a footnote to the novel, Reade refers readers
to the 1846 Parliamentary return of railway subscribers, D. Morier Evans's book
The 1847–1848 Commercial Crisis (1849), and 'pamphlets and journals of the
day' (152 n2) to verify the truth of the portrait. By the 1850s, with the railway
bubble burst, corrupt Victorian financiers like Hardie had simply graduated to
other kinds of fraud.[12] Walter Watts stole £70,000 from the Globe Insurance
Company before being caught and convicted in 1850, then committing suicide
at Newgate. Other cases of embezzlement, forgery and fraud followed – at the
Royal British Bank, at the Crystal Palace Company, even in the Treasury – though
the most remarkable cases were those of Leopold Redpath and William Pullinger,
who together managed to steal more than half a million pounds. During the
1850s Redpath made off with £240,000 from the Great Northern Railway by
forging sums and signatures on papers showing transfers of stock, and in 1860
Pullinger embezzled £263,000 from the Union Bank using similar devices. Such
cases provided plenty of documentary material upon which Reade could base his
corrupt banker in *Hard Cash*.

More to the point, they were cases of explicitly textual fraud – forgeries, copies
and falsifications of documents – with suggestive affinities to a very particular
form of piracy that Reade and other authors knew very well. In *Jure Divino* in
1706, Defoe complained of the 'Gentlemen-Booksellers, that threatened to Pyrate'
his work, and Joseph Addison and Richard Steele used piracy this way three
years later in the *Tatler* (qtd. in Aravamudan 100; Temple 164). In 1753, Samuel
Richardson complained when Irish 'pirates' published an unauthorized edition
of *Sir Charles Grandison* (Temple 157). By the nineteenth century such textual
appropriations, reproductions and corruptions were commonly called 'piracy', as
were infringements of patents, trademarks and other original designs. The subject
consumed Reade, who spent great resources prosecuting those who robbed authors
of proprietary rights. In 1853, when he was unknown and would have benefited
from any interest in his writing, Reade threatened to sue the manager of a theatre
where the actress Fanny Stirling had used two of his plays in her repertoire during
a provincial tour (Elwin 97). Four years later he sued George Bentley and later
T.H. Lacy, and in 1862 he won a judgement against B.O. Conquest of the Grecian
Theatre for unauthorized performances of *It Is Never Too Late To Mend* (Elwin
127; Dickens 9: 404). He also wrote two treatises on literary copyright: *The Eighth*

---

[12]   For an excellent swift review of the highest-profile cases of financial fraud between
1840 and 1860, see John Hollingshead's 'Convict Capitalists' in *All the Year Round* 3
(1860): 201–4. For the definitive work on these scandals, however, see D. Morier Evans's
Facts, Failures and Frauds (1859), which provides extraordinary detail – often including
court transcripts – regarding 10 of the most prominent mid-century cases, including those
of George Hudson ('the railway king'), Walter Watts, John Sadleir, Leopold Redpath and
William Pullinger. As Evans writes in his first chapter, 'With temptations to crime infinitely
multiplied, and with impediments reduced to a minimum … the last twenty years afford
materials for one of the darkest pages in the commercial history of this country' (1).

Commandment (1860), a long complaint against piracy and other copyright abuses; and 'The Rights and Wrongs of Authors' (1875), which appeared first in letters to the *Pall Mall Gazette*. As a novelist and playwright, he was frustrated by the ability of hacks to make his novels into plays before he did so himself. Each time an author produced a new work, Reade complained 'the pirates rush in and share, and undersell, and crush, and kill' (*Readiana* 181). By 1861, largely because of *The Eighth Commandment*, Reade was a leading authority on copyright, so much so that Dickens – no simpleton when it came to his commercial interests – solicited advice about his proceedings against Samuel Lane of the Britannia Theatre.[13] Three months later, when Reade won an injunction prohibiting Lacy from publishing *It Is Never Too Late To Mend* as a play, Dickens wrote to 'congratulate [Reade] heartily, on [his] victory over the accursed brood of pirates' (9: 404).

Yet Reade's relation to literary piracy was not simple, at least partly because he had such a finely nuanced sense of the forms that such piracy might take. In some ways he was an inveterate literary pirate himself, making a career of adapting others' work to the London stage and borrowing shamelessly from newspapers and magazines to collect sensational events for his plots. In 1851 he adapted Tobias Smollett's *Peregrine Pickle* for the stage, and he produced several adaptations and translations from the French: *Angelo* (1851), *The Ladies' Battle* (1851), *The Lost Husband* (1852) and *The Courier of Lyons* (1854). Even later he continued to annoy other authors with such conduct, for example by dramatizing *Ralph the Heir* (1872) without Anthony Trollope's permission and laying 'violent hands on Tennyson's *The Promise of May*' (Elwin 192). He also compiled the sensational incidents of his first popular novel, *It Is Never Too Late To Mend*, from *Times* articles and Parliamentary blue-books describing the 1853 scandal at Birmingham Gaol, and in the decades that followed – like many sensation novelists – he continued to draw incidents directly from the contemporary press.[14] In short, Reade's authorial practice seems often to have been at odds with his vigorous attacks on literary pirates. Elton Smith explains this contradiction by arguing that Reade believed 'that some legal safeguards should exist; but, since they did not, he had simply exercised his rights' (49). Really, the issue is more complex. Reade cared little about piracy as an artistic matter, but he did worry

---

[13]   Lane had announced a dramatic version of Dickens and Collins's 1860 Christmas story 'A Message from the Sea' on 6 January 1861 – a piracy that Dickens and Collins had attempted to foreclose by publishing their own dramatic adaptation in mid-December, just before the story appeared in *All the Year Round* (Dickens 9: 366–7).

[14]   As I describe in *The Self in the Cell: Narrating the Victorian Prisoner* (New York and London: Routledge 2003), Reade drew extensively from published accounts of the Birmingham Gaol scandal in writing *It Is Never too Late To Mend*, rarely even taking much trouble to disguise the names of the victims or assailants (82–3, 86–90). But as Richard Altick has shown convincingly in *The Presence of the Present: Topics of the Day in the Victorian Novel* (Columbus: Ohio State UP, 1991), sensation novelists relied almost invariably on incidents they found in the popular press.

that it created '[i]nsecurity of property', which 'saps public and private morality [... and] corrupts alike the honest and the dishonest' (*Readiana* 171). Though he eschewed concern for the artistic implications of his borrowings, then, he tried hard to guarantee rights of literary property. At a time when – as both Andrew Knighton and Kate Mattacks demonstrate – inadequate copyright laws allowed hacks to make free with others' books, Reade often volunteered to pay writers whose works he had translated and adapted. Long before he had made a penny by his pen, Reade paid Auguste Maquet £40 for the English rights to *Le Château Grantier*, which failed on the English stage but become the basis for Reade's novel *White Lies* (1857).[15] And despite Trollope's irritation, Reade voluntarily paid him half of the receipts for his adaptation of *Ralph the Heir* (Smith 46). Reade may not have been a terribly original writer, then, but neither was he – at least by his own definition – a pirate.

This is the broad view that *Hard Cash* offers: of piracy, not just as the racially charged, almost caricatured seafaring crime against the *Agra*, but also – and perhaps more dangerously – as the subtle programme of financial and textual frauds that Hardie engages in, and that threatened to destabilize property throughout the mid-Victorian capitalist sphere. Reade is not Dickens, and *Hard Cash* offers no comprehensive view of the shortcomings of 'the system'; but even in its narrowness, *Hard Cash* manages to be at once about greed, deception, the problems of wealth and property, and transgressive material and sexual desire. Its plot is punctuated by textual corruptions that disrupt commercial and sexual economies even as they mimic, too, the abridgements, reproductions and misappropriations that Reade blamed in cases of literary piracy for engendering 'insecurity of property' and, as a consequence, moral decay. Dodd is correct to identify Hardie as the 'pirate' at the heart of the novel, for the corrupt banker is an amalgam of Reade's imaginative engagement with the term – a pirate, that is, of a distinctly modern kind. Embezzler, forger, charlatan, seducer, even literary hack: Hardie is all of these. As a result, he is also the centrepiece of *Hard Cash*'s concern with piracy and an implicit assertion that commercial England has less to fear from exotic others than from the piratical depredations of its own home-grown scoundrels and villains.

II

The novel's initial insinuations about piracy and race begin to dissolve, in fact, from the moment they appear. Fighting for their lives against the pirates, the

---

[15]   Elwin asserts that Reade was scrupulous to a fault in the case of Maquet, who pressed Reade to accept a contingency agreement that provided for a refund of £20 if his adaptation was not performed within two years. That contingency became a reality and Maquet returned half of Reade's money, but in an exceptional display of integrity Reade repaid Maquet when he profited from the publication of *White Lies* (Elwin 131).

white Britons, too, turn barbarous: 'drunk with battle … naked to the waist, grimed with powder, and spotted like leopards with blood' (164). As the obvious difference between the sailors and their dark assailants narrows, the novel begins to distinguish carefully between the non-whites aboard the *Agra*. Ramgolam, the narrator writes, is a 'Caucasian darky', refined by his service to the Beresfords until he has become a 'compound of dignity and servility and of black and white' (136). He is mannerly, well dressed and well groomed, a master of the politest and most elaborate forms of spoken English. Vespasian, meanwhile, is the stock African-American of nineteenth-century fiction: simple, good-natured, prone to malapropisms and instinctively subservient to his racial betters. Though the novel takes pains to make Ramgolam the 'whiter' character, events show that the difference is not what it seems. Vespasian fights bravely against the pirates while Ramgolam hides in a meal-sack and, later, after Dodd is wounded, creeps into his cabin to steal the £14,000. In part, Ramgolam's cowardice and treachery are no more than what English readers expected of the Indian 'character' in the years just after the Mutiny. But they underscore, too, the novel's broader thesis about race: that 'whiteness' is a moral rather than a physical proposition, and that even the whitest bodies may harbour dark designs. Preparing to draw Ramgolam forth from the meal-sack, Vespasian apostrophizes him as 'dat ar niggar' and remarks 'Dis yar bag white outside, but him nation black inside' (178). He means literally to point out that Ramgolam is hiding in the sack, but his words offer another meaning. Ramgolam emerges from the sack with 'his black skin powdered with meal' – whitened, but black as the devil inside (179). Conversely, Vespasian thwarts Ramgolam's attempted theft of the hard cash and helps Dodd later to fight off the French robber, André Thibout.

Whatever its melodramatic qualities and easy assertions about race, then, *Hard Cash*'s account of the piratical attack on the *Agra* is no straightforward racial parable. On the contrary, as Dodd makes his way to England, the novel registers two parallel thematic moves: away from the view of dark skin as simply indicative or determinative of moral character, and away, too, from the conception of piracy as an obviously exotic seafaring crime. Making the black, bronze and yellow pirates in the eastern seas only the first of several threats to Dodd and his hard cash, the novel situates the attack on the *Agra* along a trajectory of piratical acts – by Ramgolam, Thibout and eventually Hardie – each one committed nearer to home and by whiter, more 'civilized' pirates. *Hard Cash* thus makes Dodd's voyage from the colonial margins back to England read paradoxically as a return to the heart of darkness, a dangerous approach to the epicentre of the piratical and insatiable Victorian commercial sphere. As it turns out, Dodd has more to fear from double-entry bookkeeping, the Bank of Barkington and the other machinery of modern finance than from pirate ships with wild crews and booming 12-pounders – more to fear from rapacious Englishness than from Malay barbarity or the 'Indian character'. Among the novel's would-be villains, Hardie emerges as the exemplary pirate, uniting and in some senses combining the meanings of the term within a single portrait of rapacity, cruelty and textual and sexual power.

Long before Dodd encounters pirates on the high seas, Hardie appears as the novel's original avaricious villain, losing his and the bank's money and then covering the losses by plundering £5,000 from his children's trusts. At first, he resists the temptation to try to get rich through the railways and is therefore Barkington's '[a]ntidote to the universal mania' (152) warning customers that even if England 'could be sold, with every building, ship, quadruped, jewel, and marketable female in it, it would not fetch the money to make these railways' (153). But like real Victorians ruined by the same cause, Hardie rushes headlong into financial destruction because, after years of patient accumulation, he cannot bear to see 'paupers making large fortunes in a few months' (153). Literally, Hardie's and the bank's failures are no more than financial problems, part of the public sphere of commercial transaction. Implicitly, however, they are blows to domesticity, a point that the narrator underscores by cataloguing the 'respectable persons, reduced to pauperism in that one day' (286) all across the town. Mr Esgar, formerly 'a respectable merchant' (287) but ruined by the bank's collapse, flees to America without settling accounts and thus passes 'his ruin on to others' (288); John Shaw, 'a steady footman' (288) about to marry and purchase a public house, loses his life's savings and hangs himself; and Blanche Lunley, the 'sunshine of the poor', reputedly dies of 'grief' when she learns that Hardie has draw out and lost even her last salvation, her Consols (290). The novel also suggests that Hardie's violation of his children's trusts constitutes a threat of a special kind: to the English social principle that makes property a genuine legacy, passed forward from father to son instead of travelling in the other direction. The novel figures this problem metaphorically in Hardie's refusal to let Alfred and Julia marry, reducing Julia to a harlot 'to be bought and sold'(128) on the marriage market and underscoring that Hardie's aim is to prevent his son – sexually, as in property – from coming into his own. Hardie's plundering thus upsets financial and sexual economies in the novel, diverting both property and desire from their proper course.

Hardie accomplishes these thefts textually – in effect, through literary piracy – appropriating, reproducing and corrupting the considerable array of financial and other documents that litter the novel. His original crime is neither imprudent speculation nor the perfectly legal plunder of his children's trusts. Rather, as Skinner discovers, Hardie's crimes begin like those of most real mid-century embezzlers: with 'falsifying accounts' (245) and 'fabricating a balance-sheet' (246) to conceal his and the bank's insolvency. Having once intruded upon Hardie's confidence in these matters, Skinner elaborates the frauds by paying his fellow townsman, Maxley, in Bank of Barkington notes, an act of textual piracy that translates Maxley's original banknotes into worthless scrip, stripping away the capital from the very man who authored its accumulation. Hardie and Skinner also steal Dodd's hard cash through piracy of another kind, purloining the receipt that proves he deposited the money in the first place. When Hardie learns later that Detective Green plans to waylay and search him for the pocketbook that contains the hard cash, he turns literary pirate in earnest, generating a thoroughly fictitious and adulterated packet of papers and receipts – a remarkable tissue of textual frauds, adapted even to include pictures of his children – decked out as the pocketbook he always carries. As a final touch, the falsified pocketbook even contains a self-exculpatory account of the hard cash:

> This day Alfred told me to my face I had fourteen thousand pounds of Captain Dodd's. We had an angry discussion. What can he mean? Drs. Wycherley and Osmond, this same day, afflicted me with hints that he is deranged, or partly. I saw no signs of it before. (387–8)

The counterfeit documents thus reinforce his fraudulent institutionalization of his son, which is itself effected through a series of textual deceptions. Peggy Black's false letter lures Alfred to Silverton, and Drs Wycherley and Spears sign certificates that consign him to the asylum. These last are neither illegal nor *prima facie* meant to deceive, but they are, as the novel shows, the products of a 'system' that permits private asylums to profit more by securing and keeping patients than by curing them. Along with purloined letters, false accounts of Alfred's conduct and dishonest affidavits filed with the court, this 'system' first keeps Alfred institutionalized, then postpones his suit against his uncle and father. It creates 'insecurity of property' precisely because it relies upon textual records but without distinguishing true texts from false ones, originals from copies and complete accounts from abridgements, adaptations and frauds. The protracted legal contest is thus in many ways a parable of literary piracy, not to mention a demonstration of the consequences of textual instability within English financial and legal practice.

This demonstration is bound up, moreover, with the novel's insistence that such piracies, localized in Hardie, have implications beyond the financial and textual. As his willing cruelty to his son suggests, Hardie is thoroughly *piratical*: cruel, alienated and reviled, but also a figure of sexual power and transgressive desire. When the bank breaks, Hardie locks himself away behind shuttered windows and locked doors, 'wrapped in his own plans [... and] deaf to the anguish of his clients' (287). Hearing that Dodd wants to see him at the bank, Hardie imagines that Mrs Dodd has sent her husband to say that 'his girl will die if she can't have my boy, etc. As if I care who lives or dies' (251). Greedy and pitiless, plotting even against Skinner, his fellow-schemer, Hardie removes with Jane and Peggy to the seclusion of Musgrove Cottage where, he writes wistfully to Dr Sampson, 'none but true friends will come near' (295). Even this implicit plea for fellowship is a textual ploy, since Hardie invites Sampson to dinner to learn from him whether Dodd has recalled anything about the hard cash. For Hardie, the geographical move to the social margins thus parallels his move to the margins of the law; it is a piratical tactic that provides space for his continued financial and sexual transgressions. At Musgrove Cottage, under the same roof with his evangelical daughter, Hardie carries on an affair with Peggy, the illegitimacy of which is figured along moral and class lines and heightened by her role as Hardie's accomplice. While Alfred should spend his wedding night in sexual bliss, Peggy helps to plunge him into a frenzy of another kind. Strapped to a bed in his cell at Silverton Grove House,

Alfred 'struggled, he writhed, he bound: he made the very room shake, and lacerated his flesh … [t]he perspiration rolled down his steaming body' (416). The scene's ecstatic but sterile energy reminds us of the ways in which Hardie's machinations disrupt sexual flows, too – of the ways in which he stands as the novel's great threat to English commercial and domestic life, as the new pirate of the modern age.

In this sense, it is fitting that Hardie's schemes collapse because Dodd, the valorous sea-captain, arrives to defeat the 'pirate' by reclaiming his property from Skinner's dead hand. It is also fitting that the property is not the hard cash; rather, it is the receipt – a pirated text – that establishes Dodd's claim to his money and shows that Alfred is right about the £14,000. The original cash has been invested and spent, but Dodd and Alfred do finally get their money because Hardie's investments in the Old Turks begin suddenly to prosper the day after the trial. Like most Victorian villains, Hardie is punished, for he is driven mad eventually by his obsession with hard cash. But the financial success that his investments enjoy is thematically crucial, for it is at once a plot contrivance that permits the wronged characters to prosper and an illustration of the danger that piracy poses in the world of the novel. Freed from piracy, the novel can again become *productive*, not just in the sense of producing an end to its attenuated plot but also in ways that matter deeply to its thematic concerns and social critique. *Hard Cash* is fairly haunted by the horror of unbridled consumption: in the fortunes and lives swallowed by Hardie's speculations; in the image of Drayton House consumed by fire; in the grotesque episode with Maxley, who is nearly killed by eating the very mouse that he poisoned for devouring his garden; in the several characters, including Maxley, Hardie and Dodd, consumed utterly by thoughts of money.[16] Amid these images, the pirate stands as the quintessential insatiable subject, the *hostis humani generis* but also the *homo economicus* whose rapacity disrupts commercial and domestic stability and threatens the novel with insanity, destruction and death. Hardie's defeat permits the novel to close amid financial and sexual plenitude, even superabundance. Just as the Old Turks begin to increase and multiply, so Alfred and Julia marry and she presents him 'with a lovely boy' (680). Just weeks later '[a]s so often happens after a long separation, Heaven bestow[s] on Captain and Mrs. Dodd another infant to play bout their knees' (680). The pirate vanquished, Albion Villa 'show[s] symptoms of bursting' and can 'no longer hold all the happy inmates' (680). *Hard Cash* thus ends in an image of domesticity restored – saved, not from racial savagery at the other end of the globe, but from domestic perils rooted in the financial heart of England.

---

[16]   Ann Grigsby points out correctly that '[t]he characters in *Hard Cash* who actually suffer from insanity, do so because of a compulsive preoccupation with money. Richard Hardie, David Dodd, and James Maxley form fixations on cash and become unable to consider any other issue' (155). See Grigsby's 'Charles Reade's *Hard Cash*: Lunacy Reform through Sensationalism.' *Dickens Studies Annual* 25 (1996): 141–58.

III

By mounting this attack against the sins of mid-Victorian materialism, *Hard Cash* earns a place alongside Dickens's *Little Dorrit* (1855–1857) and Trollope's *The Way We Live Now* (1875) as an important mid-century critique of corruption and financial malpractice. Hardie is a more thoroughly but less powerfully drawn Merdle, a precursor to the elaborate and racialized corruptions of Augustus Melmotte. Like these characters he is, too, a distinctly modern villain and fraud who reflects the apparently limitless deceptions that were possible in Victorian England's emerging capitalist sphere. But it is not quite true, as Ann Grigsby charges, that the novel flatly 'condemn[s] Victorian respectability based on materialism' (155). If anything, it reminds us of the fine line that Victorian authors like Reade (and Dickens and Trollope) walked by critiquing mid-century rapacity even as they exercised every proprietary right they could claim. Perhaps no Victorian author dealt more ruthlessly than Reade did with publishers, and certainly none worked harder to revise the legal tangles that secured authors' rights. This may explain why *Hard Cash* distinguishes so carefully between the kind of materialism that drives people to industrious accumulation and the other, piratical sort characterized by unjust seizures, textual frauds, and unending consumption. The novel never criticizes Dodd for getting rich in that supreme capitalist venture, colonialism, nor does the novel lament Alfred's return to prosperity. In fact, Alfred's principled accumulation of capital permits Hardie and Co. to rise again, wipe out 'the last disgraceful episode, and [return] to the past centuries of honor and good credit' (687).

The novel's deliberate injunction, then, is to moral and material prosperity, so that *Hard Cash* remains less an attack on Victorian materialism or the capitalist 'system' than on the individual corruptions of Victorian financiers. *Hard Cash* is in this sense a portrait of the moral growing pains of modern financial life, and of the new forms of the same old piracy that had lured individual Britons since the days of William Kidd or perhaps even Sir Francis Drake. To the extent that this is true, *Hard Cash* revises and reifies the pirate story, doing for it what other sensation novels were simultaneously doing for the Gothic by reinvesting the formal apparatus of the genre with recognizably domestic terrors. The greatest act of piracy in *Hard Cash*, then, may be textual after all, for it inheres in Reade's attempt to adapt the pirate genre for the purpose of rendering a decisively domestic critique – and for the purpose, too, of making a little money along the way.

Chapter 12

The Pirates of Penzance:
The Slaves of Duty in an Age of Piracy

Abigail Burnham Bloom

The Victorian obsession with duty to crown and country began and ended with sea-faring men. The concept was most famously articulated by Lord Nelson in 1805 when he signalled before the battle of Trafalgar, 'England expects that Every Man will do his Duty.' In fact, Nelson had originally stated, 'Nelson confides that every man will do his duty' (Vincent 582). The signal officer suggested 'expects' rather than 'confides' as it is in the vocabulary of the telegraphic signal book and does not need to be spelled out letter by letter. The concept was broadened from the individual leader, 'Nelson', to the nation for which they fought, 'England', for loyalty was expected to the leader in battle but more importantly to the country they all served. 'Duty' had to be spelled out, but the word was retained. Nelson hoped his signal would inspire his men through confirmation of the accepted belief that men must sacrifice their lives to their commander and country, for a higher purpose and for the benefit of others within their society. Nelson was mortally wounded in this battle, and as he lay on his deathbed he said, 'Thank God I have done my Duty' (Vincent 582). For Nelson personally, his belief in acting appropriately brought him comfort as he died.

The virtue of the concept of duty both towards the self and the state was accepted throughout most of the Victorian period. Thomas Carlyle wrote in *Sartor Resartus* (1831), 'Hence also our Whole Duty, which is to move, to work, – in the right direction' (Bk. II, Ch. 4). To work in the right direction would bind one personally to the concept of duty as well as to one's country. George Eliot is reported to have stated, 'the words *God, Immortality, Duty* – pronounced, with terrible earnestness, how inconceivable was the *first*, how unbelievable the *second*, and yet how peremptory and absolute the *third*' (F. Myers). Having lost her traditional religious belief, Eliot's sense of morality stemmed from her own belief in the importance of duty. Through the era the concept was gradually expanded to include the separate roles of men and women in everyday life. John Ruskin described the roles of each in *Sesame and Lilies* (1865): 'The man's duty as a member of a commonwealth, is to assist in the maintenance, in the advance, in the defence of the state. The woman's duty, as a member of the commonwealth, is to assist in the ordering, in the comforting, and in the beautiful adornment of the state' (80). Duty was accepted and promoted as an important component of good conduct. Men would do their duty to their country through serving in war and during peacetime by contributing to the advancement of the state through their work, while a woman's duty to the state primarily involved her supportive role through her duty to her husband and family. The concept of duty to the state resides behind Alfred, Lord Tennyson's admiration for the doomed soldiers in his poem 'The Charge of the Light Brigade' (1854). Queen Victoria was both symbol and supporter of the virtue of duty. On the day she became queen in 1837 she recorded in her journal, 'Since it has pleased Providence to place me in this station, I shall do my utmost to fulfil my duty towards my country' (qtd. in Munich 279n). As representative of Great Britain, Victoria personified the idea of duty.

Towards the end of the nineteenth century this strict adherence to duty began to be questioned as men and women debated their roles in society For example, in Mary Cholmondeley's 1899 best-selling novel, *Red Pottage*, personal duty, based on a middle-class religious foundation, becomes an excuse for immoral behaviour. Those members of society who lack imagination and the ability to see beyond the obvious wield the concept of duty as an instrument for enforcing tyranny over others. Oscar Wilde wrote in his 1891 essay 'The Soul of Man under Socialism' on the virtue of individualism to the state because 'Individualism does not come to man with any sickly cant about duty, which merely means doing what other people want because they want it; or any hideous cant about self-sacrifice, which is merely a survival of savage mutilation' (155). As Wilde describes duty, the term no longer has the positive resonance that it held earlier in the century. The concept of duty had become such a source of hypocrisy and double-dealing, as men and women attempted to use it to further their own interests, that W.S. Gilbert and Arthur Sullivan satirized it in their 1879 operetta *The Pirates of Penzance*, subtitled *The Slave of Duty*.[1] The satire is gentle, leaving the audience not with the sense that duty should be abandoned altogether, but that duty loses its virtue when performed automatically and without thought.

Gilbert sustained a respect for duty to the state stemming from his father's service as a naval surgeon and his own military involvement. He attempted to fight in the Crimean War but was too young. Gilbert later served in the home service Militia and attained the rank of captain. When he left the Militia in 1878, he was

---

[1] The history of the performance of this work is complicated by Gilbert and Sullivan's attempts to outwit copyright pirates. Gilbert and Sullivan were beset by American theatrical pirates who would steal their material if it were not copyrighted by being performed first in the United States. In order to secure British copyright, *The Pirates of Penzance* was first performed as a public reading following a performance of another opera at Paignton, Devon, on 30 December 1879, then had a world premiere in New York on 31 December 1879, and an official British premiere in London on 3 April 1880. The subtitle was 'Or, Love and Duty' at Paignton, while other productions used 'The Slave of Duty'. The initial title elevates the concerns of love to as much prominence as duty, while the later title indicates the greater focus on duty. Because Gilbert kept tinkering with the libretto, variations in wording and additions and deletions occur throughout the opera. Gilbert and Sullivan pirated their earlier operetta by using the song 'Climbing over rocky mountain' from *Thespis* in *The Pirates of Penzance* (*Definitive Libretto*).

made an honorary Major (Ffinch 24). In *The Pirates of Penzance* Gilbert questions the concept of duty through the presentation of the major characters. Each must decide whether to act in a way to benefit himself or for a greater cause. To make his point, Gilbert employs the satiric weapons of topsy-turvydom, inverting normal expectations so that the pirates are sympathetic and the police fearful, and *reductio ad absurdum*, taking the inclinations of the characters to a ridiculous level. Each of the major characters has a singular approach to the concept of duty that is brought to a head at the end of each act as the characters worship a concept larger than themselves. At the end of the first act the characters bow down before poetry, but their dedication is short-lived. Resolution comes at the end of the second act by the submission of the pirates to the ultimate symbol of all that is British, Queen Victoria. The movement in the operetta is from self-interest and escape from society, to devotion to something higher than the self; duty to self becomes duty to society. By satirizing the concept of duty, Gilbert thus causes each member of his audience to examine his or her own concept of duty.

The Pirates: Allegiance to Themselves

Based in the west-coast town of Penzance, the pirates of Penzance operate in the sea around Cornwall, which had been the territory of the ferocious pirates known as the Killigrews during the seventeenth century (Glinert 796). Although we hear of the pirates of Penzance's feats on the water, we only see them on land. Rather than being the villains of the piece, the pirates are the most sympathetic of characters and the most moral. They have become pirates in order to escape from civilization. As Frederic asks them to return to England with him, the Pirate King says, 'I don't think much of our profession, but contrasted with respectability it is comparatively honest' (I.134–'5). He then sings, 'Away to the cheating world go you, / Where pirates all are well-to-do' (I.140–41).[2] These men sought to escape from society by becoming pirates; while on the sea they abide by their own rules and government. The pirates have freed themselves from their duty of allegiance to England, but they have also retained a moral code, as exemplified by their behaviour to orphans. On the high seas Lord Nelson represented an extension of crown and country, whereas the pirates act on their own. They have no higher allegiance than themselves.

The pirates, in an early version of the operetta, agreed to the apprenticeship because when it was said that Frederic sought, '"a respectable line of life" we thought he meant a pirate' (198);[3] the fact that the pirates did not realize a mistake was being made and that they assume others might recognize that theirs is the

---

[2]   Although the Pirate King is generally without a name, his name was given as Richard on the opening night programme in New York, 31 December 1879.

[3]   This reference is to the Paignton version of *The Pirates of Penzance*, which Bradley includes in *The Completed Annotated Gilbert and Sullivan*, 198.

morally superior choice of professions is attested without a wink by the pirates. Gilbert parodies conventional morality by having the pirates proclaim their superiority throughout the performance. Their behaviour is constant while they are pirates; it is only when they rejoin society that they revert to behaving like those around them.

As a result of his virtue, his sympathy and his energy, the Pirate King stands out as the central figure of the drama He is a romantic figure sharing traits with literary pirates who have been wronged and who have, like Byron's Corsair, resorted to piracy in order to escape the injustice of the world. He resembles the gentleman who becomes a pirate because of the corruption of society and the lure of the freedom of the life of the pirate. Although we do not learn his specific back-story, the Pirate King was a peer of the realm who strayed, and he comments several times on the corruption of British society. In many ways the piece is a satire of other popular nineteenth-century ideas of the pirate. Yet the Pirate King is more than that. Despite his being a parody, he becomes a great character in his own right.[4] His blindness as to why others might see him as an anti-social character endears him to the audience.

In 1805 a sailor in the navy would have been expected to fight and lay down his life for his leader and his country, but the situation had changed dramatically by 1879. In Gilbert's libretto, the loss of importance of duty as a concept can be seen in the situation of the majority of English seamen. The pirates of Penzance are orphans and have a sentimental penchant for others who have lost their parents. Thus, they allow any orphans they overtake in battle to go freely. Because this proclivity has become widely known, whenever the pirates defeat a ship in battle, the captured seamen claim to be orphans. Frederic, who has been apprenticed to the pirates, reveals that everyone on the last three ships they overtook turned out to be an orphan and so they released them, 'One would think that Great Britain's mercantile navy was recruited solely from her orphan asylums – which we know is not the case' (I.91–3). In the world of Gilbert and Sullivan, the pirates act with gentlemanly respect and sympathy for the downtrodden in society, while members of the navy lie to save their lives. While this scenario would seem to fit with the topsy-turvy nature of Gilbert's imagination, it also suggests the manner in which the idea of duty to the state was changing within the larger Victorian world.

Frederic: The Slave of Duty

Frederic, the titular slave of duty, is representative of traditional Victorian society. He performs what he sees as his responsibilities without consideration for the

---

[4]   This is evident in Wilford Leach's 1983 film *The Pirates of Penzance*, which followed Joseph Papp's Broadway version of the opera. Frederic was played by the unknown and unprepossessing Rex Smith, while the well-known actor Kevin Kline played the more significant role of the Pirate King.

unusual circumstances in which he is operating. Frederic became a pirate because his father, seeing that he was 'so brave and daring' (I.43) as a child, wanted to apprentice him to a pilot. His nurserymaid, Ruth, being hard of hearing, misheard the word and apprenticed him to a pirate until his twenty-first birthday.[5] Taken from his home as a young man and apprenticed to the pirates, Frederic nevertheless has retained an exacting respect for duty. As in many nineteenth-century literary models, Frederic's morals are in his blood. He retains his upper-middle-class values, despite years spent in another lifestyle. Frederic declares himself to be a slave of duty, 'As a child I was regularly apprenticed to your band. It was through an error – no matter, the mistake was ours, not yours, and I was honour bound by it' (I.35–7). Paradoxically, Frederic has a legal contract with a group that is outside the law, yet feels honour-bound to abide by its terms.

Gilbert satirizes the established order of society by causing the audience to reexamine Frederic's blind obedience to duty. Frederic states that 'when stern Duty calls, / I must obey' (II.303–4), and his ludicrous behaviour is maintained throughout the operetta. As James Helyar states, Gilbert 'consciously carried the accepted conventions to ludicrous extremes to make their absurdity evident to all, not with bitterness or indignation, but with hilarity' (7). By mocking the idea of duty, Gilbert causes his audience to simultaneously laugh and to consider it seriously. Rather than enjoying the freedom of escape from his apprenticeship, Frederic has bound himself to his sense of duty. Frederic performs his duty in four primary ways: firstly by remaining a pirate although his family had meant to make him a pilot; secondly by arranging the extermination of the pirates when he is no longer one of them; thirdly by agreeing to stay with the pirates when the terms of his indenture are examined more carefully; and fourthly by revealing to the pirates that Major-General Stanley has lied to them. Frederic acts according to his duty when he is with the pirates by supporting their acts and revealing to them why they have been failures as buccaneers. The pirates consistently perform in a gentlemanly manner, using rules they believe to be correct, such as never harming orphans and never attacking a party weaker than themselves. Because the audience never sees the pirates involved in cut-throat behaviour, their moral behaviour is preserved. Frederic is buffeted by changes in his fortune, while the pirates make their own decisions. Frederic never changes in his idea of duty, in contrast to the pirates who ultimately adopt allegiance to a higher duty.

While the pirates have developed a separate society worthy of their loyalty, Frederic believes the only creditable society is that under the domain of the British crown.[6] The Pirate King responds to Frederic's exhortation to come back

---

[5]   Ruth claims in her explanatory song about Frederic that she is hard of hearing, but we see no evidence of this in the remainder of the operetta.

[6]   In one version of the opera, the pirates are shown not only to have developed more moral laws than the rest of society, but unusual laws within their own community. The Pirate King is king because he serves others, not as a leader, but by taking care of his men in the most menial of ways:

to civilization with him by pointing out the difference between life on land and life as a pirate: 'Oh, better far to live and die / Under the brave black flag I fly, / Than play a sanctimonious part, / With a pirate head and a pirate heart' (I.136–9). In the Pirate King's view, the real pirates operate on land. Frederic recognizes his changed position when he addresses the pirates, believing his apprenticeship is over: 'Individually, I love you all with affection unspeakable, but, collectively, I look upon you with a disgust that amounts to absolute detestation. Oh! pity me, my beloved friends, for such is my sense of duty that, once out of my indentures, I shall feel myself bound to devote myself heart and soul to your extermination!' (I.65–9). Again we see the sentimentality and virtue of the pirates as they weep out of their sympathy and pity for Frederic's situation, ignoring the fact that it means death for them!

End of Act I: The Search for Meaning in Love and Poetry

Marriage traditionally marks a milestone of adulthood and as such it establishes one's place in society. Consequently, when Frederic rejoins society, it is his duty to get married. When Frederic believes he has left the pirates, his first thought is to find a woman to be his wife. Aside from his nursemaid Ruth, who worked as a 'piratical maid-of-all work' (I.58) while Frederic was an apprentice, Frederic has never seen a woman. Frederic remarks that he does not want to take Ruth from the pirates, 'In justice to her, and in consideration for you, I will leave her behind' (I.116–17), yet the pirates are not eager for her to remain with them. Although Frederic uses the word 'duty', here he seems to take advantage of it and to think of his duty as what he really wants to do. Even the 'slave of duty' can fall into the hypocrisy of the age. Frederic hedges on the idea of duty in that he knows that he does not want to marry Ruth because of her age, yet simultaneously believes he owes her allegiance for her fidelity. Frederic is cleared of the complication of Ruth when he finds that she has lied to him about her appearance. In the strongest language of the play and the most emotional, operatic and melodramatic music, Frederic accuses Ruth of deliberate deception: 'Oh, false one, you have deceived me!' (I.200). Because of what Frederic sees as her dishonesty, he is able to abandon her without conscience. With Ruth out of the way, the field is open.

> But to cook your meals I don't refuse
> And I black piratical boots and shoes!
> I clean your knives, I bake your bread –
> I light your fires – I make your beds ...
> For if I said I'd rather not
> (I know you! I know you!)
> You would depose me like a shot! (Paignton version, 196)
> In this version, the Pirate King remains king not by noble acts, but by acting as a servant.

Frederic seeks a wife by appealing to women's desires to rescue him from his unfortunate position. Coming upon the daughters of the Major-General, Frederic urges them to look to their sense of duty:

> Oh, is there not one maiden breast
> Which does not feel the moral beauty
> Of making worldly interest
> Subordinate to sense of duty?
> Who would not give up willingly
> All matrimonial ambition,
> To rescue such a one as I
> From his unfortunate position? (I.299–306)

He looks for a woman who feels it is more important to rescue her husband rather than be raised by him within society in order to make an advantageous marriage. Once Mabel steps forward and volunteers, her sisters remark in an aside, 'had he not been / A thing of beauty, / Would she be swayed by quite as keen / A sense of duty?' (I.338–41). For Mabel, duty and desire go hand in hand and she may be putting her 'worldly interest' on hold by marrying someone without any prospects of employment. However, she can reconcile her fleshly desires with her sense of duty by choosing a handsome man. Mabel is not unaware of Frederic's physical charms as she relates 'Did ever maiden wake / From dream of homely duty, / To find her daylight break / With such exceeding beauty?' (I.388–91). 'Homely duty' becomes a nice pun here, suggesting both Mabel's appearance and her wifely duties to her family. Her dream, much like Frederic's, is of duty mixed with physical attractiveness. Although Mabel may be motivated by self-interest, she comes to adopt Frederic's view of duty. She admires Frederic's noble act in returning to the pirate band and says to the police about Frederic, 'He has done his duty. I will do mine' (II.371–2).

The end of the first act shows Major-General Stanley in apposition to the pirates, but there are many parallels between them. Both are leaders of fighting men and both sing songs in support of their profession. The Pirate King sings praise of his situation by saying he will 'live and die a Pirate King' (I.135); while the Major-General proclaims himself to be 'the very model of a modern Major-General' (I.453). The Pirate King proclaims his moral superiority in his song by claiming not to be as corrupt as other kings,

> When I sally forth to seek my prey
> I help myself in a royal way:
> I sink a few more ships, it's true,
> Than a well-bred monarch ought to do;
> But many a king on a first-class throne,
> If he wants to call his crown his own,
> Must manage somehow to get through
> More dirty work than ever I do. (I.151)

The Pirate King suggests that although his profession is considered immoral, in actuality he does less 'dirty work' than other kings. Indeed, because of their moral behaviour the men do not do very well as pirates.

The Major-General reveals the limitations of his own education, noting that although he possesses all kinds of knowledge 'in matters vegetable, animal and mineral', of military knowledge he 'Has only been brought down to the beginning of the century' (I.492). He has been educated as a gentleman, not a military leader. The comparisons emphasize the exemplary behaviour of the pirates. They have taken to the high seas to live an honest life; the Major-General has bought a baronial manor. With his wealth, this impostor has attempted to purchase class and even ancestors, another kind of piracy. The pirates have sought to change their position through marriage with the Major-General's daughters. When the Major-General objects to having pirates as sons-in-law, the Pirate King responds, 'We object to Major-Generals as fathers-in-law. But we waive that point. We do not press it. We look over it' (I.416–17). Here again, the pirates retain the moral high ground, although, of course, few would mind having a Major-General in a family, while no one would want a pirate. Yet within the confines of the play, the Major-General has been dishonest in his dealing with the pirates by lying to them about his status as an orphan in order to prevent them from marrying his daughters.[7] When the pirates recognize his lie they vow his destruction. Although through much of the drama the pirates act in accord with the romantic fiction of decadent Byronic corsairs, their more cut-throat behaviour is revealed in their proclamation that they will kill the Major-General. However, this threat never comes to pass. When all is resolved at the end of the performance, the pirates and the Major-General will be one family, and the pirates will no longer be orphans.

The pirates of Penzance are not opposed to every aspect of British society; they bow down to poetry at the end of Act I, but they do not change their behaviour. At the end of the first act, the stage is divided by the two flags representing two different ways of life: the pirates' Jolly Roger, the symbol of piracy; and the Union Jack, the flag of Great Britain held by an official emissary Major-General Stanley (see Figure 12.1). The two columns of figures, marching under their different flags, even have text coming between them.

In the second illustration (see Figure 12.2) the groups have come closer together. The Pirate King and the Major-General wave their flags across a cut in the rocks. They acknowledge each other and the camps are not so separate – the pirates dance beneath both flags and the daughters of the Major-General flirt with the pirates. In the song sung at the end of Act I, the Major-General debates

---

[7]   In an earlier version of the play, the Major-General states that his 'parents close to us are dwelling' (*Complete Annotated G&S*, 222); in the final version the Major-General's lie is of a peculiar kind as his ancestors have been purchased along with his mansion. Frederic asserts however that 'he never was [an orphan]!' (II.251). The inability of the pirates to have open and honest discourse with the Major-General is shown through their miscommunication and confusion over the words 'orphan' and 'often'.

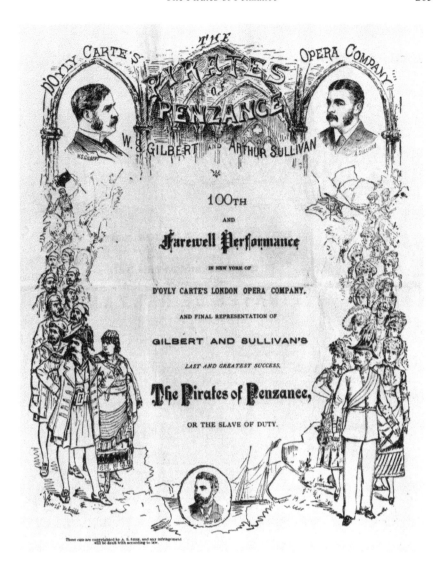

Figure 12.1   Programme, *The Pirates of Penzance* by W.S. Gilbert, composed by
               Arthur Sullivan, D'Oyly Carte's London Opera Co., Fifth Avenue
               Theatre, New York City, 5 June 1880. Front cover

the difference between an 'innocent fiction' (I.577) and a 'regular terrible story'
(I.579). All of the men, however, come briefly together by bowing down to poetry.
But this cannot keep them together.

The end of the first act is balanced with the end of Act II. The action of the
second act ends with the Pirate King and the rest of the pirates bowed down before

Figure 12.2   Programme, *The Pirates of Penzance* by W.S. Gilbert, composed by
Arthur Sullivan, D'Oyly Carte's London Opera Co., Fifth Avenue
Theatre, New York City, 5 June 1880. Back cover

the Queen. Ultimately the Union Jack, symbol of British unity, wins over the
Jolly Roger as the pirates return to the fold. The operetta, which appeared to be
primarily concerned with Frederic's restoration to society, becomes about causing

the Pirate King to recognize his allegiance to Great Britain. No longer motivated by self-interest, the pirates take their proper place within the larger society.

Frederic and the Police: Duty and Destruction

While he was apprenticed to the pirates, Frederic was obliged by his sense of duty to act as a pirate; when his apprenticeship is over, he adopts society's attitude towards his former associates. Armed with the love of Mabel and believing he is free, Frederic arranges for the pirates' destruction by leading the policemen to annihilate them. Frederic looks forward to the coming conflict: 'At last I may atone, in some slight measure, / For the repeated acts of theft and pillage / Which, at a sense of duty's stern dictation, / I, circumstances victim, have been guilty' (II.139–42). However, Frederic's plans are thwarted when the Pirate King discovers a 'most ingenious paradox' (II.180): Frederic was apprenticed by the pirates until his twenty-first birthday and since he was born on leap year day, Frederic's indenture is far from over. The pirates do not insist on his remaining with them; rather, they appeal to his sense of duty. Mabel tries to convince Frederic that he need not stay, but he replies that 'when stern Duty calls, / I must obey' (II.304–5). A pirate once again, Frederic plans to return in 1940 to claim his beloved. He also dutifully reveals to the pirates that Major-General Stanley is not an orphan at all.

Frederic's subservience to duty is laughable because of the mechanical nature of his blind obedience. He fights with the pirates against the police in an act of duty seen as noble by his beloved Mabel, but which is incomprehensible to the police themselves. Mabel explains Frederic's situation to the police by telling them, 'his heroic sacrifice to his sense of duty has endeared him to me tenfold. He has done his duty. I will do mine. Go ye and do yours' (II.370–72). Although Mabel's motivation is not innate, she sees Frederic's nobility of subservience to duty as a model for all.

The police, like soldiers and sailors, are the protectors of society and must often put their own lives on the line for the benefit of others. However, the police in *The Pirates of Penzance* are realistic; they love immortality in song and story, but in their lives they see the world from different vantage points. The girls encourage them by singing, 'Go, ye heroes, go and die!' (II.85). But the police are not eager for death and glory; they are lovers of life and respect this quality in others. The police sing of the difficulty of their situation, 'When constabulary duty's to be done ... A policeman's lot is not a happy one' (II.402–4). The police see even a criminal's capacity for the enjoyment of life. Inspired by the women, their situation and the songs they sing, the police proceed against the pirates. Like Frederic, the police do their duty without any pleasure in the action itself; they are realistic, unlike the young ladies to whom the situation appears romantic. Through Gilbert's topsy-turvy method the police are sympathetic to the criminals and fearful of being hurt, yet the police submerge their own desires (not to mention that of the criminals) to their duty. They behave in the manner they believe is correct and proceed in a mechanical way. Arthur Sullivan's music, combined with Gilbert's lyrics, reflects the thinking of the policemen and underlines the focus of the play. The policemen march forward to a musical theme punctuated by the automated sound of 'Tarantara', repeating over and over again the last syllable of the word. What was originally the sound of an exhilarating trumpet call becomes a forced march forward. As with Frederic, the automatic, repetitive behaviour of the police leads to humour rather than pathos.

End of Act II: Duty to Queen and Country

At the start of the second act of the operetta, there would seem to be no reconciliation possible between the agents of civilization, the police and the Major-General, and the agents of escape, the pirates. Yet the conflict between society and escape is not completely serious, as Robert Higbie writes, 'We see they are unresolvable, but they do not arouse anxiety in us because we are made to feel that we need not try to resolve them, that they are so pointless they are not worth the effort. Thus Gilbert presents conflict only to offer us a comic evasion of it' (66). Yet the irresolvable conflict between the forces of society and the pirates is (artificially) resolved at the end of the performance.[8] Although the pirates win the struggle against the police, the police charge the pirates to yield 'in Queen Victoria's name!' The pirates cannot resist this command, for 'with all our faults, we love our Queen' (II.575). Their duty to themselves has been remade into duty to their monarch and their state. Unlike Frederic or the police, the pirates are motivated to do their civic duty by love and not blind obedience. The police officers reveal their own soft spots as they take out their handkerchiefs and weep at the sight of the pirates kneeling to the Queen. One further revelation awaits. As the pirates are being taken away, Ruth proclaims that they are all 'noblemen who have gone wrong' (II.584). The Major-General orders that the pirates, 'Resume your ranks and legislative duties, / and take my daughters, all of whom are beauties' (II.588–90). The pirates will take their proper places in society as Peers of the Realm and husbands. They will have a new duty to their country and family.

Pirates, known as a law unto themselves and a means of escaping societal laws, become, in the hands of Gilbert and Sullivan, subject to the very laws they had once sought to escape. While the pirates chided Frederic for leaving them to find

---

[8]   The impulse not to have it resolved can be seen by the *New York Times* 29 February 1940 article, 'Frederic Goes Free' (18), announcing that Frederic is finally out of his indentures and wishing him good luck on his ventures, echoing the opening chorus of pirates in the opera. They note within the article that Frederic may have miscalculated the time of his indenture because 1900 was not a leap year due to the fact that the earth takes a little less than 365 and a quarter days to orbit around the sun (centennial years are only leap years when evenly divisible by 400), and he may indeed have four more years to serve as an apprentice.

a place among the society in which 'pirates all are well-to-do', these men, who defied society, have become its leaders. Once restored to normal life, the pirates do their duty to their Queen and country as automatically as Frederic. There is humour in the mechanical, automatic nature of their action, and still more in the absurdity of the response. As with Frederic earlier in the operetta, the pirates' sense of duty has been taken to its *reductio ad absurdum*. The pirates have lost the certainty of their own moral superiority that they had as pirates. By 1879 it is only those who reside apart from society, like the pirates of Penzance, who can live moral lives. Having voluntarily removed themselves from society, they now return. Those within society who follow the dictates of duty reveal the hypocrisy of the civilized world. We can only hope that the incorporation of the reformed pirates into society changes society as well, which was intimated in the advertisement for the Glimmerglass Opera production of the *Pirates of Penzance* in 2006. In their advertisement Queen Victoria wears a pirate's eye patch, perhaps pointing to the way in which the Major-General's brand of piracy had infiltrated society at even the highest levels.

Gilbert's satiric treatment of the concept of duty in *The Pirates of Penzance* causes the audience to rethink the importance of duty and whether it should be followed blindly. Thus, the police have questioned duty but have gone ahead despite their hesitation; Frederic has obeyed his sense of responsibility without question, and the pirates have obeyed with love and suddenly found themselves upstanding members of a society from which they had previously been outcasts. Having been exposed as peers, they cannot escape their duty within the realm any longer. In becoming part of society, the pirates are subject to the same values as Frederic and the police. But duty has become mechanical and automatic; it no longer retains the fervour of a way of living and of dying expressed by Lord Nelson.

The operetta establishes the conflict between the desire for escape from society and the need to perform one's duty. Outside society, one can live by moral laws as the pirates do, but within society, one has to live by established laws. The finale, sung by the entire cast, addresses 'Poor wandering ones!' (II.590), which first looks to the pirates who have strayed, but finally reaches out to the audience, all of whose members have strayed at one point or another, and welcomes all back into society. Like the pirates, we must be part of the mainstream to enjoy the privileges of love of country and marriage, and as part of that society we must do our duty towards it. The treatment of duty in *The Pirates of Penzance* indicates that by the end of the nineteenth century, the obsession with duty evidenced by Lord Nelson was subject to challenges. It would take the social criticism of Oscar Wilde and George Bernard Shaw, and perhaps the horrific experience of the Great War, to completely turn accepted Victorian wisdom on its head. But W.S. Gilbert had begun the transformation of the idea of duty by making it a subject for satire and a matter of choice and discussion for the theatre-going public.

Chapter 13

'Dooty is Dooty': Pirates and Sea-Lawyers in *Treasure Island*

Alex Thomson

Compared with 'pieces of eight' or 'sixteen men on a dead man's chest', 'Dooty is dooty' may not be the first phrase that comes to mind when thinking of *Treasure Island*. Yet Long John Silver's tautologous watchword is repeated four times in Stevenson's most famous pirate tale, and the whole narrative is saturated with the discussion of duty. This phrase provides the key to three interlocking problems. It directs us to the book's break with what Stefan Collini has called the 'unreflective Kantianism of Victorian moral commonplaces' (63). The depiction of the pirates in *Treasure Island* holds up a mirror to a society characterized, as Collini puts it, by 'a tendency to extend the category of duty as widely as possible' (98) and in which, as Stevenson sketches out in the posthumously published fragment 'Lay Morals', the idea of duty has become both constrictive and debilitating. This underscores the fact that not only Jim's profit on the adventure, but also his very survival, depend on his capacity for *action*, understood to be exactly that which cannot be accounted for within a model of duty based on obligation and calculation. Finally, Stevenson's development of a literary form that models precisely this relationship highlights what Jacques Derrida describes as the 'fabular' mode of existence of the law and provides a basis for rethinking the cultural and political fantasy of the pirate. Introducing 'Lay Morals', Stevenson describes communication as a hermeneutic process: 'the speaker buries his meaning; it is for the hearer to dig it up again' (5). In the case of *Treasure Island*, the phrase 'dooty is dooty' supplies the crucial missing co-ordinates without which the book remains incomplete, like the duplicate map drawn up by the officers to keep the site of the treasure hidden from their mutinous crew.

I

In a tale characterized not so much by the disappearance of the rule of law as by the proliferation of competing legal and moral frameworks, is it surprising that the pirate crew of *Treasure Island* (1883) should be not merely argumentative but thoroughly litigious? When he inadvertently walks back into the hands of the buccaneers he believes he has already bested, Jim Hawkins is forced to defend himself by conjuring up the spectre of their future trial: 'if you spare me, bygones are bygones, and when you fellows are in court for piracy, I'll save you all I can' (152). But it rapidly becomes clear that the motley remnants of the pirate band are more interested in running their own kangaroo court. Long John Silver's comment 'First and last, we've split upon Jim Hawkins' (152) becomes uncannily prophetic as the dispute over Jim's fate leads to the arraignment of Silver before the pirate council. The subsequent desecration of Dick's Bible to provide the paper on which the Black Spot is inscribed implies the break-up of their association. Stevenson, who follows closely Johnson's account of pirate articles in *A General History of the Pyrates* (1724), must know that to sign up with a pirate band requires 'an Oath taken on a Bible, reserved for that Purpose only' (Johnson 213).[1] 'It'll do to kiss the book on still, won't it?' asks Dick. 'A Bible with a bit cut out!', Silver replies: 'Not it. It don't bind no more'n a ballad-book' (161). Yet the symbolic dissolution is really only an echo of the crew's prior betrayal by the opportunistic Long John Silver while they hold their deliberations: 'I'm on squire's side now' (155).

Gulled by Silver into abandoning their attempted deposition, the pirates reinstate the leader they have dared to challenge. Silver's disavowal of the mistakes they attribute to him may be a desperate piece of rhetorical showmanship, but his fundamental rebuke has some validity. This is the second time the crew have challenged Silver's authority: the first presentation of the Black Spot (we now discover) having taken place on landing, and having led to the disastrous – because premature – mutiny. Their insubordination, although entirely in accordance with the rules laid down in the articles, is their downfall. Pouring scorn on their pious belief in due process, Silver reminds us that part and parcel of the degeneracy of *Treasure Island*'s pirates is their quaint and irresponsible addiction to a heavily legalistic but formally democratic mode of decision-making. 'You always was brisk for business, and has the rules by heart George, as I'm pleased to see' (158), he comments sarcastically. Or to use Silver's own phrase, his crew turn out to be 'sea-lawyers' (61). A sea-lawyer, as Smyth's *Sailor's Wordbook* (1867) defines it, is 'an idle "long-shorer", more given to question orders than to obey them. One of the pests of the navy as well as of the mercantile marine' (*OED*, 2nd def.). Although he refers to the officers and gentlemen on board the *Hispaniola*, who must be murdered to keep their mouths shut, Silver might as well be describing the motley crew who scupper his own mercenary venture.

Revisionist historians have confirmed Stevenson's depiction of piracy as an egalitarian or even democratic affair. But they place a much more positive emphasis on the law-bound nature of the pirate life. Building on a hint thrown out by Christopher Hill that the pirates of the late sixteenth and early seventeenth century might have preserved not only radical ideas but also alternative forms of non-hierarchical social organization, Peter Linebaugh and Marcus Rediker have

---

[1]   Although Manuel Schonhorn ascribes authorship to Daniel Defoe, scholarly opinion no longer supports this attribution.

argued that 'the pirate ship was democratic in an undemocratic age' (162).[2] Their project offers something like a counter-mythology of piracy. Reading contemporary political concerns back into the historical record, they depict the pirate ship as not only egalitarian but 'multinational, multi-cultural and multi-racial' (Linebaugh 164); the pirates of the Golden Age had 'self-consciously built … a subversive alternative to the prevailing ways of the merchant, naval and privateering ship and a counterculture to the civilization of Atlantic capitalism with its expropriation and exploitation, terror and slavery' (Linebaugh 172). The formal equality of the pirate council, and the guaranteed autonomy of the pirate, over whom the Captain's command was absolute only in the heat of battle, are a reminder of an earlier age when most seamen were equal partners in the profits of an expedition, rather than wage-labourers, and a potent counterweight to the ill-treatment of sailors by many ships' officers in both navy and merchant marine.

If Stevenson's pirates are to be regarded as democratic, however, it is in the sense of mob rule current at the time of which he is writing, and might rather be ranked alongside the contemporary complaints cited by the revisionists Linebaugh and Rediker that 'there is so little Government and Subordination among [pirates], that they are, on Occasion, all Captains, all Leaders' (163). Craven, intemperate and bibulous, Stevenson's pirates are obsessed with their own pirate codes and conventions: 'This crew has its rights like other crews' (154) comments one unnamed marauder. The contrast with Long John Silver is particularly striking. Where Billy Bones was struck down by apoplexy on receipt of the Black Spot back in the Admiral Benbow Inn – as if a single piece of paper embodied the full force of the law – Silver seems to be not so much exempt from the strictures of the pirates' code as immune to them. Like much of Stevenson's work, *Treasure Island* is intensely aware of its own literary appropriation of oral narration, and literacy becomes the figure of the boundary between the pirates' submission to the law and Silver's overcoming of it.[3] 'Ah! 'Deposed' – that's it, is it?' asks Silver when he reads what is written on the Black Spot (158), but as Jim turns this 'curiosity' over in his hands he sees that the word has been misspelled: 'Depposed' (162). That their hastily assembled document is already disintegrating confirms the insubstantial nature of the pirates' access to textual authority. Jim has it beside him at the time of writing but 'not a trace of writing now remains beyond a single scratch, such as a man might make with his thumb-nail' (162).

Literate, cunning and 'a man of substance' (38), Silver's control of language is directly linked to his ability to dissemble, and in particular, to manipulate the distance between pirate myth and pirate reality. Not only can Silver change sides at will, but he is so far in appearance from what is already (by the 1750s, presumably) pirate legend that Jim is so fully taken in at Bristol as to fail to identify him with

---

[2]   See Christopher Hill's 'Radical Pirates' in the *Collected Essays of Christopher Hill*. Volume 3 (Brighton: Harvester, 1986): 161–87.

[3]   See Penny Fielding, *Writing and Orality: Nationality, Culture and Nineteenth-Century Scottish Fiction* (Oxford: Clarendon P, 1996).

the phallic horror haunting his dreams ('a monstrous kind of creature who had never had but the one leg, and that in the middle of his body' (3)). Like those pirate ships that would sail under innocent colours before running up the skull and crossbones when their unsuspecting victim was close at hand, Silver's true nature is hidden beneath the surface: 'he was too deep, and too ready, and too clever by me ... I would have gone bail for the innocence of Long John Silver' (44). Silver is fluent in the languages of the pirate and of the gentleman: too clean to be the one-legged figure of Jim's dreams, and on the voyage home no longer a murderous villain but 'the same bland, polite, obsequious seaman of the voyage out' (186). Silver's savings, remarked several times in the novel, also distance him from his mess-mates. Ben Gunn, who spends £1,000 within 20 days, is more typical of a group whose mythic propensity to bury their treasure is belied by the historical account of their profligacy, although some certainly managed to make fortunes, and others regularly dispatched money home to wives and family.[4]

We must therefore ask whether Silver is even a pirate in Stevenson's social diagram? His relationship to the outlaws among whom he lives is more akin to that of the aristocratic James Durie in Stevenson's later novel *The Master of Ballantrae* (1889). Silver was quartermaster for Flint's ship, as Durie is for Captain Teach's. However, it has been suggested by historians that the quartermaster may often have held the real power on a pirate ship, and again Stevenson concurs, hinting that even Flint was afraid of Silver. We might treat Silver's disavowal of his leadership accordingly: '"No, not I," said Silver. "Flint was cap'n"' (57). As quartermaster, the Master faces Teach down on more than one occasion and finally bests him with curt arrogance and a shoddy joke, in the style of the late twentieth-century action-movie hero: 'Heretofore you have been called Captain Teach, but I think you are now rather Captain Learn' (*Master* 46). Silver and the Master share more than circumstantial traits, however: both have a propensity for extreme violence when necessary, but more disturbingly, a charming manner and a treacherous eloquence which compels at least respect, and at most devotion, in their acquaintances.

Significantly, Ballantrae also combines the roles of outlaw and lawgiver, for it is at his instigation that 'laws were passed in imitation of a pirate by the name of Roberts' (41) on board Teach's ship. The reference is to Johnson's history, but the latter describes the articles as more or less ubiquitous in the world of the maritime marauders: 'the principal Customs, and Government, of this roguish Commonwealth; which are pretty near the same with all Pyrates' (213). Stevenson turns typical pirate governance into a device of Ballantrae's (who insists on maintaining Teach as Captain for the same reason) to better manipulate his fellow rogues. Both the Master and Long John Silver appear to subject themselves to pirate law, but also to flaunt it or manipulate it at will. This ambiguous position is consistent with both their distinction among the pirates themselves – *with* them perhaps, but not *of* them – and Stevenson's own anxieties, evident in his essay

---

[4]   See Robert C. Ritchie's *Captain Kidd and the War Against the Pirates* (Cambridge, MA: Harvard UP, 1986): 119–21, 229–30.

'The Day After Tomorrow', about the threat to liberty posed by the combination of levelling and authoritarian tendencies in that 'stealthy change which has come over the spirit of Englishmen and English legislation' which he names 'Socialism' (472). 'Lay Morals' suggests that Stevenson's apparent rejection of duty in *Treasure Island* would be continuous with a notion of freedom conceived in terms of the alternative between conformity and manhood.

Stevenson's individualism has proven hard for recent critics to stomach; like the historian, those literary hermeneuts who have come looking for buried political treasure are mostly interested in his work as representing a 'reality' about the rights and wrongs of which they are already certain. In *Empire Boys* Joseph Bristow remarks on the anxiety of late nineteenth-century critics concerning popular fiction, yet seems to perpetuate that anxiety, albeit from a different political perspective, when he depicts such writing as right-wing and imperialistic in orientation. He suggests that 'the Robinsonade is modified, particularly in Stevenson's hands, into a kind of popular romance highly admired by conservative apologists for the novel' (Bristow 93). *Treasure Island* is damned by comparison with Stevenson's own subsequent work, and in particular with *The Beach of Falesá* (1893) which Stevenson himself described as 'the first realistic South Sea story', complaining that 'everybody else who has tried, got carried away by the romance' (qtd. in Bristow 122). However, it is by no means apparent that romance and realism are mutually exclusive terms in Stevenson's work, as an anonymous reviewer who praised the 'healthy realism' of *Treasure Island* seems to appreciate: '[the pirates'] profession is not set forth in a dangerous halo of romance' (Maixner 128).[5] Stevenson sees a combination of the 'realistic and ideal' as the fundamental principle of successful representative art, and in his essays on romance, his animus is directed largely against naturalism, which he sees as burdening the clear delineation of reality with an unhealthy cult of facts ('A Note' 78).[6] Because of, rather than despite, its romance form we should expect to find the book that Robert Fraser describes as the 'founding text in the revival of quest romance' (26) as a confrontation with rather than an escape from reality.

II

His essay on Victor Hugo plays the same founding role for Stevenson the man of letters that *Treasure Island* does for the novelist. Written when he was only 24 – as he acknowledges in the Preface to *Familiar Studies of Men and Books* – this essay, which first found him the patronage of the *Cornhill* magazine, sets out in its essentials the theory of the novel that was to be expanded in his later, better-known

---

[5]   Harvie also suggests that, like other criminals in Stevenson, his pirates are 'realistically drunken and repellent' (119).

[6]   See also Stevenson's 'A Gossip on Romance' and 'A Humble Remonstrance' in *Memories and Portraits*.

essays. Writing of Hugo, Stevenson argues that while 'Romance is a language in which many persons learn to speak with a certain amount of fluency … there are few who can ever bend it to any practical need, few who can ever be said to express themselves in it' ('Victor Hugo', 54). Hugo is one of the few who can establish a moral significance as the essence of his romances. But this moral is an 'organizing principle'; Stevenson is not interested in 'the novel with a purpose', 'the model of incompetence' in which 'the moral [is] clumsily forced into every hole and corner of the story, or thrown externally over it like a carpet over a railing' (147).

If a conception of moral purpose guides both Stevenson's theory and practice of romance, though, *Treasure Island* has certainly struck its critics as morally ambiguous. The novel puns extensively on the terminological confusion between the gentry and the pirates, and as Naomi Wood points out: 'the reactions of gentlemen of fortune and gentlemen of fortune to the idea of seven hundred thousand pounds of buried treasure is strikingly uniform' (69). As in the case of Silver, authority in the novel is bestowed not by one's place in social or legal hierarchies so much as by the ability to exploit other men's propensity to deference. In the early chapters, the authority of Squire Trelawney and Doctor Livesey seems to be merely formal, and once at sea it is distinctly precarious. Captain Smollett is alternately practical and comic in his devotion to duty, and his punctilious raising of the Union Jack over the stockade serves only to draw the pirate's cannon-fire.

The central question of *Treasure Island* might be posed in the following way: what does it mean to do one's 'dooty'? But the prime feature of 'dooty' being that it requires no other justification, it just *is* one's duty – Silver repeats 'dooty is dooty' as if it explained itself tautologically – there is no clear answer. Does dooty mean obedience to military, naval or legal procedures? Or conformity to pirate codes? Dooty is what binds Silver and his piratical comrades not only to their allotted tasks on board ship under Smollett's command, but also to their own lore and edicts: 'the crew has tipped you the black spot in full council, as in dooty bound; just you turn it over, as in dooty bound, and see what's wrote there' (158). Yet if it seems as if not only good men but also pirates are hemmed in, bound up in their dooties, it should also become apparent that 'dooty' may not mean that much after all. 'If I die like a dog, I'll die in my dooty' (72) protests honest seaman Tom; yet Silver and Jim seem to change sides at will. Silver's claim to have 'come back to [his] dooty' (177) when he returns to Smollett's command has a hollow ring. 'Dooty' should be absolute, or it is nothing, not binding after all. However, if a Bible can become like a ballad-book, so we might see that duty is also variable, or at the very least context-specific.

What Jim learns from Silver is the priority of action, considered as that which cuts through 'duties'. Where his litigious crew is really at fault, concludes Silver, is 'you hain't got the invention of a cockroach' (161). It is the power of action as a form of tactical invention, closely linked to command over language, that marks Jim's accession to maturity in the novel; and it is the excess of action over duty that the novel confirms through its narrative structure and organization. That action breaks with moral order is the key not only to the novel's own 'moral' organization, but also to Stevenson's conception of romance and his life-long struggle with the authority of Scott's novels. As he comments in the Hugo essay, what separates Scott from Fielding is 'a sense of the subtle influences that moderate and qualify a man's personality; that personality is no longer thrown out in unnatural isolation, but is resumed into its place in the constitution of things' ('Victor Hugo', 34).[7] The romance of adventure is that in which man no longer appears as wholly self-willed: a 'change in the manner of regarding men and their actions' ('Victor Hugo', 34), that is not only the formal, but the thematic or moral truth of *Treasure Island*.

The novel pivots on three moments of what Jim describes as the 'mad notions that contributed so much to save our lives' (72), the first of which comes when Jim slips over the side of the *Hispaniola* to go ashore with the pirates. It is a sudden thought that occurs to him, and which he regrets almost instantly, although it turns out to have been for the best. The 'second folly, far worse than the first' (117) comes when he abandons his companions in the blockhouse. This is rather more premeditated, as Jim has the opportunity to take provisions and weapons. His third notion is to cut the *Hispaniola* adrift, and this is clearly associated by Jim with his first two acts of 'truantry' (119). Hemmed in by competing notions of obligation, Jim's agency constitutes itself through the flagrant transgression of all protocols and codes and Jim feels these actions to be derelictions of duty, fearing that the accusation of desertion might be levelled at him with some justice.

Stevenson proposes one interpretation of this structure. Livesey's response when he hears of Jim's adventures is: 'there is a kind of fate in this ... every step it's you that saves our lives' (168). Equally, it is providence to which Ben Gunn attributes his place on the island, a nod from Stevenson to Defoe (93). The challenge of *Robinson Crusoe* is that the book could be convincingly either what it appears to be, a primer in providential religion, or a dissection of religious belief as compensatory delusion. Stevenson would have relished this irony, and it seems that he has laid the same trap both for Ben Gunn and for Jim. His actions, which he cannot explain, appear in retrospect as if they had been fated all along. Their success justifies what are at the time derelictions of duty. Jim's own mutiny and piracy are nothing of the sort, because they turn out to be heroic – having been proven profitable – by the subsequent turn of events.

This complication of the relationship between temporality and legitimacy can be linked to a common feature of pirate life – and death – suggesting that the strongest insight into pirate history in Stevenson's book comes from its structural characteristics rather than from surface details. A pirate's return is always uncertain because of the suspended legality of the crew's actions while on the high seas. It is often political circumstances in their home port that will determine whether what was licensed on departure will turn out to have been tolerated on return. In an uncertain legal and political context the pirate's real dilemma, as Jim discovers, is that actions can only be approved or condemned after the event,

---

[7]   Stevenson was later to develop this idea in 'A Gossip on Romance' into the difference between the novel of character and the novel of adventure.

while decisions have to be taken in the suspension of the applicable laws. Silver is the only member of the cast to show an explicit awareness of this fact, as he faces down the challenge of the Black Spot, overturning legal jurisdiction with the interpretative power of persuasion which is always called upon to supplement mere 'dooty'. Jim's moments of folly become legitimate decisions after the event, through a process of *post facto* rationalization which obliterates their irrational and contingent foundations.

In *The Human Condition* Hannah Arendt gives a description of the structure of action which perfectly characterizes *Treasure Island*, once we recognize that the moral lies in the excess of action over ordinary morality, or duty: 'To act, in its most general sense, means to take an initiative, to begin … It is in the nature of beginning that something new is started which cannot be expected from whatever may have happened before' (177–8). In other words, an action needs to be distinguished from the following of a rule: an action is inventive, it depends upon the suspension of any possible condition by which it could be predicted or determined. It follows that action is precisely what a conception of duty cannot teach us. Like Stevenson, Arendt specifically links action to speech: 'with word and deed we insert ourselves into the human world' (176). Most strikingly of all, she links action to storytelling, the narration by which the agent is retrospectively constituted: 'stories, the results of action and speech, reveal an agent, but this agent is not an author or producer' (184). The implied distinction is between *praxis* and *poesis*, between an action which inaugurates, and a making according to some particular end. Jim can tell the story of his actions, but cannot become their author: this is the significance of his retrospective narration, beyond its testament to his literacy. Providence, Arendt suggests, is one of those terms by which men 'tried to solve the perplexing problem that although history owes its existence to men, it is still obviously not made by them' (185).

The link between speech and action is confirmed in Stevenson's own account of the genesis of *Treasure Island*: 'The beginner must have a slant of wind, a lucky vein must be running, he must be in one of those hours when the words come and the phrases balance of themselves – even to begin' ('My First Book' 193). Yet nothing is certain until the book is done: 'And having begun, what a dread looking forward is that until the book shall be accomplished! For so long a time the slant is to continue unchanged, the vein to keep running; for so long a time you must hold at command the same quality of style; for so long a time your puppets are to be always vital, always consistent, always vigorous' ('My First Book' 193). Reworking the traditional topoi of inspiration in a maritime idiom which also suggests something like gold mining, Stevenson stresses that only the end will ever justify the audacity of beginning.

So develops an easy equivalence between the act of writing and the actions of the romance hero. Stevenson's numerous acts of literary piracy in *Treasure Island* are recounted in his essay in great detail, but they were already acknowledged in the prefatory poem which captures the author's place alongside 'Kingston, or Ballantyne the brave / Or Cooper of the wood and wave' as tellers of 'the old romance' (xxx). To begin is an act of style: the inscription of one's unique presence amongst one's elders and betters, which can only be an act of unlicensed violence, the staking of a claim that can only be proved through its own success. This is frontier work, or, not to put too fine a point on it, piracy. Through a paradox that Heidegger explores in his essay on the work of art, only the existence of the artwork bestows on its creator that title which alone could have authorized beginning in the first place.[8] That writing's legislative dimension exceeds its representational function is also one of the lessons Jim must learn. What he also finds out is that such literary self-creation is necessarily violent, and deeply anarchic. The foundation of the law depends on the murderous suspension of the law. Whereas in *Peter Pan* Barrie keeps the pirates at a reassuring distance (Never Land) and offers us the choice between growing up and submitting to the law – returning with Wendy – or remaining exiled from it forever with Peter, Stevenson teaches us that to become oneself requires the contravention of social custom. The writing and reading of literature becomes an image of that making and remaking of the law on which *bildung* depends, and which runs athwart the discourse of 'duty'.

III

'The instant of decision is madness' (Derrida, *Writing* 30): Jim's transition to adulthood can be helpfully set alongside Jacques Derrida's citation of Kierkegaard, in both early and more recent texts.[9] For there to be a decision, Derrida argues, there must be impossibility. If I did not have to choose between two equally persuasive or compelling actions, if I were not faced with a dilemma which could not be referred to any particular tribunal or law to determine the correct course of action, I would not be called upon to make a decision. So we are only really speaking of a decision when there is a situation which cannot be overcome without something like Jim's moments of truantry. Each such decision, which can only occur in the suspension of any and every law which might determine its outcome, marks the invention, the 'mystical foundation', of a new law in setting a course by which one can steer. But it can only be seen as such afterwards: since in the decision there are no criteria against which to judge it; and if it could be anticipated in advance it would be the unfolding of a programme rather than the taking of a decision. Derrida suspends the possibility of simply identifying freedom with action, on which Arendt's account depends: 'the decision makes the event, but it also neutralizes this happening that must surprise both the freedom and the will of every subject' (Derrida, *Politics of Friendship* 68).

---

[8] See Martin Heidegger's 'The Origin of the Work of Art', in *Basic Writings* ed. David Farrell Krell (London and New York: Harper Collins, 1993): 139–212.

[9] See, for example, Derrida's more recent 'Force of Law: The "Mystical Foundation of Authority"', trans. Mary Quaintance, Drucilla Cornell et al. (eds), *Deconstruction and the Possibility of Justice* (New York: Routledge, 1992): 26.

Jim's more or less impulsive breaks with what he knows to be his duty can be seen, with the hindsight he himself employs in telling his story, as such inventions of the law. But what stands out, and this is why Long John Silver is so clearly the figure best equipped to guide the lad, is that the founding of the law takes place in a constitutive moment of illegality. The old law must be broken, the new law does not yet apply and so the moment of law-making is a kind of disruptive interzone. *Treasure Island* – in which the outcomes of Jim's actions are deferred until the plot resolves and one side or other wins – prolongs and sustains this moment. Derrida comments: 'In the founding of the law or in its institution, the same problem of justice will have been posed and violently resolved, that is to say buried, dissimulated, repressed. Here the best paradigm is the founding of the nation-states or the institutive act of a constitution' ('Force of Law' 24). Derrida's essay 'Declarations of Independence' first cast this as a performative structure: the signatories of the United States Constitution are not yet legally the representatives of the body they are claiming to bring into being. This does not invalidate the Constitution, but it may require us to rethink our notion of legality somewhat.[10]

Where *Treasure Island* specifically anticipates Derrida is in its romance form. In his essay on Kafka's 'Before the Law', Derrida argues that the mode of existence of the law must be fabular. Because the law denies its own historicity, it presents itself as eternal; it cannot be accounted for on the basis of a history or a legal anthropology. Of Freud's hypothetical foundation of the law in the killing of the primal father, Derrida comments 'this pure and purely presumed event nevertheless marks an invisible rent in history. It resembles a fiction, a myth, or a fable' ('Before the Law' 199). Situated before (in relation to) the law, we cannot conceive or account for a time before (prior to) the law, and therefore an origin of the law. The law's origin is neither ahistorical, nor is it available to factual reconstruction: the law belongs to fiction.

If we accept the account I have offered of the connection between action and romance, and of Stevenson to Derrida, it should become clear that the political lesson offered by *Treasure Island* runs deeper than that of the revisionists. As historians, they rely on the possibility of distinguishing the 'romance' from the 'reality', as David Cordingly's popular pirate history promises. Yet this distinction is put into question in Stevenson's model of the literary artwork. Replying to Henry James in 'A Humble Remonstrance', Stevenson suggests that James's essay should really have been called 'the Art of Narrative' (J. Smith, 87). Like Scott, Stevenson rejects the moralizing distinction between novel and romance, which derives from contrasting their relationships to 'reality'. The final lines of the prefatory poem – 'may I / And all my pirates share the grave / Where these and

---

[10]   The connection to *Treasure Island* may not be wholly anachronistic. John D. Moore remarks that 'Stevenson's notion of narrative is intriguing in its anticipation of speech act theory' (439), while Derrida himself links Austin back to Nietzsche in *Limited Inc*. See Moore's 'Emphasis and Suppression in Stevenson's *Treasure Island*: Fabrication of the Self in Jim Hawkins' Narrative', *CLA Journal* 34 (June 1991): 436–52.

their creation lies!' (xxx) – collapse the distinction between author and character, and glorifies the romancers themselves as buccaneers. In doing so Stevenson turns *Treasure Island* itself into a figure of literature, conceived as an inventive act of piracy committed against 'history' understood as linear, sequential, progressive. The flora of the island are Californian rather than Caribbean; but accuracy of correspondence to a specific real topography or history is by the by. After all, the story of the book, as opposed to the story in the book, begins with Stevenson's founding act of cartographic invention.[11]

When it comes to pirates, *Treasure Island* does conform to a relatively consistent historical framework in a way which *The Master of Ballantrae*, a more obvious historical allegory in its concern with the effects of the '45, is not: Teach died in 1718, according to the same account from which Stevenson draws his description of the pirate. However this consistency is beside the point – not least because a 'realistic' reading of *Treasure Island* must fall victim to such challenges as Ritchie's response to the legend of Captain Kidd's treasure: 'the idea of burying loot on a tropical island would have struck [the men who turned to piracy] as insane' (229–30). So although licensed to invent freely by the conventional assurance of its fictional status, romance for Stevenson does not mean an indifference to history, nor does it mean a story located in some ahistorical mythic realm. Rather, by exposing the mechanisms of the law, *Treasure Island* can call into question the legislative distinction between history and fiction which seeks to rule one version of the pirate in and another out. The romance is not anti-realist, and it is entirely consistent for Stevenson to be praised for both his romance and his realism: but romance is stronger than realism, in being able to challenge the forms of narrative legitimization that seek to demarcate fact and fiction. The centrality of Johnson's *General History* to both Stevenson's work – he had a copy of the book sent out to him while he was writing *Treasure Island* – and to the revisionist project suggests not only the intense ambivalence of the documentation of pirate life but also its scarcity. That this text lies at the origin of all fictional and historical depictions of pirates suggests that it can be consistently judged to belong to neither one nor the other mode of story-telling.

The mythology of the pirate is based on a simple topological model. As exotic outsider, or as drunken hooligan, the pirate derives his status from being outside or beyond the law, a situation doubled in the case of the notorious female pirates. The revisionist model offered by Linebaugh and Rediker does not put this into question, but takes pirate democracy to be the figure of a virtuous and self-organizing community bound only by its own conventions, enforced socially, rather than via government. For Linebaugh and Rediker pirate democracy is set up outside or beyond the law. It may impose its own rules – indeed this is what constitutes it as a form of society rather than merely the anarchy as which it is reviled – but it is defined in opposition to majority state power. Pirates are exceptions,

---

[11] Elaborated in 'My First Book'; the story is continued in 'The Persons of the Tale', a metafictional encounter between Smollett and Silver.

the existence of whom proves the rule about the rest of maritime venture in its unredeemed capitalist form. This is to reverse our perspective on piracy: no longer simply illegal, illegitimate and outlawed, being outside of the law becomes the very virtue of the pirate. Excepting themselves from illegitimate frameworks of legality confers a legitimacy on their actions. The historians presume a topological model of legality based on a simple opposition in which the majority fall within the law, but a minority fall without; their analysis of pirate democracy inverts our conventional distribution of value within the figure (an inversion whose affective path has already been mapped in the popular romance of the heroic swashbuckler) rather than threaten the overall schema.

The consequences of these observations are striking. The lesson of *Treasure Island* is clearly not simply either the value of abiding by the law – since Jim's success depends on breaking rules – or the virtue of transgression, since Jim positions himself on the side of law, against the pirates. What the book opens up instead is an image of the law that is not governed by the topological figure of inside / outside. The performative and illegal foundation of legality that Jim discovers suggests that the border between legitimate and illegitimate passes through the innermost parts of the law itself, indeed bisects the law at its origin. The pirates are, as Stevenson has shown us, as subject to the law of the law as everyone else, however debatable and negotiable their particular laws might be. The pirate can no longer be opposed to the law-abiding citizen as either simply the degenerate and irresponsible law-breaker; but nor can the inverse argument be sustained – that he or she is the virtuous political opponent of an illegitimate legality. What the figure of the pirate exposes, and what Jim learns to manipulate, is that the origin of the law lies in an improvisational violence, a violence which can never be acknowledged or accounted for by the law. Stevenson's account is anarchic: not in the sense of opposing the vigour of chaos to the entropy of order, nor in the political celebration of an alternative vision of human co-operation and autonomy, freed from oppressive authority, but in exposing the void at the origin of the law, an exposure pre-eminently of the order of romance.

Chapter 14

Staging the Pirate: The Ambiguities of Representation and the Significance of Convention

Victor Emeljanow

The tradition of nineteenth-century pirate representation demonstrates a complex intertwining of the strands of popular literature and theatre. Popular theatrical performances included the latest technological developments, and their scripts appropriated fictional narratives and scenes from contemporary painting. Equally, novelists and painters used the theatrical staging of situation and character as modes of representation. As Martin Meisel points out, 'the shared structures in the representational arts constitute not just a common style but a popular style' (4). At the same time, Meisel argues, nineteenth-century arts and entertainment aspired 'to a union of inward signification, moral and teleological as well as affective, with a weighty, vivid, detailed and documented rendering of reality' (13). It is within this context that the pirate becomes a key figure in the complex discourse of performance conventions, which themselves embody outward signification and the desire for verisimilitude.

Any discussion of the representation, or staging, of the pirate must therefore acknowledge the contributions of the actors who impersonated him and the dramatic genres of melodrama, burlesque and pantomime, which enabled audiences to position the pirate within the world of archetypal villainy and heroism, or in that of mocking ironization. Equally important in the development of this representation is the appropriation of melodramatic narratives by the emerging industry of juvenile literature from 1851 onwards and the representation of these narratives in the miniaturized toy theatres of the so-called Juvenile Drama from 1811 onwards. In this chapter I shall consider the development of the stage pirate in the nineteenth century by examining popular dramas like *Peter Pan* and *The Red Rover* alongside less well-known works (including private, domestic performances like those of the juvenile theatre) to reflect upon the dramatic forces that combined to shape the image of the stage pirate that we know and love today.

As *Pirates of the Caribbean* draws its inspiration from the flamboyant impersonations of Tyrone Power and Errol Flynn, so in turn their films drew inspiration from the novels of Rafael Sabatini and the representations of pirates by Howard Pyle for magazines like *Scribner's* and *Harper's Monthly* (Figure 14.1).

Figure 14.1   Howard Pyle, 'Captain Keitt', *Harper's Monthly*, August 1907

Pyle's contribution to the iconography of the pirate cannot be overestimated and goes back to his first contribution to *Scribner's* in 1877, appearing three years before Gilbert and Sullivan's *Pirates of Penzance*.[1] In the preface to his *Book of Pirates*, Pyle outlined the perennial attractiveness of the pirate figure:

> Courage and daring, no matter how mad and ungodly, have always a redundancy of vim and life to recommend them to the nether man that lies within us, and no doubt his desperate courage, his battle against the tremendous odds of all the civilized world of law and order, have had much to do in making a popular hero of our friend of the black flag. (xiv)

In the 1890s, Pyle also published illustrated editions of Defoe's *Robinson Crusoe* and Stevenson's *Treasure Island* for Scribner's Illustrated Classics and of Charles Johnson's 1724 *General History of the Robberies and Murders of the*

---

[1]   Pyle's first significant depiction of pirates was 'The Buccaneers and Marooners of the Spanish Main', in *Harper's Magazine* in 1887.

Most Notorious Pyrates.[2] He thus allied himself to both an eighteenth-century tradition of representation and, more closely, to Stevenson's novel, itself regarded as 'the apotheosis of the 'penny dreadful' (Darton 295).

Pyle's comments about the liminal position of the pirate as a popular hero/ villain reflect contemporary perceptions of piracy and the pirate. For example, Samuel Walkey's protagonist in 'The King of the Seas' describes his reactions to La Valle, his pirate opponent: 'I could not help a great dash of admiration flooding my heart at his inimitable coolness – his perfect nonchalance' (180). Similarly, writing of *Treasure Island* in 1888, Henry James lauded Stevenson's Long John Silver as 'one of the most picturesque ... most genially presented villains in the whole literature of romance. He has a singularly distinct and expressive countenance, which, of course, turns out to be a grimacing mask. Never was a mask more knowingly, vividly painted' (qtd. in Carpenter 155). James's comments illustrate an ambiguity embedded in representations of pirates, deriving from their links to popular magazines and juvenile literature in particular. Moreover, James's references to the 'picturesque', 'the expressive countenance' and the 'grimacing mask' connect descriptions of villainy to its performance, to the essential theatricality of the piratical persona and, obliquely, to the direct influence of theatre conventions and practices.

Juvenile magazines appealed to the same clientele who regularly purchased the scenes and characters that were used in juvenile theatres. The magazines modelled their stories on the earlier adventure novels of Frederick Marryat, W. H. Kingston and R. M. Ballantyne. They also shared many of the same values: 'to entertain and instruct, to inculcate approved value systems, to spread useful knowledge, to provide acceptable role models' (J. Richards 3). The juvenile or toy theatres enabled children to share the experience of an exciting melodrama at home and to recreate for themselves the performances of popular actors and their theatrical contexts. In an article about juvenile theatre, Frank Jay describes the close connection between juvenile theatres and the emerging industry in the 1860s of juvenile fiction. He points to the fact that Edwin J. Brett, a founder of the long-running magazine *Boys of England*, launched the publication in November 1866 with a serial *Alone in the Pirates' Lair*, together with a toy theatre version – 'a complete new Play' – of the same name, 'consisting of eight scenes, seven sheets of characters, six wings, and foot-pieces, and a large stage front' (qtd. in Jay).[3]

This commercial crossover suggests the absorption of an older tradition to launch a new venture for a new market. The industry of toy theatres actually coincides with the heyday of melodrama. Skelt began his business in the early 1840s, while William West inaugurated the fashion for publishing juvenile plays in 1811 and continued his business until 1832. West went to great lengths to engrave representations of famous actors like Edmund Kean and T. P. Cooke and selected plays that represented the

---

2 In his collection *The Buccaneers and Marooners of America* (London: Fisher Unwin, 1891).

3 From *Boys of England*, 27 November 1866: 16.

current melodramatic taste, including *Black Ey'd Susan* and *The Red Rover*.[4] In his *Memories and Portraits*, Stevenson devotes a whole chapter to juvenile theatres and remembers with effervescent pleasure the acquisition of sets of Skelt's *Juvenile Drama* in Edinburgh, referring directly to the plays he had possessed as a child, including *The Red Rover*, *My Poll and My Partner Joe*, *The Smuggler* and *Der Freischutz*.[5] These 'penny plain and twopence coloured' (198) were to influence his later work profoundly: 'Out of this cut-and-dry, dull, swaggering, obtrusive, and infantile art, I seem to have earned the very spirit of my life's enjoyment; met there the shadows of the characters I was to read about and love in a late future' (209).

The Red Rover undoubtedly helped shape elements of *Treasure Island* and it is therefore worth pausing to consider why this play was so enduring and influential. *The Red Rover*, a version of J. Fenimore Cooper's novel by Edward Fitzball, was staged at London's Adelphi theatre on 9 February 1829. Cooper's novel had been published in London and Paris in 1827 and adapted for the stage as early as 1828 in the United States.[6] Cooper had made it clear that his portrayal of the Red Rover was intended 'to show the manner in which men of the fairest promise can be led astray by their wayward passions, and to prove how narrow the boundaries become between virtue and vice' (427). These ambiguous attributes would appeal to any actor-manager. Fitzball himself was one of the most successful melodramatists of the first half of the nineteenth century. He adapted Cooper's *The Pilot* for the Adelphi in 1825 and wrote *The Flying Dutchman: or, the Phantom Ship* for the same theatre in 1827. Both of these came under the management of Frederick Yates, a charismatic and versatile actor who played the title role of the Red Rover [Figure 14.2]. *The Times* thought he played the role 'with great spirit' ('Adelphi Theatre' 3); and Henry Crabbe Robinson, who had seen the production on 17 March 1829, found that he 'looked the bold pirate to perfection and his powers of mimicry made him an excellent performer of characters in disguise' (127). *The Stage or Theatrical Inquisitor* felt that the staging elements would ensure the production's success: 'The story is much altered from the novel … but there is sufficient life, bustle, burning, blazing and dancing … to make it a favourite for some time with the public' (*The Stage or Theatrical Inquisitor*, February 1829, 102). By September 7 it was being produced at the Surrey theatre (the old Royal Circus) with T. P. Cooke given top billing as the resourceful sailor, Fid, and the Rover played by the theatre's manager, David Osbaldiston.[7]

---

[4]   See Ralph Thomas, 'Juvenile Drama', *Notes and Queries*, 18 October 1873, quoted by Jay.

[5]   Originally published as an article in *The Magazine of Art*, April 1884.

[6]   In a version by Samuel Chapman at the Chestnut theatre, Philadelphia, 28 February 1828. The version was staged at the Lafayette theatre, New York on 26 May 1828 and continued to be performed as late as 1879. (See James Rees's *Old Drury of Philadelphia: A History of the Philadelphia Stage, 1800–1835* (Philadelphia: U of Philadelpha P, 1932), 138.)

[7]   On the continuing popularity of versions of the play see John D. Gordan, 'The Red Rover Takes the Boards', *American Literature* 10.1 (March 1938): 66–75 and George Speaight's *Juvenile* (London: Macdonald, 1946).

Figure 14.2   J. K. Green, 'Characters and Scenes in *The Red Rover*' (1842)

The play was billed as a 'nautical burletta' at the Adelphi; at the Surrey it was simply announced as a 'nautical drama'. The Adelphi, situated on the Strand in the heartland of London's West End, was closer to the two patent theatres, Covent Garden and Drury Lane. They were the only theatres licensed to perform the 'legitimate' drama. As an 'illegitimate' theatre, the Adelphi risked being prosecuted for performing plays that contained dialogue. Yates was sufficiently diplomatic to use the old, and increasingly irrelevant category of 'burletta' to describe *The Red Rover*, despite the fact that by 1829 the distinctions between 'legitimate' and 'illegitimate' plays were blurred and often ignored.[8] South of the Thames and outside the City of Westminster, the Surrey, since its days as the Royal Circus, had been rebuilt to cater

---

[8]   The burletta was defined as 'a drama in rhyme which is entirely musical; a short piece of recitation and singing, wholly accompanied more or less by an orchestra', George Colman, *Random Records*, 1830, 146 quoted in George Rowell, *The Victorian Theatre* (Cambridge: Cambridge UP, 1978), 10.

for the large numbers of local residents as well as for a wider, more affluent audience. *The Red Rover* was added to a programme which contained Douglas Jerrold's long-running *Black Ey'd Susan* and emphasized the attractiveness of T. P. Cooke, who played in both. Just as at the Adelphi the play had been a vehicle for Yates, so at the Surrey it became a vehicle for a star performer of British sailors.

As contemporary reviews indicate, the performance of the stage pirate reflected the public's appetite for spectacular theatrical display. Audiences also responded to the performance of the pirate's persona – the mask referred to by Henry James – which allowed the actor to demonstrate a capacity for deception, disguise and illusion. The list of costumes for *The Red Rover* production included disguise elements like flaxen and grey wigs that allowed the Rover to conceal his real identity. For the Pirate, the costume is 'a blue jacket trimmed with gold lace, red stocking tights, red waistcoat, white petticoat, trowsers [sic], blue cloth cap hanging down at the side, black belt, mantle shoes and buckles' (*The Red Rover*, Dicks' Standard Plays, No. 450, nd, I.viii). The illustration [Figure 14.3] captures the moment of revelation as the Rover discards his cloak and flourishes the red flag that identifies him to Fid and to the hero, Lieutenant Wilder:

> ROV: You start: are there no king's ships but those of England? No flags but those of George? What think you of the lily of France? (*takes up a white flag, waves it and drops it.*) Or the gorgeous Spaniard? (*Unfurls another flag as before.*) or the Portuguese? (*Displays a third flag.*) You see I boast the colours of all nations.
> WIL: And which of the colours do you yourself assume?
> ROV: This. (*Waving a crimson flag and throwing off his mantle*) Behold and know me! (*Music*)
> WIL: The Red Rover?
> ROV: Ay, the Red Rover! (*Music. Strikes a gong which is hanging near R. 3rd. E. And the deck is filled with whole crew, all armed*) (I.viii)

The script emphasizes the deceptive nature of the pirate, able to hide behind the colours of a flag. Moreover, the staging of the Rover revealing himself by unfurling, waving and dropping four separate flags is both flamboyant and dramatic. The illustration, which depicts the scene where the Rover reveals himself as a pirate, has been adjusted to include many more crew on stage, further emphasizing the scene's theatricality. It also adjusts the persona of the pirate to reflect a young, slightly androgynous young man, not the 32-year-old of Yates's theatrical portrait, in order to tap into contemporary expectations and images of the pirate.

At the same time, however, the theatrical performance fleshes out Cooper's original plans for his characters. When Madame de Lacy, who, together with her daughter, has been abducted by the pirate, pleads for their lives when confronted by a mutinous crew intent on their deaths, the Rover responds: 'Lady, this is bold language to sound in the ears of a blood-seeking, remorseless pirate, since 'tis plain you believe me such; but know, that vengeance is at hand – such vengeance as the hunted and denounced freebooter best likes, and is proud to inflict – mercy' (II.xiv).

Figure 14.3   Edward Fitzball, *The Red Rover*, frontispiece to Dicks' Standard
Plays, No. 450 (undated, possibly 1843)

The disparity between the Rover's outward show and inner sensitivity, public
reputation and private nobility, emphasizes the complexity of Cooper's character.
The play ends as the chief mutineer, Sam Cutreef, shoots the Rover, and the comic
tailor Hector Homespun, sets the ship on fire:

> ROV (laughing hysterically): Ha, ha, ha! So best: his ship shall be the Rover's
> funeral pile. (*The flames issue from the hatchway – Re-enter the crew from both
> cabins. – The ship is seen burning – she begins to sink with the Crew-some fall-
> some ascend the rigging, others struggling as the ocean overwhelms them-Mast,
> rigging and Crew, all sink with the vessel.-The Red Rover is seen combating the
> waves, and at last meets his fate. – The Dart is seen at the back, with Lieutenant
> Wilder, Madame de Lacy, and Gertrude aboard, and Fid clinging outside the
> vessel, as the curtain descends.*)

The script contains no references to the novel's original eighteenth-century setting and any references to the Rover's involvement in the slave trade are suppressed. Nor is the play influenced by elements of the Romantic 'man of loneliness and mystery/scarce seen to smile, and seldom heard to sigh' (Byron, *Corsair* I.173–4). The contemporary relevance of the production would have received an additional boost from the report in *The Times* on the day of its opening at the Adelphi that 40 pirates captured off the coast of Africa were undergoing their final examination in court ('The Forty Pirates' 3). More significantly, in terms of the crossover between the traditions of representation, the portrait of Yates, combining a reasonably accurate portrait of the actor with a highly conventionalized melodramatic posture of aggression and defiance, is drawn from J. K. Green's *Juvenile Drama* published in 1842.[9] Green himself was influenced by earlier representations of pirates, including those of J. C. Cross.

In 1851 Green published a halfpenny set of *Blackbeard the Pirate; or the Jolly Buccaneers*, originally published by West in 1824. Both owe their origins to J. C. Cross's *Blackbeard; or, the Captive Princess*, first performed on 9 April 1798, but not published until 1809. Jane Moody has argued for the significance of Cross's contribution to the evolution of melodrama and that the publication of his plays in 1809 'indicates the emergence of the minor play as a text to be read and imagined in the closet, not simply enjoyed as a theatrical spectacle' (30). The plays would provide a fertile resource for the juvenile drama and encourage other publishers like Cumberland, Duncombe and Lacy to issue collections of minor plays for performance.

Cross would have read one of the many editions of Captain Charles Johnson's *A General History of the Robberies and Murders of the Most Notorious Pyrates*, as well as Charles Johnson's (not the same man) *The Successful Pyrate*, first performed at Drury Lane in 1712 and published in 1713. From *The General History* he would have obtained the appearance of Blackbeard:

> Captain Teach assumed the cognomen of Black-beard, from that large quantity of hair, which, like a frightful meteor, covered his whole face … The beard was black, which he suffered to grow of an extravagant length; as to breadth, it came up to his eyes, he was accustomed to twist it with ribbons, in small tails, … and turn them about his ears: in time of action, he wore a sling over his shoulders, with three brace of pistols, hanging in holsters like bandoliers, and stuck lighted matches under his hat, which appearing on each side of his face, his eyes naturally looked fierce and wild, made him altogether such a figure, that imagination cannot form an idea of a fury, from Hell, to look more frightful. (Johnson, 84–5)

From Johnson's play, he acquired a plot that used the exploits of another actual pirate, Henry Avery (also known as 'Every' or 'Avary', but possessing a number of other aliases). Avery was notorious for seizing the magnificent and heavily armed

---

[9]   By the end of 1829 at least two publishers of juvenile drama, William West and I. J. Dyer, had already brought the play out (Speaight 216–17).

vessel, the *Ganj-i-Sawai* from the Emperor Aurangzeb in 1694 and legend has it that he also captured the Grand Mughal's daughter. Cross blended these two elements in what was advertised as 'a new grand spectacle, consisting of music, dance and action' at the Royal Circus. Blackbeard was to be played by Mr Crossman, who would appear in a 'grand equestrian entree' ('Jones's Royal Circus' 1) immediately before. Cross was carefully keeping within the terms of the Licensing Act of 1737, which prohibited the use of spoken dialogue in theatres other than the patent ones.[10] There are no descriptions of Blackbeard in the play itself. Perhaps spectators already knew the persona from engravings, or the character was regarded as merely a plot device whose actions determined his role. Certainly Cross pays little attention to historical facts or to geographical consistency. Avery's exploits took place near Madagascar, while Blackbeard's occurred along the North American coast and in the West Indies. The play is presented as a spectacular display of the various facets of villainy. Blackbeard (Figure 14.4)[11] is a villain prepared to murder his wife, Orra, when she resents his obvious attraction to the captured princess Ismene, as well as a fellow sailor who refuses to shoot the young hero, Abdallah. At the end of the play, Blackbeard is wounded by the hero (not by the historically accurate Lieutenant Maynard who subsequently decapitated him in 1718) and falls overboard.

Despite its historical inaccuracies, the melodramatic forms and techniques of the staging reflected prevailing interests in the recreation of naval engagements, Eastern exoticism and even Gothic spectral visitations. The play opens with a song in which the pirates extol the virtues of grog and the jollity of a pirate's life, a necessary device included in most subsequent nautical melodramas. Blackbeard joins in and demonstrates his prowess by shooting out a candle with his pistol. The crew also contains a prototypical British sailor, William, along with his girlfriend Nancy, disguised as a member of the crew. The setting of cabins and decks, a staple of nautical drama, is complemented by locations in both Madagascar and the West Indies:

> [he] extinguishes the lights; she becomes much agitated; he approaches her, drags her to the sopha [sic], solicits, threatens, etc. When a groan is heard, and THE APPARITION OF ORRA rises! Stalks across the stage, and vanishes. – Blackbeard, with his sword drawn, apparently defying it-Ismene is horror struck. (x, 41)[12]

---

[10] The Royal Circus had been built as a speculative venture in 1782 to cater to the rapidly expanding population of south London and to challenge Astley's Amphitheatre for spectacular displays of horsemanship.

[11] The illustration, as that of Yates, is like a studio portrait of a performer frozen in a characteristic moment. Some attention has been paid, however, to the costuming which figures the skull and crossbones and Blackbeard's distinctive beard. Though the actor depicted is A. V. Campbell, the manager of Sadler's Wells theatre 1825–32, it can represent the original since no illustrations of Crossman survive.

[12] This reference is to the scene and page number.

Figure 14.4   A. V. Campbell, 'Mr. Campbell as Blackbeard the Pirate'

Blackbeard is clearly portrayed as a villain, ruthless and totally unsentimental in his attitudes towards women and his crew, a far cry from the Red Rover and his innate sense of decency.

Though naval dramas would continue to find a place on the popular stage – especially among the huge Drury Lane autumn melodramas – until the end of the nineteenth century, by mid-century the memory of British naval exploits had dimmed. The pirate's lair and the high seas had been replaced by the drawing room and the streets as the primary locations for exploration of 'wayward passions' and the 'narrow boundaries between virtue and vice'. Certainly, as we have seen, the pirate continued to thrive in the pages of boys' magazines and the cut-outs of the juvenile drama, where the figure's menace and ruthlessness found a place. On stage the performance of those qualities was mitigated by a growing middle-class self-consciousness about the simplistic values of melodrama and their old-fashioned modes of expression. Nevertheless, even if audiences were becoming less tolerant of 'the grimacing mask' of the performer and more inclined to favour restraint and understatement, their fondness for burlesque and pantomime gave the pirate figure a lasting place on the popular stage. Within these two genres the ambiguities of the pirate could be explored and given a fresh meaning.

The complexities of the stage pirate are typically expressed in H. J. Byron's *Robinson Crusoe; or Harlequin Friday and the King of the Caribee Islands!*, performed at the Princess's theatre on 26 December 1860. The work, labelled 'a Grotesque Pantomime Opening', contains three pirates: Cutpurse, Gougeye and their captain, Will Atkins. The names of the first two signal their direct descent from Cutreef in *The Red Rover*. The other name is a deliberate fusion of William, a name long identified with the sailor from *Blackbeard* to *Black Ey'd Susan*, and a surname associated with the unromantic ordinariness of tradesmen and servants. It was an unlikely name for a figure described as a 'freebooter, smuggler, pirate, buccaneer and blackguard'. This ironic juxtaposition was further enhanced for the audience by the fact that the role was played by J. G. Shore who, by 1858, was identified with *jeune premier* roles.[13] Moreover, by 1860 the Princess's theatre had established a stellar reputation. Charles Kean had developed it as a venue for elaborately staged Shakespeare and the 'gentlemanly melodrama' of Dion Boucicault in the 1850s, and it had become a bastion of middle-class respectability. For pirates to appear at the Princess's theatre, then, is seemingly at odds with the theatre's apparent aims, or perhaps a reflection of the wholesale assimilation of the pirate into nineteenth-century cultural life.

H. J. Byron was particularly noted for his burlesques of melodrama and his verbal pyrotechnics, and this is reflected in his production of *Robinson Crusoe*. When Atkins enters in Scene 1, the stage directions describe him as 'a buccaneer of the true Cobourg stamp, enveloped in a rough pea jacket, and covered with every variety of offensive weapon' (i, 254).[14] He also has 'a piece of black plaister [sic] which extends the entire length of his countenance'. However, as he kneels at the feet of the heroine, Pretty Jenny Pigtail, he exclaims:

> You are my government; by persecution
> You have induced in me a revolution.
> I used to smoke and drink and use bad language;
> But now my bosom is a prey to *anguiage*. (i, 255)

His followers also demonstrate an incompetence that belies their appearance. When Jenny tries to run away, they run after her 'and missing her come whack

---

[13] J. G. Shore had worked at the Adelphi theatre and would join Marie Wilton and H. J. Byron when they took over the management of the Prince of Wales's theatre in 1864. See C. E. Pascoe, *The Dramatic List* (London: David Bogue, 1880) sv. J. G. Shore.

[14] All references to the play include scene and page number and are drawn from Michael Booth's recension of the text in *English Plays of the Nineteenth Century*, volume 5 (Oxford: Oxford UP, 1975). See also Lacy's edition, volume 49, nd. http://victorian.worc.ac.uk.

against each other; this is repeated, and they come with a thump against Atkins, who strikes them and seizes Jenny' (i, 256). She struggles ineffectually, but when the hero, Robinson Crusoe, enters: 'He knocks down the two Ruffians with back-handed blows, and floors Atkins with a driver; then stands C. With Jenny insensible in his arms. Picture' (i, 257). All three pirates then run off, cowardly and powerless. The Indians who appear on a desert island in Scene 3 'brandishing their tomahawks fiercely' (iii, 264) are rendered just as ineffectual by their predilection for rum. After Jenny is abducted by Atkins, she appears on stage 'with her hair down ... and the wild, determined manner of melodramatic heroines in the Third Act' (v, 270). She seizes a large pistol from Atkins and 'stands at bay':

> Come on at once! [Wildly] Ha, ha, ha, ha!

To which Atkins replies:

> Miss P., you're not at the Victori-a.
> Though the lorn damsels there you thus burlesque, you
> Will find no gallant tar comes to the rescue. (v, 270)

Atkins collapses in fright when he sees the Indians. At the end of Scene 7, Crusoe and Atkins confront each other. Atkins and Crusoe run on stage 'à la Macbeth' and 'à la Macduff' respectively, while Atkins is attacked by Crusoe's Goat and Parrot. The first part of the pantomime concludes with:

> a terrific combat, the Goat and Parrot acting as seconds. At last Crusoe misses his foot and falls ... Atkins is about to despatch Crusoe when Jenny rushes out and wards off the blow; at the same time the Dog flies on, and fastening on to the neck of Atkins as in canine dramas, drags him to the ground. They rise, swing around, roll over, down to the footlights and back again, etc. (vii, 277)

The action is interrupted by the figure of Liberty, who transforms the scene into the Golden Grotto of Christmas and the main characters into Harlequin, Columbine and Pantaloon in preparation for the comic scenes of the harlequinade, the traditional pantomime ending.

The ambiguities of the pirate figure are now played out on stage as a clash between modes of representation. Reference to an acting style appropriate to the Victoria theatre (and its older identity as the Coburg) prompts the audience to recognize an outmoded performance style that made it laughable and to congratulate themselves on their sophisticated appreciation of irony. W. S. Gilbert would capitalize on this affectionate parody of the outdated (and, by inference, working-class) theatrical conventions in a conservative middle-class forum later in the century.

Gilbert had long been associated with burlesques and to a lesser extent pantomime. In fact, by 1870 he was identified as a 'leviathan of burlesque' (qtd. in Stedman, *W. S.*

Gilbert 62).[15] Before he wrote *The Pirates of Penzance*, he had already penned *Our Island Home*, an 1870 play featuring pirates. The conceit of having Frederic as an indentured pirate apprentice is taken from that play, as is the statement in the earlier play by the melodramatic pirate chief, Captain Bang, that as a child he had been taken by his nurse to the seafront to be apprenticed to a pilot (Stedman, *Six Comic Plays* 140). Yet Gilbert hadn't originally conceived of the play as being about pirates. Ian Bradley states that the provisional title of the play, *The Robbers*, points to a story that had been originally conceived as a tale of burglars and policemen, and the shift to piracy only took place while Gilbert was in the United States (86). The entry of the pirates in Act 2 of *Pirates of Penzance*, clutching burglars' tools, preserves some of the spirit of the original play, although it renders the pirates somewhat ambiguous.

Critical reviews did not always emphasize the importance of the pirates to the plot. After the performance required to preserve the play's copyright at Paignton's Bijou theatre on 30 December 1879, *The Pirates of Penzance* opened in New York at the Fifth Avenue theatre the following night. The review in the *New York Times* makes no reference to the pirates and focuses on the humour of the absurd situation and the abilities of the performers. When it opened in London at the Opera Comique on 3 April 1880, however, references to the comic opera's antecedents were clearly noted:[16] 'The plot is well described as a satirical burlesque upon the conventional romance of buccaneering, and the sentimentalities of the pirates' career on the stage and in fiction' (*Musical Times* 444).[17]

The nexus between the stage representations and those in juvenile fiction was further emphasized by the *Stage Directory* (1 May 1880) that compared the humour of the play to that of a 'children's story-book'. The representation of the pirates 'dressed picturesquely after the Red Rover style, with red caps, short jackets, and skirts reaching to the knee' (*Dramatic Notes* 20) preserved the tradition of the earlier play in its toy theatre manifestations, and its relevance to children received a fresh impetus when D'Oyly Carte rehearsed *H.M.S. Pinafore* and *The Pirates of Penzance* with juvenile companies aged between 10 and 13 as Christmas specials (Beatty-Kingston, 80–82).

The opening of the play preserves a connection with *Blackbeard* in that both begin with a rousing chorus that glorifies the pirate life. However, the attitude of the Pirate King toward his crew differs from the earlier play. He is not the ferocious, dominating figure of a Blackbeard. Indeed, in the licensing copy of the play the Pirate King plays a menial role, not preserved in the final staged version, that erodes his role as a leader:

> But to cook your meals I don't refuse
> And I black piratical boots and shoes

---

[15]   See *The Graphic*, 18 April 1870.

[16]   The Opera Comique had opened in 1870 in the West End as a home for comic opera, French comedy and musical extravaganzas. D'Oyly Carte became its manager in 1874 and had been responsible for *The Sorcerer* (1877) and *H.M.S. Pinafore* (1878).

[17]   Quoting the review in the *Paignton and Newton Directory*, 31 December 1879 of the copyright performance.

I clean your knives, I bake your bread
I light your fires – I make your beds … (Paignton version, Gilbert 196)

The pirates themselves have all the trappings of ferocity, but, as Abigail Burnham Bloom notes in her discussion of 'duty', their opera-bouffe context completely undermines their marauding intentions. A reviewer for *The Graphic* notes that:

the pirates themselves and their mock-ferocious Captain, are a strange lot … The strong sense of 'duty' entertained by these pirates, their tender sympathy for orphans, and 'with all their faults' their loyal attachment to the Queen and reverence for 'our House of Lords', are unique in the history of sea marauders. (371).

The illustration [Figure 14.5] of the 'paradox scene' in Act 2 preserves the characteristic pose of earlier pirate representations but is undercut by the absurd parallelism of Ruth the pirate maid's stance and the imperturbability of Frederick in the face of their threats. The setting of a ruined chapel recalls the context of Gothic melodrama and its connection with Romantic antecedents.[18] The 'pirates' of Penzance are, of course, ultimately revealed to be men of noble birth, which explains their inadequacies as swashbucklers and their inability to terrify. Far more appropriate in his villainy and capacity to fill audiences with dread was Captain Hook of J.M. Barrie's *Peter Pan* who, along with Long John Silver, has to be one of the quintessential pirate rogues of the long nineteenth century.

Captain Hook's development as a pirate was not, however, entirely straightforward and the dramatization of piracy in *Peter Pan* was as complicated and ambiguous as it had been for a number of Hook's predecessors. Writing in 1934, the year of her father Gerald's death, Daphne du Maurier evoked his performance as Captain Hook in *Peter Pan*, which had opened at the Duke of York's theatre on 27 December 1904. From her description, it would appear that the performer had retreated from Gilbert's absurd faux pirates and restored the dark violence that had been present in Cross's *Blackbeard*:

When Hook first paced his quarter deck in the year 1904, children were carried screaming from the stalls, and even big boys of twelve were known to reach for their mother's hand in the friendly shelter of the boxes. How he was hated, with his flourish, his poses, his dreaded diabolical smile! That ashen face, those blood-red lips, the long, dank, greasy curls; the sardonic laugh, the maniacal scream, the appalling courtesy of his gestures; and that above all most terrible of moments when he descended the stairs and with slow, most merciless cunning poured the poison into Peter's glass … Gerald *was* Hook; he was no dummy dressed from Simmons'

---

18   The drawing of the Pirate King is a reasonably accurate depiction of Richard Temple, who created the role and had a long association with the D'Oyly Carte Company. He would go on to play the Mikado (1885) and in revivals of *The Pirates of Penzance* thereafter.

Figure 14.5 'The Paradox Scene' from *The Illustrated Sporting and Dramatic News*, 10 April 1880

in a Clarkson wig, ranting and roaring about the stage, a grotesque figure whom the modern child finds a little comic. He was a tragic and rather ghastly creation who knew no peace, and whose soul was in torment; a dark shadow; a sinister dream … He was the spirit of Stevenson and of Dumas, and he was Father-but-for-the-grace-of-God; a lonely spirit that was terror and inspiration in one. (110–11)

Thus, Gerald du Maurier appeared to have captured an authentic pirate, closer to Howard Pyle's illustrations than to a staged replica or a composite of inherited theatrical conventions. Nevertheless, the description is undoubtedly coloured by his daughter's fascination with Gothic romanticism and her own complex obsession with him as a man. The account may, therefore, owe as much to Daphne du Maurier's fascination with Byron's *Corsair* and memories of performances of *The Flying Dutchman* as to her recollections of the actual production of *Peter Pan*. Indeed, since she was only three years old at the time of the production, it is questionable that she would have remembered so much of it. She probably witnessed one of the revivals in which her father reprised the role and she would have been familiar with the text of the play which Barrie had resisted publishing until 1928.

The evolution of the pirates in *Peter Pan* was a complex one. Much has been written about Barrie's obsession with the Llewelyn Davies family and its effect on his writings about children,[19] but the portrayal of Captain Hook is also a product of Barrie's tastes in reading and theatregoing. He had certainly read *Treasure Island* and Ballantyne's *Coral Island* (Green 407), as well as Charles Johnson's 1724 history; he had seen *The Pirates of Penzance* and he was determined that his pirates would not be Gilbert and Sullivan travesties, a point he made to the designer William Nicholson. Yet even at the outset his intentions were compromised. Du Maurier refused to wear 'a wig of purple chenille, arranged to look like snakes' (Steen 98) for Hook, and on the first night he covered a complicated scene change by performing impersonations of Henry Irving in *The Corsican Brothers*, Beerbohm Tree as Svengali in *Trilby* and John Martin Harvey in *The Only Way*, Freeman Wills's adaptation of Dickens's *A Tale of Two Cities*. Hardly surprisingly, Irving's grandson Laurence, who saw du Maurier as a child, remembered Hook played 'with touches of parody, that were echoes of the Lyceum' (Irving 87), the theatre where his grandfather had made his reputation. Based on du Maurier's performances, then, Hook was both a thrillingly piratical figure as well as a humorous one.

The published version of the play reveals further complications to the depiction of Hook. Barrie added material to the play after the publication of his novel version, *Peter Pan and Wendy* in 1911, and elaborated in the whimsical account of Hook's supposed career at Eton published in *The Times* in 1927.[20] Hook's first appearance on stage in Act II is described in the stage directions:

---

[19]   See Andrew Birkin, *J.M.Barrie and the Lost Boys* (London: Constable, 1979).

[20]   'Captain Hook at Eton, a strange story' appeared in the 8 July 1927 number of *The Times* and was republished in the collection *M'Conachie and J.M.B: Speeches* (New York: Scribners' Sons, 1939).

cadaverous and blackavized, his hair dressed in long curls which look like black candles about to melt, his eyes blue as the forget-me-not and of a profound insensibility, save when he claws, at which time a red spot appears in them. He has an iron hook instead of a right hand ... He is never more sinister than when he is most polite, and the elegance of his diction, the distinction of his demeanour, show him one of a different class from his crew ... This courtliness impresses even his own victims on the high seas, who wrote that he always says 'Sorry' when prodding them along the plank ... At his public school they said of him that he 'bled yellow'. In dress he apes the dandiacal associated with Charles II ... (II, 27–8)[21]

Later in Act IV as he is about to poison a sleeping Peter Pan, Barrie qualifies Hook's intentions: 'Does no feeling of compassion disturb his sombre breast? The man is not wholly evil: he has a Thesaurus in his cabin, and is no mean performer on the flute. What really warps him is a presentiment that he is about to fail' (IV, 60).

This portrait of a gloomy, meditative villain is captured in the illustration (Figure 14.6) as Hook contemplates his plans to make the captured Boys walk the plank:

The terrified Boys are prodded up and tossed about the deck.
Hook seems to have forgotten them; he is sitting by the barrel with his cards. (V.i.65).

At the end of the play, Hook's plot to blow up the ship is thwarted and Peter Pan is revealed to be unscathed:

At this sight, the great heart of Hook breaks. That not wholly unheroic figure climbs the bulwarks murmuring 'Floreat Etona', and prostrates himself into the water, where the Crocodile is waiting for him open-mouthed. (V.i.65)

The remaining pirates retain the trapping of ferocity in their costuming, but they are no more effectual than the pirates of Byron's pantomime or Gilbert's operetta. They are despatched by the Boys in Act V, who prove more than a match for their cutlasses and pistols, and are sustained by their patriotism. They sing the national anthem when they are about to walk the plank and respond enthusiastically to Wendy's advice that their real mothers would 'hope [their] sons will die like English gentlemen' (V.i.66–7). Thus, the moral and educational values enshrined in *Chums* and *Boys' Own Paper* and the performance values of burlesque and pantomime are never far from the surface.[22]

---

[21]   References are to act and page number of the Samuel French edition of Barrie's *Peter Pan*.

[22]   The pantomime and burlesque pedigree was further reinforced by the production's indebtedness to the achievements of the Conquest family at the Surrey theatre, whose pantomimes in the 1890s saw the demonstration of a flying apparatus that enabled mid-

Figure 14.6   Gerald du Maurier as Captain Hook, *The Sketch*, 4 January 1905

When Hook exults at the prospect of making his captured boys walk the plank, his speech is punctuated by the sound of his confederate Smee tearing pieces of calico to make the pirates' clothes and stitching them together on a sewing machine. Smee, played by George Shelton, with his spectacles and description as a 'Nonconformist pirate', is a direct descendant of Homespun, the captured tailor in *The Red Rover*. Even Hook's speeches contain elements of parody, in particular, his outlandish oaths 'split my infinitives', 'uvula and tonsils' and 'By Gaius and Balbus'. All these touches restore an ambiguity that may not have been part of Barrie's original plans and contributed nothing to Daphne du Maurier's memory of her father's performance. Certainly the critics saw du Maurier's

---

air dances, underwater scenes and electrically enhanced fairies. See Frances Fleetwood, *Conquest: The Story of a Theatre Family* (London: Allen, 1953), 161–2.

interpretation as a burlesque of piracy: *The Times* described his performance as 'luridly melodramatic' ('Duke of York's Theatre' 4); his use of 'expurgated oaths and melodramatic airs, is a splendid piece of burlesque' (qtd. in Agate 135).[23] Even if du Maurier performed Hook as 'elegant and *stylisé* to the last degree' in 1904, the depiction of the pirates contained elements that ensured that their eccentric behaviour would become ultimately indistinguishable from parody: 'The pirates … gradually became more and more Gilbert-and-Sullivan, and finally ended up as Sullivan-and-water' (Steen 98).

Perhaps Alfred Noyes writing in 1905 sums up best the traditions of pirate representation and the place of *Peter Pan* within that tradition:

> What pirates these are … that might have stepped straight out of the red and yellow illustrations of an old broad-sheet ballad; pirates of the imagination … not earthly, but ideal pirates, who wear boat-cloaks and big boots and blood-spotted bandages round the head. Each of them is the delightful essence and consummation of a thousand conventions … It is the last word on pirates. It is the story of pirates reduced to the simplest terms; stripped of unnecessary details and realities, and made eternal as boyhood. For 'grown-ups' it has an exquisite humour. It is like a delicious and subtle parody of all the pirate stories … and yet it is as real and vivid as 'Treasure Island.' … I had a great choking thought during those wonderful twopenny-coloured episodes – if only Robert Louis could have been there to see them! (114).

It would appear, therefore, that by 1904 staging the pirate had reached a point where it could develop little further. The pirate in the nineteenth century had been a key figure in the complex discourse of conventions of performance and 'inward signification', of historical fact and 'figural truth' (Meisel 4) that informed the shared structures of nineteenth-century representational arts. It would now be left to the new medium of film to untangle the strands of representation and select for its own purposes the elements of juvenile adventurism or mocking irony that would best suit its purposes and a new market.

---

[23] Unidentified review, 27 December 1904.

Chapter 15

Bram Stoker's *The Mystery of the Sea*: Law and Lawlessness, Piracy and Protectionism

Carol A. Senf

Published in 1902, *The Mystery of the Sea* is the first novel that Bram Stoker produced after the collapse of the Lyceum Company made the 55-year-old Stoker entirely dependent on his own talents. At this point Stoker, who had written sporadically whenever he could take time away from his responsibilities, first to the Irish Civil Service and later to Henry Irving and the Lyceum, became a full-time writer. Frequently pressed for money, Stoker experimented with most of the popular genres of his day, as Andrew Maunder and David Glover demonstrate. Eager to argue against those who see him only as a Gothic writer, Maunder points to 'Stoker's diversity as a writer in terms of genre, form and subject matter' (9) and describes him as 'indelibly linked to the popular fictional genres of the late-nineteenth and early-twentieth centuries' (9). Similarly Glover notes that his own study reads Stoker 'as he most wanted to be read, as a popular writer' (6). Given the fact that the nineteenth century was, as Grace Moore comments in the introduction to this collection, 'the great age of the literary pirate', and that Stoker also grew up on the coast, it is not surprising that he would write at least one novel that touches on a figure who appeared in popular literature during the nineteenth century, the romantic figure of the pirate. What is interesting to me, however, and what this chapter addresses is the way that Stoker refocuses his youthful interest in a romantic figure from the past to address contemporary social issues – including the state's responsibility to its citizens and the balance of world power at a time when, because of industrialism and imperialism, important changes were taking place throughout the world. As a result, *The Mystery of the Sea* is not just Stoker's experiment with a popular form but a work that uses the romantic figure of the pirate for social commentary.

The sea figures as a backdrop for much of what Stoker wrote, and biographer Paul Murray observes that its pervasiveness in Stoker's writing was noted by his contemporaries:

> The impact of the sea beside which he had grown up is also evident in Stoker's writing. The anonymous author of a profile of Stoker in the *Literary World* in 1905 divided his fiction into two categories, the supernatural and the marine with *The Watter's Mou'* (1895), *The Mystery of the Sea* and *The Man* specimens

of the latter, 'for they all possess a paramount attraction in their sea-scapes and sea-scenes'. (28)[1]

Another biographer, Barbara Belford, traces Stoker's love of the sea back to his early childhood years as an invalid when he listened to his mother tell stories of Ireland and her own family's place in Irish history:

> Here was the genesis of his fascination with storms, shipwrecks, and sea rescues, with pirate coves, buried treasure, and the unknown. And always the sea, particularly the angry sea. In his imagination Stoker envisioned mist-clouded sails protecting cargoes of gold and silver, jewels and coins. He conjured up scenes of vast caves filled with whiskey brought in by the smugglers who stealthily oared in and out of the hidden coves around Clontarf. (15)

The Mystery of the Sea includes most of the elements that Belford mentions, including two sea rescues, buried treasure and a heroine who is proud of the fact that she is descended from Sir Francis Drake. In fact, she even displays a jewelled brooch that she inherited from the Drake family:

> I have been looking up the history of the time since I saw you, and I found that Admiral de Valdes when he was taken prisoner by Sir Francis Drake at the fight with the Armada was kept, pending his ransom, in the house of Richard Drake, kinsman of Sir Francis. How the Drake family got possession of the brooch I don't know; but anyhow I don't suppose they stole it. They were a kindly lot in private, any of them that I ever knew; though when they were in a fight they fought like demons. The old Spanish Dons were generous and free with their presents, and I take it that when Pedro de Valdes got his ransom he made the finest gift he could to those who had been kind to him. That is the way I figure it out. (138)

Historians might question Marjory's loyalty to her ancestor, arguing that Drake was as much a pirate as an explorer and that he captured Valdes and the Spanish galleon *Rosario* because it was known to be carrying treasure (both funds to pay Spanish soldiers as well as valuable cargo from the New World). For example, Philip Gosse, who wrote at least three books on piracy (*The Pirate's Who's Who*, 1924; *My Pirate Library*, 1926; and *The History of Piracy*, 1932) in addition to numerous studies of natural history,[2] says it is 'hard to determine ... whether Francis Drake was a pirate or no' (*History of Piracy* viii)[3] because he held 'openly or by

---

[1]   Murray cites *Literary World*, 15 November 1905.

[2]   He was also the grandson of the naturalist Philip Henry Gosse, founder of marine biology, and son of the literary critic and biographer Edmund Gosse.

[3]   Additional information on Drake can be found in a variety of sources, including *Francis Drake Privateer: Contemporary Narratives and Documents*. Ed. John Hampden

implication a commission from the Crown' (*History* viii) and was therefore linked to legitimate political authority, especially during time of war when the monarch was likely to loosen whatever control he or she had over such individuals. Janice E. Thomson characterizes Drake as a privateer or Sea Dog, but demonstrates that his actions were no less violent for their semi-legitimacy:

> These private adventurers, in collusion with the English Crown, engaged in all kinds of violent activities directed against Spain in the New World. Besides plundering Spanish ships and settlements, such sea Dogs as Drake, Cavendish, Clifford ... and Raleigh engaged in what might be termed state-sponsored terrorism. For example, Drake extorted large ransoms from two Spanish colonial cities by threatening to burn them to the ground. He actually destroyed three other cities. His sack of Peru netted him and his backers £2.5 million and repaid his backers, including Elizabeth, '47 for 1'[4] ... Other Sea Dogs behaved similarly, plundering, destroying, and extorting their way to fame and fortune in England and sharing their loot with the English Crown. (23)[5]

The numerous wars in which various European nations were involved provided profound economic incentives for monarchs to overlook the violent behaviour associated with piracy, and the economic opportunities, high adventure and drama associated with such maritime entrepreneurs provided an incentive to these individuals as well. Reminding his readers of the pirate adventurers of the past by suggesting a family relationship between Sir Francis Drake and his heroine, Marjory Anita Drake, Stoker nonetheless distinguishes his hero and heroine from such romantic figures and shifts much of his emphasis to contemporary social issues, including the war in Cuba and the plight of Scottish fishermen.

Whether one calls them pirates, privateers or Sea Dogs, it is not surprising that these often violent and romantic figures became a subject for literature, or that Stoker, who seemed to keep his fingers on the pulse of the reading public, would write about

---

(University: U of Alabama P, 1972) and Julian Corbett, *Sir Francis Drake* (1890; repr. New York: Haskell House Publishers Ltd, 1968). The latter begins by emphasizing the romance associated with Drake:

Of all the heroes whose exploits have set our history aglow with romance there is not one who so soon passed into legend as Francis Drake. He was not dead before his life became a fairy tale ... His exploits loomed in mythical extravagance through the mists in which, for high reasons of State, they soon remained enveloped, and to the people he seemed some boisterous hero of a folk-tale outwitting and belabouring a clumsy ogre. (1)

[4]   Thomson cites Louis Kronenberger, 'People on Spits and Other Niceties', *Atlantic Monthly*, September 1969, 106.

[5]   Stoker even suggests in *Mystery* that, while piracy had been made illegal by the time he wrote the novel, war often provides opportunities for individuals who might have turned pirate in previous centuries: 'There were many scoundrels, such as chiefly come to the surface in war time, who would undertake any work, however deadly, however brutal, however dangerous. Such villains might be at work even now!' (125)

them. Stoker is not just a popular writer, however. Reading his fiction, I share Andrew Maunder's assessment that Stoker is 'more varied, powerful and socially aware than many critics have allowed for' (11). Considering his youthful interest in piracy and mysteries connected with the sea, along with his mature concern with social issues, it is no surprise that he came to diminish Marjory's resemblance to her famous pirate ancestor in order to focus on these social issues in *The Mystery of the Sea*. For example, Stoker examines the responsibility of the state to protect the lives of the weak and suggests that the pirates of his day are little more than criminals. Thus Marjory, like her famous ancestor, aligns her fortune with the nation she has sworn to support. Unlike him, however, she is willing to subordinate her personal interest in either fame or fortune to the greater social good, especially when it comes to the question of protecting the poor and weak. That she also marries the barrister Archie Hunter links her to those who are interested in adhering to the current law, rather than operating outside it or attempting to accrue wealth only for herself. Equally interesting is a connection that Stoker may have been considering as he wrote. As Thomson's study demonstrates, the world's great nations were working during the nineteenth century to abolish privateering as an alternative to state naval power. One of the chief documents to articulate this change was the Treaty of Paris (16 April 1856), which was signed by the governments of France, Britain, Russia, Prussia, Austria, Sardinia and Turkey; one purpose was 'to establish a uniform doctrine' on 'Maritime Law in time of War' (71). Although the Treaty of Paris was signed while Stoker was still a schoolboy, his novels often incorporate legal issues. As an attorney himself, Stoker would have been aware of changes in the law, which he wove into his fiction. He was also interested in major changes taking place in world politics. By setting *Mystery* during the Spanish–American War of 1898, Stoker reveals his awareness of the political balance of power and also brings in two additional players who had not signed the original treaty, Spain and the United States, both of whom Thomson mentions by name: 'After Congress declared war, the United States issued a presidential proclamation in which it declared that it would abide by all of the provisions of the Declaration of Paris, including the ban on privateering' (76). She adds that Spain allowed ships of the Spanish mercantile navy to sail but held them to the statutes and jurisdiction of the navy, for all intents and purposes banning privateering as well.

While piracy was disappearing at the time *Mystery* was written, it is entirely relevant to look at Marjory Drake's character in terms of piracy or privateering. The two terms are often used interchangeably, but piracy technically refers to individuals who have no affiliation, no matter how tenuous, with a legitimate state. A privateer, on the other hand, has some kind of relationship to the official government. Hence the same individual might be a pirate at one time, a privateer at another. Thus, despite her ancestry, and relationship to Sir Francis Drake, there is little reason to see Marjory Drake as a pirate, privateer or Sea Dog. Even though I admire Lisa Hopkins's analysis of *The Mystery of the Sea*, I disagree with her characterization of Marjory as a pirate, who 'as ironically befits a descendant of Sir Francis Drake' is 'demoted from legitimate combatant to pirate' (96). In fact,

I argue in this chapter that everything Stoker tells us about Marjory demonstrates the ways in which she differs from her famous ancestor.

Archie Hunter, Stoker's narrator, has already begun to fall in love with Marjory when he meets with two diplomats and acquaintances, Adams of the American Embassy in London and Cathcart of the British Embassy in Washington, who tell him of Marjory's background. Cathcart tells Archie, who at the time does not even know her full legal name, that Marjory is an American heiress who had given a battleship to the American government after learning of Spanish atrocities on Cuban civilians:

> To this end she bought a battle ship that the Cramps[6] had built for Japan. She had the ship armed with Krupp[7] cannon which she bought through friends in Italy; and went along the Eastern coast amongst the sailors and fishermen till she had recruited a crew. Then she handed the whole thing over to the Government as a spur to it to take some action. The ship is officered with men from the Naval Academy at Annapolis; and they tell me there isn't one of the crew – from the cabin boy to the captain – that wouldn't die for the girl tomorrow. (117)

Donating a battleship to an established government would thus seem to be precisely the opposite of piracy as Gosse defines it, quoting the 'Privy Council in 1873 (in A.G. for Hong-Kong *v*. Kwok-a-Sing) … definition of Piracy given in Rex *v*. Dawson 1696' as:

> Piracy is only the sea term for robbery within the jurisdiction of the Admiralty … If the mariner of any ship shall violently dispossess the master and afterwards carry away the ship itself or any of the goods with a felonious intention in any place where the Lord Admiral hath jurisdiction this is robbery and piracy. (*History of Piracy* 317)

Despite her admiration for her famous ancestor, Marjory's gift reveals how much she differs from Drake. Indeed, Stoker emphasizes that everything Marjory

---

[6]   Located in Philadelphia, the Cramps shipyard was one of the nation's largest for nearly 100 years. As I discuss in *Science and Social Science in Bram Stoker's Fiction* (Westport, CT: Greenwood, 2002), Stoker is extremely interested in all kinds of technological developments. For example, he becomes positively eloquent describing the sophisticated equipment he will use to dig for the Spanish treasure that he suspects is buried on his property. Stoker, having barely escaped being blown up when he and Irving travel by boat through a mine-bed, is enthusiastic about seeing the mock naval battle later in the day. (See Bram Stoker, *Personal Reminiscences of Henry Irving*. Vol. II. New York: Macmillan, 1906, 268 for a description of the episode that figures in the background of *Mystery*.)

[7]   At the turn of the century, the German industrial dynasty was known as the world's premier weapons manufacturer.

does is both legal and done for the express purpose of advancing the power and authority of a legitimate state.

Although Marjory is definitely interested in the treasure of the Spanish Armada that Archie discovers after figuring out the cipher and determining where the long-lost treasure had been buried, both her concern for the law and her lack of willingness to commit violence also suggest that she is no pirate. Indeed, Stoker is careful to demonstrate that Archie and Marjory have a legal right to the long-buried treasure that they find on his property. Not only had Stoker studied law (he began legal study in 1886 and was called to the Bar in 1890), but he also invests his narrator with the same kind of legal training:[8]

> When I was about eight and twenty I found myself nominally a barrister, with no knowledge whatever of the practice of law and but little less of the theory, and with a commission in the Devil's Own – the irreverent name given to the Inns of Court Volunteers. (11)

Certainly, Archie would need all his legal training to determine whether he was entitled to the treasure that he found. If the laws regarding piracy were confusing, the laws regarding hidden treasure are equally so, and Archie also needs to understand how the Scottish laws regarding treasure differ from the laws in England:

> The Scotch law is much the same as the English; and as we are in Scotland, we are of course governed by the former. The great point of difference, seen with the eyes of a finder is that in Scotland the fraudulent concealment of Treasure Trove is not a criminal offence, as it is in England. Thus, from my point of view, I have nothing to fear as to results; for though by the General Police Act[9] the finder is bound to report the find to the Chief Constable, the statute only applies to things found on roads or in public places. So far as this treasure is concerned, it may turn out that it can, in a sense, be no treasure trove at all. (254–5)

Archie goes on to cite William Blackstone, whose *Commentaries on the Laws of England* (1765–69) is a compilation of English common law and thus the guidebook to English law and precedent:

> According to Blackstone, treasure trove is where any money or coin, gold, silver, plate or bullion is found hidden *in* the earth or other private place, the owner thereof being unknown. If found *upon* the earth, or in the sea, it belongs,

---

[8]   Almost all of Stoker's biographers identify Archie as Stoker's most obviously autobiographical character, and both his legal training and his prowess as a swimmer connect to his creator.

[9]   Passed in Scotland in 1847, this legislation empowers local authorities in various ways.

not to the Crown, but to the finder, if no owner appears. It is the hiding, not the abandoning, which gives the Crown the property ... The right of the Crown is ... limited to gold or silver, bullion or coin. It extends to nothing else. (255)

Thus, even if Archie and Marjory had to forfeit the silver and gold coins they find, it appears that they would be entitled to keep the remaining treasures, especially the rubies that Marjory finds so enchanting. Of course, Archie has an added incentive in that the wealth would make him financially equal to Marjory. Admitting that he has a 'comfortable, though not great fortune' (11), Archie is concerned that he might be accused of being interested in Marjory only because of her wealth; and Marjory had earlier given him a false name because she is cautious of fortune hunters. As the novel progresses, though, the wealth diminishes in importance, so much so that by the end, both Archie and Marjory come to realize that human relationships, most significantly their love for one another, are far more important than material treasure. Indeed, Don Bernardino, a descendant of the man who had funded the Spanish Armada and consequently a man who is interested in reclaiming his family's lost treasure, decides that Marjory's honour is more important than the treasure, and the novel concludes with the reconciliation of Marjory and Don Bernardino:[10]

> Strangest of all was the finding of Don Bernardino. The body of the gallant Spanish gentleman was found washed up on the shore behind the Lord Nelson rock, just opposite where had been the opening to the cave in which his noble ancestor had hidden the Pope's treasure. It was as though the sea itself had respected his devotion, and had laid him by the place of his Trust. Marjory and I saw his body brought home to Spain when the war was over, and laid amongst the tombs of his ancestors. We petitioned the Crown; and though no actual leave was given, no objection was made to our removing the golden figure of San Cristobal which Benvenuto had wrought for the Pope. It now stands over the Spaniard's tomb in the church of San Cristobal in far Castile. (340–41)

Seeing Don Bernardino as 'gallant' and a 'gentleman' reveals that Marjory has changed her mind regarding her former opponent. While she had earlier seen him only as a Spaniard and therefore her enemy, she has learned to respect him as a human being. Certainly the reference to 'the Lord Nelson rock' links Don Bernardino to one of England's greatest naval heroes. He is thus officially seen as English rather than Spanish. The descendants of people who had fought on opposite sides in the battle of the Spanish Armada against England had previously argued over who had greater rights to the treasure. Now it appears that political differences inherited from the past are abandoned, and Marjory is cleansed of her ancestor's taint of piracy. While her famous ancestor had sailed the high seas searching for wealth, Marjory is passionate about bringing justice to all people. Siding with the

---

[10]   See Hopkins for a discussion of this reconciliation, 97.

downtrodden of the world also separates Marjory from the aggressive imperialism of *fin-de-siècle* Britain. Indeed the treasure becomes unimportant, so much so that Stoker does not indicate what happens to the rest of the treasure, which is on a ship that sinks in a storm.

If Marjory is redeemed of charges of piracy primarily because of her interest in justice rather than treasure, there remains one group that might be characterized as authentically piratical, individuals who meet the definition Gosse includes in *The History of Piracy*:

> Webster defines a pirate as 'a robber on the high seas, one who by open violence takes the property of another on the high seas, especially one who makes it his business to cruise for robbery or plunder; a freebooter on the seas; also one who steals in a harbour.' (viii)

A group of thieves that operates both on land and at sea kidnaps Marjory, gains control of the whaler *Wilhelmina* and takes it into international waters. However, they might also be defined as kidnappers, blackmailers or thieves since they abduct Marjory and plan to hold her for ransom, as well as stealing the treasure from Archie's house.

In addition to their connection to the high seas, though, the names that Stoker gives the men in this group suggest the colourful identities often adopted by pirates:

> 'Feathers' is none other than Featherstone who was with Whisky Tommy – which was Tom Mason – in the A.T. Stewart ransom[11] case. If those two are in it, most likely the one they called the 'Dago' is a half-bred Spaniard ... That Max that she named, if he's the same man, is a Dutchman; he's about the worst of the bunch. Then for this game there's likely to be two Chicago bums from the Levee, way-down politicians and heelers. It's possible that there are two more; a man from Frisco that they call Sailor Ben – what they call a cosmopolite for he doesn't come from nowhere in particular; and a buck nigger from Noo Orleans.[12] A real bad 'un he is ... His words made my blood run cold. Was this the crowd, within whose danger I had consented that Marjory should stand. The worst kind of scoundrels from all over the earth. (285–6)

---

[11]   Alexander Turney Stewart (1803–76), an Irish American entrepreneur, made his fortune in the dry goods business and was at the time of his death one of the richest men in New York. Shortly after his death, his body was stolen and held for ransom. For an excellent discussion of this case and its ramifications for *Mystery*, see Hopkins 98–101.

[12]   Stoker often depicts the racial other as especially horrifying. Not only is Dracula presented as vaguely 'Eastern',, but Oolanga in *The Lair of the White Worm* is another demonic African. The monstrous other in Stoker's fiction is often a racial other, and Sean Grass's essay in this volume on Charles Reade's *Hard Cash* also looks at pirates as racial others.

The Chief of the Secret Service describes this gang as 'blackmailers' instead of pirates, a term that refers to individuals who extract money by means of intimidation, not necessarily through the threat of exposure or censure. While he reinforces their cruelty, however, he also connects them to the Romantic figure of the pirate by highlighting their bravery or 'pluck':

> 'You don't know these wretches,' said the chief of the latter 'They are the most remorseless and cruel villains in the world; and if they are driven to bay will do anything however cruel or base. They are well plucked too, and don't know what fear means. They will take any chances, and do anything to get their way and protect themselves. If we don't go right in this matter, we may regret it to the last of our days.' (280)

The reference to their bravery suggests that Stoker is still thinking of the romantic popular figure of the pirate. However, Stoker's emphasis on legitimate political authority demonstrates how far he had moved away from the mainstream figure. Indeed, his pirates are common criminals despite their courage. They would seem to be no match for the combined forces of the governments of the United States and Great Britain. Ironically, though, Marjory is finally saved by the heroic Archie, who swims out to the ship on which she is held captive, kills several of her captors and manages to help her to escape. Most of the pirates who are not killed by Archie perish ignominiously during a storm at sea:

> The storm continued for a whole day, growing rougher and wilder with each hour. For another day it grew less and less, till finally the wind had died away and only the rough waves spoke of what had been. Then the sea began to give up its dead. Some seamen presumably those of the *Wilhelmina* were found along the coast between Whinnyfold and Old Slains, and the bodies of two of the blackmailers, terribly mangled, were washed ashore at Cruden Bay. The rest of the sailors and of the desperadoes were never found. Whether they escaped by some miracle, or were swallowed in the sea, will probably never be known. (340)

The unmourned deaths of the pirates and the fact that Archie does not even mention what happened to the treasure that had led to the loss of so many people suggest that Stoker is moving away from the traditional pirate tale because he wants to focus on social issues. As I detail later in this chapter, Stoker is more concerned with the atrocities committed against Cuban peasants and the economic hardships of the herring fisherman from Cruden Bay than he is in pirates. His emphasis on such matters serves to turn the reader's attention to contemporary problems.

Stoker certainly seems intent on redeeming Marjory of her pirate lineage, and this would correspond with Gosse's assertion that piracy was dying out in the nineteenth and earlier twentieth centuries. Indeed, Gosse links the last of the pirates to the American slave trade, suggesting that pirates were inclined to prey on the most vulnerable. He also suggests that technology of the kind that so fascinates Stoker was at least partially responsible for the demise of piracy:

> The modern age seems to have done away with piracy, save in an occasional and bastard form, as it has done away with many more attractive expressions of human activity. What with thirty-five knot cruisers, aeroplanes, wireless and above all the police power of the modern state, there seems very little chance for the enterprising individual to gain a living in this fashion and still less for capital so invested to earn a satisfactory return for the risk involved. (297–8)

Neither Marjory nor Archie feels the need to turn to piracy, though they are willing to risk a great deal for love or for protection of the weak. Indeed, Marjory seems to have become involved in politics initially because of her interest in protecting Cuban civilians from Spanish atrocities. Telling Archie of Marjory's decision to purchase a battleship for the United States, the diplomat Cathcart makes it clear that she had been motivated by the fate of the rural non-combatants who, during the Cuban Revolution of 1895–98, were relocated by the military to concentration camps, where a number died as a result of poor food and miserable sanitary conditions: 'At the time the reports kept crowding in of the Spanish atrocities on the *reconcentrados*; when public feeling was rising in the United States, this girl got all on fire to free Cuba' (117). While she herself attributes her hatred of Spain partially to the destruction of the USS *Maine* (in Havana harbour in 1898), she is consistent about attributing her loathing to their persecution of the weak and helpless: 'I hate them! Nasty, cruel, treacherous wretches! Look at the way they are treating Cuba! Look at the *Maine!*' (68). By stressing Marjory's passion regarding the fate of the *reconcentrados* Stoker is careful not to identify her with hawkish Americans, who used the phrase 'Remember the *Maine*' to express their desire for military intervention against Spain. While hawkish Americans may have wanted to substitute one military power for another, as well as establish US hegemony in the Western hemisphere, Marjory seems more concerned with justice for the Cuban peasants, and she is willing to use military force to effect that justice.

Marjory's sympathy for the underdog is consistent with another scene in the novel that otherwise seems to make little sense aside from the fact that it introduces the reader to Archie's gift of Second Sight, the ability to see what is not immediately present to the senses.[13] Early in the novel, Archie arrives at Cruden Bay for his annual visit. Calling himself 'nominally a barrister' (11), he also reveals his interest in the lives of the people in the area around him. Noting in passing that he 'had been thinking of the decline of the herring from the action of the trawlers in certain waters, and fancied this would be a good opportunity to get a local opinion' (18), he poses his question to a local fisherman.

---

[13]   In addition to Archie and Gormala MacNiel in *Mystery*, both Rupert Sent Leger and his aunt, Janet MacKelpie (*The Lady of the Shroud*), are gifted with Second Sight.

The fisherman responds with anger directed against both 'the trawlers and the laws which allowed them to do their nefarious work' (18). What is especially interesting here is Stoker's apparent sympathy with the local fishermen, whose traditional means of making a living is jeopardized by a kind of perfectly legal theft on the high seas.[14] The fisherman, Lauchland Macleod, describes the impact of large-scale ships that use dragnets to catch fish. Because these nets are dragged through the water at great depths, they have the potential to replace traditional fishing methods or, in Macleod's words, render 'certain fishing grounds, formerly most prolific of result to the fishers ... absolutely worthless' (18). Stoker has Macleod describe the pitfalls of dragnets precisely and poetically:

> Suppose you be a farmer, and when you have prepared your land and manured it, you sow your seed and plough the ridges and make it all safe from wind and devastatin' storm. If, when the green corn be shootin' frae the airth, you take your harrow and drag it ath'art the springin' seed, where be then the promise of your golden grain? (18)[15]

Although Archie clearly admires Macleod and describes him as a golden man, it is also evident that Stoker sees him as something of an anachronism. His criticism of the trawlers makes no impact on their legal piracy, and he himself is drowned returning from a fishing expedition. Indeed, Archie sees him as the last in a long line of 'victims of the Cruden Skares' (35), the procession of individuals who had drowned in the waters near Cruden Bay.

The reference to the drowning of Lauchland Macleod and Stoker's interest in the fishing industry is a minor episode in a novel that seems to focus on mystery and romance rather than on mundane reality. Nonetheless it brings readers back to the point that Maunder makes quite eloquently at the beginning of his study, the importance of seeing Stoker as a multi-faceted writer who is as much concerned with the world of his own day as he is with Gothic fantasy and high drama: 'Whilst acknowledging the importance that present-day readers ascribe to *Dracula*, this study suggests that there are other dimensions to Stoker's work that are worth acknowledging' (9). Over the past 30 years, scholars have teased out many of those other dimensions to *Dracula*. Now that *Mystery* is back in print in the United States, perhaps scholars in the US and elsewhere will begin to devote more attention to this lesser novel as well, seeing its references to pirates and piracy as Stoker's way of focusing on problems that he saw were important to his world. Readers are

---

[14]   John Peck's recent study, *Maritime Fiction: Sailors and the Sea in British and American Novels, 1719–1917* (Basingstoke: Palgrave, 2001), also explores piracy as a metaphor for capitalist robber barons, noting parallels between business and piracy. Tamara Wagner's chapter in this volume also demonstrates the similarities in piracy and commerce.

[15]   In fact, in 2007 a number of countries passed legislation to prevent the kind of overfishing that occurs when dragnets are used.

fortunate that Stoker grew up on the coast and was driven by economic necessity to write popular fiction during a period when the romantic pirates and privateers of previous centuries were being replaced by maritime capitalists, and that he was aware of the similarities in these seemingly dissimilar groups of people.

Chapter 16

Piracy and the Ends of Romantic Commercialism: Victorian Businessmen Meet Malay Pirates

Tamara S. Wagner

The Powers of the West have been busy here, as in other quarters of the world; but in spite of their new-born political importance only a languid interest has, for the most part, been excited in the countries themselves and in the problems to which their affairs have given rise. The failure of the lands of southeastern Asia to make a strong appeal to the imagination of the peoples of Europe is to be ascribed, however, not to their intrinsic unimportance, nor yet to any lack of wealth, of beauty, of charm, or of the interest that springs from a mysterious and mighty past. The reason is to be sought solely in the mere accident of their geographical position.

Hugh Clifford, *Further India*, 1

When pirates are sighted in Catherine Gore's *Adventures in Borneo* (1849), they are fascinatingly indeterminate, vaguely exoticized in a symptomatic fusion of figures and tropes commonly associated with the Far East in the mid-nineteenth century. Even as they are traced to a specific island (Borneo) and tribe (the Illanuns), their description remains strikingly vague. It conjures up an amorphously exotic danger to be mastered. The figure of the pirate comes to embody indeterminacy itself, an admixture that underscores the denial of any affiliation to a nation or empire. Piracy is shown to present a danger to imperialist commerce through its very doubling of its expansionism, its absorption of different regions and its negotiation of a cosmopolitanism that is perceived, first and foremost, as a threat. It simultaneously provides a narrative structure that is endorsed as a defining tale of imperialist adventure. In this dual fictionalization of British ventures further out into the East, the pirate ship is likened to commercialized exotica as drawing-room paraphernalia. This collapses 'the Orient' into a stylized depiction of a domestic item: 'a strange sail, which, when pointed out by their exclamations, I could liken only to the curiously-rigged boats or junks one sees sailing in the air on some Japan screen or Chinese tea-box' (Gore 99–100). This projection of traditional orientalist tropes into Southeast Asia, contained as they are in imported luxury products, pinpoints complex issues in the functions of 'the exotic' in the Victorian novel, while specifically underscoring central ambiguities in the region's representation as a curiously elusive imaginary.

As late as 1904, Hugh Clifford was to write of the 'failure of the lands of southeastern Asia to make a strong appeal to the imagination of the peoples of Europe' (1). Clifford was a colonial administrator who had entered the Civil Service of the Protected Malay States in 1883, aged 17, and eventually became Resident of Pahang, Governor of the Straits Settlements and High Commissioner for the Malay States. When he set out to describe 'the lands of southeastern Asia', he attempted to locate the cause of this imaginative failure in 'the mere accident of their geographical position' (1), and yet he clearly felt that such a marginalization had to be an indicator of more than a merely accidental belatedness of the British in the region. It was an omission that moreover belied the presence of rival imperial powers.

If colonial Malaya was to produce its own English-language fiction only in the last decades of the nineteenth century, the region itself had, in fact, already featured as a site of ethnographic narratives as well as of exotic projection ever since the first European settlements in Southeast Asia.[1] Yet it was Borneo's problematic positioning in the imperialist geopolitics of the time, implicated as it was in the management of piracy, that especially formed a decisive focus point for the complexities of commercial imperialism. When Clifford bemoaned Britain's status as a relative latecomer in the region, his comments on the lack of fictional productions may have been inextricably entwined with an underpinning imperialist agenda, yet he also repeatedly deplored the impact of what he tellingly lumped together as the 'Powers of the West' (1). For Clifford, Southeast Asia's absence from the literary map of Victorian Britain would do a disservice as much to the region's 'charm [and] the interest that springs from a mysterious and mighty past' as to the empire's stake in it. His conflicted agenda, I wish to suggest, thus revealingly testifies to the ambiguity with which attitudes towards British settlements there were generally invested.

As Clifford's lifelong fascination with the divergent cultures he encountered in Southeast Asia can be said to feed directly into his works, his fictional writing was indisputably propelled primarily by ethnographical interest. What is perhaps the most significant for the Malaya's position in British fiction is indeed that he self-consciously defined what he saw as the more representative function of his anecdotal sketches against the celebration of a certain aestheticized amorphousness in Joseph Conrad's 'Malay novels'.

---

[1]   This included the fiction both of colonial administrators like Clifford himself as well as writing by the English-educated Straits Chinese. *The Straits Chinese Magazine* ran from 1897 to 1907. By contrast, Multatuli's *Max Havelaar*, set on Java (now part of Indonesia), was first published in Dutch in 1859. Although it was translated into a number of European languages within the next few years (Baron Alphonse Nahuys's English translation was published in 1868), its impact on British colonial fiction of the region was sparse and diffuse. See Tamara Wagner's 'Oriental Halves and Unlovely Hybrids: Rewriting Racialisation and Discourses on Degeneration in Victorian Southeast Asia'. *Science and Race*. Spec. issue of *Journal of Commonwealth Studies* 5 (2007): 197–218. Colonial literature in the Philippines was thriving from the sixteenth century onwards, seeing its heyday in the nineteenth.

Conrad's Southeast Asia was indisputably a vaguely evoked Orient, in which enigmatic pirates featured as intriguing projections on various metaphorical levels. This aestheticization could not be any more different from the ethnographic sketching that Clifford had in mind when he underscored the region's indeterminacy as another, or 'further', India, and which he endeavoured to provide in his own fictional writing. A juxtaposition of their divergent renditions of the Far East and the presence of rival imperial powers in the nineteenth century hence brings out the ambiguities that the region's literary representation not only engendered, but also helped to express. At the same time, I also wish to situate both their works firmly in the context of the changing functions of the region's elusive literary imaginaries in British fiction throughout the second half of the nineteenth and the beginning of the twentieth centuries. Drawing on the largely anecdotal sketches by colonial officers as well as on novels as diverse as Gore's *Adventures in Borneo* of 1849 and G.A. Henty's *In the Hands of the Malays* of 1905, I furthermore seek to argue that these narratives of piracy bring out the region's representative role as an imaginary space in which orientalist adventure and the issues of commerce met and merged.

'To Bankok! Magic name, blessed name. Mesopotamia wasn't a patch on it': Narrating Victorian Southeast Asia

The first-person narrator of Conrad's early Malay story 'Youth' signs up in the English merchant service in order to realize heavily orientalist fantasies of a magical East: 'To Bankok [sic]! Magic name, blessed name. Mesopotamia wasn't a patch on it. Remember I was twenty, and it was my first second-mate's billet, and the East was waiting for me' (*Eastern* 14). This East is vague and indeterminate, connected to youth, recalled in a nostalgic retrospect. Ban Kah Choon tellingly terms Conrad's eulogies on Southeast Asian seascapes 'purplish and romantic', although he proceeds to emphasize that 'it would be a mistake to dismiss [them] on these grounds. Behind the expressive gestures are intense feelings for the moment that heighten our awareness of the unique qualities of the land' (x). Ban of course reads Conrad specifically with this recreation of nineteenth-century Singapore and Malaya (now Malaysia) in mind. As he says of the retraceable routes of 'The End of the Tether', it 'is to be transported irresistibly back to the Singapore of the 1880s, and to have the scenes and life of that period recreated for us' (xxiv). Clifford, for one, would have disagreed. Such a reading moreover makes light of the allegorical levels that underpin Conrad's writing.

Recently, there has been new interest in the ways in which Conrad's narratives of Southeast Asia formed part of and critically reacted to the ethnographic literature of the time. Benita Parry's *Conrad and Imperialism* (1983) began to explore the ways in which Conrad transformed colonial writing to compose instead 'a fiction at odds with the traditional assumptions of the genre' (5). Parry even suggested that, 'through Conrad's multiple tellings, the story of the Other and the white man in the outposts of empire became theirs as well as ours' (119). Heliena Krenn's *Conrad's Lingard Trilogy* (1990), Andrea White's *Joseph Conrad and the Adventure Tradition* (1993) and Christopher Gogwilt's *The Invention of the West: Joseph Conrad and the Double-Mapping of Europe and Empire* (1995) have proceeded to reconsider the long-spurned question of whether, or how far, Conrad's fiction reflects the realities of the colonial British and Dutch Empires. Drawing attention to representational issues, they engage with the changing conceptualization of 'the exotic', 'the Orient' and the impact of the empire in Victorian fiction and an emergent modernism. Andrea White speaks of Conrad's double vision, pointing out the ways in which he demythologized and disrupted the imperial subject constructed in his earlier writing. More recently, Robert Hampson's *Cross-Cultural Encounters in Joseph Conrad's Malay Fiction* (2000) has focused on a textual tradition of 'writing Malaysia' (2) to situate what he terms Conrad's 'Malay fiction' within a postcolonial project of analysing 'cross-cultural encounters, cultural identity, and cultural dislocation' (23).

Much has been made in recent discussions of the ambiguously (self-)ironic detailing of the disillusioning incursion of a 'Western voice' into the magic East in 'Youth'. The hopeful narrator finds his first encounter with the alluring East dismantled by a reflection of 'the West': 'And then, before I could open my lips, the East spoke to me, but it was in a Western voice. A torrent of words was poured into the enigmatical, the fateful silence ... The voice swore and cursed violently; it riddled the solemn peace of the bay by a volley of abuse' (36). Christopher Gogwilt has analysed this clash of the Victorian (commercial) adventurer's great expectations and the sordid side of imperialist trade as a central encounter in Conrad's implicit critique of imperialism to suggest that it is a moment of the evolving historicity of the term 'the West'. The sudden proliferation of the English usage of 'the West' as a term for European nation-states at the turn of the nineteenth century, Gogwilt argues, reflects a 'new sense of global cultural proportion emerging from the "new imperialism" of the 1890s', and 'Youth' illustrates the way in which this 'rhetorical invention of the West' propels this development (*Invention* 25). Robert Hampson likewise stresses that '[t]he conqueror's silent triumph over an unseen landscape is replaced by this vituperative assertion of Western power' and, furthermore, that this 'Western voice' is itself 'divided, hybridised' (7). It is a mirror-version of the recurrent concern with racial and cultural hybrids in Conrad's fiction. Elsewhere I have addressed the region's role in the formation of occidentalist – as opposed to and entwined with orientalist – literary representations in detail.[2]

The 'Western voice', then, means business in more senses than one. In Clifford's words, the 'Powers of the West' have been busy here. Their 'busi-ness' disrupts the enigmatic silence, shatters the expectations of a first encounter with 'the East' and reminds the narrator (and the reader) that it is the merchant service that has

---

[2]   See Wagner, 'Oriental Halves', 197–218, and *Occidentalism in Novels of Malaysia and Singapore, 1819–2004* (Lewiston, Queenston and Lampeter: Edwin Mellen P, 2005), ch. 1.

taken the would-be orientalist out East in the first place. Adventure and commerce form two sides of the same coin in Conrad's imperialist writing, as they coincide, collide and counterpoise each other. A brush (or identification) with native pirates constitutes the meeting-point of trade, rival colonial powers and the smuggling enterprises that externalize the piratical ventures underlying commercial policies and practices.

In *Almayer's Folly* (1895), the first of Conrad's 'Malay trilogy' – with the symptomatically geographically vague subtitle, *A Story of an Eastern River* – Conrad introduces the problematics of imperialist commerce, or commercial imperialism, by focusing on an emblematic meeting of Malay pirates and European businessmen in the waters surrounding the Malayan Archipelago:

> It was the point in the islands where tended all those bold spirits who … invaded the Malay Archipelago in search of money and adventure …, not disinclined for a brush with the pirates that were to be found on many a coast as yet, making money fast, they used to have a general 'rendezvous' in the bay for purposes of trade and dissipation. (6–7)

The pirate at once functions as a metaphorical projection for the threat presented by native resistance or 'infection' and for the savagery of Victorian commercialism. Commerce and piracy are contrasted, then conflated. In analysing the changing topos of piracy, this chapter situates it firmly within narratives of a self-styled 'benign' commercialism that was at the centre of imperialist self-definitions.

The last decades have seen an in-depth discussion of imperialism's pervasiveness in the domestic Victorian novel and a tracing of imperialist ventures home. Ever since Edward Said's influential studies, retrospective postcolonial readings of colonial texts have become an established strategy – so much so that their very commonness has recently given rise to re-examinations of their premises and ends. Raphael Samuel has already suggested that orientalism was 'by no means necessarily a pathological affair' (76). Nigel Leask has likewise stressed the importance of a more balanced approach to avoid either restating 'exploded myths of empire' or lapsing into the 'rhetoric of blame which presumes that all European travellers were uniformly racists, jingoists, or imperialists' (4). In a recent essay, Erin O'Connor speaks of the urgent need for a 'post-postcolonial criticism' (*passim*). As this reassessment of the literary representation of the Malay pirate is firmly situated within the current redirection in Victorian studies beyond the impasses created by purely contextual analysis, it is also necessary to stress the narratives' own self-conscious engagement with the conflicting demands of historical or ethnographical interest and aesthetic appreciation.[3]

---

[3]   O'Connor particularly protests against what she terms 'Victorientalism': a 'mining of a distant, exotic, threatening but fascinating literature to produce and establish a singularly self-serving body of knowledge elsewhere' (227).

This re-evaluation is precisely what singles out the shifting narrative functions of Southeast Asia in British fiction as such a remarkably revealing point-of-entry into discourses on the literary uses of the exotic in Victorian culture at large. Pinpointing debates at the time, Clifford repeatedly deplored Conrad's lack of interest in ethnographic accuracy. In his review of Conrad's *Almayer's Folly*, 'Mr Joseph Conrad at Home and Abroad', he even referred to Conrad's 'complete ignorance of Malays and their habits and customs' (v). Conversely, in his 'Author's Note' to *A Personal Record*, Conrad later staged a dialogue between himself and Clifford that pivoted on this divergence of administrators' ethnographical mapping and 'his own particular East of which I had but the mistiest, short glimpse' (142). It is because of the importance of such debates in the ongoing 're-presentation' of the region that a discussion of often conflicting cultural myths of the British presence in Southeast Asia achieves a particular poignancy in the reappraisal of its literary transformation.

Early European Filibusters and the Myth of British Benign Commercialism

What Clifford attempted to describe as 'further India' was a region alternately known as 'Asia of the Monsoons' and a part of the East Indies in a commercial, rather than a geographical, definition. The contested term 'Southeast Asia' was coined only after World War II as a descriptive entity that is now thought of as comprising Brunei, Burma, Thailand, Laos, Cambodia, Vietnam, Malaysia, Singapore, Indonesia and the Philippines, although geographical demarcations continue to be disputed (Osborne 4). The 'southeastern Asia' Clifford had in mind, by contrast, extended only to territories of British commercial interest – a self-styled benevolent interest that he sharply contrasted with early Portuguese incursions: 'the misconduct of the early European filibusters which put the East forever on the defensive, and caused the name of the white man to stink in the nostrils of the brown peoples' (34). In *Further India*, he set self-congratulatory eulogies on British paternalism against earlier European atrocities: 'We of this latter age know how much, in the fullness of time, the rule of the white man had served to ease the people of the Malay Peninsula at least' (63).

Clifford's conceptualization of the imperialist presence in British Malaya and, he argued, its regenerative function for the Malays formed an outgrowth of a Romantic commercialism that had been pivotal to the region's earliest representation in British colonial writing. It had been instituted, perhaps most markedly, by the founder of Singapore, Thomas Stamford Raffles in the early nineteenth century; defining British intervention against Portuguese and, increasingly, Dutch 'filibusters' underscored a parallel juxtaposition of native piracy and British benign commerce. This set of contrasts soon found its nemesis in the deliberate conflations in fictional amalgams of smugglers, corrupt traders and outcast Malay chiefs driven to piratical ventures.

British interest in the region came intriguingly late, and this is surely important for its appeal to readers of adventure stories, just as the emphasis on trade rather than territory accounts partly for the central role of commerce in fiction. Piracy represented a meeting-point for these two sides of the region's literary potential, while the corresponding narrativization of Dutch imperialist despotism formed an inviting entry-point for 'benign' intervention. Although the British East India Company had set up a trading-port on Penang, an island off the coast of the Malayan Peninsula, in 1786, the Dutch continued to dominate European trade in Southeast Asia. The Napoleonic Wars provided the decisive opening. In 1811 the British took over Java in order to protect it from the French – at least temporarily breaking the Dutch hold over the region. Although Java was returned after the defeat of Napoleon, British free-trade policies had made decisive incursions into Southeast Asia, and these policies contrasted usefully with early filibusters and, as Raffles put it in his *History of Java* (1817), the despotic slavery practised by the Dutch:

> The Dutch Company, activated solely by the spirit of gain, and viewing their Javan subjects with less regard or consideration than a West-India planter formerly viewed the gang upon his estate, because the latter had paid the purchase-money of human property which the other had not, employed all the pre-existing machinery of despotism, to squeeze from the people their utmost mite of contribution, the last dregs of their labour, and thus aggravated the evils of a capricious and semi-barbarous government, by working it with all the practised ingenuity of politicians and all the monopolising selfishness of traders. (vol.1, 151)

Raffles, a clerk in the East India House, had first come out to Malaya in 1805. In 1811 he was appointed Lieutenant-Governor of Java, an office he held until the Peace of 1815. As Lieutenant-Governor of Bencoolen in Sumatra, he endeavoured to foil attempts by the Dutch to regain a monopolistic hold over trade in the Malayan Archipelago. The Anglo-Dutch Treaty of 1824 stipulated that the British give up Sumatra in exchange for Malacca on the Malayan Peninsula. Meanwhile, however, Raffles had founded an additional base on Singapore, where he proposed a commercial 'factory'. Established in 1819, this strategic port-city soon surpassed Penang in its profitability, and the Straits Settlements, comprising Singapore, Malacca and Penang, were officially formed in 1826, consolidating the British presence in the region. Once tin mines were discovered in Perak in 1850, the hinterland became of increasing importance. In 1867 the British Straits Settlements were transferred from the Government of India to become a Crown Colony directly under the control of the Colonial Office in London – a good indication of their rapidly developing significance.

By the 1870s, Singapore had become the world's chief rubber sorting and export centre, a hub of commercial imperialism. In 1877 Frederick William Burbidge, on his way to collect plants in Borneo for a Chelsea horticultural firm, called it the 'Liverpool of the East' (14). In the 1890s, the British Empire controlled Penang, Province Wellesley (facing Penang Island), Malacca and Singapore as well as Perak, Selangor, Pahang and the nine states of Negri Sembilan, to be united as the Federated Malay States in 1896, and to a degree, the state of Johore; by 1914 the entire peninsula was under British control. Still, in his 1869 *The Malay Archipelago*, Alfred Russell Wallace emphasized that a vast region remained largely uncharted beyond 'few and scanty' British possessions:

> To the ordinary Englishman this is perhaps the least known part of the globe. Our possessions in it are few and scanty [and] few persons realise that, as a whole, it is comparable with the primary divisions of the globe, and that some of its separate islands are larger than France or the Austrian empire. (1)

Its potential for exploration, commercial expansion and literary setting was thus by no means limited to trading-ports.

While resident colonial administrators such as Clifford preferred to set their anecdotal sketches in the areas most familiar to them, Conrad used Singapore as a point of departure at best, focusing instead on remote outposts. Borneo especially presented a unique case at the centre of commercial disputes. Rajah Brooke, the White Rajah of Borneo, has hence invariably been read as the inspiration for Conrad's 'Lingard trilogy'. This trilogy, comprising *Almayer's Folly* (1895), *An Outcast of the Islands* (1896) and *The Rescue* (1920), critically reacted to the racial typecasting of the traders, sailors, clerks and different immigrant populations that passed through and populated the region at the time. Most importantly, its focus on the Dutchman, Almayer, demystified projections of aggressive imperialism on to European 'others'. Instead, white men were lumped together as interchangeable intruders from 'the West'.

In *Almayer's Folly*, the Dutch officers who visit the eponymous antihero among the run-down commercial buildings on Borneo that epitomize his (and the empire's) demise, bemusedly humour his speculations on British expansion. With consummate irony, Almayer's privileging of British interest is the subject of ridicule:

> They listened and assented, amazed by the wonderful simplicity and the foolish hopefulness of the man, till Almayer carried away by his excitement, disclosed his regret at the non-arrival of the English, 'who knew how to develop a rich country,' as he expressed it. There was a general laugh amongst the Dutch officers at that unsophisticated statement. (36)

Romantic commercialism had run to seed. Earlier in the century, Raffles had significantly combined his ethnographic interest in a region he considered alluringly exotic with economic theories of the commercial benefits of imperialist rule, the vilification of the Dutch serving in a twofold capacity in negotiating imperialist involvements with smugglers, marauders and Malay 'sea-robbers'.

Raffles repeatedly blamed the Dutch for having 'very much diverted [commerce] from its ancient course by the restrictive system of Dutch colonial policy' (vol.1, 193). John Crawfurd, the second British Resident of Singapore, put it even more pointedly in his *History of the Indian Archipelago* (1820): 'conduct of the nature here related brought the European character into the greatest discredit with all the natives of the Archipelago, and the piratical character which we have attempted to fix upon them, might be most truly retaliated upon us' (vol.3, 235). The Dutch were cast as indirectly responsible for native piracy, which additionally underscored images of their despotism.[4] Ironically, while 'benign' promotion of free trade was channelled into a Victorian paternalism premised on Romantic commercialism, the 'suppression of piracy' became a favoured slogan that helped to extend commerce while feeding into ideals of beneficial, civilizing imperialist intervention.[5]

The more incriminating details of Victorian capitalism could be expunged, as it were, from imperialist rhetoric when they were shown to have been confined to the foreign and especially a rival commercial power, yet as Conrad's fiction shows, this was by no means an uncontested strategy. Lacking Conrad's self-referential irony, Clifford disconcertingly projected commercial violence primarily on to Chinese shopkeepers. Philip Holden speaks of 'the spectre of commerce' (41) in Clifford's negative depictions of Chinese commercial rapacity, a spectre engendered by 'a disavowal of the fact that the flag followed trade' (57). Clifford's often oddly situated defence of the Malays (as well as of British interference) at the expense of the Chinese, however, presents an unusual case, and I shall come back to his curiously nostalgic evocation of legendary pirates of the past. The common practice in political rhetoric was to 'justify' intervention by poising it against Malay piratical ventures. The new commercial networks closely replicated

---

[4]   Anthony Forge, in 'Raffles and Daniell: Making the Image Fit'. *Recovering the Orient: Artists, Scholars, Appropriations*, eds Andrew Gerstle and Anthony Milner (Chur, Switzerland: Harwood Academic Publishers, 1994), 109–50, argues that Raffles's emphasis on the differences between Dutch and British colonial systems is clearest in his views on the economic nature of the Javanese, whom he tellingly casts as 'civilized' and therefore, 'like all civilised men, an example of "economic man"' (109). See also Mary Catherine Quilty, *Textual Empires: A Reading of Early British Histories of Southeast Asia* (Clayton, Victoria: Monash Asia Institute, 1998): the concept of mutually beneficial self-interest imbued late-eighteenth-century liberal economics with its morality, and Romantic commercialism as it was deployed by Raffles and reformulated by his successors at once built on and participated in these discourses on benign commerce (*passim*).

[5]   Tarling suggests a double caveat: 'If, however, matters of judgement and motivation are involved, it is also necessary to be fair to the Europeans who believed they were suppressing piracy' (*Piracy* 1). See Tarling's *Piracy and Politics in the Malay World: A Study of British Imperialism in Nineteenth-Century South-East Asia* (Melbourne: F.W. Cheshire, 1963; repr. Nendeln, Liechtenstein: Kraus Reprint, 1978).

Asian maritime empires and were thus implicated in the redirection of piratical and other commercial ventures to a remarkable extent.[6]

Brooke's Commerce with the Pirates: A Narrative of Imperialist Ambiguities

Piracy's role in nineteenth-century discourse on the end, or ends, of Romantic commercialism was indisputably multifarious, and fictional representations of the various pirates of the region reflect this in markedly different ways. If it was central to political rhetoric regarding Malaya, it was definitional in the attempts to create a British Borneo. Cultural myths circulating about Brooke, the White Rajah, inspired some of the most lasting literary topoi. Brooke's ventures, in fact, engendered a fascination with commercial ventures that were defined against piracy, yet, as a result, included it in a peculiar fashion. The expedition for the 'suppression of piracy', Henry Keppel was to write in his minute account of the *Expedition to Borneo of H.M.S. Dido for the Suppression of Piracy* (1846), opened up Borneo 'to commerce and civilisation' to 'bestow happiness on its inhabitants' (vol.1, 164). It became a mythologized enterprise that newly united adventure and commerce to reinvest imperialist expansion in the name of trade with the excitement of exploration. Tarling speaks of Brooke's 'Rafflesian aspirations' (*Fall* 37): '[i]ntervention in the eighteenth century was a commercial technique; with Raffles it was part of a grandiose imperial scheme; with Brooke it [was] intimately connected with his own individuality' (*Britain* 38). Under the Anglo-Dutch Treaty, Borneo had been left to the Dutch. It was Brooke's intervention as an individual rather than an East India Company employee that made British commerce possible without any direct interference on the part of the empire.[7]

---

[6]   The Bugis, among other maritime traders, played a specifically versatile part in Britain's commercial incursions. As Nicholas Tarling has extensively shown, they actively encouraged the smuggling of British 'country traders' (*Piracy passim*). The establishment of Singapore formed a 'pivot of their trading operations in the archipelago ... a springboard for their enterprises in Malaya, Sumatra and Borneo, a staging port for their pilgrims en route to Mecca, and an important centre for the dissemination of knowledge and information' (Christian Pelras. *The Bugis*. Oxford: Blackwell, 1996, 150–51). In Victorian fiction, Bugis and Malay pirates are regularly conflated; the terms were used interchangeably. Pelras stresses that '[a]lthough their name may sound familiar to readers of Conrad's novels', the Bugis' 'former reputation as pirates is almost entirely without foundation' (3–4). Like the Malays, from whom they are distinguished in recent anthropological studies, the Bugis belong to the Austronesian peoples of maritime Southeast Asia. Based originally in Sulawesi, which was colonized by the Dutch in the seventeenth century, they played a multifarious part in the trade the British redirected to Singapore (Pelras 150–51).

[7]   The son of an East India Company official, Brooke was first an officer in the Indian Army, but was wounded in 1825, during the Anglo-Burmese War. He visited the Straits Settlements for the first time in 1830. When his father left him a substantial fortune, he returned to Southeast Asia as an explorer. He became Rajah of Sarawak, Governor of

Owen Rutter's *The Pirate Wind: Tales of the Sea-Robbers of Malaya* (1930), for example, revealingly plays into precisely this eulogy of 'Rafflesian aspirations' as it details how Brooke accepted the rule of Sarawak in order to 'free the Borneo seas from the scourge of the pirates' (92). Even more importantly, ideals of benign commercialism and individualist exploration formed a mixture that struck a chord in the cultural myths of Southeast Asian pirates:

> Trading, thus understood, was the occupation of ambitious men who played an occult but important part in all those national risings, religious disturbances, and also in the organised piratical movements on a large scale which, during the first half of the last century, affected the fate of more than one native dynasty and, for a few years at least, seriously endangered the Dutch rule in the East. (Conrad, *Rescue* 67–8)

This passage from *The Rescue*, the last in Conrad's *Lingard* trilogy, sums up this overarching interest in commerce. In Conrad's novels, commercial failure structures the themes of disillusionment and exile, as they link trade to organized piratical movements, and European smugglers to indigenous as well as imperialist concepts of commerce with their respective savagery. That the White Rajah's conflicted role had inspired the *Lingard* trilogy has revealingly been the starting-point for critical reassessments of the novels ever since John Dozier Gordan's 1938 article 'The Rajah Brooke and Joseph Conrad'.[8] Lingard significantly never finds the Eastern river that promises commercial gain, and in Almayer the same 'Rafflesian aspirations' meet cultural myths that circulated about the Dutch 'half-caste' Olmeijer at the time. While it is undoubtedly in Almayer's failure that Raffles's (and Brooke's) commercial idealism truly runs to seed, the piratical savagery of the 'spectre of commerce' is also inherent in Lingard's mythologized adventures: a vanquishing of pirates that aligns his commercial ventures with piracy in more ways than one.

In *Almayer's Folly*, the Dutch, instead of featuring as vilified projections of European commerce themselves, pointedly style the 'smart business transactions' of the gentlemen-traders of Brooke's ilk 'English pedlars':

Labuan and Commissioner and Consul-General to the Sultan and Independent Chiefs of Borneo. Compare Tarling's *Imperialism in Southeast Asia: 'A Fleeting, Passing Phase'* (London: Routledge, 2001), 55–6.

   [8] In *Conrad's Eastern World* (Cambridge: Cambridge UP, 1966), Norman Sherry suggests that Conrad drew on various such 'white rajahs' of the Malay region, while more recent studies have concentrated on the ways in which these models become transformed in fiction with emphasis on the demystification of the Brooke myth. As Hampson puts it, 'when Conrad draws on material relating to Sir James Brooke, he is not using an esoteric figure, but rather someone who ... had a place in the popular imagination' (1). See also White 104; Gogwilt, *Invention* 76.

The Dutch merchants called those men English pedlars; some of them were undoubtedly gentlemen for whom that kind of life had a charm; most were seamen; the acknowledged king of them all was Tom Lingard, he whom the Malays, honest or dishonest, quiet fishermen or desperate cut-throats, recognised as 'the Rajah-Laut' – the King of the Sea. Almayer had heard of him before he had been three days in Macassar, had heard the stories of his smart business transactions, his loves, and also of his desperate fights with the Sulu pirates, together with the romantic tale of some child – a girl – found in a piratical prau by the victorious Lingard. (7)

Almayer marries the female pirate, and while much has been made of Conrad's concern with hybridity as embodied by their daughter (Hampson 105–7), what really drives the story is commercial speculation and its initial contrast with piracy. Money is at the heart of this venture into cross-cultural marriage, the adventurer's imagination zooming in on the dowry of Lingard's adopted daughter, pictured as a pirate's loot: 'He was gifted with a strong and active imagination, and in that short space of time he saw, as in a flash of dazzling light, great piles of shining guilders, and realised all the possibilities of an opulent existence' (10). Ironically, Lingard's profits have been swallowed up by his explorations.

The slow decay of business ventures indicates not so much the end of the 'Rafflesian' adventure, but its ingrained financial side. Andrea White has suggested that Almayer's dreams are all the wrong ones: they are dreams of a 'diminished commercial world' (122), which helps to explain why 'the same Bornean jungles described by Brooke are unfamiliar to readers of Conrad' (27). The East's enigmas in Conrad's fiction have always something nightmarish about them, and the phantasmagoria is the dark underbelly of 'smart business transactions'. The adventure tradition of pirates and their commercial suppression comes to an end. The White Rajahs' demystification eclipses their fictionalization. The cultural myths of Brooke account for the growing attraction of Borneo in pirate novels, yet they do so in changing ways that track shifts in the representation of orientalized piracy in the second half of the nineteenth century.

When the prolific novelist and playwright Catherine Gore turned to a vaguely 'exotic' setting in *Adventures in Borneo* half a century earlier, she significantly dedicated the novel to Brooke 'by an admirer of his energy, firmness, and moderation'. The novel ends with yet another eulogy on his putatively enlightening interventions:

Darkness is no longer over the land. … Under the auspices of one of the most energetic and honourable adventurers of modern times, a new territory has been colonised, wither commerce may steer, unmolested, her richly-freighted fleets; – secured by the triumphant authority of the British flag, from all fear of a recurrence of those evils which signalised my own ADVENTURES IN BORNEO. (260)

Predating the wealth of imperialist adventure stories of the late-Victorian age, Gore's novel features a diminutive boy as its main protagonist and first-person narrator. Shipwrecked, orphaned and wounded by pirates off the coast of Borneo, he is nursed back to health by a well-intentioned tribe. He is subsequently captured by pirates, put on the slave-market and fortuitously rescued by his uncle, whose arrival foreshadows Brooke's.

Set before Brooke's expeditions to the region, the novel shows the helpless child-hero relying on just such an intervention: 'I had been so accustomed, from my childhood, to hear of Britannia ruling the waves, and of the British flag being sovereign in India, that I was firmly convinced some fort, or factory, or colony must be attainable' (172–3). Such endorsement of commercial imperialism remains centre stage, absorbing the structures and tropes of the exoticized narratives of exploration. It was these narrative structures that became pivotal in later adventure tales, which in their stead subsumed the underpinning imperialist ideologies. In James Greenwood's *The Adventures of Reuben Davidger* (1865), for example, the titular hero stows away on board a ship and is taken captive by Dyaks on Borneo, thus setting the same scene as Gore's novel. However, while the boy's face is covered during the decisive piratical attack in the earlier novel, coyly veiling the events, heroic fights with 'sea-robbers' wielding 'their terrible krisses, sharp as razors, ... and the stone-headed clubs' (83) are detailed with relish in Greenwood's novel. The ending sees the hero return triumphantly, his friends and family 'taking me, by my brown skin and the rings in my ears, for a distinguished foreigner' (355).

In John Conroy Hutcheson's *The Penang Pirate* (1885), furthermore, the crew can even be seen 'to prepare for a fresh struggle with all the alacrity and glee of schoolboys going out for an unexpected holiday' (56). The popularity of these narratives of adventurous encounters with Malay pirates was to prove so lasting that even late twentieth-century fictionalizations of Southeast Asia contained references to Victorian adventure tales. A striking example is George Rocker's *Escaped Singapore; Heading Homewards*, an account of his experience of being shipwrecked during World War II, published in 1990: '"When I was young," said Ronald, "I used to love reading tales of Malay pirates and their wavy-bladed *kris*; but I never thought that I'd meet them for myself"' (112). A personal account of wartime Southeast Asia is narrated through the lens of Victorian adventure tales as an influential literary source.

By far the most memorable of these tales was indisputably G.A. Henty's *In the Hands of the Malays* (1905). It was one of the most exoticized: doubly set in a remote region in the year 1669 and, hence, before the British Empire's incursion into the region, among a Dutch merchant community on Batavia. In contrast to both Clifford's and Conrad's self-conscious negotiation of their representation of Britain's rival imperialist powers, the Dutch protagonist stands in for a European presence in general. He saves the settlement from a massacre and is duly rewarded as 'the hero of the occasion' (54). In this, he is in striking opposition to the threatening pirate of unknown origins: 'It would have been difficult to fix his nationality. The outline of the face was Arab; the colour of the skin showed that though one or other of his parents had been white, the other had been either Arab or Malay' (7). From Gore to Henty, narratives of piracy capitalize on exotic indeterminacies, eschewing the anecdotal detailing mainly employed by colonial administrators. The pirate Sea Tiger in Henty's adventure tale is an unclassifiable hybrid and an indeterminate threat, his tiger-like qualities at once investing him with savage courage and aligning him with exotic fauna. In her study of 'somatic fictions', politics of fitness and imperialist ideology, Athena Vrettos speaks of a hermeneutic uncertainty: Victorian racialism conceived non-white races as less sensitive than the 'civilized' white middle classes. Either hereditary factors or repeated exposure to hardship were seen to have fostered the 'savage's' physical resilience, yet stamina was also understood as an attribute necessary for evolutionary survival (Vrettos 147).[9] As a conclusion to this map of fictional pirates and the ways in which they were inspired by, and conversely impinged on, the myths circulating at the time, I shall trace the narrative functions of such ethnographic mapping.

The Victorian Adventures of the Malay Pirate: Remapping Ethnographic Myths

When Alfred Russell Wallace set out to detail 'the races of man' in *The Malay Archipelago*, a work he notably dedicated to Darwin, he divided the various tribes into two main 'races' – the Malays and the Papuans of New Guinea. Yet he was somewhat at a loss to account for what he termed 'intermediate' tribes that might be 'formed by a mixture of the two' as opposed to 'the true Malay races' or the 'Malays proper' (446). This indeterminacy played directly into the cultural mythologization of the 'Malay pirate'. In Hutcheson's *The Penang Pirate*, racial casting sets up the Malay as a 'half-Chinese' (36) 'mulatto' (26): 'short, thick-set, black-haired, and yellow-visaged' (23) with a 'low Mongolian type of face' (27). Indiscriminately 'mixed', Malay crewmen are at the bottom rack of the ship's (racial) hierarchy. The 'white men on board' include Snowball 'as one of us, although he is a nigger' (24), who asserts 'with dignity' that he knows he 'isn't 'xactly like you white gen'lemen; but den I isn't a nasty mulatto like dem poor trash' (26). Pirate narratives set in colonial Southeast Asia cast a very different light on the changing attitudes to and literary uses of racial categories that were emerging at the time.[10]

---

⁹   See also Robert J.C. Young's *Colonial Desire: Hybridity in Theory, Culture and Race* (London: Routledge, 1995), 92–3.

¹⁰   It has even been argued that the notion of a 'Malay race' was developed in the course of the nineteenth century, as colonial administrators lumped together a number of diverse ethnic groups. See C. Mary Turnbull, *A Short History of Malaysia, Singapore and Brunei* (Singapore: Graham Brash, 1981), 4; Philip Holden, *Modern Subjects/Colonial*

In 1849, Catherine Gore used a sleight-of-hand polarization of the natives into harmless and dangerous tribes that skirted the issues of innate racial characteristic that became so central to late-Victorian colonial fiction. In the wake of Darwin's cataclysmic works, concepts of racial distinctiveness, together with fears of degeneration or racial suicide, were increasingly at the centre of ongoing reconceptualizations. As Sean Grass notes in his chapter, a subplot in Charles Reade's *Hard Cash* (1863) illustrates the new emphasis on racial indeterminacy in invocations of an 'exotic' threat very pointedly. The eponymous 'hard cash' is fated to be nearly lost for good as a result of the very mundane, domestic 'piracy' of embezzlement in a suburban area in England, its safe delivery through various threats at sea meant to underscore the affinities between corrupt businessmen and savage pirates.[11]

Of indeterminate origins, Reade's pirates are, via Portuguese filibusters, linked to colonial investments – the 'crew was a mixed one: the captain was believed to be a Portuguese' (139). The ship turns loose a 'wild crew of yellow Malays, black chinless Papuans, and bronzed Portuguese' (164). Hutcheson's *The Penang Pirate* likewise conjures up 'such ferocious looking ruffians as herd together in Eastern seas' (61). In Reade's novel, however, physical courage 'parted the races': 'the Papuans and Sooloos, their black faces livid and blue with horror, leaped yelling into the sea, or crouched and whimpered; the yellow Malays and brown Portuguese, though blanched to one colour now, turned on death like dying panthers' (169). Blanched to one colour, they share a praiseworthy savagery with 'white Britons, drunk with battle now, naked to the waist, grimed with powder, and spotted like leopards with blood' (164). This is a far cry from the sympathetic 'noble savages' of Gore's novel, while it also anticipates the grudging admiration for Henty's Sea Tiger.

The most intriguing development, however, is the steady infusion of a curious nostalgia into the fictionalization of the Malay pirate at the end of the nineteenth century. This additional twist perhaps most poignantly articulates the ambiguity in the representation of Britain's imperialist encounters in the region. To an extent, as Grace Moore discusses, it forms part of Darwinian concerns with degeneration at large, and this further contributes to a self-conscious reappraisal of the imperialist mission itself. Clifford's *In Court and Kampung* (1897), for example, refers to the passing of the Malay in 'his natural state': 'Such changes have been wrought in the condition of the Malay on the West Coast, during the past twenty years of British Protection, that there one can no longer see him in his natural state. He has become sadly dull, limp, and civilised' (3). *The Real Malay: Pen Pictures* (1907) by Frank Swettenham, a colonial administrator who had worked with Clifford on an eventually uncompleted Malay dictionary, may all too blatantly assert the white man's duty to 'civilize' Malaya: 'My object is to show that when the British

---

Texts: Hugh Clifford and the Discipline of English Literature in the Straits Settlements and Malaya 1895–1907 (Greensboro, NC: ELT Press, 2000), 2–4.

[11]   I discuss Reade's novel in more detail elsewhere (Wagner, *Occidentalism* ch.1).

Government at last consented to interfere in Malay affairs, ... *the result obtained has been strikingly satisfactory*' (19). Yet the ambiguous nostalgia that is so pivotal in Clifford's works nevertheless also runs through Swettenham's fiction. In the preface to *Malay Sketches* (1895), he speaks of his attempt to recall 'that Golden Peninsula, 'twixt Hindustan and Far Cathay, from whence the early navigators brought back such wondrous stories of adventure' (ix).

Although it has been suggested that Clifford endeavoured to argue that Britain's benevolent imperialism engendered a commitment to the 'regeneration' of the Malay race (Holden 41), his novels, moreover, became increasingly more expressive of muted resignation. Clifford's *Sally: A Study* (1904) and *Saleh: A Sequel* (1908) readdress degeneration, redeploying the topos of *amok* as a defining racial characteristic and, most importantly, redirecting projections of commercial rapacity.[12] Illustrating a poignant end of the literary eulogies of the Malay pirate, the novels trace the story of Rajah Saleh, a Malay educated in England who returns as a stranger to cast off his education, becomes an insurgent and ultimately runs *amok*. An 'unlovely hybrid' (169), he epitomizes 'the uneasy blending of the civilisations of Asia and the West' (140) in colonized Malaya: '[t]he tangle and topsy-turvydom, the crooked vision and the distorted travesty of the truth which result from looking at the West through the eyes of the East, and of judging the Oriental from the standpoint of the European' (165). Suicidal insurgence is sparked off by muddled financial accounts. Chinese shopkeepers are slaughtered, their shops 'pillaged and plundered' (236), while romantic pirate stories are reduced to the undignified end of common thieves:

> [T]he assailants were sneaking off into the forest like the blood-stained thieves they were. The Past, looked at through the glamour of romance – the fierce unfettered Past of a thousand stories – had appealed to [Saleh] with a wonderful force; now that it had been revived and had been made actual in the Present, it filled him with horror, disgust, and shame. Indeed, indeed the English had robbed him of many things. (236)

The English have robbed Saleh of his glorious pirate's past. This is a sad end indeed for Saleh, his (foreign) fictions of his people, as well as ideals of benevolent interference. 'May God forgive us for our sorry deeds and for our glorious intentions' (253), beseeches the narrator of *Saleh*.

The end of *Further India* marks a similar disillusionment mixed with nostalgia: 'Our task is now completed: the tale is told, and Chryse the Golden stands revealed to us, robbed of its magic and its mystery, just a common fragment of the earth upon which we also tread' (Clifford 345). Saleh's end embodies the death of a Romantic commercialism that has run aground in an imperialist commercialism that is exposed as an outgrowth of, rather than a benign counterpoise to, piracy.

---

[12]   On *amok* in the fiction of Conrad, Clifford and Swettenham see also Holden 102–4; Gogwilt 58.

The ambiguous nostalgia expressed in the later novels of Conrad and Clifford, in fact, have thereby initiated a persisting representation of a Southeast Asia revealed and deprived in more senses than one, in which the pirate and what he represents functions at once as robber and robbed, holding up a distorted mirror to the commercial orientalist.

Bibliography

'Adelphi Theatre'. *Times* 10 February 1829: 3.

Admari, Ralph. 'Ballou, the Father of the Dime Novel'. *American Book Collector* (September–October 1933): 121–9.

Agate, James. *Those Were the Nights*. London: Hutchinson, 1946.

Alexander, Christine. *The Early Writings of Charlotte Brontë*. Oxford: Basil Blackwell, 1983.

——. 'Readers and Writers: *Blackwood's* and the Brontës'. *The Gaskell Society Journal* 8 (1994): 54–69.

Allen, Kristie. '"Confound the Pirates!" Nautical Melodrama and the Anti-Slave Trade in the Making of the British Nation State'. *Nineteenth Century Studies* 24 (2010): page references unavailable at the time of going to press.

Anderson, Benedict. *Imagined Communities: Reflections on the Origin and Spread of Nationalism*. 1983. New York and London: Verso, 1991.

'Another Extra Double New World' (advertisement). *New World* 4 (14 May 1842): 322.

Antony, Robert J. *Like Froth Floating on the Sea: The World of Pirates and Seafarers in Late Imperial South China*. Berkeley: Institute of East Asian Studies, U of California, 2003.

Aravamudan, Srinivas. *Tropicopolitans: Colonialism and Agency, 1688–1804*. Durham, NC and London: Duke UP, 1999.

Arendt, Hannah. *The Human Condition*. Chicago: U of Chicago P, 1998.

'Art. III. – 1. *Narrative of Events in Borneo and Celebes, Down to the Occupation of Labuan* … London: Reeve, Benham, and Reeve, 1848'. *Edinburgh Review* 88 (1848): 63–94.

'Art. IX. – A Letter to a Member of Parliament, on the Slavery of the Christians at Algiers. By Walter Croker, Esq. of the Royal Navy. London, Stockdale, 1816'. *Edinburgh Review* 26 (1816): 449–57.

Ashby, Nanette M. *Charles Sealsfield, 'The Greatest American Author': A Study of Literary Piracy and Promotion in the 19th Century*. Stuttgart: Charles Sealsfield Gesellschaft, 1980.

Ashley, Leonard R.N. 'Gilbert and Melodrama'. *Gilbert and Sullivan*: Papers presented at the international conference held at the University of Kansas in May 1970. Ed. James Helyar. Lawrence: University of Kansas Libraries, 1970: 1–6.

Avery, Gillian. *Childhood's Pattern: A Study of the Heroes and Heroines of Children's Fiction, 1770–1950*. London: Hodder and Stoughton, 1975.

Baer, Joel H. '"The Complicated Plot of Piracy": Aspects of English Criminal Law and the Image of the Pirate in Defoe'. *Studies in Eighteenth-Century Culture* 14 (1985): 3–28.

Bakhtin, Mikhail. *Rabelais and His World*. Trans. Hélène Iswolsky. Bloomington: Indiana UP, 1984.

Ballantyne, R.M. *The Coral Island*. 1857. n.p. Regent Classics, The Thames Publishing Co., n.d.

——. *The Gorilla Hunters*. 1861. n.p. Bibliobazaar, 2007.

——. *The Pirate City*. 1874. Gloucester: Dodo Press, 2007.

——. *The Madman and the Pirate*. 1883. n.p. Tutis Digital Publishing Pvt Ltd, 2008.

Ballou, Marturin Murray. *The Belle of Madrid; or, The Unknown Mask. A Tale of Spain and the Spanish*. Boston, MA: F. Gleason, 1849.

Ban, Kah Choon. 'Introduction'. *The Eastern Stories*. By Joseph Conrad. New Delhi: Penguin, 2000.

Bankson, Douglas H. *Charles Reade's Manuscript Notecards for* Hard Cash. Diss., U of Washington, 1954.

Barker, Benjamin. *The Bandit of the Ocean; or, the Female Privateer*. New York: De Witt, 1855.

——. *The Land Pirate; or, the Wild Girl of the Beach*. Boston: Gleason's, 1847.

Barnes, James J. *Authors, Publishers, and Politicians: The Quest for an Anglo-American Copyright Agreement, 1818–1854*. Columbus: Ohio State UP, 1974.

Barrett, Daniel. 'Play Publication, Readers and the "Decline" of Victorian Drama'. *Book History* 2.1 (1999): 173–87.

Barrie, J.M. *Peter Pan*. 1911. New York: Grosset & Dunlap, 1911.

——. 'Captain Hook at Eton, a Strange Story' *The Times*, 8 July 1927, 15–16.

——. *Peter Pan*. London: Samuel French, n.d.

Barrow, John. *Travels in China*. London: T. Cadell and W. Davies, 1804.

——. *Some Account of the Public Life and a Selection from the Unpublished Writings of the Earl of Macartney*. 2 vols. London: T. Cadell and W. Davies, 1807.

[Barrow, John.] 'Free Trade to China'. *Quarterly Review* 50 (1833–34): 430–67.

Beatty-Kingston, W. 'Our Musical Box', *The Theatre*, 2 February 1885, 80–82.

Belford, Barbara. *A Biography of the Author of Dracula*. New York: Alfred A. Knopf, 1996.

Benjamin, Walter. *The Arcades Project*. Intro. Howard Eiland, trans. Howard Eiland and Kevin McLaughlin. Cambridge, MA: Harvard UP, 2002.

Benson, Peter. 'Gleason's Publishing Hall'. *Publishers for Mass Entertainment in Nineteenth-Century America*. Ed. Madeleine B. Stern. Boston, MA: G.K. Hall, 1980: 137–45.

Birkin, Andrew. *J.M. Barrie and the Lost Boys*. London: Constable, 1979.

Bodenheimer, Rosemarie. '*North and South*: A Permanent State of Change'. *Mary Barton*. Ed. Thomas Recchio. New York: Norton, 2008.

Bonaparte, Felicia. *The Gypsy-Bachelor of Manchester: The Life of Mrs. Gaskell's Demon*. Charlottesville: UP of Virginia, 1992.

Booth, Michael R. *English Plays of the Nineteenth Century*. 5 vols. Oxford: Clarendon Press, 1976.

——. *The Theatre in the Victorian Age*. Cambridge: Cambridge UP, 1991.

Boyd, Kelly. *Manliness and the Boys' Story Paper in Britain*. Basingstoke: Palgrave Macmillan, 2003.

Brantlinger, Patrick. *Rule of Darkness: British Literature and Imperialism, 1830–1914*. Ithaca, NY and London: Cornell UP, 1988.

Bratton, J.S. *The Impact of Children's Fiction*. London: Croom Helm, 1981.

Brewster, Mary. *'She Was A Sister Sailor': The Whaling Journals of Mary Brewster, 1845–1851*. Ed. Joan Druett. Mystic, CT: Mystic Seaport Museum, 1992.

Bristow, Joseph. *Empire Boys: Adventures in a Man's World*. London: HarperCollins Academic, 1991.

'British Connexion with China', *The Gentleman's Magazine* new series 1 (1834): 123–30.

Brontë, Charlotte. *Jane Eyre*. London: Penguin, 1996.

Brontë, Patrick Branwell. *The Poems of Patrick Branwell Brontë*. Ed. Victor A. Neufeldt. New York: Garland Publishing, 1990.

——. *The Hand of the Arch-Sinner: Two Angrian Chronicles of Branwell Brontë*. Ed. and reconstructed Robert G. Collins. Oxford: Clarendon Press, 1993.

——. *The Works of Patrick Branwell Brontë: An Edition*. 4 vols. Ed. Victor A. Neufeldt. New York: Garland Publishing, 1997–99.

Brown, David Blayney. *Turner and Byron*. London: Tate Gallery, 1992.

Bryant, William Cullen, Francis L. Hawks and Cornelius Mathews. 'An Address to the People of the United States in Behalf of the American Copyright Club'. New York: n.p., 1843.

Bulwer-Lytton, Edward. *Pelham, or the Adventures of a Gentleman*. New York: Kensinger Publishing, n.d.

Burbidge, Frederick William. *The Gardens of the Sun; or, A Naturalist's Journal on the Mountains and in the Forests and Swamps of Borneo and the Sulu Archipelago*. London: John Murray, 1880.

Byron, Lord. *Byron's Letters and Journals* (vol. 3). Ed. Leslie Marchand. Cambridge, MA: Belknap, 1974.

——. *The Complete Poetical Works*. 7 vols. Ed. Jerome McGann. Oxford: Clarendon Press, 1980–93.

——. *The Corsair*. 1814. Byron, *The Complete Poetical Works* 3: 148–214.

——. *The Ravenna Journal*. London: First Edition Club, 1928.

Carlyle, Thomas. *Sartor Resartus and On Heroes and Hero-Worship, and the Heroic in History*. Middlesex: Echo, 2007.

Carpenter, Kevin. *Desert Isles and Pirate Islands: The Island Theme in Nineteenth-Century English Juvenile Fiction*. Frankfurt: Peter Lang, 1984.

'Carriers' Address of the *Corsair*'. *Corsair* 1 (4 January 1840): 683.

Casarino, Cesare. *Modernity at Sea: Melville, Marx, Conrad in Crisis*. Minneapolis: U of Minnesota P, 2002.

Chew, Samuel. *Byron in England: His Fame and After Fame*. New York: Russell and Russell, 1965.

Clifford, Hugh. 'Mr Joseph Conrad at Home and Abroad'. *The Singapore Free Press and Mercantile Advertiser*, 1 September 1898: 142.

——. 'The Art of Mr Joseph Conrad'. *Living Age*, 10 January 1903: 120–23.

——. *Further India: Being the Story of Exploration from the Earliest Times in Burma, Malaya, Siam and Indo-China*. London: Lawrence and Bullen, 1904.

——. *In Court and Kampung: Being Tales and Sketches of Native Life in the Malay Peninsula*. Singapore: Graham Brash, 1989.

——. *Saleh: A Prince of Malaya*. Singapore: Oxford UP, 1989.

Cohen, Daniel E. *Pillars of Salt, Monuments of Grace: New England Crime Literature and the Origins of American Popular Culture, 1674–1860*. Commonwealth Center Studies in American Culture. New York and Oxford: Oxford UP, 1993.

Cohn, Bernard. 'Representing Authority in Victorian India'. *The Invention of Tradition*. Eds Eric Hobsbawm and Terence Ranger. Cambridge: Canto, 1983, 165–209.

Collini, Stefan. *Public Moralists: Political Thought and Public Life in Britain 1850–1930*. Oxford: Clarendon Press, 1991.

Collins, Robert. *The Hand of the Arch-Sinner: Two Angrian Chronicles of Branwell Brontë*. By Branwell Brontë. Oxford: Clarendon Press, 1993.

Collins, Wilkie. 'A Sermon for Sepoys'. *Household Words* 27 February 1858: 244–27.

Conrad, Joseph. *A Personal Record*. London: J.M. Dent, 1919.

——. *Almayer's Folly: A Story of an Eastern River*. London: J.M. Dent & Sons, 1947.

——. *The Rescue: A Romance of the Shallows*. New York: W.W. Norton, 1968.

——. *The Eastern Stories*. Ed. Ban Kah Choon. London: Penguin Books, 2000.

Cooper, J.F. *Sea Tales: The Writings of J.F. Cooper*, New York: Literary Classics of the United States, 1991.

Corbett, Julian. *Sir Francis Drake*. 1890; rpt New York: Haskell House Publishers Ltd, 1968.

Cordingly, David. *Under the Black Flag: The Romance and the Reality of Life Among the Pirates*. New York: Random House, 1995.

Cowie, Alexander. *The Rise of the American Novel*. New York: American Book Co., 1948.

Cox, Jeffrey N. 'The Ideological Tack of Nautical Melodrama'. *Melodrama: The Cultural Emergence of a Genre*. Eds Michael Hays and Anastasia Nikolopoulou. Basingstoke: Macmillan, 1999, 167–89.

Craig, George. 'Blown Away!' *Household Words*, 17 March 1858: 348–50.

Crawfurd, John. *History of the Indian Archipelago, Containing an Account of the Manners, Arts, Languages, Religions, Institutions, and Commerce of its Inhabitants*. 3 vols. London: Frank Cass, 1820.

[Crawfurd, John]. 'Chinese Empire and Trade'. *Westminster Review* 21 (1834): 221–56.

——. 'Voyage of Ship *Amherst*'. *Westminster Review* 20 (1834): 22–47.

Creighton, Margaret S. and Lisa Norling, eds. *Iron Men, Wooden Women: Gender and Seafaring in the Atlantic World, 1720–1920*. Baltimore and London: Johns Hopkins UP, 1996.

Crowther, Andrew. *Contradiction Contradicted: The Plays of W.S. Gilbert*. Madison: Fairleigh Dickinson UP/London: Associated UP, 2000.

Darton, F.J. Harvey. *Children's Books in England: Five Centuries of Social Life*. 3rd edn. Cambridge: Cambridge UP, 1982.

Davis, Jim, ed. *The Britannia Diaries of Frederick Wilton*. London: Society for Theatre Research, 1992.

Dawson, Graham. *Soldier Heroes: British Adventure, Empire and the Imagining of Masculinities*. London and New York: Routledge, 1994.

Defoe, Daniel. *Captain Singleton*. 1720. Ed. Shiv K. Kumar. New York: Oxford UP, 1990.

——. *Defoe's Review, Reproduced from the Original Editions*. 1704–13. 22 vols. Ed. Arthur Wellesley Secord. New York: Columbia UP, 1938.

Dekker, Rudolf M. and Lotte C. van de Pol, *The Tradition of Female Transvestism in Early Modern Europe*. Basingstoke: Palgrave, 1997.

De Pauw, Linda Grant. *Seafaring Women*. Boston: Houghton-Mifflin, 1982.

Derrida, Jacques. *Writing and Difference*. Trans. Alan Bass. London: Routledge, 1981.

——. 'Before the Law'. Trans. Avital Ronell and Christine Roulston. *Acts of Literature*. Ed. Derek Attridge. London: Routledge, 1992.

——. 'Force of Law: The "Mystical Foundation of Authority"'. *Deconstruction and the Possibility of Justice*. Trans. Mary Quaintance, Drucilla Cornell et al. New York: Routledge, 1992.

——. *The Politics of Friendship*. Trans. George Collins. London and New York: Verso, 1997.

Dickens, Charles. *The Letters of Charles Dickens*. 12 vols. Eds Madeline House, Graham Storey and Kathleen Tillotson. Oxford: Clarendon Press, 1965–2002.

Dickens, Charles and Wilkie Collins. 'The Perils of Certain English Prisoners, and Their Treasure in Women, Children, Silver, and Jewels'. 1857. *Charles Dickens: The Christmas Stories*. London: J.M. Dent, 1996.

Disraeli, Benjamin. *Vivian Grey*. London: R. Brimley Johnson, 1904.

Downing, Clement. *A History of the Indian Wars*. Lahore: Al-Birundi, 1978.

Dramatic Notes, April 1880 (London: David Bogue, 1881): 20.

Druett, Joan. *Hen Frigates: Wives of Merchant Captains Under Sail*. New York: Simon & Schuster, 1998.

——. *She Captains: Heroines and Hellions of the Sea*. New York: Simon & Schuster, 2000.

Dugaw, Dianne. *Warrior Women and Popular Balladry, 1650–1850*. New York and Cambridge: Cambridge UP, 1989.

'Duke of York's Theatre: "Peter Pan; Or, The Boy Who Wouldn't Grow Up"'. *Times* 28 December 1904: 4.

Du Maurier, Daphne. *Gerald*. 1934. London: Gollancz, 1948.

——. *The Infernal World of Branwell Brontë*. London: Gollancz, 1960.

Dunae, Patrick A. 'Boys' Literature and the Idea of Empire, 1870–1914'. *Victorian Studies* 24.1 (Autumn 1980): 105–21.

Dutheil, Martine Hennard. 'The Representation of the Cannibal in Ballantyne's *The Coral Island*: Colonial Anxieties in Victorian Popular Fiction'. *College Literature* 28.1 (Winter 2001): 105–22.

Earle, Peter. *The Pirate Wars*. New York: St Martin's, 2003.

Edmonds, Sarah Emma. *Nurse and Spy in the Union Army, Comprising the Adventures and Experiences of a Woman in Hospitals, Camps, and Battle-Field*. Hartford, CT: W.S. Williams & Co., 1865.

Elfenbein, Andrew. *Byron and the Victorians*. Cambridge: Cambridge UP, 1995.

Elwin, Malcolm. *Charles Reade*. London: Jonathan Cape, 1931.

The Era. 11 December 1853, issue 794.

Evans, D. Morier. *Facts, Failures and Frauds: Revelations Financial Mercantile Criminal*. 1859. New York: Augustus M. Kelley, 1968.

Exquemelin, A.O. *Bucaniers [sic] of America: or, a true account of the ... assaults committed ... upon the coasts of the West Indies by the Bucaniers [sic] of Jamaica and Tortuga ... especially, the ... exploits of Sir H. Morgan ... written originally in Dutch, by J. [or rather A. O.] Esquemelin ... now ... rendred [sic] into English*. 2 vols. London: W. Crooke, 1684–85.

Fay, Peter Ward. *The Opium War, 1840-1842*. 1975. New York: Norton, 1976.

'Fanny Campbell'. *Biography Index*. New York: H.W. Wilson Co., 1968, 7: 167.

Feather, John. *Publishing, Piracy and Politics: An Historical Study of Copyright in Britain*. London: Mansell, 1994.

Felluga, Dino Franco. *The Perversity of Poetry: Romantic Ideology and the Popular Male Poet of Genius*. Albany: State U of New York P, 2005.

Ffinch, Michael. *Gilbert and Sullivan*. London: Weidenfeld & Nicolson, 1993.

Fischler, Alan. *Modified Rapture: Comedy in W.S. Gilbert's Savoy Operas*. Charlottesville: UP of Virginia, 1991.

——. 'Drama'. 1999. *A Companion to Victorian Literature and Culture*. Ed. Herbert Tucker. Oxford: Blackwell, 2005.

Fleetwood, Frances. *Conquest: The Story of a Theatre Family*. London: Allen, 1953.

Fox, Grace. *British Admirals and Chinese Pirates: 1832–1869*. London: Kegan Paul, Trench, Trubner & Co., 1940.

Fraser, Robert. *Victorian Quest Romance: Stevenson, Haggard, Kipling and Conan Doyle*. Plymouth: Northcote House, 1998.

Garber, Marjorie. *Vested Interests: Cross-Dressing and Cultural Anxiety*. New York: Routledge, 1992.

Gaskell, Elizabeth. *North and South*. Ed. Patricia Ingham. Harmondsworth: Penguin, 1995.

Gerassi-Navarro, Nina. *Pirate Novels: Fictions of Nation Building in Spanish America*. Durham, NC: Duke UP, 1999.

Gérin, Winifred. *Branwell Brontë*. London and New York: T. Nelson, 1961.

——. *Elizabeth Gaskell: A Biography*. Oxford: Clarendon Press, 1976.

Gilbert, W.S. and Arthur Sullivan. *The Complete Annotated Gilbert and Sullivan*. Ed. Ian Bradley. Oxford: Oxford UP, 1996.

Glinert, Ed, ed. *The Complete Gilbert & Sullivan*. London: Penguin Books, 2006.

Glover, David. *Vampires, Mummies, and Liberals: Bram Stoker and the Politics of Popular Fiction*. Durham, NC: Duke UP, 1996.

Gogwilt, Christopher. *The Invention of the West: Joseph Conrad and the Double-Mapping of Europe and Empire*. Stanford: Stanford UP, 1995.

Gordan, John Dozier. 'The Rajah Brooke and Joseph Conrad'. *Studies in Philology* 35 (October 1938): 613–34.

Gore, Catherine. *Adventures in Borneo*. London: Henry Colburn, 1849.

Gosse, Philip. *The History of Piracy*. 1932. New York: Burt Franklin, 1968.

——. *My Pirate Library*. 1926. With an introductory note by Sir Edmund Gosse. New York: Burt Franklin, 1970.

Graham, Gerald S. *The China Station: War and Diplomacy, 1830–1860.* Oxford: Clarendon/Oxford UP, 1978.

The Graphic, 10 April 1880: 371.

Green, R.L. *Fifty Years of Peter Pan*. London: Peter Davies, 1954.

Greenberg, Michael. *British Trade and the Opening of China, 1800–42*. Cambridge: Cambridge UP, 1951.

Greenwood, James. *The Adventures of Reuben Davidger; Seventeen Years and Four Months Captive Among the Dyaks of Borneo*. London: Ward, Lock & Co, 1865.

Grey, Charles. *Pirates of the Eastern Seas (1618–1723): A Lurid Page of History*. Port Washington, NY: Kennikate Press, 1933.

Grigsby, Ann. 'Charles Reade's *Hard Cash*: Lunacy Reform through Sensationalism'. *Dickens Studies Annual* 25 (1996): 141–58.

Gutzlaff, Charles. *Journal of Three Voyages along the Coast of China in 1831, 1832, & 1833*. Intro. W. Ellis. 3rd edn. London: Thomas Ward, [1840].

'Gutzlaff's *Journal*'. *Quarterly Christian Spectator* 5 (1833): 591–612.

'Gutzlaff's *Three Voyages, & c.*' *Eclectic Review* 3rd series 11 (1834): 369–92.

Haley, Bruce. *The Healthy Body and Victorian Culture*. Cambridge, MA: Harvard UP, 1978.

Hampson, Robert. *Cross-Cultural Encounters in Joseph Conrad's Malay Fiction*. Basingstoke: Palgrave, 2000.

Hannabuss, Stuart. 'Ballantyne's Message of Empire'. *Imperialism and Juvenile Literature*. Ed. Jeffrey Richards. Manchester: Manchester UP, 1989: 53–71.

Hargreaves, Reginald. *Women-at-Arms: Their Famous Exploits Throughout the Ages*. London: Hutchinson & Co., 1929.

Harvie, Christopher. 'The Politics of Stevenson'. *Stevenson and Victorian Scotland*. Ed. Jenni Calder. Edinburgh: Edinburgh UP, 1981.

Hay, John C. Dalrymple. *The Suppression of Piracy in the China Sea, 1849*. London: Edward Stanford, 1889.

Heidegger, Martin. *Basic Writings*. Ed. David Farell Krell. London and New York: Harper Collins, 1993: 139–212.

Helyar, James, ed. *Gilbert and Sullivan*: Papers presented at the international conference held at the University of Kansas in May 1970. Lawrence: University of Kansas Libraries, 1970.

Henty, G.A. *In the Hands of the Malays and Other Stories*. London: Blackie and Son, 1905.

Herndon, Ruth Wallis. 'The Domestic Cost of Seafaring: Town Leaders and Seamen's Families in Eighteenth-Century Rhode Island'. *Iron Men, Wooden Women: Gender and Seafaring in the Atlantic World, 1700–1920*. Baltimore, MD: Johns Hopkins UP, 1996.

Hevia, James L. *Cherishing Men from Afar: Qing Guest Ritual and the Macartney Embassy of 1793*. Durham, NC: Duke UP, 1995.

Hibbert, Christopher. *The Great Mutiny: India, 1857*. New York: Penguin, 1985.

Higbie, Robert. 'Conflict and Comedy in W.S. Gilbert's Savoy Operas'. *South Atlantic Bulletin* 45.4 (November 1980): 66–77.

Hill, Christopher. *Collected Essays of Christopher Hill, Volume 3*. Brighton: Harvester, 1986.

Hobsbawm, Eric. *The Age of Empire: 1875–1914*. New York: Vintage, 1989.

Holden, Philip. *Modern Subjects/Colonial Texts: Hugh Clifford & the Discipline of English Literature in the Straits Settlements & Malaya 1895–1907*. Greensboro, NC: ELT Press, 2000.

Hopkins, Lisa. *Bram Stoker: A Literary Life*. New York: Palgrave Macmillan, 2007.

Houtchens, Laurence H. 'Charles Dickens and International Copyright'. *American Literature* 13 (1941): 18–28.

Howard, David, John Lucas and John Goode. *Tradition and Tolerance in Nineteenth-Century Fiction: Critical Essays on Some English and American Novels*. London: Routledge & Kegan Paul, 1966.

Howarth, Patrick. *Play Up and Play the Game: The Heroes of Popular Fiction*. London: Eyre Methuen, 1973.

Hughes, Helen. *The Historical Romance*. London: Routledge, 1993.

Hutcheson, John Conroy. *The Penang Pirate, and The Lost Pinnace*. London: Blackie and Son, 1885.

Ingham, Patricia. 'Introduction'. *North and South*. By Elizabeth Gaskell. Harmondsworth: Penguin, 1995, xii–xxviii.

Irving, Laurence. *The Precarious Crust*. London: Chatto & Windus, 1971.

Jarvis, Louise. 'Dames at Sea: A History of Female Sailors Proves that Women Can Be Bloodthirsty, Too'. Review of Joan Druett, *She Captains: Heroines and Hellions of the Sea*. *New York Times Book Review*, 26 March 2000: 15.

Jarvis, Robin. *The Romantic Period: The Intellectual and Cultural Context of English Literature, 1789–1830*. Harlow: Pearson Longman, 2004.

Jay, Frank. *Peeps into the Past: Being a History of Old-Time Periodicals, Journals and Books* (Third Series). London 1919. The Online Books Page <http://onlinebooks.library.upenn.edu>. Accessed 15 February 2008.

Jeans, Peter D. *Seafaring Lore and Legend*. New York: McGraw-Hill, 2004.

Jerrold, Douglas. *The Writings of Douglas Jerrold. Volume 8: Comedies and Dramas*. London: Bradbury and Evans, 1854.

——.*Black-Ey'd Susan*. 1829. London: T.H. Lacy, 1855.

——. *Black-Ey'd Susan*. 1829. *Nineteenth-Century Plays*. Ed. George Rowell. Oxford: Oxford UP, 1953.

——. *Black Ey'd Susan*. London: Dicks, n.d. [1829].

Johnson, Capt. Charles [Daniel Defoe?]. *A General History of the Robberies and Murders of the Most Notorious Pyrates*. 1724. Ed. Manuel Schonhorn. Columbia: U of South Carolina P, 1972.

Jones, John Bush. 'Gilbertian Humor: Pulling Together a Definition'. *The Victorian Newsletter* 33 (Spring 1968): 28–31.

'Jones's Royal Circus'. *Times* 9 April 1798: 1.

'Journal of the Continental Congress, November 25, 1775'. *Naval Documents of the American Revolution*. Ed. William Bell Clark. Washington, DC: The US Navy Department, 1966, 2: 1131, 1174–82.

Karraker, Cyrus H. *Piracy Was a Business*. Rindge, NH: Richard R. Smith, 1953.

Keay, John. *The Honourable Company*. New York: Macmillan, 1991.

Keppel, Henry. *Expedition to Borneo of H.M.S. Dido for the Suppression of Piracy: With Extracts from the Journal of James Brooke, Esq. of Sarawak (Now Agent for the British Government in Borneo)*. 2 vols. London: Chapman and Hall, 1846.

King, Dean. Foreward. *The Black Ship*. By Dudley Pope. New York: Henry Holt & Co., 1998: ix–xii.

Konstam, Angus. *The History of Pirates*. Guildford, CT: The Lyons Press, 1999.

Krenn, Heliena. *Conrad's Lingard Trilogy: Empire, Race, and Women in the Malay Novels*. New York: Garland Publishing, 1990.

Kuang Xinnian. 'Xun zhao shi qu de shi ye' [In Search of the Lost Vision]. Wen yi li lun yu pi ping, *Theory and Criticism of Literature and Art* 4 (2002). 3 January 2011 <http://www.chinese-thought.org/whyj/002380.htm>.

Lacy, Thomas. 'Assignments Book 1' *Samuel French Archive*. MS 81/2366, Box 1. Victoria & Albert Theatre Museum, London.

——. 'Assignments Book 2' *Samuel French Archive* MS 81/2366, Box 2. Victoria & Albert Theatre Museum, London.

Leask, Nigel. *Curiosity and the Aesthetics of Travel Writing, 1770–1840*: 'From an Antique Land'. Oxford: Oxford UP, 2002.

[Lindsay, Hugh Hamilton and Charles Gutzlaff]. *Report of Proceedings on a Voyage to the Northern Ports of China in the Ship Lord Amherst*. 2nd edn. London: B. Fellowes, 1834.

Linebaugh, Peter and Marcus Rediker. *The Many-Headed Hydra: Sailors, Slaves, Commoners, and the Hidden Story of the Revolutionary Atlantic*. Boston, MA: Beacon Press, 2000.

Lister, Thomas Henry. *Granby*. New York: Harper, 1826.

Lloyd's Weekly Newspaper, 11 December 1853, issue 577.

Lowell, James Russell. 'A Fable for Critics'. *Complete Poetical Works of James Russell Lowell*. Boston, MA and New York: Houghton, Mifflin and Co., 1849: 113–50.

Mabee, Frank. 'The Spithead Mutiny and Urban Radicalism in the 1790s'. *Romanticism* 13.2 (2007): 133–44.

Mackie, Erin Skye. 'Welcome the Outlaw: Pirates, Maroons, and Caribbean Countercultures'. *Cultural Critique* 59 (2005): 24–62.

Maclagan, Michael. *'Clemency' Canning*. London: Macmillan, 1962.

Maixner, Paul, ed. *Robert Louis Stevenson: The Critical Heritage*. London: Routledge, 1981.

Malgonkar, Manohar. *Kanhoji Angrey, Maratha Admiral*. London: Asia Publishing House, 1959.

Mangan, J.A. and James Walvin, eds. *Manliness and Morality: Middle-Class Masculinity in Britain and America, 1800–1940*. Manchester: Manchester UP, 1991.

Mann, Herman. *The Female Review: or, Memoirs of an American young lady, whose life and character are particularly distinguished, being a Continental soldier for nearly three years in the late American War*. Dedham, MA: Nathaniel and Benjamin Heaton, 1797.

Marchand, Leslie. *Byron: A Biography*. 3 vols. New York: Knopf, 1957.

Marryat, Captain Frederick. *The Pirate*. Philadelphia, PA: Carey and Hart, 1836.

Marshall, P.J. and Glyndwr Williams. *The Great Map of Mankind: British Perceptions of the World in the Age of Enlightenment*. London: J.M. Dent & Sons, 1982.

Maunder, Andrew and Grace Moore, eds. *Victorian Crime, Madness and Sensation*. Aldershot and Burlington, VT: Ashgate, 2004.

Maunder, Andrew. *Bram Stoker*. Tavistock: Northcote House Publishers Ltd., 2006.

McGill, Meredith L. *American Literature and the Culture of Reprinting, 1834–1853*. Philadelphia: U of Pennsylvania P, 2003.

McKee, Christopher. *A Gentlemanly and Honorable Profession: The Creation of the U.S. Naval Officer Corps, 1794–1815*. Annapolis, MD: The Naval Institute Press, 1991.

Meisel, Martin. *Realizations*. Princeton, NJ: Princeton UP, 1983.

'Memorial of A Number of Persons Concerned in Printing and Publishing … Remonstrating Against the Enactment of an International Copy-Right Law'. *Senate Documents* (27th Congress, 2nd Session, June 1842): 323.

Miller, Lucasta. *The Brontë Myth*. London: Anchor, 2005.

Moncrieff, W.T. *The Mistress of the Mill*. 1849. London: T.H. Lacy, 1850.

Moody, Jane. *Illegitimate Theatre in London 1770–1840*. Cambridge: Cambridge UP, 2000.

Morgan, James Appleton. *Law of Literature*. 2 vols. New York: James Cockcroft & Company, 1875.

Morgan, Susan. *Sisters in Time: Imagining Gender in Nineteenth-Century British Fiction*. New York and Oxford: Oxford UP, 1989.

The Morning Chronicle, 6 December 1853, issue 27130.

'Mr. Willis's First Letter from England'. *Corsair* 1 (6 July 1839).

Munich, Adrienne Auslander. 'Queen Victoria, Empire, and Excess'. *Tulsa Studies in Women's Literature* 6.2 (Autumn 1987): 265–81.

Murray, Lieutenant [Marturin Murray Ballou]. *Fanny Campbell, Female Pirate Captain*. Boston, MA: Gleason's, 1845.

Murray, Paul. *From the Shadow of Dracula*. London: Jonathan Cape, 2004.

The *Musical Times*, 1 February 1880: 444.

Myers, Frederic W.H. 'Criticisms and Interpretations'. Bartleby.com <http://www.bartleby.com/309/1001.html> 19 December 2009.

Myers, Janet C. *Antipodal England: Emigration and Portable Domesticity in the Victorian Novel*. New York: SUNY P, 2009.

Nadal, Goncal Lopez. 'Corsairing as a Commercial System: The Edges of Legitimate Trade'. *Bandits at Sea: A Pirates Reader*. Ed. C.R. Pennell. New York and London: New York UP, 2001: 125–36.

Nan Mu. 'Ya pian zhan zheng yi qian Ying chuan A Mei Shi De Hao zai Zhongguo yan hai de zhen cha huo dong' [The British *Ship Amherst*'s Reconnaissance in China's Coastal Waters before the Opium War]. *Jin Bu Ri Bao* [*The Progressive Daily*] 13 September 1952: 2.

Nayder, Lillian. 'Class Consciousness and the Indian Mutiny in Dickens's "The Perils of Certain English Prisoners"'. *SEL: Studies in English Literature, 1500–1900* 32.4 (Autumn 1992): 689–705.

——. *Unequal Partners: Charles Dickens, Wilkie Collins, and Victorian Authorship*. Ithaca, NY: Cornell UP, 2002.

Nelson, Claudia. *Boys Will be Girls: The Feminine Ethic and British Children's Fiction 1857–1917*. New Brunswick and London: Rutgers UP, 1991.

Neufeldt, Victor A. *The Works of Patrick Branwell Brontë*. 3 vols. New York: Garland Publishing, 1997–99.

Newbury, Michael. *Figuring Authorship in Antebellum America*. Stanford: Stanford UP, 1997.

Newlyn, Lucy. *Reading, Writing, and Romanticism: The Anxiety of Reception*. New York: Oxford UP, 2000.

Nietzsche, Friedrich. *Collected Writings*. Trans. Walter Kaufmann. New York: Modern Library, 2000.

Nordau, Max. *Degeneration*. 1895. Introduction by George L. Mosse. Lincoln and London: U of Nebraska P, 1993.

Noyes, Alfred. 'The Boy Who Wouldn't Grow Up'. *The Bookman* (December 1905): 114.

O'Connor, Erin. 'Preface for a Post-Postcolonial *Criticism*'. *Victorian Studies* 45.2 (2003): 217–46.

Oddie, William. 'Dickens and the Indian Mutiny'. *The Dickensian* 68 (January 1972): 3–15.

Orwell, George. 'Boys' Weeklies'. 1940. *Critical Essays*. London: Secker & Warbug, 1960, 61–91.

——. 'Charles Reade'. 1940. *The Collected Essays, Journalism and Letters of George Orwell*. vol. 2. Eds Sonia Orwell and Ian Angus. New York: Harcourt, Brace, and World, 1968: 34–7.

Osborne, Milton. *Southeast Asia: An Introductory History*, 7th edn. St Leonards: Allen & Unwin, 1997.

Paravisini-Gebert, Lizabeth. 'Cross-Dressing on the Margins of Empire: Women Pirates and the Narrative of the Caribbean'. *Women at Sea: Travel Writing and the Margins of Caribbean Discourse*. Eds Lizabeth Paravisini-Gebert and Ivette Romero-Cesareo. New York and Basingstoke: Palgrave, 2001: 59–97.

Park, Hyungji. '"The Story of Our Lives": *The Moonstone* and the Indian Mutiny in *All the Year Round*'. *Negotiating India in the Nineteenth-Century Media*. Eds Douglas Peers and David Finkelstein. New York: Palgrave Macmillan, 2000: 84–109.

Parry, Benita. *Conrad and Imperialism: Ideological Boundaries and Visionary Frontiers*. London: Macmillan, 1983.

Pascoe, C.E. *The Dramatic List*, London: David Bogue, 1880.

Paxton, Nancy. 'Mobilizing Chivalry: Rape in British Novels about the Indian Uprising of 1857'. *Victorian Studies* 36.1 (Autumn 1992): 5–30.

Peck, John. *Maritime Fiction: Sailors and the Sea in British and American Novels, 1719–1917*. Basingstoke: Palgrave, 2001.

Pelras, Christian. *The Bugis*. Oxford: Blackwell, 1996.

Pennell, C.R., ed. *Bandits at Sea: A Pirates Reader*. New York: New York UP, 2001.

Peters, Catherine. *The King of Inventors: A Life of Wilkie Collins*. Princeton, NJ: Princeton UP, 1991.

Peters, Laura. '"Double-dyed Traitors and Infernal Villains": *Illustrated London News*, *Household Words*, Charles Dickens and the Indian Rebellion'. *Negotiating India in the Nineteenth-Century Media*. Eds Douglas Peers and David Finkelstein. New York: Palgrave Macmillan, 2000: 110–34.

Petitt, Clare. *Patent Inventions: Intellectual Property and the Victorian Novel*. Oxford: Oxford UP, 2004.

Phillips, Walter Clarke. *Dickens, Reade and Collins: Sensation Novelists*. New York: Columbia UP, 1919.

Pionke, Albert. 'Secreting Rebellion: From the Mutiny to *The Moonstone*'. *Victorians Institute Journal* 28 (2000): 109–40.

Poovey, Mary, ed. *The Financial System in Nineteenth-Century Britain*. Oxford: Oxford UP, 2003.

Pratt, Mary Louise. *Imperial Eyes: Travel Writing and Transculturation*. London: Routledge, 1992.

Prestige, Colin. 'D'Oyly Carte and the Pirates: The Original New York Productions of Gilbert and Sullivan'. *Gilbert and Sullivan*: Papers presented at the international conference held at the University of Kansas in May 1970. Ed. James Helyar. Lawrence: U of Kansas Libraries, 1970: 113–48.

PuruShotam, Nirmala Srirekam. *Negotiating Language, Constructing Race*: *Disciplining Difference in Singapore*. Berlin: Mouton de Gruyter, 1998.

Pyle, Howard. *The Book of Pirates*. New York: Harper, 1921.

——. *The Buccaneers and Marooners of America*. London: Fisher Unwin, 1891.

'The Quarter Deck'. *Corsair* 1 (16 March 1839): 1.

Quayle, Eric. *Ballantyne the Brave*: *A Victorian Writer and His Family*. Chester Springs, PA: Dufour Editions, 1967.

Raffles, Thomas Stamford. *The History of Java*. 2 vols. London: Black, Parbury, and Allen, Booksellers to the Hon. East-India Company, and John Murray, 1817.

Reade, Charles. *Hard Cash*. 1863. London and Glasgow: Collins Clear-Type P, n.d.

——. *Readiana: Comments on Current Events*. 1882. Paris and Boston, MA: The Grolier Society, n.d.

Reade, Charles L. and Rev. Compton Reade. *Charles Reade, D.C.L., Dramatist, Novelist, Journalist: A Memoir*. New York: Harper, 1887.

Rediker, Marcus. *Between the Devil and the Deep Blue Sea: Merchant Seamen, Pirates, and the Anglo-American Maritime World, 1700–1750*. New York and Cambridge: Cambridge UP, 1987.

——. 'The Seaman as Pirate: Plunder and Social Banditry at Sea'. *Bandits at Sea: A Pirates Reader*. Ed. C.R. Pennell. New York and London: New York UP, 2001: 139–68.

——. *Villains of All Nations: Atlantic Pirates in the Golden Age*. Boston, MA: Beacon Press, 2004.

——. 'The Pirate and the Gallows: An Atlantic Theater of Terror and Resistance'. *Seascapes: Maritime Histories, Littoral Cultures, and Transoceanic Exchanges*. Eds Jerry H. Bentley, Renate Bridenthal and Kären Wigen. Honolulu: U of Hawai'i Press, 2007: 239–50.

The Red Rover, Dicks' Standard Plays, No. 450, n.d.

'Remarks on the Proposed International Copyright Law'. *New World* 4 (12 March 1842): 173.

Revitt, Paul J. 'Gilbert and Sullivan: More Seriousness than Satire'. *Western Humanities Review* 19 (1965): 19–34.

Richards, Jeffrey. *Imperialism and Juvenile Literature*. Manchester: Manchester UP, 1989.

Richards, T. Addison. 'Idlewild: The Home of N.P. Willis'. *Harper's New Monthly Magazine* 26 (January 1858): 145–66.

Rigney, Ann. *Imperfect Histories: The Elusive Past and the Legacy of Romantic Historicism*. Ithaca, NY: Cornell UP, 2001.

Ritchie, Robert C. *Captain Kidd and the War Against the Pirates*. Cambridge, MA: Harvard UP, 1986.

Robertson, Fiona. *Legitimate Histories: Scott, Gothic, and the Authorities of Fiction*. Oxford: OUP, 1994.

Robinson, Henry Crabbe. *The London Theatre 1811–1866: Selections from the Diary of Henry Crabbe Robinson*. Ed. Eluned Brown. London: STR, 1966.

Rocker, George. *Escaped Singapore; Heading Homewards*. Singapore: Graham Brash, 1990.

Rowell, George, ed. *Nineteenth-Century Plays*. Oxford: Oxford UP, 1953.

Ruggles, Benjamin. Report, *Senate Documents* (June 1838): 494.

Ruskin, John. *Sesame and Lilies*. 1865. Rev. edn. New York: James B. Millar, 1884.

Rutter, Owen. *The Pirate Wind: Tales of the Sea-Robbers of Malaya*. Singapore: Oxford UP, 1986.

Said, Edward. *Orientalism*. Harmondsworth: Penguin, 1978.

——. *Culture and Imperialism*. London: Chatto & Windus, 1993.

Sampson, Robert. *John L. O'Sullivan and His Times*. Kent, OH: Kent State UP, 2003.

Samuel, Raphael. *Island Stories: Unravelling Britain. Theatres of Memory, Volume II*. Ed. Alison Light with Sally Alexander and Gareth Stedman Jones. London and New York: Verso, 1998.

'Sargeant Talfourd's Speech, on Moving the Second Reading of the Bill for Extending the Term of Copyright in England, February 27th, 1839'. *Corsair* 1 (6 April 1839): 54–6.

Saunders, David. 'Dropping the Subject: An Argument for a Positive History of Authorship and the Law of Copyright'. *Of Authors and Origins: Essays on Copyright Law*. Eds Brad Sherman and Alain Strowel. Oxford: Clarendon Press, 1994: 93–110.

Schlyter, Herman. *Karl Gützlaff: Als Missionar in China*. Lund, Sweden: C.W.K. Gleerup: 1946.

——. *Der China-Missionar Karl Gützlaff und Seine Heimatbasis*. Lund, Sweden: C.W.K. Gleerup, 1976.

Schor, Hilary. *Scheherezade in the Marketplace: Elizabeth Gaskell and the Victorian Novel*. New York and Oxford: Oxford UP, 1992.

Scott, Walter. *The Pirate*. 1822. Edinburgh: Robert Cadell, 1842.

——. *Waverley; or, 'Tis Sixty Years Since*. 1814. Ed. Claire Lamont. Oxford and NY: Oxford UP, 1986.

Seguin, Marilyn. *Where Duty Calls: The Story of Sarah Emma Edmonds, Soldier and Spy in the Union Army*. London: Branden Books, 1999.

Seville, Catherine. *Literary Copyright Reform in Early Victorian England: The Framing of the 1842 Copyright Act*. Cambridge: Cambridge UP, 1999.

Sharpe, Jenny. 'The Unspeakable Limits of Rape: Colonial Violence and Counter-Insurgency'. *Genders* 10 (Spring 1991): 25–46.

Shelley, Percy Bysshe. *The Complete Poems of Percy Bysshe Shelley*. New York: Modern Library, 1994.

Sherman, John and Nathaniel Parker Willis. *Trenton Falls, Picturesque and Descriptive*. New York: N. Orr & Co., 1868.

Ship Amherst. Return to an Order of the Honourable the House of Commons, dated 17 June 1833 ... [London]: House of Commons, 1833. Reprinted in *Irish University Press Area Studies Series, British Parliamentary Papers: China*. Vol. 39. 127–233.

Smith, Elton E. *Charles Reade*. Boston, MA: Twayne, 1976.

Smith, Henry Nash. *Virgin Land: The American West as Symbol and Myth*. 1950. Cambridge, MA: Harvard UP, 1970.

Smith, Janet Adam, ed. *Henry James and Robert Louis Stevenson: A Record of Friendship*. London: Rupert Hart-Davis, 1948.

Smith, Leonard V., Rev. *Mutiny: A History of Naval Insurrection* by Leonard F. Guttridge. *The Journal of Military History*, 58.3 (July 1994): 523–4.

Smythe, George Sydney. 'Social Piracy; or, The Rovings, Roamings, Motions, Locomotions, Peregrinations, Pouncings, Manoeuvres, and Maraudings, Great Larcenies and Petty Larcenies of Mr. and Mrs. Hawke and the Young Hawkes'. *New Monthly Magazine* 72 (1844): 1–17, 168–79, 351–62.

Snodgrass, Judith. *Orientalism, Occidentalism, and the Columbian Exposition: Presenting Japanese Buddhism to the West*. Chapel Hill: U of North Carolina P, 2003.

Snow, Edward Rowe. *True Tales of Pirates and their Gold*. New York: Dodd Mead, 1957.

The Stage or Theatrical Inquisitor, February 1829: 102.

Stallybrass, Peter and Allon White. *The Politics and Poetics of Transgression*. London: Methuen, 1986.

Stanley, Jo, ed. *Bold in Her Breeches: Women Pirates Across the Ages*. San Francisco and London: Pandora, 1995.

Starkey, David. 'Pirates and Markets'. *Bandits at Sea: A Pirates Reader*. Ed. C.R. Pennell. New York and London: New York UP, 2001: 107–24.

Staunton, George [Thomas]. *An Historical Account of the Embassy to the Emperor of China, Undertaken by Order of the King of Great Britain*. London: Printed for John Stockdale, Piccadilly, 1797.

St Clair, William. 'The Impact of Byron's Writings: An Evaluative Approach'. *Byron: Augustan and Romantic*. Ed. Andrew Rutherford. Basingstoke: Macmillan, 1990: 1–25.

Stedman, Jane. *Six Comic Plays by W.S. Gilbert*. London: Routledge, 1969.

——. *W.S. Gilbert: A Classic Victorian and his Theatre*. New York: Oxford UP, 1996.

Steen, Marguerite. *William Nicholson*. London: Collins, 1943.

Stephens, John Russell. 'Lacy, Thomas Hailes (1809–1873)', *Oxford Dictionary of National Biography (ODNB)*. Oxford UP, September 2004. 1 January 2008. <http://www.oxforddnb.com/articles/15/15862>.

Stevenson, Robert Louis. 'The Day After Tomorrow'. *The Contemporary Review* 51 (April 1887): 472.

——. *Familiar Studies of Men and Books*. New York: Dodd, Mead & Co., 1887.

——. *Lay Morals and Other Papers*. London: Chatto & Windus, 1911.

——. *Memories and Portraits*. New York: C. Scribner's Sons, 1910.

——. 'My First Book'. *Treasure Island*. Ed. Emma Letley. Oxford: Oxford UP, 1985.

——. 'A Note on Realism'. Vol. XXIV Waverley Edition. London: Waverley Book Co., 1925.

——. *Treasure Island*. Ed. Emma Letley. Oxford: Oxford UP, 1985.

——. *The Master of Ballantrae*. Ed. Adrian Poole. Harmondsworth: Penguin, 1996.

Stoker, Bram. *The Mystery of the Sea*. 1902. Ed. Carol A. Senf. Kansas City: Valancourt Books, 2007.

Stoneman, Patsy. *Elizabeth Gaskell*. 2nd edn. Manchester: Manchester UP, 2006.

Stuart, Reginald C. *United States Expansionism and British North America, 1775–1871*. Chapel Hill: U of North Carolina P, 1988.

Super, Robert Henry. *The Chronicler of Barsetshire: A Life of Anthony Trollope*. Ann Arbor: U of Michigan P, 1988.

Sutcliffe, E.G. 'Charles Reade's Notebooks'. *Studies in Philology* 27 (1930): 164–211.

Sutton, Max Keith. *W.S. Gilbert*. Boston: Twayne/G.K. Hall, 1975.

Swettenham, Frank. *Malay Sketches*. London: John Lane, 1895.

——. *The Real Malay: Pen Pictures*. London: John Lane, 1907.

Tarling, Nicholas. *The Fall of Imperial Britain in South-East Asia*. Singapore: Oxford UP, 1993.

Temple, Kathryn. 'Printing Like a Post-Colonialist: The Irish Piracy of *Sir Charles Grandison*'. *Novel: A Forum on Fiction* 33.2 (2000): 157–74.

Tennyson, Alfred, Lord. *Idylls of the King*, 'The Passing of Arthur'. *Tennyson: A Selected Edition*. Ed. Christopher Ricks. Berkeley and Los Angeles: U of California P, 1989.

Terry, Rachel. *Reading the Brontës: An Introduction to Their Novels and Poetry*. Oxford: Alden Group, 2000.

'The Life-Boat – A Sketch'. *Corsair* 1 (7 March 1840): 831.

'The Forty Pirates'. *Times* 9 February 1829: 3.

Thomson, Janice E. *Mercenaries, Pirates, and Sovereigns: State-Building and Extraterritorial Violence in Early Modern Europe*. Princeton, NJ: Princeton UP, 1994.

Tigges, Wim. 'A Glorious Thing: The Byronic Hero as Pirate Chief'. *Configuring Romanticism*. Eds Theo O'haen, Peter Liebregts and Wim Tigges. New York: Rodopi, 2003.

Trelawny, John Edward. *The Adventures of a Younger Son*. London: Richard Bentley, 1854.

Trevelyan, George. *Cawnpore*. London: Macmillan and Co., 1865.

Trocki, Carl A. *Prince of Pirates: The Temenggongs and the Development of Johor and Singapore, 1784–1885*. Singapore: Singapore UP, 1979.

Trollope, Anthony. *The Small House at Allington*. New York: Penguin, 1991.

——. *The Last Chronicle of Barset*. New York: Penguin, 2002.

——. *The Eustace Diamonds*. New York: Penguin, 2004.

Trumpener, Katie. *Bardic Nationalism: The Romantic Novel and the British Empire*. Princeton, NJ: Princeton UP, 1997.

Turley, Hans. *Rum, Sodomy, and the Lash: Piracy, Sexuality, and Masculine Identity*. New York: New York UP, 1999.

Turnbull, C.M. *A Short History of Malaysia, Singapore and Brunei*. Singapore: Graham Brash, 1981.

Uglow, Jennifer. *Elizabeth Gaskell: A Habit of Stories*. London: Faber & Faber, 1993.

Vallar, Cindy. 'The Lure of Piracy: Reality vs. Romanticism'. *Pirates and Privateers: The History of Maritime Piracy*. Ed. Cindy Vallar <http://www.cindyvallar.com/romanticism.html> (16 January 2008).

Vincent, Edgar. *Nelson: Love & Fame*. New Haven: Yale UP, 2003.

'Voyage of the *Amherst* to Northern China'. *Eclectic Review* 3rd series 10 (1833): 326–43.

Vrettos, Athena. *Somatic Fictions: Imagining Illness in Victorian Culture*. Stanford: Stanford UP, 1995.

Walker, Robert. *The Female Soldier, or, The Surprising Life and Adventures of Hannah Snell*. 1750. Ed. and intro. Dianne Dugaw. Los Angeles: W.A. Clark Memorial Library, 1989.

Walkey, Samuel. 'The King of the Seas'. *Chums* 8.374 (8 November 1899): 180ff.

Wallace, Alfred Russell. *The Malay Archipelago: The Land of the Orang-Utan, and the Bird of Paradise, a Narrative of Travel, with Studies of Man and Nature*. 1869. Singapore: Periplus, 2000.

Ward, Ralph T. *Pirates in History*. Baltimore: York Press, 1974.

Watkins, Daniel. *Social Relations on Byron's Eastern Tales*. London and Toronto: Associated UP, 1987.

Weinberg, Albert Katz. *Manifest Destiny: A Study of Nationalist Expansionism in American History*. 1935. Chicago: Quadrangle Books, 1963.

Welsh, Alexander. *The Hero of the Waverly Novels: With New Essays on Scott*. 1963. Princeton, NJ: Princeton UP, 1992.

White, Andrea. *Joseph Conrad and the Adventure Tradition: Constructing and Deconstructing the Imperial Subject*. Cambridge: Cambridge UP, 1993.

Wiener, Harold. 'Byron and the East: Literary Sources of the "Turkish Tales"'. *Nineteenth-Century Studies*. Eds Davis, Herbert, William DeVane and R.C. Bald. New York: Greenwood, 1968: 89–129.

Wilde, Oscar. *The Soul of Man under Socialism and Selected Critical Prose*. Ed. Linda Dowling. London: Penguin, 2001.

Williams, Carolyn. 'Parody, Pastiche, and the Play of Genres: The Savoy Operas of Gilbert and Sullivan'. *The Victorian Comic Spirit: New Perspectives*. Ed. Jennifer A. Wagner-Lawlor. Aldershot: Ashgate, 2000: 1–21.

Williams, Harry T., Richard N. Current and Frank Freidel. *A History of the United States to 1877*. 1959. 3rd edn. New York: Alfred A. Knopf, 1969.

Willis, Nathaniel Parker. *Dashes at Life with a Free Pencil: Part IV – Ephemera*. 1845. New York: Garrett Press, 1969.

Wilson, Frances, ed. *Byromania: Portraits of the Artist in Nineteenth- and Twentieth-Century Culture*. New York: St Martin's, 1999.

Winnifrith, Tom, ed. *Poems of Patrick Branwell Brontë: A New Annotated and Enlarged Edition of the Shakespeare Head Brontë*. New York: New York UP, 1983.

Wood, Naomi. 'Treasure Island and the Romance of Money'. *Children's Literature* 26 (1998): 61–85.

Wren, Gayden. *Most Ingenious Paradox: The Art of Gilbert and Sullivan*. Oxford and New York: Oxford UP, 2001.

Wright, T.R. *Elizabeth Gaskell, 'We Are Not Angels': Realism, Gender, Values*. Basingstoke: Macmillan, 1995.

Wu Haimin. 'Zou xiang Baierni: Zhongguo ban quan bei wang lu' [Toward Berne: A Memorandum on Copyright in China]. December 1992. Yifan Public Library (shuku.net). 3 January 2010 <http://www.shuku.net/novels/baogaowenxue/zxberni/zxberni.html>.

Young, Alfred F. *Masquerade: The Life and Times of Deborah Sampson, Continental Soldier*. New York: Alfred A. Knopf, 2004.

Young, Robert J.C. *Colonial Desire: Hybridity in Theory, Culture and Race*. London: Routledge, 1995.

Index

Adams, John, 122n
Addison, Joseph, 188
Alexander, Christine, 41, 43, 46n, 49
Allen, Kristie, 9
Altick, Richard D., 189n
Anderson, Benedict, 99
Angrey, Kanhoji, 48, 49, 54
Angria, 4, 41–58
Antony, Robert, 61
Arendt, Hannah, 5, 218
Ashby, Nanette M., 83
Avery, Captain, 2, 17, 46, 230–31
Avery, Gillian, 166n

Baer, Joel H., 66n, 185
Baker, Thomas A., 83n
Bakhtin, Mikhail, 46, 47
Ballantyne, R.M., 225
    The Coral Island, 6, 165–79, 182, 238
    Gascoyne, the Sandal-Wood Trader, 38n, 176n
    The Gorilla Hunters, 168
    The Madman and the Pirate, 6, 38n, 165–79
    The Pirate City, 170n
    Rob the Rover, 38n
Ballou, Maturin Murray, 95–115
    Fanny Campbell, Female Pirate Captain, 95–115
Balzac, Honoré de, 79
Bankson, Douglas H., 187
Barker, Benjamin, 95
Barnes, James J., 80, 88, 93n
Barrett, Daniel, 140
Barrie, J.M., 178, 186
    Peter Pan, 6, 22, 29, 33, 38, 107–108, 219, 223, 236, 238, 239, 240
Barrow, John, 60, 62, 63, 64, 70
Beatty-Kingston, W., 235
Beckford, William, 28

Beechey, Captain, 122n
Belford, Barbara, 244
Benson, Peter, 97, 115
Bentley, George, 188
Berne Convention, 136
Birkin, Andrew, 238n
Blackbeard, see Teach, Edward
Blackstone, William, 248
Blackwood's Edinburgh Magazine, 46, 53, 58n
Bligh, Captain William, 122n
Blossom, HMS, 122
Bodenheimer, Rosemarie, 119n, 124
Bonaparte, Felicia, 119n, 123, 124
Bonaparte, Napoleon, 44, 52, 57n, 118, 119
Bonny, Anne, 17, 18n, 96, 100n
Boone, Charles, 49
Booth, Michael R., 140n
Boucicault, Dion, 136, 141, 183n, 233
Bounty, HMS (ship), 122
Boys of England, 38, 225
Boys' Own Paper, 239
The Boys Standard, 38
Braddon, Mary Elizabeth, 136n
    Lady Audley's Secret, 136n, 139n
Bradley, Ian, 199n, 235
Brando, Marlon, 122n
Brantlinger, Patrick, 66n, 150, 155, 157, 162, 171, 183n
Bratton, Jacky, 136
Brett, Edwin J., 225
Bristow, Joseph, 171, 176, 215
British East India Company (see East India Company)
Brontë, Anne, 41–2, 43
Brontë, Charlotte, 41–2, 43, 46n, 58n
    Jane Eyre, 23, 35n
Brontë, Emily, 41–2, 43
    Wuthering Heights, 35n
Brontë, (Patrick) Branwell, 4, 41–58

And the Weary are at Rest, 42n
Glass Town saga, 43
The Pirate, 41
The Hand of the Arch-Sinner, 42n
Brooke, Sir James (Rajah), 262, 264, 265n,
    266, 267
Brother Jonathan, 82, 83, 93n
Brown, David Blayney, 36
Brummel, Beau (George Bryan
    Brummel), 32
Bryant, William Cullen, 89
Buckstone, J.B., 136
Bugis, 264
Burbidge, Frederick William, 261
Burg, B.R., 27n
Burke, Edmund, 86
Burney, Fanny
    Camilla, 32
Burns, Robert, 184
Butler, Samuel
    The Way of All Flesh, 31–2n
Byron (Clara) Allegra, 23
Byron, Lord George Noel Gordon, 20,
    23–39, 50, 178, 239
    Childe Harold's Pilgrimage, 31, 51
    The Corsair, 1, 4, 11, 12, 14–19, 20,
        21, 23, 27, 29, 31, 35, 36, 62, 67,
        74, 86, 200, 229, 238
    Don Juan, 27n, 36, 51, 52
    'The Giaour', 51
    Lara, 27n, 37n
    Manfred, 27n, 31
    'Prisoner of Chillon', 27n
    Ravenna, 25
Byron, Henry, 136
Byron, H.J., 233–4

Calico Jack, see Rackham, John
Campbell, A.V., 231–2
Canning, Charles (1st Earl, known as
    'Clemency Canning')153
Carey, Henry, 143n
Carlyle, Thomas 24n
    Sartor Resartus, 197
Carpenter, Kevin, 38, 166, 167, 176, 225
Carroll, Lewis (Charles Lutwidge
    Dodgson), 47
Casarino, Cesare, 85, 86

Cawnpore Massacrre, 149–64
Chakravarty, Gautum, 150n, 153n
Chapman, Samuel, 226n
Chew, Samuel, 25n
Cholmondley, Mary, 198
    Red Pottage, 198
Choon, Ban Kah, 257
Christian, Fletcher, 122
Clay, Henry (Senator), 80
Clifford, Hugh, 255, 256, 257, 260, 262,
    263, 267, 269, 270, 271
    Sally, a Study, 270
    Saleh: a Sequel, 270
Clive, Robert (Colonel), 49, 57–8n
Clough, Arthur
    Amours de Voyage, 31
Cohn, Bernard, 152
Coleman, John, 183
Coleridge, Hartley, 43
Coleridge, Samuel Taylor, 28, 43, 81
Collini, Stefan, 211
Collins, Robert, 41, 43, 45, 48
Collins, Wilkie, 2,7–8, 149–64, 174n, 183n
    'Perils of Certain English Prisoners',
        149–164, 182
Colman, George, 227n
Conquest, B.O., 188
Conrad, Joseph, 171, 255–71
    Almayer's Folly, 259, 260, 262
    An Outcast of the Islands, 262
    The Rescue, 262, 265
    Youth, 257
Cooke, J., 48n
Cooke, T.P., 140, 143, 225, 226, 228
Cooper, James Fenimore, 99, 229
    The Pilot, 38
    The Red Rover, 7, 38, 223, 226–9, 233,
        235
    The Sea Lions, 38
    The Wing-Wing, 38
Corbett, Julian, 245n
Corbould, Richard, 37
Cordingly, David, 2, 3, 4, 5n, 10, 17n, 96n,
    105n, 220
The Cornhill, 184, 215
The Corsair (journal), 6, 79–93
Coutts, Angela Burdett, 149
Cowie, Alexander, 28n

Cox, Jeffrey N., 142
Craig, George, 7, 149
Crawfurd, John, 68n, 69, 72, 263
Crimean War, 133, 152, 198
Croker, Walter, 186n
Cross, J.C., 230, 231, 236
Crystal Palace Company, 188
Cuban Revolution (1895–98), 252
Cunningham, John William, 23

Dampier, William, 36n
Darwin, Charles, 268, 269
    On the Origin of Species, 169
Davis, Jim, 147
Davis, Nuel Pharr, 150n
Deazley, Ronan, 139n
Dechang, Zhang 61n
Defoe, Daniel, 8, 36n, 66, 95, 186, 188,
    212n
    Captain Singleton, 9, 11, 18, 29n, 46n,
        56, 96, 185–6
    The King of Pirates, 29n
    Moll Flanders, 56, 167n
    Robinson Crusoe, 11, 18, 46n, 166n,
        224, 233
Degeneration, 165–179, 269, 270
Dekker, Rudolf M., 95
Delacroix, Eugene, 37n
Deleuze, Gilles, 91
De Pauw, Linda Grant, 1, 98n
De Quincey, Thomas, 43
Derrida, Jacques, 5, 211, 219, 220
Dickens, Charles (Boz), 2, 6, 79, 81, 82,
    83, 85, 149–164, 174n, 183n, 189,
    190
    All the Year Round, 150, 184
    *American Notes for General
        Circulation*, 89
    Household Words, 7–8, 149–164
    Little Dorrit, 195
    Oliver Twist, 80
    'Perils of Certain English Prisoners',
        149–164, 182
    The Pickwick Papers, 80
    A Tale of Two Cities, 238
Dicks, John, 137, 143, 144, 228
Disraeli, Benjamin, 151, 153
    Vivian Grey, 32

Dobree, Bonamy, 122n
The Dollar, 89
Donaldson versus Beckett, 91
Downing, Clement, 49
D'Oyly Carte Opera Company, 235, 236n
Drake, Sir Francis, 10, 27, 54, 65, 195,
    243–54
Dramatic Authors' Society, 136, 141
Dramatic Copyright Act (1833), 141, 147
Druett, Joan, 112n
Dugan, James, 122n, 123n
Dugaw, Dianne, 95, 106
Duncombe, John, 136, 137, 143, 145, 230
Du Maurier, Daphne, 44, 236, 238, 240
Du Maurier, George,
    Trilby, 238
Du Maurier, Gerald, 236, 238, 240, 241
Dyer, J.J., 230

Earle, Peter, 184n, 186n
East India Company (EIC), 49, 58, 59–77,
    264n
Eclectic Review, 69, 73
Edinburgh Review, 184, 186n
Edmonds, Sarah Emma, 96n
Elfenbein, Andrew, 25n, 30, 34
Eliot, George (Mary Ann Evans), 197
    Felix Holt, the Radical, 31n
Elwin, Malcolm, 183n, 190
The Era, 133n, 134
Esquemeling, John (see Exquemelin,
    Alexander)
Evangelical Magazine, 72
Evans, D. Morier, 188
The Examiner, 134
Exquemelin, Alexander, 12, 29n

Fay, Peter Ward, 63n, 65
Feather, John, 82
Felluga, Dino Franco, 26
Ffinch, Michael, 199
Fielding, Penny, 213n
Finden, William, 37n
First War of Indian Independence, see
    Indian 'Mutiny'
Fischler, Alan, 140n
Fitzball, Edward, 135, 226, 229
Fleetwood, Frances, 239n

Flynn, Errol, 223
French, Samuel, 139
Freud, Sigmund, 220
Forge, Anthony, 263n
Foucault, Michel, 84n
Fox, Grace, 61n
Fraser, Robert, 215
French Revolution, 27
Fuseli, Johann Heinrich, 37

Gable, Clark, 122n
Garber, Marjorie, 107
Gaskell, Elizabeth Cleghorn, 117–131
   Cranford, 123
   The Grey Woman, 119
   Lois the Witch, 119
   The Manchester Marriage, 123
   Morton Hall, 119
   'My French Master', 119
   North and South, 5, 10, 117–131, 177
   Sylvia's Lovers, 119, 123
Gay, John, 143
George I, 58
Gérin, Winifred, 44, 123
Gerassi-Navarro, Nina, 62, 98, 99
Gilbert & Sullivan, 197–209, 241
   HMS Pinafore, 235
   The Mikado, 236n
   The Pirates of Penzance, 5, 22, 38,
      197–209, 224, 234, 235–6, 238
Gilbert, W.S., see also Gilbert & Sullivan,
      140, 234, 236, 239
Gladstone, William Ewart, 3
Gleason, Frederick, 97, 98, 113, 114
Glimmerglass Opera, 209
Glinert, Ed, 199
Glover, David, 243
Gogwilt, Christopher, 258, 265n, 270n
Golding, William, 171n
   Lord of the Flies, 171n
Gordan, John D., 226, 265
Gore, Catherine, 9, 25, 268, 269
   Adventures in Borneo, 255, 257, 266–7
Gosse Edmund, 244n,
Gosse, Philip, 1, 3, 17, 244, 247, 250n, 251
Gosse, Philip Henry, 244n
Gow, John, 28n
Graham, Gerald S., 70

The Graphic, 235, 236
Gray, James, 96
Great Northern Railway, 188
Greeley, Horace, 93n
Green, J.K., 227, 230
Greenberg, Michael, 62, 65n
Greenwood, James, 9, 267
Grey, Charles, 55
Grigsby, Ann, 194n, 195
Griswold, Rufus, 85
Gutzlaff, Charles, 10, 59–77

Haimin, Wu, 76
Haley, Bruce, 169
Halifax Guardian, 58
Hall, Staurt, 101n
Hampden, John, 244n
Hamilton, Captain Sir Edward, 118
Hampson, Robert, 258, 265n
Hannabuss, Stuart, 165, 167
Harper's, 93n, 223, 224n
Harris, J.A. (Mrs), 183n
Harvey, John Martin, 238
Hastings, Warren, 57n
Hazlewood, Colin H., 136n, 139n
Hay, John C. Dalrymple, 61n
Heidegger, Martin, 219
Helyar, James, 201
Henty, G.M., 9, 268, 269
   In the Hands of the Malays, 257, 267
Hermione, HMS (ship), 117, 118, 121, 123,
   131
Hevia, James L, 64n, 65
Hibbert, Christopher, 150n, 151n, 152, 153
Higbie, Robert, 208
Hill, Christopher, 87, 212, 213n
Hobhouse, John (1st Baron Broughton), 31
Hobsbawm, Eric, 157
Holcroft, 137n
Holden, Philip, 263, 268n, 270
Hollingshead, John, 188n
Honoré, Ann, 141n
Hopkins, Lisa, 246, 249n, 250n
Houtchens, Lawrence H., 83
Howard, Trevor, 122n
Howarth, Patrick, 166, 168
Hudson, George, 188n
Hughes, Thomas, 167

Hughes, Winnifred, 184n
Hugo, Victor, 215–7
Hutcheson, John Conroy, 9, 267, 268, 269

Indian 'Mutiny' (1857), 7, 133–4,
      149–164, 182, 191
Illustrated London News, 133n
Ingham, Patricia, 119n, 122, 123, 124, 125
Ingram, Joseph Holt,
      Lafitte The Pirate of the Gulf, 28n
Irving, Henry, 238, 247n
Irving, Washington, 83

James, Louis, 143n
James, Henry, 220, 225, 228
James, William, 117n
Jay, Frank, 225
Jarvis, Louise, 106
Jarvis, R., 12, 16
Jeans, Peter D., 117
Jeffries, Sabrina, 24n
Jerrold, Douglas,
      Black Ey'd Susan, 7, 9n, 133–147, 226,
      228
Jerrold, W. Blanchard, 139
Johnson, Charles (Captain), 1, 19, 20–22,
      214, 230, 238
*A General History of the Robberies and
      Murders of the Most Notorious
      Pyrates, 1*,2, 11–16, 18, 46, 47, 48,
      49, 96, 212
Johnson, Charles, 230
Joyce, Valentine, 122n

Kafka, Franz, 220
Kean, Charles, 233
Kean, Edmund, 225
Keats, John, 28
      'Ode to a Nightingale' 28n
Keay, John, 49
Kelsey, Harry, 65
Keppel, Henry, 264
Kidd, William (Captain), 2, 27, 185, 195, 221
Kierkegaard, Soren, 219
King, Dean, 119
Kingsley, Charles, 29n, 167
      Westward Ho!, 29n, 182
Kingston, W.H.G., 38, 225

Klausman, Ulrike, 96, 105n
Kline, Kevin, 200n
Knight, Stephen, 167n
Konstam, Angus, 4
Krenn, Heliena, 258
Krentz, Jayne Ann, 24n
Kronenberger, Louis, 245n

Lacy, T.H., 7, 133–147, 188, 189, 230, 233n
      Lacy versus Rhys, 138
Lafitte, Jean 27
Lane, Samuel, 189
Leach, Wilfred, 200n
Leask, Nigel, 259
Le Bris, Michel, 105n
Lemon, Mark, 136, 137n
Leveridge, Richard, 143n
Lewis, C.S., 43
Lewis, Matthew, 28
Lewis, Michael Arthur, 122, 123n
Lindsay, Hugh Hamilton, 10, 59–77
Linebaugh, Peter, 5, 113, 212, 213, 221
Lister, Thomas Henry,
      Granby, 32
Literary Copyright Act (1842), 135–6, 138,
      141, 147
Lloyd, Frank, 122n
Lloyd's Weekly Newspaper, 133n
Locke, John, 86, 87
Lord Amherst (ship) 60
Lowell, James Russell, 85
Lucas, John, 118n
Lytton, Edward Bulwer (1st Baron Lytton),
      24n, 25, 79
      Pelham, 32

Mabee, Frank, 123
Macartney mission (1792), 60, 62, 64, 65, 69
Mackie, Erin, 45
Maixner, Paul, 215
Malgonkar, Manohar, 49
Manzoni, Alessandro, 99
Manwaring, George Ernest, 122n, 123n
Maquet, Auguste, 190
Marchand, Leslie, 31
Marcus, J.G., 117n
Marjoribanks, Charles, 59, 67
Marryat, Frederick (Captain), 66, 225

The Pirate, 34, 38
Marshall, P.J., 63
Marx, Karl, 69n
Mason, Connie, 24n,
Mather, Cotton, 66
Maunder, Andrew, 169n, 243, 246, 253
Mayhew, Edward, 93
McGill, Meredith, 82, 87
McKee, Christopher, 118
McQueen, James, 53
Meisel, Martin, 223
Melville, Herman,
    Moby Dick, 51n, 113
Milestone, Lewis, 122
Miller, Lucasta, 44
Missionary Register, 72
Moncrieff, William T., 141–2
Monroe, James (President), 104
Moody, Jane, 230
Moore, John D., 220
Morgan, Henry, 27, 29, 71
Morgan, James, 86, 87
Morgan, Susan, 130
Morning Chronicle, 134n
Morton, Edward, 141n
Morton, John Maddison, 137, 138n
Morton, Thomas, 138n
Munich, Adrienne, 198
Murray, Paul, 243
Musical Times, 235
Myers, Frederic W.H., 197
Myers, Janet C., 7, 113

Nadal, Rafael, 89
Nahuys, Alphonse (Baron), 256n
Napoleonic Wars, 2, 27
Nayder, Lillian, 8, 151, 157
Nelson, Horatio (Admiral Lord), 197, 199, 209
Newbolt, Henry, 167
Newbury, Michael, 84
Newlyn, Lucy, 86
New Monthly Magazine, 187
New World, 82, 83, 88, 90
New York Times, 208
Nicholson, William, 238
Nietzsche, Friedrich, 29
    Ecce Homo, 29n
Noble, Mark, 37

Nordau, Max, 169, 178
North Star (ship), 184
Noyes, Alfred, 241

O'Connor, Erin, 259
Oddie, William, 150
Opium War, Chinese, 9, 59, 61, 62
Orwell, George, 98, 183n,
Osbaldiston, David, 226
O'Sullivan, John L., 102n
Oxenham, John, 29

Pall Mall Gazette, 189
Paolino, Ernest N., 104
Papp, Joseph, 200n
Paravasini-Gebert, Lizabeth, 98n, 108
Park, Hyunggji, 150
Parker, Bonnie, 107
Parker, Richard, 131n
Parry, Benita, 257
Parry, William Edward, 48n
Pascoe, C.E., 233n
Paxton, Nancy, 153
Peacock, Thomas Love, 25
    Nightmare Abbey, 25
Peck, John, 9, 253
Pelras, Christian, 264
Pennell, C.R., 3, 11, 17n, 22, 96n
Peters, Catherine, 150n, 154
Peters, Laura, 150n, 152, 156
Phillips, Walter Clarke, 183n
Pigot, Hugh, 117
Pionke, Albert, 151
Pirates of the Caribbean, 1, 10, 223
Planché, J.R., 137n
Polk, James (President)
Poovey, Mary, 188
Pope, Dudley, 117n, 118n
Porter, T.O., 6, 79–93
Power, Tyrone, 223
Pratt, Mary Louise, 63, 68, 69n, 110, 113
Pullinger, William, 188
Pyle, Howard, 223, 224, 225, 238

Qing China, 59–77
The Quarterly Christian Spectator, 75
The Quarterly Review, 70
Quayle, Eric, 166

Quilty, Mary Catherine, 263n

Rackham, John (Calico Jack), 29
Radcliffe, Ann, 28
Raffles, Thomas Stamford, 260, 261, 263,
    264, 265, 266
Rasor, Eugene L. 122n, 123n
Read, Mary, 17, 18n, 96, 108
Reade, Charles,
    Hard Cash, 8–9, 181–195, 269
    It is Never Too Late to Mend, 183n,
      187n, 188, 189
    A Terrible Temptation, 183n
    White Lies, 190
Reade, John Edmund, 31
Rediker, Marcus, 5, 28, 42n, 47, 48, 50n,
    51n, 55n, 56, 57, 58, 91, 96n, 105,
    185, 212, 213, 221
Redpath, Leopold, 188
Rees, James, 226n
Reynolds, David S., 98n
Reynolds' Newspaper, 134n
Rhys, Horton, 138n
Richardson, Samuel, 188
    Sir Charles Grandison, 188
Rigney, Ann, 18, 19, 20
Ritchie, Robert, 96n, 214n
Robertson, Fiona, 12
Robertson, T.W., 135
Robinson, Henry Crabbe, 226
Robinson, Kenneth, 154
Rocker, George, 267
Rodgers, Woodes, 54, 58
Rose, Mark, 84n
Rowell, George, 227n
Ruggles, Benjamin, 89
Rupert, Prince 29
Ruskin, John, 24n
    Sesame and Lilies, 197
Rutter, Owen, 265

Sabatini, Rafael, 22, 223
Sadleir, John, 188n
Sahib, Nana (Dhondu Pant), 152
Said, Edward, 151, 259
Saint-Amour, Paul K., 84
Sampson, Deborah, 96
Sampson, Robert, 102n

Samuel, Raphael, 259
Sandwich, HMS, 131
Saunders, David, 84
Schlyter, Herman, 71, 72
Schornhorn, Manuel, 105n, 212n
Schor, Hilary, 123
Scott, Sir Walter, 20, 22, 27, 36, 46n, 81,
    99, 102, 178, 186n, 220
    The Bride of Lammermore, 28n
    Ivanhoe, 19, 28n
    The Pirate, 4, 11, 12, 19, 20, 28, 33, 34
    Rob Roy, 19
    Waverley, 19, 110
Selby, Charles, 140n
Selkirk, Alexander, 57
Semmel, Bernard, 65n
Seville, Catherine, 81, 88n, 134n, 140
Shakespeare, William 44, 95
Sharpe, Jenny, 153, 158
Shaw, George Bernard, 209
Shelley, Mary Wollstonecraft, 31, 33n
Shelley, Percy Bysshe, 26, 30, 31,
    Drama, 33n
    'Ode to Autumn', 50
    Queen Mab, 26
Shelton, George, 240
Sherman, John, 85
Sherry, Norman, 265n
Shore, J.G., 233
Silver-Fork Novel, 32
Singleton, Henry, 37
Smith, Elton, 183n, 189
Smith, Henry Nash, 95
Smith, Janet Adam, 220
Smith, Leonard V., 121
Smith, Rex, 200n
Smollett, Tobias
    Peregrine Pickle, 189
Smythe, George Sydney, 187, 212
Snell, Hannah, 96, 100n, 108
Snow, Edward Rowe, 98n
Society for the Diffusion of Useful
    Knowledge, (SDUK), 88
Society for the Promotion of Christian
    Knowledge (SPCK), 88
Sons of Britannia, 38
Southey, Robert, 81
Spanish-American War (1898), 246

Spanish Armada, 249
Sparrow, Captain Jack (see *Pirates of the Caribbean*)
Speaight, George, 226n, 230n
St. Clair, William, 31, 36
The Stage, 226
Stage Directory, 235
Stallybrass, Peter, 47
Stanley, Jo, 1, 2, 96n
Starkey, David, 90
Staunton, George, 63, 66, 67
Stedman, Jane, 234
Steele, F.O., 98n
Steele, Richard, 188
Stephens, John Russell, 137
Stevenson, John, 123
Stevenson, Robert Louis, 3, 165n, 178, 211–222, 241
    The Beach of Falesá, 215
    'The Day After Tomorrow', 215
    Familiar Studies of Men and Books, 215
    'A Gossip on Romance', 215, 217
    'A Humble Remonstrance', 215
    'Lay Morals', 211, 215
    The Master of Ballantrae, 214, 221
    Memories and Portraits, 215, 226
    Treasure Island, 5, 22, 29n, 33, 166n, 186, 211–222, 224n, 225
    'Victor Hugo', 215–7
Stewart, Alexander Turney, 250n
Stirling, Edward,
    A Struggle for Gold, 134
Stirling, Fanny, 188
Stoker, Bram,
    The Lady of the Shroud, 252n
    The Lair of the White Worm, 250n
    The Mystery of the Sea, 10, 243–254
Stoneman, Patsy, 122, 123
Stowe, Harriet Beecher, 183n
    Uncle Tom's Cabin, 183n
The Straits Chinese Magazine, 256n
Stuart, Reginald C., 103
Sullivan, Arthur, see Gilbert & Sullivan
Sutcliffe, E.G., 187n
Sutherland, John, 115
Swettenham, Frank, 269, 270
Swift, Jonathan, 66
    Gulliver's Travels, 36n

Talfourd, Thomas Noon, 81, 82, 135
Tarling, Nicholas, 263n, 264n
Taylor, Jenny Bourne, 169n
Teach, Edward, 1, 13–14, 16, 29, 185, 221, 231–2, 236
Temple, Richard, 236n
Tennyson, Alfred, Lord, 177
    'The Charge of the Light Brigade', 198
    Idylls of the King, 177
    The Promise of May, 189
Terry, Rachel, 58
Thomas, Ralph, 226n
Thompson, Mowbray, 183n
Tigge, Wim, 36n
The Times, 184n, 189, 226, 229, 238, 240
Tindal, Matthew, 185
Tome, Sandra, 83n
Townsend, Elton, 184n
Treaty of Paris, 246
Tree, Beerbohm
Trelawny, Edward John, 31
Trevelyan, G.O., 153
Trollope, Anthony, 4, 23–39, 189–90
    Can You Forgive Her?, 24
    The Eustace Diamonds, 23–39
    The Last Chronicle of Barset, 25
    Ralph the Heir, 189–90
    The Way We Live Now, 195
Trollope, Frances (Fanny), 23n
Trumpener, Katie, 110
Turley, Hans, 2, 8n, 10, 11, 14, 17, 27n, 45, 55n, 154, 157, 160n, 161, 186
Turnbull, C. Mary, 268n

Uglow, Jennifer, 119, 123

Van de Pol, Lotte C., 95
Verdi, Giuseppe, 37n
Victoria, Queen, 198, 208, 209
Virno, Paolo, 90
Vrettos, Athena, 268

Walker, Robert, 96
Walkley, Samuel, 225
Wallace, Alfred Russell, 262, 268
Walpole, Horace, 28
War of Spanish Succession, 184

Ward, Ralph, 186
Wars of Liberation (South America), 2
Waterloo, Battle of, 44
Watkins, Daniel, 12, 15
Watson, Charles (Admiral), 49
Watts, Walter, 188
Webster, Benjamin, 133, 134, 135
Weinberg, Albert Katz, 101
Wellington, the Duke of (Arthur
        Wellesley), 44, 48n, 55
Welsh, Alexander, 18
West, William, 225, 230n
The Westminster Review, 68, 69, 72
Wheaton versus Peters, 87, 91
Wheeler, Hugh (General), 153n
Wheeler, Ulrica (also known as Margaret
        Frances Wheeler), 153n
Wheelwright, Julie, 96n, 98n
White, Allon, 47
White, Andrea, 258, 265n, 266
Whitman, Walt, 99
Wiener, Harold, 37n
Wilde, Oscar, 198, 209
        The Soul of Man Under Socialism, 198

Wilks, Thomas Egerton, 138–9n
Williams, Glyndwr, 63
Williams, Harry T., 102
Willis, Nathaniel Parker, 6, 79–93
        Pencillings by the Way, 82
Wilson, Frances, 25n, 30
Wilton, Marie, 233n
Wood, Naomi, 216
Woodman, Richard, 117n, 118n, 122n, 123n
Woodmansee, Martha, 84n
Wordsworth, William, 81
        'Lines Composed Above Tintern
                Abbey', 28n
        The Prelude 28n
World Trade Organization, 76
World War One (1914–1918), 209
Wright, Terence, 126, 130n

Xinnian, Kuang, 59

Yates, Frederick, 226, 227, 228, 229, 231
Yonge, Charlotte M., 166n
Young Folks, 3
Young, Robert J.C., 268n